Understanding
and Assessing
Child Sexual
Maltreatment

Second Edition

To
Lemuel Adolphus Johnson
December 15, 1941, to March 12, 2002
My much missed brother
Who always respected my scholarship
Even though we worked in different worlds

Understanding and Assessing Child Sexual Maltreatment

Second Edition

Kathleen Coulborn Faller
The University of Michigan

SAGE Publications
International Educational and Professional Publisher
Thousand Oaks ▪ London ▪ New Delhi

For information:

Sage Publications, Inc.
2455 Teller Road
Thousand Oaks, California 91320
E-mail: order@sagepub.com

Sage Publications Ltd.
6 Bonhill Street
London EC2A 4PU
United Kingdom

Sage Publications India Pvt. Ltd.
B-42, Panchsheel Enclave
Post Box 4109
New Delhi 110 017 India

Printed in the United States of America

Library of Congress Cataloging-in-Publication Data

Library of Congress Cataloging-in-Publication Data
Faller, Kathleen Coulborn.
Understanding and assessing child sexual maltreatment / Kathleen Coulborn Faller.
    p. cm.
Includes bibliographical references and index.
ISBN 0-7619-1996-1 (C) — ISBN 0-7619-1997-X (P)
1. Child sexual abuse-Psychological aspects. I. Title.
HV6570 .F347 2003
362.76—dc21   2002151159

This book is printed on acid-free paper.

03 04 05 10 9 8 7 6 5 4 3 2 1

Acquisitions Editor: Margaret Seawell
Editorial Assistant: Alicia Carter
Production Editor: Melanie Birdsall
Copy Editor: Elisabeth Magnus
Typesetter: C&M Digitals (P) Ltd
Indexer: Kathy Paparchontis
Cover Designer: Janet Foulger

Contents

Preface   vii

Acknowledgments   xi

PART I: WHAT CONSTITUTES SEXUAL MALTREATMENT?   1

1   Professional Roles and the Extent of Child Sexual Maltreatment   3

2   Definitions and Signs of Child Sexual Maltreatment   19

**PART II: COLLABORATING WITH INSTITUTIONS HAVING
MANDATORY AND LEGAL OBLIGATIONS**   53

3   Working With Protective Services and the Police   55

4   Collaborating With Attorneys and Working With the Courts   73

PART III: DATA COLLECTION AND DECISION MAKING   103

5   Child Interviews When Sexual Abuse Is Suspected   105

6   The Context of Child Interviewing   141

7   Decision Making in Child Sexual Abuse   163

PART IV: SEXUAL ABUSE IN SPECIAL CONTEXTS   189

8   Sexual Abuse in Family Foster Care   191

9   Sexual Abuse in Day Care   215

10 Sexual Abuse Allegations in Divorce   237

References   273

Name Index   291

Subject Index   299

About the Author   307

Preface

This book is written for practitioners who encounter cases of child sexual abuse. Although it will be useful for professionals from many fields, its primary audience is mental health practitioners who must work closely with other professionals, such as child protection workers and lawyers, on these complex cases.

Because this is a book for practitioners, literature reviews are not exhaustive. Rather, relevant works are cited. In addition, because there are many gaps in research-based knowledge about child sexual abuse, much of the guidance and many of the opinions derive from clinical experience. I regard information based upon clinical experience to be as valid and useful as research-based knowledge in practice with sexual abuse cases. I believe these two sources of knowledge can complement one another.

Throughout the book, I use the pronouns *she* and *her* to refer to children who are thought to have been sexually victimized and the pronouns *he, him,* and *his* to refer to those suspected of sexual abuse. This decision about pronouns was made for stylistic purposes and acknowledges that, to date, the majority of identified victims of sexual abuse are female and the majority of identified offenders are male. However, this is not meant to imply that there are no male victims, who now represent between one fifth (National Child Abuse and Neglect Data System [NCANDS], 2001) and one third (Faller, 2000a) of identified victims. Nor should this decision allow us to ignore the existence of female sex offenders, who are being identified in increasing numbers (e.g., Davin, Hislop, & Dunbar, 1999; Elliot, 1993; Faller, 1995; Mathews, Matthews, & Speltz, 1989; Mendel, 1995; Rosencrans, 1997).

The original edition of this book was published in 1990. The field of child sexual abuse has changed since then, in part by the generation of new knowledge. In addition, the field of child sexual abuse has bifurcated, so that the professionals and knowledge base that are child or victim focused are somewhat separate from the professionals and knowledge base related to sex offenders. It was not possible in this edition to do justice to the considerable developments in both child and offender research and practice. Most of the material in the original version of this book focused on the child victim. To incorporate the new knowledge related to the child and keep the book manageable, the chapter related to offenders has been eliminated.

A second way in which the field of child sexual abuse has changed is by what has been termed the "backlash" (e.g., Myers, 1994). When the first edition of this book was published, the backlash was an emerging development (e.g., Hechler, 1988; Wexler, 1990), but it has grown greatly since then. The backlash has several facets. It involves a challenge to Child Protective Services (CPS) as a government program. "Backlashers" assert that CPS is characterized by over-intrusiveness—running roughshod over family privacy; underintrusiveness—failing to rescue children who are in genuine jeopardy; and incompetence (e.g., Eberle & Eberle, 1986; Gardner, 1991, 1992b). In addition, professionals, such as those in mental health, who work collaboratively with CPS are said to be part of the "child abuse industry." The implication is that they substantiate cases in order to line their own pockets. Consider this excerpt from an editorial in the *Wall Street Journal* (2001):

> With the passage of the Mondale Act of 1974, otherwise known as the Child Abuse Prevention and Treatment Act, came also the large cottage industry of child advocates, self-proclaimed experts in abuse, and of course citizen hot lines, sources of anonymous—not to mention overwhelmingly false—accusations of abuse. ("The Funding Fount," 2001, p. A14)

Child sexual abuse cases, victims, and professionals have been the particular target of the backlash. The trustworthiness of children and adults reporting sexual abuse is a subject of great debate (e.g., Ceci & Bruck, 1993, 1995; False Memory Syndrome Foundation, 1992; Loftus & Ketchem, 1991; Yapko, 1994). Forensic interviewers, evaluators, and therapists are being attacked for incompetence (e.g., Wood & Garven, 2000), for having an "agenda," and for gullibility—believing their clients.

Professionals who work in the child sexual abuse field are on the defensive. To a large extent, the backlash has set the research agenda for child sexual abuse—the weaknesses of children's memory and their suggestibility and strategies to avoid false accounts. The backlash has also affected practice, governing how mental health professionals and others conduct interviews and provide treatment. The emphasis is on the danger of false allegations of sexual abuse rather than on the danger of being sexually abused and not disclosing the abuse. Children have lost their voice. An important goal of this book is to provide a considered response to the backlash but also a response that takes into account the needs of children.

The book is divided into four parts. Part I is an introductory section of two chapters that focuses on professional roles, the extent of child sexual abuse, definitions, and indicators. Part II has two chapters. One deals with the agencies having mandated roles: CPS and law enforcement. The other provides information on the legal system and working with lawyers. Part III consists of three chapters and addresses the practice of assessment in child sexual abuse. A chapter on the child interview addresses interview structure, questioning techniques, and the use of media or props. Another chapter covers the larger context in which the child interview takes place; it includes material on various models for investigation or assessment of an allegation of sexual abuse, a short review of the literature on children's memory and suggestibility, and a summary of research and practice relevant to disclosure of sexual abuse. Finally, a chapter on decision making addresses how professionals go about making a decision about the likelihood of sexual abuse once they have gathered all their data. Part IV deals with three special situations: (a) sexual abuse in day care, (b) sexual abuse in foster care, and (c) allegations of sexual abuse in divorce cases.

Acknowledgments

I wish to acknowledge the University of Michigan School of Social Work's support of my scholarly work, including this book. The school strongly encourages faculty in research and knowledge development endeavors. Indicative of that support is the provision of editorial assistance to faculty. Thus, I would like to thank Terri Torkko, who read the manuscript in its entirety and gave invaluable editorial suggestions.

I want to thank my colleagues, especially Mark Everson, who are concerned about children's welfare, for their contributions to the field of child sexual abuse. Mark and I have presented collaboratively over the years, and I have learned a great deal from him, as reflected in numerous references to his work, both published and unpublished. The knowledge Mark and other colleagues have developed, both research and practice based, is reflected in this book.

I want to thank Terri Hendrix from Sage Publications. If it had not been for Terri, I would not have thought to produce a second edition of *Understanding Child Sexual Maltreatment*. In fact, because of advances in knowledge about child sexual abuse, the second edition is substantially a new book requiring a different title, *Understanding and Assessing Child Sexual Maltreatment*.

Last, and perhaps most important, I want to thank my husband, Lincoln Faller, and my daughter, Helen McIntosh Faller, for being my family, supporting my career, and tolerating my workaholism.

PART I

What Constitutes Sexual Maltreatment?

1

Professional Roles and the Extent of Child Sexual Maltreatment

Introduction: Why Professionals Need to Know About Child Sexual Maltreatment

As recently as 50 years ago, sexual abuse of children was thought to be extremely uncommon. Thus, in 1955, Weinberg, in a landmark work on incest, estimated that the rate of incest among young children in the United States was only about one per million. Today, researchers in sexual abuse believe that as many as one in three or four American females and one in 6 to 10 males are sexually abused during their childhoods (Bolen & Scannapieco, 1999; Faller, 1988a; Finkelhor, 1979a, 1984; Peters & Wyatt, 1986; Russell, 1983; Saunders, Villeponteaux, Lipovsky, Kilpatrick, & Veronen, 1992).

These recent findings lead to a conclusion that most professionals whose employment brings them into contact with children can expect to encounter cases of child sexual maltreatment. These include professionals from agencies mandated to address child sexual abuse—public child welfare agencies, law enforcement agencies, and the courts. But they also include professionals in educational, health, and mental settings.

Child welfare professionals—protective services, foster care, adoption, and institutional care workers—will provide services to many children with a history of sexual abuse. Child welfare workers are responsible for investigation, case management, and intervention in cases of child sexual abuse. Currently, sexual abuse cases constitute between 10% and 15% of the 3 million children reported each year to Child Protective Services (CPS) (Petit & Curtis, 1997;

U.S. Department of Health and Human Services [USDHHS], Children's Bureau, 1998; Wang & Daro, 1998) and between a fourth and half of the children removed by public child welfare agencies from their homes (Portland State University, 1996; S. Kelly, personal communication, September 1988). Many sexually abused children experience difficulties in functioning, especially during adolescence, and are placed in institutional care. In some residential treatment programs, between 50% and 100% of children are victims of sexual abuse (e.g., D. De Palma, personal communication, September 5, 1994; M. Rosensweig, personal communication, November 1994).

Because sexual abuse is both a child protection problem and a crime, law enforcement and the courts are inevitably involved. In many communities, law enforcement and CPS jointly investigate allegations of intrafamilial sexual abuse. Law enforcement is responsible for gathering information to determine if there are acts that warrant criminal prosecution, and CPS is responsible for issues of child safety. All involuntary intervention in child sexual abuse—removing the child, mandating certain interventions, and incarcerating the offender—must be sanctioned by a juvenile, family, or criminal court. In addition, allegations of sexual abuse sometimes are brought to the domestic relations or divorce court.

School personnel, including regular classroom teachers, special education teachers, school counselors, and school administrators, will encounter many children who may have been sexually abused. In fact, school staff are first among professionals in the number of cases they report to child protection agencies (USDHHS, Children's Bureau, 1998). Cases are usually discovered when children reveal their abuse to persons whom they trust, often in school. In addition, child protection workers, wanting to interview children about possible abuse, away from the influence of their families, typically come to the child's school to do this. Moreover, behavior and sometimes emotional problems that result from sexual abuse may require intervention by school social workers, counselors, and teachers in school.

Professionals from all disciplines in health care settings may see sexually abused children. Physicians are the professionals who have been mandated reporters of child maltreatment the longest. Children come to them and other health care personnel for medical exams related to possible child sexual abuse. Often cases of sexual abuse are discovered in medical settings when children are brought in for care of sequelae of sexual abuse, or even for unrelated conditions.

Staff in mental health settings will regularly encounter children for whom there are concerns about sexual abuse. The effects of sexual abuse bring children to mental health outpatient settings as well as to psychiatric facilities. Furthermore, adults who were victimized as children, who never revealed their maltreatment and/or never received treatment, present in mental health settings with a wide range of sequelae of sexual abuse—sexual dysfunction, problems in intimate relationships, substance abuse, depression and suicidal ideation, and problems of self-esteem.

The following case example illustrates the roles of various professionals.

Case Example: Mary, a 5-year-old, was acting out sexually in her prekindergarten class. She was "humping" her stuffed teddy bear and asking boys in her class to touch her "inside peepee." When this first happened, Ms. A, her teacher, spoke to Mary's mother, April. April told Ms. A that they had been homeless for a while, living in a park, and she thought some of the older boys in the park might have done something to Mary. She did not know their names. Ms. A consulted with her principal, and they decided not to report the behavior to CPS. However, 2 days later, Ms. A caught Mary in the bathroom teaching two other girls how to touch their "inside peepee."

Ms. A made a report to CPS. A worker and a police officer came to Mary's school, and they attempted to interview her using a structured forensic interview protocol. Mary got scared at the beginning of the interview when asked about the difference between the truth and a lie. She told them you get a "whoopin'" when you tell a lie. Also, because the police were there, she also thought she was going to jail for teaching her friends the "inside peepee" game. She said a man taught her about her "inside peepee," a nice man. She did not respond when asked who he was, where she met him, or when this happened. She then got under the table and wouldn't come out.

The CPS worker and the police then went to talk to Mary's mother, April. She lived in a nearby trailer park. A man, naked to the waist, answered the trailer door. This turned out to be mother's new boyfriend, Fred. There were three younger children in the trailer, all in their nightclothes. There were twin girls who were a year old and a 3-year-old boy who could not yet say words. April eventually emerged from the bedroom, still in her nightclothes. The CPS worker asked her to get dressed, and she and the police officer interviewed April in the police car. There was no suitable place for an interview in the trailer.

April told them she had recently separated from her violent husband, Jake. She showed them her restraining order and said that Jake had lost custody of an older child, who was not hers, for child abuse. This child was with his parents. She said Jake had recently gotten unsupervised visits with the children every other weekend. She said that Mary's humping began after these visits started. April had not asked Mary anything about the humping. She just told her to stop, that it was nasty.

The CPS worker asked April to take Mary for a medical exam and asked April if she would cooperate with a referral to a multidisciplinary team that evaluated child welfare cases. April agreed.

The team consisted of social workers, psychologists, a psychiatrist, an educational specialist, a domestic violence specialist, a substance abuse specialist, a pediatrician, and a lawyer. The team interviewed Mary three times, evaluated the three younger children, and then interviewed and tested April, Jake, and Fred, the boyfriend. They conducted a developmental assessment on Mary's younger brother and referred him for speech therapy. Mary received a second medical exam because April had taken her to the family doctor, who did not do a genital exam. There were findings consistent with digital penetration. The team obtained records from the CPS referral on Jake's oldest child and spoke with his parents. They also got other police records on Jake. Finally, the team interviewed the maternal grandmother, who provided support to April and child care to her children.

The multidisciplinary team made the following findings: Mary had been sexually abused, probably by her father, on unsupervised visits. In her second interview, Mary stated her daddy touched her "inside peepee" with two fingers when she slept with him at night. She also demonstrated how she sat on his chest and "humped." In her third interview, she said her daddy didn't do anything wrong; he was a "nice man." Her father said Mary had tried to get him to touch her vagina but he had told her no. (He then obtained a criminal defense attorney and refused to be interviewed by police or to have any further involvement in the investigation.)

The environment in Jake's house was unsafe in any case because Jake dealt drugs out of his home when the children were visiting. There was a police drug raid and the children were there. Jake had a 4-year history of drug-related arrests and was awaiting trial on drug charges.

April was overwhelmed by the responsibility of four young children. All the children showed some delays, those of the 3-year-old brother being the most marked. Fred had a substance abuse problem but no history indicating the potential to sexually or otherwise abuse children. He also worked steadily and was a support to April. However, the team felt it prudent not to assume that he would play a long-term role in the family.

The team made the following recommendations: (a) no more visits with Jake; (b) individual treatment for Mary; (c) individual treatment for April; (d) wraparound services for the family to assist April in finding better housing, help her with parenting, and assist her in obtaining concrete services for which she was eligible, including child care, food stamps, a housing subsidy, and better medical care.

The team recommended a reevaluation of the family in 6 months.

Protective services endorsed this plan and assisted April in stopping the visits by appearing on her behalf in the domestic relations court. They made the appropriate referrals so she could obtain the recommended treatment and services. The law enforcement officer was chagrined that he could not pursue criminal prosecution of Jake.

Mary's case demonstrates the importance of expertise in sexual abuse by all professionals involved with children. School personnel need knowledge about the signs and symptoms of sexual abuse. CPS and law enforcement need standardized procedures and interview protocols in order to act effectively on sexual abuse cases. But they also need to have recourse to other experts and resources, such as the multidisciplinary team, when structures designed to deal with the easiest and most straightforward cases are insufficient. As can be seen from the case example, although multidisciplinary teams need to have a spectrum of professionals with expertise in sexual abuse, they also need additional expertise to address problems that may be associated with child maltreatment. Finally, therapists must have skill in providing sexual abuse- and trauma-specific treatment.

Information that will assist professionals in these various capacities will be provided in the coming chapters, with special attention to the roles and responsibilities of mental health professionals. In this first chapter, the major concerns will be describing a philosophical orientation to sexual maltreatment that gives priority to the child's best interest and providing information on the incidence and prevalence of sexual abuse.

A Child-Centered Approach

In this section, I will suggest that the most ethically responsible position for professionals to take in the face of accusations of child sexual abuse is a child-centered one. That is, case decisions and actions should be examined through the eyes of the child. This approach is suggested to deal both with the pressures from parties with different views and agendas related to the allegation and with the professional's own responses to sexual maltreatment cases.

A major dilemma for professionals attempting to intervene in a case of suspected sexual maltreatment is the intensely competing interests. The nature of the conflict varies depending upon the relationship between the child and the alleged offender, who may be a parent, stepparent, sibling, family friend, acquaintance, stranger, or professional. Professionals may include church officials such as priests, school officials, or mental health professionals. Regardless of the relationship between the accused and the child, the stakes for the alleged offender are very high. As a consequence, he may launch a multifaceted campaign against the child and all those who support the child, including professionals.

In intrafamilial cases, what is good for the child may be absolutely opposed by the family. In part, this is because consequences of discovery and intervention for families are potentially dire. Children are often removed from their parents' care. Families are broken up. Parental rights may be terminated. Multimodal, long-term treatment can be imposed upon the family. Reputations may be ruined. Offenders and sometimes their accomplices may be criminally prosecuted, and finally those prosecuted may go to jail or prison.

In extrafamilial cases, especially if the accused is prominent in the community, consequences can be equally devastating. Extrafamilial offenders face the same legal consequences in the criminal courts as do intrafamilial offenders. In addition, families and friends may abandon them and they may face loss of employment. Some of the most challenging cases for professionals are ones in which the accused works with children and may even be a colleague.

Moreover, professionals attempting to intervene in situations in which sexual maltreatment is suspected or substantiated must be hypervigilant about their own potential biases. Sexual abuse elicits strong emotional reactions from laypersons and professionals who are exposed to it. To believe that an adult has violated this societal taboo is to stigmatize him markedly. Individuals are likely to have opposing emotional reactions, to deny or to desire retribution. Neither of these reactions is particularly child centered.

Moreover, personal characteristics of professionals, such as gender, age, personal history of sexual or physical abuse, and profession, affect responses to allegations. Using 16 vignettes of possible sexual abuse, Jackson and Nuttall (1997) examined the opinions of social workers, psychologists, pediatricians, and psychiatrists. They found that women, social workers, younger professionals, and persons with childhood experiences of physical and sexual abuse were more likely to believe that children in the vignettes had been sexually abused.

Perhaps of greater significance for the issue of a child-centered approach were Jackson and Nuttall's (1997) findings regarding case characteristics in the vignettes. These characteristics were systematically varied and have not necessarily been found to be associated with the likelihood of sexual abuse. Nevertheless, professionals in their study were less likely to believe sexual abuse when the offender was a minority, a professional, not a family member, and not a substance abuser. If the victim was a minority, was between ages 3 to 8, showed affect when describing the event, and evidenced behavior change, the respondents were more likely to believe sexual abuse. These professionals were also more likely to believe if there was protective services involvement. An oversight in the Jackson and Nuttall research is that they failed to systematically collect data on the ethnicity of the professionals they studied.

Because adults' interests—those of the accused and their supporters and those of professionals handling the case—often prevail, children may suffer additional trauma from the intervention. They may be disbelieved by professionals when they are telling the truth. They may be subjected to repeated interviews. They may receive a medical exam from someone who is insensitive or inexperienced. They may be inadequately protected from the abuser or the family. They may be removed from their homes unnecessarily or put in unsuitable placements. They may feel traumatized and humiliated by the court process, which requires them to describe to others their sexual abuse and often to submit to brutal cross-examination. Finally, they may receive inadequate or unskilled treatment.

It is critical that professionals adopt a stance that can help children cope with pressures from competing parties, can facilitate monitoring their personal reactions and prejudices, and can ensure that they are not additionally traumatized by the intervention. The best strategy is a child-centered approach. This approach dictates that all assessment, case management decisions, and interventions take into account the child's best interest.

To act in the child's best interest, the professional starts by appreciating that there are individual differences in the impact of sexual abuse on children. Factors such as age, gender, ethnicity, the relationship between victim and offender, the characteristics of sexual abuse, and the child's social situation all affect the child's response to sexual abuse. The professional must gather sufficient information about the child and the abuse to understand these factors. Second, the professional should ascertain the child's wishes—that is, what the child wants to happen in terms of intervention and ultimate case outcome. However, what the child wants may not be synonymous with her best interest. For example, a child may wish to return to her mother even though it is clear that the mother will not or cannot protect the child from further sexual abuse. In addition, the younger the child, the less she may be able to judge what is in her best interest. Therefore, a child-centered approach is one in which the professional acts in the child's best interest by taking into account individual differences in children's experience and reaction to sexual abuse and the child's wishes.

Thus, when it is initially determined that the child has been sexually abused, she should be asked what should happen. If the child says the offender should get help, that should usually result in a therapeutic approach to the abuser. If the child says the offender should go to jail, this desire should generally lead to a more punitive response. Of course, the victim may change her mind, and these changes also need to be considered.

Additional steps are part of a child-centered approach. The child's gender, ethnicity, and other individual factors should be considered in decisions about the professionals to interview and work with the child. Although gender is routinely taken into account, race rarely is. In addition, if several professionals need to know from the child what happened, instead of having the child interviewed several times, they can have a single interview videotaped, or they can view the interview with the victim from behind a one-way mirror.

Moreover, professionals may need to play leadership roles in developing appropriate community resources to support a child-centered approach. Physicians with knowledge about sexual abuse and sensitivity to the needs of victims need to be located so that children are not retraumatized by the medical exam and important medical evidence is not overlooked. As will be discussed in Chapter 9, sexually abused children have particular placement needs. Communities need to develop and support specialized facilities for sexually abused children. Finally, professionals must develop adequate treatment resources so that the damage to victims can be alleviated and, in cases where it is appropriate, families can be reunited.

Therefore, although it is important that individual professionals adopt a child-centered approach, it is also necessary for communities to do so. Multidisciplinary, multiagency collaboration, involving agencies that serve all sectors of the child population, is the best way to ensure that a child-centered approach guides service delivery. Only then will there be minimal retraumatization of the victim from intervention and maximum rehabilitation of the victim and the victim's family.

The Extent of Child Sexual Maltreatment

It is difficult to ascertain the extent of a phenomenon that is shrouded in secrecy and surrounded by shame. Adding to the problem of identification is the fact that sexual abuse usually leaves no physical traces. Therefore, information about how widespread sexual maltreatment is comes from the mouths of victims, witnesses, and perpetrators. Two main kinds of data are used to study the extent of sexual abuse: reports of sexual maltreatment to professionals who have some responsibility for intervention and studies of populations that may contain victims.

INCIDENCE RATES OF CHILD SEXUAL MALTREATMENT

Reported cases usually yield estimates of incidence rates, that is, how many cases of sexual abuse occurred within a given time frame, usually a year. By taking the number of reports and comparing that with the number of children in the population during the target year, one can calculate an annual rate of sexual abuse for the child population. There are three main sources of national incidence data: the accumulated reports of cases to child protection agencies (American Association for the Protection of Children [AAPC], 1988; USDHHS, Children's Bureau, 2001); the Fifty State Survey, data collected annually from states on child abuse and fatalities by Prevent Child Abuse America, formerly the National Committee to Prevent Child Abuse (NCPCA), a voluntary agency (Peddle & Wang, 2001; Wang & Daro, 1998; Wang & Harding, 1999, 2000); and three periodic studies called the National Incidence Studies (NIS), funded by the federal government (Sedlak & Broadhurst, 1996). Data from all of these sources reflect an increase in the numbers of child maltreatment cases reported (including child sexual abuse) over time but a decline in the proportion substantiated by CPS.

There are other sources of statistics about sexual abuse, but they are not as useful as the sources noted above. Police reports yield less reliable information because there are literally thousands of police agencies in the United States. They do not have uniform practices for collecting information about sex crimes, and there is no central data collection. National law enforcement statistics come from the FBI, but their data include only cases where a federal statute has been violated. Hospitals, courts, diagnostic facilities, and treatment agencies may collect statistics about their cases. Their findings can be enlightening but are usually restricted to one institution and thus are not very generalizable.

Although child protection agency data are the most comprehensive, even they have limitations. First, most child protection agencies handle only cases where a caretaker is involved in the maltreatment.[1] The caretaker must be the perpetrator or must be neglectful by not protecting the child from sexual abuse.[2] Many sexual abusers of children are not caretakers. Estimates vary depending upon the data source, but between one third and two thirds of sexual abusers of children are not caretakers (Faller, 1994b). In addition, many state and local child protection agencies have not systematically collected information that incidence studies ask for. Finally, there are differences in how abuse and neglect are defined and handled from state to state that affect statistics.

Official national incidence data on all types of child maltreatment began to be collected systematically in 1976 with the passage of the Child Abuse Prevention and Treatment Act of 1974. These data consist of the accumulated reports of child maltreatment to local child protection agencies that go into a central data bank, initially sponsored by the National Center on Child Abuse and Neglect (NCCAN), an agency of the federal government (AAPC, 1985, 1986, 1987, 1988,

1989). In 1986, the federal government decided to revise the data collection system and stopped gathering information altogether for 3 years. The revised system, the National Child Abuse and Neglect Data System (NCANDS), began issuing reports in 1992 (USDHHS, Children's Bureau, 1998, 2001).

Findings from NCCAN and NCANDS regarding cases reported to the child protection system follow. What they indicate is an increase in the absolute number of sexual abuse cases over 15 years, an increase in the rate per 10,000 children, and an increase in the proportion of all abuse and neglect cases represented by child sexual abuse. Thus, in 1976, only 6,000 cases of sexual abuse were reported, a rate of .86 per 10,000 children, and in 1976, sexual abuse represented only 3% of all reports of maltreatment. By 1986, this figure had climbed to 132,000 cases, a rate of 20.89 per 10,000 children, and represented 15% of all cases of maltreatment (AAPC, 1988). From the NCANDS data system, statistics from 1990 indicate that sexual abuse remained about 15% of reports, but by 1996 the proportion had declined to 12.3% of the total reports of child maltreatment. However, because the total number of reports continues to increase, 12.3% represents about 369,000 reports (USDHHS, Children's Bureau, 1998).

Because data from the Fifty State Survey (Wang & Daro, 1998; Wang & Harding, 1999) are available a year earlier than NCANDS data and include additional information, they are frequently used to supplement NCANDS findings. Like the NCANDS data, these findings reflect a recent decline in the proportion of sexual abuse reports. Whereas in 1986 sexual abuse represented 16% of reports, in 1997 sexual abuse reports were only 7%, or about 223,650 cases. That percentage and number have increased a little in the last few years; in 1999 10% of reports were for sexual abuse, or about 324,400 (Peddle & Wang, 2001; Wang & Harding, 1999).

Findings from NCANDS and NCPCA are limited to cases that are reported to CPS. NIS (Sedlak & Broadhurst, 1996; USDHHS, 1981, 1988) conducted in 1980, 1986, and 1993 gathered information on cases known to professionals, including those known and not known to CPS. The researchers collected information from professionals in 29 counties chosen to be representative of the country as a whole who were mandated reporters (law enforcement, school personnel, hospital staff, treatment providers, court staff). In addition, they examined records of CPS in those counties. These studies projected estimates of total numbers of maltreated children, determined changes over time in numbers and types of child maltreatment being identified by professionals, and ascertained the proportion of these cases known to protective services. These studies employed two different standards, harm and endangerment, for defining child maltreatment. The harm standard is more stringent and in the case of sexual abuse would exclude a case if the offender was not a parent or parent substitute. For example, if the offender was a babysitter or a teenager, the case would not be counted under the harm standard but would be counted under the endangerment standard (Sedlak & Broadhurst, 1996).

In 1993, NIS-3 estimated that 217,000 children, or 32 per 10,000 children, were sexually abused under the harm standard and that 300,200 children, or 45 per 10,000 children, were sexually abused under the endangerment standard (Sedlak & Broadhurst, 1996). Unlike the NCANDS and NCPCA data, the NIS-3 data showed an increase in the rate of sexual abuse from 19 per 10,000 children in 1986 to 32 per 10,000 in 1993. Possibly a decline in sexual abuse cases was not detected because it was too recent.

Of the 1993 sexual abuse cases defined by the harm standard, 42% were investigated by CPS. The research methodology did not allow for the researchers to discern if a case was reported to CPS but not investigated by them. However, there was a significant decline in the proportion investigated from 72% in 1986 to 42% in 1993 (Sedlak & Broadhurst, 1996). Interestingly, a slightly higher percentage of identified sexual abuse cases defined as endangerment, 44%, was investigated by protective services, but there was a comparable pattern in decline in percentage investigated in 1993 (44%), compared to 1986 (75%) (Sedlak & Broadhurst, 1996).

Another enlightening source of information about the incidence of sexual abuse is a Gallup poll of a representative sample of 1,000 U.S. parents, conducted in 1995. Among other questions, this poll asked parents if their children had been sexually abused during the past year. Almost 2% of parents reported that their children had been. This figure projects to over 1 million children, a rate 10 times the number of cases substantiated in 1995 by CPS. Approximately 300,000 cases were reported to CPS that year, and about a third of these were substantiated by child protection agencies (Finkelhor, Moore, Hamby, & Straus, 1997; Moore, Gallup, & Schussel, 1995). The Gallup poll data may be an underestimate because parents may be loath to implicate themselves. Nevertheless, it is probably more inclusive than the NCANDS data, which would include only cases in which a caretaker was the abuser or had failed to protect a child from sexual abuse.

Finally, Jones and Finkelhor (2001) recently examined both the NCANDS and the Fifty State Survey and reported that both data sets reflected a 26% decline in the number of reports of child sexual abuse from 1993 to 1998 and a 31% decline in the number substantiated. They noted that the reporting trend was consistent with the reporting trends of other violent crimes—rape, battering, and overall rates for violent crime—and they argued on this basis that the decline represented, at least in part, a reduction in incidence of sexual abuse. However, they also pointed out that reporting failures by victims, their families, and professionals, as well as system changes causing fewer cases to be substantiated, could be reflected in these data. Although this research was based upon two important sources of information about incidence of sexual abuse, it did not take into account the Gallup poll findings of 1993 or the NIS research.

Incidence data indicate that child sexual abuse is experienced by a substantial proportion of children. Until recently, consistent increases in numbers of cases of child sexual abuse were identified. There are a variety of possible explanations for the recent leveling off and decline of cases being reported. It is possible, as Wang and Daro (1998) optimistically suggested, that this chronic problem has finally been exposed and that there are no longer substantial numbers of silenced children. However, this interpretation, which implies that the dominant pattern is one of chronic sexual abuse, is not supported by the data. Prevalence data suggest that single instances of sexual abuse are common. In addition, it is possible that public education about sexual abuse, increased professional awareness, and threats of criminal prosecution are serving as a deterrent for potential sex offenders and thereby protecting children.

However, other explanations are probably more likely. Although there have always been skeptics about sexual abuse, beginning in about 1985 doubts about children's accounts of sexual abuse began to increase. There have been challenges to both the children and to professionals who support them. The skepticism about allegations of sexual abuse is reflected in the media, in opinions of some professionals, in what happens in the courtroom, and in assertions by those accused. Arguably this "backlash" could have a dampening effect on children's willingness to disclose. Probably more likely is a decrease in willingness of adults, both professionals and nonprofessionals, to bring concerns about sexual abuse to the attention of CPS.

THE PREVALENCE OF CHILD SEXUAL MALTREATMENT

Accounts by adults of having been sexually maltreated as children give an estimate of the prevalence of sexual abuse—that is, how many people experience sexual abuse while growing up. Such studies generally consist of population surveys that may cover a range of topics but also ask about sexual maltreatment during childhood. This information is gathered using a variety of methods: by telephone, by having participants fill out questionnaires, or by face-to-face interviews with respondents. In addition, a range of populations are surveyed: (a) volunteers; (b) special populations, such as persons seeking treatment or college students; and (c) samples representative of the general population.

Because studies are conducted in different ways, using different populations, and with varying definitions of sexual abuse, their results differ. A seminal study was that conducted by Finkelhor (1979a) of men and women from six New England colleges and universities. He found that 19.2% of women and 8.9% of men reported experiences of sexual abuse during childhood. It is assumed that proportions in a college population are lower than those in the general population because the sequelae of sexual abuse can affect academic performance. Finkelhor's results startled the child welfare community and led to an appreciation of the seriousness of the problem of child sexual abuse.

Some later research found that even higher proportions of Americans had been sexually victimized. Studies yielding the highest proportions were those involving face-to-face interviews with adult women in which researchers matched ethnicity and gender of respondent and interviewer. Using a broad definition of sexual abuse, Russell (1983), whose subjects consisted of a representative sample of 930 women from the San Francisco area, found that 54% had experienced sexual abuse before the age of 18. When the definition was narrowed to include only sexual contact, the percentage was 38%. The proportion of women found by Wyatt (1985) to have been sexually abused was even higher, 62% (45% when the definition included only sexual contact abuse). Her sample was a stratified probability sample of 248 black and white women from the Los Angeles area, and her interview approach was comparable to Russell's. Although these two studies involved only women and both surveyed California populations, their results are sobering.

Data on sexual abuse of women derived from two studies by Saunders et al. (1991, 1992) highlight the impact of methodology on reported prevalence rates. The studies both employed the same definition of sexual abuse but differed in data collection methods. One involved a representative national sample, surveyed by trained female telephone interviewers. The second was a probability sample of women in Charleston County, South Carolina, interviewed face to face by trained female research assistants. The 4,008 respondents (weighted sample) in the national study reported a rate of child sexual abuse of 13.3% (N:534). In contrast, the 391 women in the Charleston study report a sexual abuse rate of 33.5% (N:131). The differences in the proportion of women reporting sexual abuse probably reflect the difference in data collection methods—that is, the superiority of face-to-face information gathering—rather than unusually high rates of victimization in Charleston County. This interpretation of the findings is congruent with high rates noted in the face-to-face studies by Russell (1983) and Wyatt (1985).

Research on the sexual abuse of men has not been as extensive and has consistently found that lower proportions of men than women report victimization. The results of two studies provide information about how methodology affects findings. A study by Risin and Koss (1987) of close to 3,000 males attending institutions of higher education in the United States noted that 7.3%

of them had experienced some form of sexual abuse before the age of 14. The definition employed in this study included noncontact as well as contact sexual abuse and required that there be a significant age discrepancy between the victim and the offender, that some form of coercion be present, and that the offender be a caregiver or authority figure. When these findings are compared to those from studies of women, boys are more likely than girls to be victimized by someone outside the home and to be victimized by women.

Fromuth and Burkhart's (1987) sample was also college-aged men, theirs coming from two universities and totaling 582 subjects. They varied the definition of sexual abuse and found that this affected the proportion of men defined as sexually abused. Factors that were varied included the maximum victim age, whether there needed to be an age differential between a victim and offender, whether coercion had to be present, whether noncontact behaviors were included, and whether the victim had to experience the sexual abuse as negative. Proportions of male subjects defined as sexually maltreated varied from 4% to 24% with these manipulations in definition.

A telephone survey conducted by the *Los Angeles Times* (Crewdson, 1988) is notable because it was large (involving 2,627 persons), it included both men and women, and it consisted of a national sample. The *Los Angeles Times* survey found that 22% of respondents reported sexual victimization as children— 27% of women and 16% of men.

In recent years, researchers have begun to undertake meta-analyses on prevalence studies, aggregating several studies so that the numbers are larger and samples more inclusive, and then producing estimates of prevalence. Gorey and Leslie (1997) examined findings from 16 cross-sectional studies involving nonclinical populations. They reported a victimization rate of 22.3% among female respondents and 8.5% among males. However they argued that these rates might well be inflated because samples with lower response rates reported higher sexual abuse estimates and those who failed to respond were more likely not to have been sexually abused. These researchers also noted the impact of definition on prevalence, stating that if a narrow definition was employed the prevalence rates declined even more. They concluded with a conservative victimization estimate of 12% for women and 5% for men.

Gorey and Leslie's (1997) findings were challenged by Bolen and Scannapieco (1999) with regard to their methodology, most importantly their inclusion of some nonrandom samples and exclusion of some important random sample studies and their failure to take into account the number of screen questions for sexual abuse. Bolen and Scannapieco's own meta-analysis involved only studies with random samples and examined the effect of the following independent variables on the prevalence rate of sexual abuse: (a) number of male and female respondents, (b) response rate, (c) year of the survey, (d) number of screen questions, (e) type of survey, (f) region, (g) upper age limit for the victim, (h) level of sexual contact, (i) age differential between victim and offender, and (j) age of respondent. They estimated female prevalence rates at between 30% and 40% and male prevalence rates at more than 13%. They noted that the small number of studies of males made it difficult to arrive at a prevalence estimate for men. Factors that predicted higher rates among females were more screen questions, fewer respondents, and more recent data collection. For men, predictors of higher rates were telephone interviews and more screen questions.

Regardless of which meta-analysis more accurately reflects the state of the U.S. population, these findings indicate that sexual abuse is a significant problem for children and adults in our country. It is not a rare occurrence. Therefore, professionals who work with children need to know about sexual maltreatment and how to intervene to help victims, offenders, and their families.

Notes

1   Some child protection agencies cover cases in which caretakers are not necessarily parents: for example, day care center cases, sexual abuse in foster care, sexual maltreatment of children in institutions, and abuse by school personnel.

2   Of course, child protective agencies handle all kinds of maltreatment, not merely sexual maltreatment.

2

Definitions and Signs of Child Sexual Maltreatment

M ost professionals who work with children receive training in the signs and symptoms of child sexual abuse as part of their postprofessional education. However, child sexual abuse encompasses a wide spectrum of acts, and there is disagreement about both when and whether some sexual acts are abusive. Moreover, some training provided in the 1970s and 1980s about indicators of sexual abuse has been determined to be incorrect, and new findings are constantly emerging. This chapter will address both definitions and signs of sexual abuse.

A Definition

Three different components of a definition of sexual abuse will be discussed in this section: (a) the types of sexual behavior, (b) the parameters of abusive versus nonabusive sexual encounters, and (c) patterns of sexual abuse.

TYPES OF SEXUAL BEHAVIORS

The types of behavior presented in Table 2.1 are usually included in a definition of sexual abuse. Each type is defined according to its subcategories, and an example of the behavior involving children is given.

Table 2.1　　　Types of Sexually Abusive Behavior

Definition	Example
1. Noncontact sexual abuse	
a. Sexual comments to the child	An 11-year-old girl is asked by a 33-year-old man to meet for "hot sex" through an Internet chat room.
b. Exposure of the intimate parts (genitals, anus, breasts) (flashing)	Older brother shows his sister his penis, asking her if she has ever seen one; shows her how he can cause an erection by rubbing it.
c. Voyeurism (peeping)	Mother's boyfriend removes the door from the bathroom so he can watch her 13- and 14-year-old daughters toileting.
d. Fetishism: having a sexual fixation on clothing or body parts (e.g., leather or rubber garments, underwear, feet, buttocks)	Grandfather takes his 12-year-old granddaughter's underwear from the hamper and uses them to masturbate.
e. Obscene phone calls	Adolescent offender calls his English teacher's wife and invites her to suck his dick. (He later masturbates while recollecting the phone call.)
2. Fondling	
a. Touching of the child's intimate parts by the offender (breasts, genitals, buttocks)	Stepfather massages 7-year-old stepdaughter's vagina while wrestling with her.
b. The offender inducing the child to touch his or her intimate parts	Mother persuades her 11-year-old daughter to caress mother's body and rub her vagina when they sleep in the same bed.
c. Fondling can be on top of or beneath the clothing.	
3. Digital or object penetration	
a. Offender placing a finger(s) in victim's vagina or anus	Day care provider inserts his finger in the anus of a 3-year-old charge.
b. Offender inducing the child to place a finger(s) in the vagina or anus of the offender	Mother requires her 6-year-old son to put four fingers in her vagina and move them in and out.
c. Offender placing an object in the vagina or anus of the victim	Father puts crayons in daughter's vagina in the course of play (takes a photograph of this)
d. Offender inducing child to place an object in the vagina or anus of the offender	Stepfather requires his 6-year-old stepdaughter to put a vibrator up his anus.

Definition	Example
4. Oral sex	
a. Tongue kissing	Five-year-old boy French-kisses his grandmother. He tells her his mom does this to him.
b. Kissing, licking, or biting other parts of the body	Ten-year-old describes how her uncle kisses her all over her body.
c. Breast sucking, kissing, licking, biting	Eleven-year-old states her grandfather sucks on her breasts and bites her nipples. He has told her that this will make them grow.
d. Cunnilingus—licking, kissing, biting, or sucking the vagina, or placing the tongue in the vaginal opening	Nine-year-old states her mom's boyfriend sucked her "wee-wee" and put his tongue inside. She says it felt weird.
e. Fellatio—licking, kissing, sucking, or biting the penis	Four-year-old describes a child care provider sucking his penis and calling this the "baby game."
f. Analingus—licking the anal opening	Brothers, ages 5 and 7, caught by foster mother engaging in analingus. They tell her their mom's friend taught them this. They say it's called "licking buttholes" and it tickles.
g. The offender may inflict these acts on the victim or require the victim to do them to him or her.	
5. Penile penetration	
a. Vaginal intercourse—penis in the vagina	Thirteen-year-old girl asserts that her mother's boyfriend, over several months, gradually put his penis farther and farther in her vagina until he achieved complete penetration.
b. Anal intercourse—penis in the anus	A 4-year-old girl bent over, pulled down her pants, and spread her buttocks, stating that's where her cousin poked her and that he put grease on her butt first.
c. Penetration is usually of the victim by the offender	

The types of sexual behavior in Table 2.1 are presented in roughly ascending order, from least serious to most serious. However, the rating of seriousness is from a professional perspective. The victim may experience a "nonserious" sexual interaction as very traumatic. For example, a 12-year-old girl may be quite overwhelmed by her father telling her that she has nicer breasts than her mother and that he wants to touch them. No sexual contact takes place, and therefore the behavior falls into the least serious category, but the child's relationship with her father is greatly damaged.

An additional illustration of the importance of victim perception is the reaction to oral-genital sex. Oral-genital sex is conceptualized as less serious than penile penetration. However, not only are some types of oral sex very intrusive, but victims may be more disgusted by oral sex than by intercourse.

An increasing type of noncontact behavior is cybersex, or virtual sex. As children have become computer literate, they have become vulnerable to manipulation by adults who engage in sexual solicitations of children on the Web (e.g., Applin & Hunt, 2001; Farley, 2001; Finkelhor & Jones, 2001; Finkelhor, Mitchell, & Wolak, 2000). Children may inadvertently or purposefully go to chat rooms, where they enter into dialogues with adults who seek to sexually exploit them. These exploitations may comprise the dialogue itself, in which the adults obtain sexual gratification from sexually explicit discourse (cybersex). Sometimes these adults try to make arrangements to meet with children for sexual encounters. In a survey of a nationally representative sample of about 1,500 children, ages 10 to 17, who use the Internet, Finkelhor and colleagues (Finkelhor & Jones, 2001; Finkelhor et al., 2000) found that during the prior year, approximately 20% had received a sexual solicitation and 25% had received unwanted exposure to naked people having sex. One fourth of the children reported that these encounters had distressed them.

The list of types of sexual abuse provided in Table 2.1 consists of the most common ones but is not all-inclusive. For example, frottage, which involves the offender obtaining gratification from contact, usually of his genitals, with the child's skin or clothing, is not included. Acts in which the offenders require that children do things to their own bodies are not in the table. Examples might be the offender inducing the child to undress, to touch him- or herself, or to put a finger or object in his or her own vagina or anus. Interfemoral (dry or vulvar) intercourse is not designated. In this activity, the penis goes between the victim's upper thighs, and, in cases involving girl victims, there may be contact with the vulvar area. Sometimes the offender uses a lubricant. Finally, attempted sexual acts are not included, although attempts to engage in sex with children are clearly abusive.

The initial sexual abuse may be at the less serious end of the continuum, but, over time, the offender may engage in progressively more serious and intrusive types of abuse. However, in other situations of sexual abuse, the initial behavior is quite serious. A progression is not always found. Finally, many studies indicate that a single incident of sexual abuse is the most common report (e.g., Faller & Henry, 2000).

THE PARAMETERS OF SEXUALLY ABUSIVE RELATIONSHIPS

The activities designated in Table 2.1 are not abusive when the parties are consenting adults. To differentiate abusive from nonabusive sexual contact, three parameters must be defined: (a) who an offender is, (b) what the age limits for a victim are, and (c) how to interpret apparently consensual sexual encounters between people at different developmental stages.

Who Is an Offender?

An act is regarded as abusive when it involves people at different developmental stages. This usually means there is a significant age differential between the offender and the victim, 5 years being the commonly employed age gap, and the offender being, of course, the older party. Thus, a situation in which a 16-year-old girl fondles a 5-year-old boy would be regarded as sexual abuse, but sexual fondling between a 5-year-old and a 6-year-old normally would not.

However, an age differential is not the only way an abusive act is differentiated from a nonabusive one. First, generally, the offender possesses superior knowledge about sex, and the victim is to some extent naive about the meaning of the sexual encounter. Second, the act is primarily for the sexual pleasure of the offender and does not represent mutual, consensual exploration. Third, there is usually a power differential between victim and offender, the offender having superior power. Power may be exercised through manipulation, various threats, or the use of force.

Therefore, child-child sexual encounters where there is no age differential can sometimes be abusive; there may be a predator child and a victim. In some cases, the victim may even be older than the predator child. For example, a 12-year-old boy might force sex on a 14-year-old girl, or an 11-year-old might trick or cajole a mentally retarded 16-year-old into sexual activity.

Predatory sexual behavior is often a sign the predator child has been previously sexually abused. Imposing sexual encounters on other children is a red flag for prior victimization.

What Is the Maximum Age for a Victim?

One of the difficulties in defining a sexually abusive relationship is making a decision about the upper age limit for a victim. In part, the age cutoff is determined by that used by Child Protective Services (CPS) and is usually 17 (National Center for the Prosecution of Child Abuse, 1997, Vol. 5). However, researchers have also had an influence upon maximum age. Some have used 18; others, 16 (Russell & Bolen, 2000). Moreover, the maximum age may vary by sex, the upper age limit for boys being younger than that for girls. For example, some researchers have used 13 as the cutoff for boys (Risin & Koss, 1987). In addition, some have used a different maximum age depending upon the age differential between victim and offender: For example, the maximum age for the victim may be 16 if the offender is at least 10 years older (Finkelhor, 1979a). Finally, a retarded victim may be chronologically an adult but developmentally a child.

There is no definitive answer to the question of what an appropriate maximum age should be. Nevertheless, it is important for professionals to consider this issue in cases where it is relevant in order to ensure that appropriate case management decisions are made.

The Issue of Consent

An issue that is related to maximum age is consent. There is an assumption that the consent must be informed—that is, the child must have a full appreciation of the significance of the sexual encounter. Finkelhor (1979b) has argued that what makes sex between an adult and a child abusive and therefore wrong is that a child cannot give informed consent, both because he or she cannot really understand the meaning of the sex and because the child is not really free to say no. Therefore, situations where children agree to cooperate or actively participate are nevertheless abusive. So too are situations where previously victimized and/or disturbed children initiate sexual encounters with adults.

What about older children? Can an adolescent consent to a sexual encounter with an adult? This judgment is influenced by the age of consent, which varies from state to state, being as low as 14 in some states and as high as 18 in others (Crewdson, 1988; Russell & Bolen, 2000). Therefore, it is difficult to arrive at a clear-cut answer. The following case example illustrates the dilemma posed by cases involving consenting adolescents.

Case Example: Mrs. M had two daughters, Alma, 10, and Jeanette, 15. The girls had been sexually abused by their father. When Mrs. M found out about this, she threw Mr. M out of the house and refused him access to the children.

After the exit of Mr. M, she got a job working for a construction company, and she had a series of boyfriends. George, age 27, was one who moved in with the family. He was highly regarded by Mrs. M and the girls because he was a college graduate. However, after he had been living with the family for 3 months, Alma told her mother that George had come into her bed and fondled her vagina and rubbed his penis back and forth between her legs. Mrs. M discovered that he had been sexually abusing Jeanette as well.

Mrs. M threw him out, as she had done with her husband. However, Jeanette went with him, informing her mother that she was in love with George. Further, Jeanette told her mother that she was fat and drank too much. It was no wonder that George preferred her (Jeanette) to her mother. Jeanette moved in with George and began working as a waitress to support herself (and him).

There is no question that George's sexual encounter with Alma was abusive. She is 17 years his junior and she objected to what he did. From a legal standpoint, George is also sexually abusing Jeanette, but she does not perceive this relationship as abusive. She declares she is in love with him. Furthermore, if it weren't already known that George had a propensity to sexually abuse children (from his molestation of Alma), his relationship with Jeanette would not be so worrisome. The fact that Jeanette is supporting George, as her mother had done before her, adds to our concern. Should protective services or the juvenile court intervene and force Jeanette to return to her mother or, alternatively, place her in care? Or should she be allowed to remain with George and perhaps learn from this mistake?

Finally, just as gender affects maximum age, so it may have an impact on consent. Sexual socialization of boys differs from that of girls. In simplified and vernacular terms, boys are taught that they should like sex and should seek it— that is, they should be the initiators. In contrast, girls are taught that they shouldn't like it too much and that they should wait to be asked. When girls are asked, they should say no. These normative differences, in part, reflect a concern about the risk of pregnancy for girls.

Gender differences in sexual socialization may affect perceptions of sexual invitations. For example, when a boy is asked to have sex with an older woman, he may experience this as a compliment and an opportunity both to learn about sex and to experience pleasure. He may tacitly or overtly give his consent. Research on boy victims supports these clinical observations (Fromuth & Burkhart, 1987). Risin and Koss (1987) found that a substantial proportion of college-age males, reporting sexual experiences during childhood, defined themselves as actively participating in sexual encounters with substantially older females that, on the basis of age criteria, would be considered abusive. This was especially likely to be the case when the offenders were baby-sitters.

PATTERNS OF SEXUAL ABUSE

One dimension of defining sexual abuse is designating the various sexual acts, as documented in Table 2.1. Another is describing patterns of sexual abuse. Dyadic sex, group sex, sexual exploitation, sex rings, and ritualistic sexual abuse will be discussed. Dyadic sexual encounters are the most common, and professionals and the public accept their existence. There are, however, less common patterns of sexual abuse that arouse greater skepticism.

Dyadic Sex

In this situation, there is one perpetrator and one victim, and the perpetrator engages in sexual activity with a child. These encounters are characteristic of both intrafamilial and extrafamilial sexual maltreatment.

Group Sex

Some sexual abuse occurs in a group context. Group sex can take a variety of forms (Burgess, 1984; Finkelhor, Williams, & Burns, 1988). A single offender may begin by initiating dyadic sex with more than one victim and then, by accident or design, have sexual encounters with two or more victims more or less simultaneously. This may happen in intrafamilial cases where, for example, a father is sexually involved with several of his children. Group sex may also be the pattern in extrafamilial sexual abuse.

Another variation of group sex involves more than one offender and generally several victims. Polyincestuous families may engage in this kind of group sex. In such families, sexual abuse is typically found intergenerationally and laterally in the extended family. Women as well as men are offenders, and often it is not possible to clearly differentiate victims from offenders. The mothers in these cases may describe themselves as forced to become involved, and older children who have previously been abused become predators (Faller, 1991a).

Group sex may also be the pattern in extrafamilial contexts: for example, in day care situations, in institutions for children, in foster care, or in camps. In these instances, there usually is a single offender, but, in some cases, multiple offenders are involved. See Chapter 9 on sexual abuse in day care and Chapter 8 on sexual abuse in foster care for further discussion of group sex.

Sexual Exploitation

Sexual maltreatment may also involve sexual exploitation of children. Children are used to produce pornography or are sold as prostitutes. Both of these activities violate federal statutes when they result in interstate transport of goods or children, and they violate state laws as well (Campagna & Poffenberger, 1988).

Child pornography may consist of children having sex with adults, with other children, or engaging in seductive or masturbatory activities alone. Photographs, videotapes, or films are then made of children engaging in these acts. Pornography may pander to persons with either heterosexual or homosexual tastes. In some cases, animals are involved or other perversions shown. Because the use of children in the production of pornography is illegal, young adults who look to be children may be employed instead. Often an issue when pornography is seized is documenting the age of the victims (Walsh, 2001).

Child pornography is produced for the gratification of adults, although those producing child pornography are not necessarily sexually attracted to children. Pedophiles, however, may make and collect pornographic pictures of their victims. These are later used for arousal, in trade (either the pictures or the children themselves), and, in some cases, to entice new victims into sexual activity (Burgess, 1984; Crewdson, 1988).

An emerging arena of concern is child pornography and adult solicitation of sex with children on the Internet. Child pornography is fairly readily available on the Internet. However, as adult models are sometimes employed in traditional pornography, so are electronic simulations of child images used in Internet pornography.

Child prostitutes are of all ages and of both sexes. Younger children will have a procurer. This may be someone who is a family member, an acquaintance of the child or family, or a pimp by profession. The circumstances in which adolescent girls prostitute are similar to those of adult women prostitutes. That is, they usually have a pimp, who at some level takes care of them, and they may be one of several girls in the pimp's stable. Adolescent male prostitutes, like adult male prostitutes, are more likely to operate independently (Campagna & Poffenberger, 1988).

Many of the older children involved in sexual exploitation are no longer living with their families (Barnitz, 2001). Typically they are runaways. Few children are actually abducted for the purpose of sexual exploitation (Crewdson, 1988; Finkelhor, Hotaling, & Sedlak, 1992; Plass, Finkelhor, & Hotaling, 1997).

Another source of children for prostitution and pornography is the developing world, especially Southeast Asia and the Philippines, although some also come from Latin America (Barnitz, 2001; Campagna & Poffenberger, 1988; Sassoon, 1988). These children may be sold by their families, abducted, or brought to the United States (or to western Europe) under false pretenses—for example, allegedly to be adopted or to be educated (Barnitz, 2001). Persons who are sexually attracted to children may also travel to developing countries on sex tours, where they have access to children who suit their tastes (Campagna & Poffenberger, 1988; Sassoon, 1988). However, most individuals from the developed countries who have sex with children in the sex trade are not pedophiles but businessmen or vacationers (Barnitz, 2001).

Finally, some parents make pornography involving their own children. In the past, when it was necessary to have a photographic laboratory to develop film and to make copies, family or amateur production of child pornography was limited. Also, the fact that professional photographic studios are required to report any person who asks to have such material developed or reproduced further inhibits persons without access to photographic equipment from producing child pornography. However, the current ready availability of video equipment, which is reasonably priced and does not require the services of a photographic laboratory, has greatly facilitated the production and copying of child pornography. It is also quite a lucrative enterprise, which further enhances its appeal.

Sex Rings

Children may also be sexually abused in sex rings. Boys are more likely to be victimized in sex rings than girls (Burgess, 1984). As best as can be discerned, sex rings are generally developed by pedophiles: that is, individuals whose primary sexual orientation is to children. In establishing sex rings, pedophiles develop for themselves, and sometimes for like-minded persons, a stable of children with whom they have sex. Pedophiles may choose professions that allow them access to children, or they may merely put themselves in situations where they can befriend and attract children (Crewdson, 1988; Faller, 1988a). Some boast special skills in selecting children who are vulnerable to sexual exploitation. These are typically children who are deprived and neglected. In addition, children from single-parent, female-headed families may be targeted. Pedophiles assert that these children lack a male role model and therefore are likely to gravitate to the male pedophile.

Usually there is a grooming or seduction process involved, in which the children are initially plied with attention, friendship, and/or gifts, and as they become emotionally or materially dependent upon the perpetrator, sexual favors are demanded. In addition, current members of the ring may be used to recruit new members. These children serve as recruiters to enhance their relationship with the ringleader and to receive additional rewards. The recruiter may emphasize the material benefits of involvement and minimize the sexual activity. Some recruiters are children who are too old to be of sexual interest to the ringleader and who engage in recruiting activities to maintain an emotional and/or material relationship with the ring leader (Burgess, 1984).

In some cases, sexual activity in sex rings is group sex: That is, sexual activities involve several children simultaneously. Children may also be encouraged to engage in sexual activities with one another. However, in other instances, the leader of the ring has a series of dyadic encounters with ring members, although the members are likely to know of one another. In some cases, a ring involves more than one perpetrator (as well as several victims) (Burgess, 1984).

Leaders of sex rings may have very narrow tastes in children. They are likely to be particular regarding the sex of the child, as mentioned earlier, preferring boys; they may be restricted in terms of the age range that interests them; and they may prefer a particular physical type in their victims. To access desirable victims, the pedophile may become part of a network with other pedophiles and share children. Photographs of these children are often taken. These may be used to facilitate the selection of desirable children, or they may be sold or traded as pornography. In addition, if members of the network have proclivities toward children of different ages, one member may pass on to another a child who is too old to be of interest to him. (See Burgess, 1984, for a further discussion of sex rings.)

Ritualistic Sexual Abuse

Yet another pattern in which children may be sexually abused is in a ritualistic context. Ritualistic abuse is maltreatment (of children and adults) that includes physical, sexual, and psychological abuse. The motivations for this multimodal abuse are thought to be various. Finkelhor et al. (1988) identified three types of cases in a study of day care: (a) true cult-based ritualistic abuse, (b) pseudo-ritualistic abuse, and (c) psychopathological ritualism. Included in the first category are cases where the abuse of children is in the context of the practice of Satanism. The second category involves individuals who may engage in similar acts but not out of religious belief, rather to instill fear and ensure children's silence. In the third category are usually the disturbed offenders like Jeffrey Dahmer, who sexually assaulted, killed, and dismembered young men.

When this book was originally published, there was a great deal of interest in and concern about ritual abuse, most child welfare professionals believed in its existence, and the federal government funded research into its characteristics and effects (Bybee & Mowbray, 1993; Goodman, Bottoms, Qin, & Shaver, 1994; Valliere, Bybee, & Mowbray, 1988; Waterman, Kelly, Oliveri, & McCord, 1993). But responses to allegations of ritual abuse have undergone a transformation in the last 10 years, so that any case involving ritual elements elicits great skepticism. In fact, it is no longer *au courant* to believe in the existence of ritual abuse (Chaffin & Stern, 2001; Myers, 1998).

There appear to be several reasons for the change in perceptions of ritual abuse. One reason for disbelief is the paucity of physical documentation of victims' reports, specifically of alleged ritual murders (Lanning, 1990). If the accumulated accounts were true, one would expect hundreds of missing children and adults to be reported and graves or ritual burial sites to be discovered. There is no such evidence. Nevertheless, some corroboration has been found (Faller, 1994c, 1996a; Snow & Sorenson, 1990; Stickel, 1993).

Perhaps the most controversial case was the McMartin Preschool case, which involved almost 400 alleged victims and a 3-year criminal trial, the most expensive in California's history (Waterman et al., 1993). In the end, charges against all but two defendants were withdrawn, one defendant was acquitted, and the jury hung twice over some counts against another defendant. This case is perceived by both professionals and the public as a false case. Yet a team of five archeologists, led by Gary Stickel, who holds an adjunct appointment in the Department of Archeology at the University of California at Los Angeles, found physical evidence of the tunnels under the day care center described by the children and approximately 2,000 artifacts, a number of which supported the children's allegations (Stickel, 1993).

Another case with corroboration is the Country Walk case in Miami, which was prosecuted by Janet Reno when she was attorney general for the State of Florida. A couple, Frank and Iliana Furster, were described as having ritually sexually abused preschoolers in their baby-sitting service. Children's stories of birds being tortured and killed and the Fursters dressing in costumes and engaging in sexual activities with one another and with the children seemed incredible. Nevertheless, Iliana Furster turned state's witness and testified against her husband, corroborating the children's statements (Hollingsworth, 1986). Later, however, when she discovered her testimony did not render her immune from incarceration, she recanted her statements.

And in a 1989 case in Matamoras, Mexico, the bodies of 12 adults who had been ritually sacrificed by a satanic cult were discovered. However, this case did not involve children, nor did it involve sexual abuse.

In addition, there is a modest body of research on cases involving ritual abuse. These studies can be categorized into research of four types (Faller, 1994c): (a) the extent of professional experience with ritual abuse (Goodman et al., 1994), (b) research on day care center cases (Bybee & Mowbray, 1993; Faller, 1988a; Finkelhor et al., 1988; Kelley, 1989, 1992b; Waterman et al., 1993), (c) research on community-based "cults" or cases (Jonker & Jonker-Bakker, 1991, 1997; Snow & Sorenson, 1990), and (d) studies of intergenerational ritual abuse (Kelley, 1992a; Leavitt, 1994; Young, Sachs, Braun, & Watkins, 1991).

The research findings include findings about the prevalence and the impact of ritual abuse. With regard to its extent, a little more than 10% of professionals involved in child welfare and mental health services delivery have encountered cases of ritual abuse. For mental health professionals, cases are fairly evenly divided between adult reports and child reports, with adult reports having more bizarre allegations (Goodman et al., 1994). The modal number of cases seen per professional was one and the median two, although 2% of respondents reported seeing in excess of 100 cases (Goodman et al., 1994). In a national study of 260 cases of sexual abuse in day care, Finkelhor et al. (1988) found that 13% of cases included allegations of ritual abuse.

A number of studies compare the functioning of children in day care who are alleged to have been ritually abused with children alleged only to have been sexually abused, using standardized measures. In these studies, the impact of ritual abuse is greater on children's functioning (Bybee & Mowbray, 1993; Kelley, 1988, 1992a, 1992b, 1993; Valliere et al., 1988; Waterman et al., 1993). Finally, a small number of studies comparing adults with histories of ritual abuse to adults with other traumatic experiences demonstrate more severe symptoms by ritually abused adults (e.g., Leavitt, 1994).

A second reason that some researchers have evidently doubted the existence of ritual abuse is the failure to identify an organized conspiracy of Satanists behind the practices (Goodman et al., 1994; La Foutaine, 1994). Professionals who believe their clients' accounts of ritual abuse have, as a consequence, been faulted (Goodman et al., 1994). It is not clear why evidence of a conspiracy is a hallmark, nor why the failure to identify one calls into question the existence of individual cases. An alternative hypothesis is there may be a loose network of offenders, similar to that found among pedophiles (Faller, 1993b).

A third and major cause of this transformation of views about ritual abuse has been the concerted campaign against those who support victims reporting ritual abuse and the victims themselves. This campaign has especially been fostered by the False Memory Syndrome Foundation, which surfaced in 1992 (e.g., Lanning, 1992; Okerblom, n.d.). The FMSF was founded by Peter and Pamela Freyd, who are both husband and wife and stepsiblings. Their daughter, Jennifer Freyd, who is a professor and memory researcher in the Department of Psychology at the University of Oregon, has stated that her parents started this organization in response to her (private) accusation that her father sexually abused her (Freyd, 1993).

The FMSF has attacked all allegations of sexual abuse, often using ritual abuse as a vehicle to demonstrate how preposterous abuse allegations are (see, e.g., the April and December 1997 [Vol. 6] issues of the *False Memory Syndrome Foundation Newsletter* and the book *The False Memory Syndrome Phenomenon* [FMSF, 1992]). The vigor of the attack against ritual abuse, like the vigor of the attack against sexual abuse in general, reinforces the belief of some professionals, myself included, that there is substance to ritual abuse.

The FMSF strategy eventually caught the attention of the media. The media's initial reaction to allegations was to sensationalize ritual abuse cases. This treatment was especially true of the talk shows, such as *Geraldo* ("Satanic Cults and Children," 1987) and *Oprah* ("Satanism," 1986; "Satanic Worship," 1988). However, "the story" that eventually replaced the horror of ritual abuse became the catastrophic injustice of false allegations of ritual abuse (e.g., Nathan, 1987).

Ultimately, the backlash against ritual abuse cases resulted in the reversal of some criminal convictions involving ritual abuse (*New Jersey v. Michaels,* 1994; *North Carolina v. Kelly,* 1995) and a number of high-profile lawsuits against clinicians who treated patients reporting ritual abuse (*Bloom v. Braun*, 2000; *United States v. Paterson*, 1999). Thus, this effort to discredit clinicians who have provided services to the survivors of ritual abuse, the survivors, and ritual abuse itself has been quite successful.

Finally, it must be said that it is difficult to believe human beings could engage in the heinous acts described by victims of ritual abuse; the enormity of allegations no doubt fuels skepticism. People cast about for alternative explanations. Nevertheless, some case descriptions are provided by individuals who appear very credible (Mayer, 1991; Ryder, 1992; Stone & Stone, 1992; Wong & McKeen, 1990), and cases continue to be identified.

Table 2.2 lists characteristics reported in cases of ritual abuse. It is included in this chapter, despite the general rejection of ritual abuse as a phenomenon, because I endorse a child or victim-centered approach to child sexual abuse. What this means is that if children report abuse with these characteristics, their accounts need to be taken seriously, although not every assertion by a child need be taken at face value. The list can be used to assist professionals who encounter cases where ritual abuse is alleged.

Table 2.2 is not an exhaustive list of characteristics but rather a list of elements commonly described in these cases. These have been divided into two sections: abuse characteristics and context characteristics. A rather disconcerting finding is that quite similar characteristics—for example, chants and ritualistic marriages—have been reported in several contexts (Crewdson, 1988; Faller, 1988d).

In the abuse characteristics section are listed those characteristics that may signal a report of ritualistic abuse. These abuse characteristics are not unique to ritual abuse, but they may be red flags that the report is of ritual abuse, and such cases may include other types of abuse as well. In addition to physical, sexual, and psychological abuse are somewhat unique types of abuse: confinement, pornography, and the use of chemicals, apparently to alter children's perceptions.

The contextual characteristics are divided into unique places mentioned by children or adults; evidence of belief systems; unique dress described by children or adults; a category termed "Accoutrements"; unusual verbal behavior; symbols, which may be wide-ranging; and any ceremonies described.

The following example is a case where I evaluated 14 children from five families.

Case Example: The abuse in this case involved a deviant subgroup of individuals in a prominent church in a small community. Altogether about 35 children reported being involved. The parents were middle-class, successful people—teachers, a radio announcer, an accountant. The ritual abuse took

Table 2.2   Characteristics of Ritualistic or Multimodal, Calculated Abuse to Children

1. Maltreatment reported by children and adults alleging ritualistic abuse

   A. Physical abuse
      1. Sadistic physical abuse
      2. Burning of the victim and others
      3. Cutting of the victim and others
      4. Torture of the victim and others

   B. Sexual abuse
      1. Group sex
      2. Coerced or cajoled sex with other children
      3. Child prostitution
      4. Child rape
      5. Object insertion into the vagina and/or anus

   C. Emotional abuse
      1. Threats of death and severe bodily harm
      2. Undermining the victim's belief system
      3. Use of omnipotence of the offender
      4. Victims witnessing apparent killing
         a   Of animals
         b. Of babies
         c. Of adults
      5. Ingestion and use of body excretions/products
         a. Feces
         b. Urine
         c. Blood
         d. Semen
         e. Apparent use of human flesh

   D. Confinement
      1. Tying up
      2. Putting victim in a grave, coffin, closet, cage

   E. Pornography
      1. Involving children with adults
      2. Involving children with other children
      3. Involving children with animals
      4. Used to sell
      5. Used to threaten children

   F. Chemicals
      1. Children describe ingestion of pills, potions
      2. Children describe receiving shots

(Continued)

Table 2.2 *(Continued)*

2. Context characteristics

    A. Places abuse occurs
        1. Outdoors (e.g., in the woods, in a special site)
        2. In churches
        3. In day care

    B. Ideology (actual belief or possible use of ideology for manipulation)
        1. Satanism
        2. Other religious belief systems
        3. Some components of Satanism
        4. Polymorphous perversity
        5. Pedophilia

    C. Dress
        1. Robes (black, white, red, purple)
        2. Animal costumes (e.g., tigers, lions, bears)
        3. Uniforms (police, doctor's coat, nurse)
        4. Masks (e.g., devil)
        5. No clothes on at all

    D. Accoutrements
        1. Altar
        2. Guns and knives
        3. Circles (drawn on the ground)

    E. Verbal/auditory
        1. Chants
        2. Songs
        3. Prayers
        4. Music

    F. Symbols
        1. Inverted crosses
        2. 666 (the devil's number)
        3. Devil
        4. Number 13
        5. Bones/skeletons
        6. Candles

    G. Ceremonies
        1. Black mass
        2. Marriages (e.g., to offenders)
        3. Marriage to Satan

place on Sunday mornings when parents were in church and children were in Sunday school or at the church baby-sitting service, during a youth group that met on Wednesday evenings, and on church outings. The abusers included two teenaged boys and their parents. One of the boys was successfully criminally prosecuted, and the other pleaded. Although two grand juries were convened to consider charges against the adults named by the children, none of the adults were indicted.

When children began reporting abuse, the pastor was mortified but supported the children and their families. The church provided education about ritual abuse and treatment for the children.

The children reported sexual abuse in the church bathroom, when they would be taken there by one of the teenaged boys. They also reported abuse in the woods near the church, in the woods next to a nearby day care center, and at an empty mansion in the community. Some children reported the two teenagers would take them to the children's houses in the church van, enter the houses, and sexually assault the children in their houses. The children were threatened that if they told, the abusers knew where they lived and would come and kill them and their parents. After telling about the abuse, a 6-year-old boy insisted on sleeping with a hockey stick by his bed so he could protect himself and his family if the abusers came to get him.

Activities described as having taken place in the church, in the woods near the day care center, and in the mansion included making the children engage in sexual activities with each other and making the children engage in sex with the adults and teenagers. The children also described adults and children wearing white, black, purple, and red robes and "cone hats like Mississippi Burning." They spoke of chants, a large circle on the ground in the woods, being made to kill animals such as rabbits and cats, and being made to kill babies. Several children described and drew a picture of a pit in the ground in the woods. The teenagers would make a child lie on the ground in the pit and require the other children to throw rocks and sticks at the child. Sometimes the child would be partially buried by rocks and dirt in the pit.

Illustrative of the detail the children provided is the following account by 9-year-old Sam, who would have been 5 at the time of the abuse. He said, "And they made us kill babies." When asked how he knew the baby was a real baby, Sam said, "It was crying. It was wrapped up in a pink blanket." He said, "Scott made me kill the baby." When asked how, he said that Scott had a knife. He drew a picture of the knife. Sam said, "Scott went, 'Here, Sam, hold the knife for a minute.' I was holding the knife and he grabbed my hand and made me stab the baby. Then he said, 'Sam, why'd you do that? Why'd you kill the baby? Now God won't love you anymore.' That made me real sad because I thought now I wouldn't be able to go to heaven and be with my grandpa." When Sam was asked why he thought the baby was killed, he said it stopped crying. When asked if the baby bled, he said there was blood all over. When asked what happened next, Sam said Scott threw the baby on the ground, but it didn't cry anymore. As to what they did with the baby, he said they buried it in the woods. He did not know exactly where. When asked if he was sure this was a real baby, he insisted it was. Sam's demeanor when he described this event was subdued and he appeared remorseful.

Additional, similar, detailed accounts were provided by all but three of the children I evaluated from this case. Moreover, the children had symptoms consistent with having the experiences they described. I have followed this case over time, beginning in 1994, and only one child has recanted, although the memories of some children have faded. Recently, the church settled a civil lawsuit involving some of the parents, acknowledging that the ritual abuse occurred.

Sam's report captures the dilemma of ritual abuse. How should professionals respond to reports of this type? One the one hand, a child describes a heinous crime and needs support. On the other, what the child has related is very difficult to believe. David Finkelhor, a pioneer in sexual abuse research and principal investigator of the national study of sexual abuse in day care (Finkelhor et al., 1988), which brought ritual abuse to professional attention, has provided an important observation. Essentially, he has noted that explanations supporting the existence of ritual abuse are not very satisfactory and that explanations asserting it does not exist are also not satisfactory (D. Finkelhor, personal communication, 1992).

Indicators of Possible Sexual Abuse Among Children

Children who have been sexually abused may show symptoms of these traumatic experiences. In this discussion of indicators, symptoms will be divided into two general categories: sexual symptoms and nonsexual indicators of possible sexual abuse.[1] In addition, asymptomatic children will be considered. An essential point is that sexual symptoms are much more likely to be related to sexual abuse than are nonsexual symptoms.

SEXUAL SYMPTOMS

When children demonstrate sexual behavior, possess sexual knowledge, and make statements about sexual activities, they may have been sexually abused. Such symptoms cause particular concern in preschool children. They are usually not old enough to have received any sex education and are unlikely to have sexually active or knowledgeable peers who might have exposed them to sexual material.

Sexual Behavior

Sexual behavior in children with a possible history of sexual abuse has been the subject of research and clinical observation. Both of these approaches to understanding child sexual behavior will be discussed in this section, as practitioners are advised to employ both approaches to understanding children's sexual behavior.

A Standardized Measure of Sexual Behavior

William Friedrich of the Mayo Clinic has been studying sexual behavior as a potential marker for sexual abuse for more than 20 years (Friedrich, 1993, 1994). He began this work using the Sexual Problems subscale of the Child Behavior Checklist (Achenbach, 1993) and eventually created the Child Sexual Behavior Inventory (CSBI), which reliably differentiates children aged 2 to 12 with a history of sexual abuse from children without a sexual abuse history (Friedrich, 1990, 1993, 1994, 1999). Patterns of normative and sex abuse-specific behaviors are differentiated for children aged 2 to 5 years, 6 to 9 years, and 10 to 12 years and are differentiated by gender. Friedrich and colleagues have conducted this research, using children with and without a history of sexual abuse from several sites in the United States and Canada. The instrument continues to be refined (Friedrich, 1999; Friedrich et al., 1996a, 1996b).

The CSBI yields a Total Score and has two subscales. One subscale is composed of developmentally normal sexual behavior, such as "Touches sex parts at home," "Touches breasts," and "Tries to look at people when they are nude." The other subscale consists of sexual abuse–specific behaviors, such as "Touches other child's sex parts," "Puts mouth on sex parts," "Masturbates with object/toy," and "Asks others to do sex acts." Items on the developmental subscale are found in children regardless of abuse history, whereas those in the sexual abuse–specific subscale are very low frequency in children without a history of abuse but are found in a substantial minority of children with a history of sexual abuse.

Professionals assessing for possible sexual abuse are advised to acquaint themselves with the CSBI and current findings for children with and without a history of sexual maltreatment. Even if the professionals cannot administer the CSBI, they may know about the child's sexual behavior. Knowledge about the significance of the specific behaviors as indicators of sexual abuse may be vital in decisions about intervention.

The limitation of the CSBI is that it relies on adult (usually the child's parent) report. This may introduce bias in that adults may either under- or overreport sexual behavior. In addition, the measure can only tap information the adult possesses; the child may have engaged in behaviors unknown to the adult. Foster parents or noncustodial parents may not report sexual behavior simply because they have not seen it.

Clinical Observations

Clinical observations and reports about sexual behavior are quite consistent with the research on the CSBI. However, clinicians often obtain qualitative information rather than just frequency of behaviors. In addition, the CSBI has a cutoff at age 12. Clinical observations include behaviors of adolescents. Six different types of sexual behavior that signal possible sexual abuse will be described in this section: (a) excessive masturbation, (b) sexual interaction with peers, (c) sexual aggression toward younger or more naive children, (d) sexual accosting of older people or adults, (e) seductive behavior, and (f) promiscuity.

Excessive Masturbation. When is masturbation excessive? Most children, and indeed most adults, masturbate. This is developmentally normal behavior for children. Generally, they discover that it feels good to touch or rub their genitals as they explore their bodies. Because it feels good, they will repeat the activity. The appropriate adult response to encountering a child masturbating is to acknowledge that it feels good but to explain to the child that masturbation is an activity to be done in private.

Signs that a child is excessively masturbating are as follows: (a) compulsive masturbation (i.e., the child cannot stop); (b) inflicting injury while masturbating (also an indication that this is compulsive behavior); (c) masturbating several times in a day; (d) inserting an object into the vagina or anus during masturbation; and (e) masturbating when upset and feeling vulnerable.

Illustrative of excessive masturbation is the following case example:

Case Example: Ms. T brought her 3-year-old daughter, Sally, to be evaluated for possible sexual abuse. The major symptom the mother complained of was masturbation. She said that she would catch Sally masturbating and tell her to stop. Sally would then go into the bedroom and her mother would catch her again. The mother said that the child would seem in a trance.

When the evaluator interviewed Sally, Sally told the evaluator that she was bad. The evaluator asked what she did that was bad. Sally replied "riding." The evaluator asked what "riding" was. Sally proceeded to demonstrate. She straddled the arm of a chair and, placing one hand on the seat of the chair and holding on to the back with the other, she rocked back and forth on the chair arm, masturbating, for several minutes. She appeared transfixed. She then got off and proceeded to "ride" the other arm of the chair. There were three other chairs with arms in the playroom and she asked if she could "ride" them as well. She took off her jeans and underpants, saying it was better that way. She appeared red from her mons veneris to her anus, apparently from "riding."

When asked where she learned about "riding," she said her grandmother taught her. She then described a range of sexual activity involving both of her grandparents.

In this case, the mother's description suggests excessive masturbation, but before seeing Sally, the evaluator wondered if perhaps the mother's punitive response was responsible for the masturbation. However, clearly what the child demonstrated in the session was excessive masturbation, and Sally then revealed the source of her "riding" behavior.

A final caution about excessive masturbation is that some deprived children may masturbate excessively. Because of a lack of stimulation and nurturance in their environment, they resort to self-stimulation and self-comfort in the form of masturbation. Moreover, as considered in the above case example, children who have been caught and punished for masturbating may develop a pattern of furtive masturbation, which can become preoccupying to the point that the behavior is excessive.

Therefore, to conclude, when there are reports of masturbation, professionals first need to determine whether the behavior is within normal limits and then need to look for the cause of the behavior, taking into account that something other than sexual abuse might be the source of excessive masturbation.

Sexual Interaction With Peers. Some children who have been sexually abused will engage in sexual activity with peers. In cases where this is the child's reaction to sexual abuse, clinical hypotheses are as follows: The child has been sexually overstimulated and as a consequence is sexually precocious. In addition, there are cases in which the sexual interaction has a compulsive quality to it, reflective of the traumatic aspect of the sexual abuse.

However, again, it is important to differentiate developmentally normal behavior from that which is more likely to be indicative of sexual abuse. Children aged 3, 4, or 5 generally discover not only that touching themselves feels good but also that other people have genitalia, some of which are different from theirs (i.e., boys and girls are different). These discoveries may occasion looking at one another's genitals and touching one another. Because the touching feels good, it may be repeated. Furthermore, if children observe adults engaged in sexual activity, they may try these acts themselves. And as children become older and learn about various forms of sexual activity, they may experiment.

Nevertheless, when children are discovered engaging in sexual activity with one another, it is important to inquire where they learned about these acts. Children may gain general knowledge about sex acts and information about the more common sexual behaviors from observation or education. For example, when children observe intercourse, they learn that adults may get on top of one another and move around, but they are unlikely to know that the penis goes in the vagina unless they observe from quite close up. And, in that case, the question of whether the children were allowed or required to watch must be explored. Of course, older children may have learned that the penis goes in the vagina as part of sex education or from other children. Therefore, when they attempt intercourse, it may well involve penetration.

In addition, children are more likely to observe or learn about fondling or genital intercourse than fellatio, cunnilingus, analingus, or anal intercourse, simply because the latter are less common and less universally accepted sexual behaviors. Thus, engaging in the latter types of behavior is more likely to be a sign of sexual abuse than engaging in the former.

The following case example is one where sexual interaction is a clue that the children have been sexually abused.

Case Example: Nannette, 6, and Dottie, 5, typically spent several weeks during the summer with their paternal grandmother. She saw little of them during the school year because she worked as a teacher's aide.

She had fixed up their father's room for them with bunk beds. (He was residing in the state prison for armed robbery.) She noted that they would usually be in the lower bunk together in the morning. She asked why they did not stay in their separate bunks, and they giggled and said that they were scared of the dark. She put a night light in the room but still would find them together in the morning. She became concerned when she noted that sometimes they had taken their pajamas off. When she queried about this, they again giggled and told her it was hot.

One night as she passed their door, she heard talking and entered the room. She found both children naked. Nannette was on her hands and knees with her buttocks up in the air, and Dottie had her finger in Nannette's anus. As the grandmother entered the room, Dottie said, "Now it's your turn to do it to me."

Their grandmother, very upset, told the girls to put their pajamas back on and go down to the living room. She then questioned them about what they were doing and where they had learned to do it. They told her that they had figured it out themselves. She made Nannette sleep on the couch and sent Dottie back to the bedroom. Because of some training she had received as a teacher's aide, she doubted their story.

The next day, thinking that the sexual play was something that their mother or her new boyfriend had instigated, she called protective services. Eventually, the children told the child protection worker that their dad used to sleep with them when their mother was at work. He would put his fingers in their "pussies" and their "butts." The part with the "pussy" hurt, but if you put a finger in the "butt" and wiggled it around, it felt good.

In this case, the behavior was of the sort unlikely for children to discover spontaneously, nor would it be something they might observe. The fact that they chose to repeat the activity they reported felt good suggests that this sexual interaction was a reaction to the sexual overstimulation aspect of their abuse.

Sexual Aggression Toward Younger or More Naive Children. Another possible symptom of sexual abuse is sexual aggression toward younger or vulnerable children. The clinical explanation here is somewhat different from that related to sexual interaction with peers. The child who has been victimized identifies with the sexual aggressor as a way of dealing with the trauma of his or her victimization. That is, the child becomes a perpetrator in order to achieve mastery over his or her own sense of vulnerability.

Children as young as 3 years have been found to exhibit this aggressive response (Cavanagh-Johnson, 1988). This kind of reaction to sexual abuse appears more common in boys than in girls. Sexual aggression is thought to be more frequently related to previous sexual abuse than the two types of sexual behaviors already described.

Such a pattern may be an acute response to the trauma of sexual maltreatment and may disappear of its own accord. However, in a number of cases, the sexual aggression becomes chronic. In the latter instances, these aggressive acts may be merely defined as sexual play when the child is young, but as the child becomes older, especially during adolescence, the child is relabeled as a perpetrator. Sadly, if the significance of the problem had been recognized earlier and adequately treated, the child might not have become an adolescent sex offender. In yet other instances, there is minimal or no sexual aggression following the sexual abuse, and sexual aggression as a response to earlier sexual maltreatment does not begin until adolescence. This syndrome is sufficiently common to be labeled "the victim to offender cycle" (e.g., Ryan & Lane, 1997). It argues for early treatment of sexual abuse, especially among boys, even if the child appears asymptomatic, and for vigilance on the part of caretakers in order to detect later hypersexual behavior.

In the following case example, sexual aggression was the outcome of sexual victimization.

Case Example: Martin, 5, and his sister, Sarah, 3, were sexually abused by their adolescent cousin, Henry. Sarah disclosed her sexual abuse to her mother, and both children were brought to treatment. Initially, Martin denied anything had happened to him and said Henry was a really nice guy. He said he wanted to be like Henry when he grew up. In the next session, Martin said that he knew something had happened to Sarah but not to him. Sarah then described Henry requiring both her and Martin to fellate him, saying that she had to tell for Martin because he was too scared.

Martin still did not admit to any abuse, but after the session in which Sarah told about his victimization, he got in her bed at night and put his hands inside her pants. She began having nightmares, but it took her several days to tell her mother what Martin had done.

When the children's mother confronted Martin, he began to tell her about his victimization by Henry. He also began to discuss this in treatment. He said that at first it was fun being with Henry. Henry would toss him up in the air, and Martin would land on the bed. Then Martin described his surprise when Henry told him to take his shirt off and Henry rubbed his penis on Martin's chest. Then Henry put his penis in Martin's mouth. Martin became very upset when he described this to the therapist, saying he couldn't make him stop. Even more distressing to Martin was having to watch Henry put his penis in Sarah's mouth and in her vagina while she cried for him to stop. Martin said he couldn't protect himself or his sister.

There was one subsequent incident in which Martin tried to pull Sarah's pants down, and she kicked him. In contrast to his aggression with his little sister, Martin was very nonassertive with male peers. In treatment, the therapist helped Martin talk about how awful it was to be tricked by someone you looked up to and not be able to do anything to stop him when he mistreated you. In addition, treatment focused on how Sarah must feel when Martin sexually abused her. Martin was helped to be more assertive with his peers and was enrolled in a karate class.

Before the sexual maltreatment, Martin seems to have very much identified with Henry. Therefore, in the early stages of treatment, he could not acknowledge that his cousin betrayed him or directly express his anger and sense of vulnerability. This identification and denial appears to have resulted in his victimizing the only person in his environment he could dominate, his little sister. Focusing on Martin's own feelings, as well as those of his sister, and teaching him more appropriate ways of achieving a sense of mastery and expressing aggression were important techniques in reducing the likelihood of repeated sexual aggression.

Sexual Accosting of Older People. Behavioral or verbal sexual advances to older persons are other symptoms of possible sexual abuse. In such instances, the apparent dynamics are somewhat different from those cited in other types of sexual interaction. The child has been socialized both to expect adults to be sexual and often to view sexual interaction as a way adults and children show they care about one another. Thus, children who have been previously sexually maltreated may invite people whom they like or value to be sexual with them. So, for example, a 4-year-old victim who had been required to fellate a number of men, liked her uncle, and said to him, "Take down your pants so I can see your penis." It is my clinical experience that girls are more likely to engage in this kind of behavior than boys. Like sexual aggression, sexually accosting older people is quite a compelling indicator of having been sexually victimized.

In the following case, a child demonstrated this symptom of sexual abuse in foster care. (See Chapter 8 for a discussion of this phenomenon in foster care.)

Case Example: Diane, 3, was removed from the home of her mother and mother's boyfriend after the boyfriend severely physically abused one of her older brothers. She was initially placed with her brothers but had to be moved because her brothers were attempting intercourse with her.

In her new placement, she was the youngest child. Her foster mother initially had no knowledge about possible sexual abuse and was quite surprised at the large size of Diane's vaginal opening. She did nothing about this observation.

She became concerned when Diane kept asking her older foster brothers and sisters to rub her tu-tu. Diane would stretch the elastic of her underpants open in the front and say, "Touch down here," or she would take the older child's hand and try to put it on her genitalia.

The foster mother became very worried at a family gathering and finally reported her suspicions to the child welfare worker. A grandfatherly friend of the family's was on the floor playing with the children. He was lying on his back, and Diane came and sat on his face and rubbed her vagina back and forth across it. Diane looked quite surprised when the man jumped up and told her she was a bad girl. She began to cry.

Eventually, it was learned that Diane's father, her mother, and the mother's boyfriend had all been involved in sexual abuse of the three children in the family.

In this case, there were symptoms that actually preceded Diane's sexual advances to both her foster siblings and the family friend. Her invitations were both behavioral and verbal.

This type of overt sexual invitation is more characteristic of younger children who do not fully appreciate the inappropriateness of their actions. However, it may also be found in emotionally disturbed children who may be much older.

Seductive Behavior. Older children who have been sexually abused are more likely than younger ones to know that overt sexual invitations are inappropriate. They learn this from the admonitions the offender may use to prevent disclosure as well as from reactions to such invitations and other information sources. Nevertheless, like their younger counterparts, they have been socialized at an early age to be sexual beings. They may persist in more subtle behaviors that may be perceived as seductive.

Mental health professionals and others who observe children acting in this manner must appreciate that this is learned behavior, a result of how their abuser(s) taught them to act. Therefore, it is important not to blame the victim for these patterns. Often victims are quite unaware that their actions are viewed as seductive. They may believe they are ugly or otherwise unappealing and may be bewildered by the responses they elicit from people to whom they behave seductively.

In addition, seductive behavior, although a "red flag," may also be exhibited by teenaged girls without a history of sexual abuse. One reason for the cutoff of the Child Sexual Behavior Inventory at 12 years is that Friedrich and colleagues found that sexual behaviors could not be used to reliably differentiate between girls with and without a history of sexual abuse once they reached adolescence (Friedrich, Grambsch, Broughton, Kuiper, & Beilke, 1991).

The following case example illustrates this type of symptom:

Case Example: Ursula, 15, ended up in foster care because of intense conflicts with her mother. She blamed her mother for the fact that her mother had lost custody of four younger siblings and for marrying two men who sexually abused Ursula.

Soon after placement, her first foster mother demanded that she be removed. The foster mother was vague about what the problems were but did say that she didn't like the way her husband responded to Ursula. Ursula was moved to a second foster home.

After Ursula had been in her second foster home about 2 weeks, she called her worker in a panic. She said she got along fine with the foster mother and liked the foster father, but she felt very anxious when she was left alone in the house with him.

Her worker went to the home to see if she could understand what the problems were. She had a meeting with Ursula and the foster parents. Ursula was dressed in very tight jeans and a tight sweater. She was a very statuesque 15-year-old. Although it was a cold, rainy day, about 10 minutes into the meeting, Ursula declared she was hot and left the room, returning in a few minutes in a pair of very short cutoff jeans. She sat with one leg draped over the arm of the chair and the other on the coffee table. Her foster father was facing her, essentially being forced to look at her crotch.

The worker quickly sensed what the problem was. She decided that she needed to talk to Ursula separately. She spoke later with Ursula about how she was sitting, noting that this might be misinterpreted by the foster father and lead to a sexual advance, which would make Ursula feel uncomfortable. Ursula was quite surprised and said she didn't understand how the foster father could think she was sexy because her face was too fat. She then went on to relate similar trouble with both the owner of the restaurant where she was working and his son. Both had been grabbing her sexually and the son had tried to force her to have sex with him in his car.

Further work with Ursula helped her to decrease behaviors that were interpreted as sexual invitations.

In Ursula's case, her previous sexual abuse by both a father and a stepfather resulted in an exaggerated style of behavior that was perceived as a sexual invitation. Not only had this led to a reaction by the foster father in her second foster home that made her uncomfortable, but it had resulted in sexual aggression by both her boss and his son. Moreover, probably the request for her removal by her first foster mother was a consequence of this woman's interpretation of Ursula's behavior as an attempt to seduce her husband.

Promiscuity. When a sexually abused girl reaches early adolescence, a consequence of her victimization may be promiscuity. She has learned at an early age that her body is for the use of others. This pattern of relating to others that was imposed when she was younger becomes a voluntary or quasi-voluntary one as she becomes older. Ironically, these victims of sexual abuse may experience little or no sexual pleasure. Many of them report they actually do not experience sexual gratification. Moreover, some adolescent victims have poor self-images as a consequence of the sexual maltreatment, and being promiscuous reinforces this self-image. For example, one victim said, "I feel like a slut, so I act like a slut."

Of course, not all promiscuous teenagers have been sexually abused. Other dynamics can lead to promiscuity. Some girls resort to sex as a way of gaining acceptance and achieving relationships. In addition, children who have not been nurtured as they have grown up may use sex as a way of relating because they are deficient in skills for developing other kinds of close relationships.

Finally, for some adolescents, promiscuity is a way of rebelling, often against their parents.

Promiscuity may be manifested as or develop into adolescent prostitution. A survey of adolescent prostitutes concluded that 90% of them had been sexually abused as children (Carlson & Riebel, 1978). A common sequence is for an adolescent victim of sexual abuse to run away to escape the sexual abuse and other problems at home and then to be faced with the need to support herself. Few jobs that underage girls can find allow them to support themselves and remain on the street. Therefore, for lack of alternatives, they resort to prostitution. Often these runaways are befriended by men whose intention is to use them as prostitutes. The case example presented here is illustrative.

> *Case Example*: Darlene first ran away from home when she was 12. She was placed in a group home. She intended to stay in the group home, but one afternoon on her way to the dentist, she met a man who offered her some cocaine. She got high with him, and when she was sober again, she had missed her dentist appointment and decided she could not return to the group home. So she went with the man. He turned out to be a pimp, who kept her and three other teenagers. He became her lover before he persuaded her to prostitute for him. However, she had little overt negative reaction to prostituting, using the term "making money" to describe the prostitution and declaring that she didn't see anything wrong with it.
>
> Darlene came to the attention of protective services at the age of 14. At the time, her pimp was in prison for rape and she was 5 months pregnant. She also had a severe case of venereal warts. Despite her circumstances, her major concern was that the baby might not be her pimp's.
>
> Her description of her family background helped explain why she had run away and gotten herself in her current situation. She said that her mother was always "bitching" at her. Further exploration revealed that the bitching was about Darlene's relationship with her stepfather. He had begun sexually abusing Darlene when she was about 6. This abuse continued until Darlene ran away. Despite the stepfather's sexual abuse, he was the more nurturing, caring parent. Darlene's mother had always perceived her as a competitor and a threat. Darlene did not initially tell her mother about the sexual abuse because her stepfather told her that her mother would throw him out. When she did finally tell her mother at 10, her mother blamed her. Then, in the face of the stepfather's denial, Darlene's mother decided Darlene was lying and was just trying to make trouble between the parents. Over the next 2 years, Darlene's mother vacillated between accusing the stepfather of sexual abuse, accusing Darlene of seducing him, and accusing Darlene of lying about it. At no time did she show any empathy for Darlene.

At 14, Darlene had a hard time conceptualizing what her stepfather had done as abuse and did not think it had negatively affected her. Because of her family background, she was quite vulnerable to relationships in which she perceived herself as being cared for, yet was being exploited. There are parallels between Darlene's perception of the sexual abuse by her stepfather and her perception of being used by her pimp as a prostitute: That is, she minimized their exploitative nature.

Sexual Knowledge

One indication of possible sexual abuse in young children is sexual knowledge beyond what would be expected for their developmental stage. Therefore, when young children know about digital penetration, ejaculation, and anal intercourse, know that adult males get erections and that the penis goes in the vagina during intercourse, and know what fellatio and cunnilingus are, what intercourse, fellatio, cunnilingus, and anal intercourse feel like, and what semen looks or tastes like, the possibility of sexual abuse needs to be carefully explored. It is necessary to find out where the children learned this information.

It is possible for them to learn about some of these aspects of sex in ways other than participation. As noted earlier, children may observe sexual activity. However, as also noted, usually they learn about the more common types of activity, fondling and intercourse, and will lack detail. In addition, they may be exposed to pornography. However, pornography that is shown on cable television is soft core: That is, no penises are shown entering vaginas, no cunnilingus or fellatio is shown, and no ejaculation occurs. In addition, when children say they have seen these acts on television, it is important to consider the possibility that children have been allowed to view pornography as a prelude to sexual abuse. Moreover, most professionals would regard having children watch pornography as inappropriate and perhaps abusive. If children report that they have seen pornography on the Internet, it is nevertheless important to determine the specific characteristics of the pornography and how they obtained access to it.

Finally, there are certain types of sexual knowledge that children cannot gain without actual participation. These include what semen tastes like, what anal or vaginal intercourse feels like, what fellatio feels like, and what cunnilingus feels like.

The following example illustrates advanced sexual knowledge.

Case Example: Ellen, 8, was alleging sexual abuse by her father and one of his friends. She said that first her father had abused her. Then he had invited his friend over and let him do it, too.

Her father said that when she was allowed to visit her maternal grandparents, she got to do anything she wanted. He knew that the grandparents rented pornographic movies and said she had probably gotten her ideas about sexual abuse from watching the movies.

Ellen refused to talk to the police officer who tried to interview her, saying she didn't like men. Men do bad things to girls. She was sent to a female expert in sexual abuse.

During the course of the interview, the evaluator asked her again about her feelings about men. She repeated that they do bad things to girls. As to what these were, she said with their dick. She was asked what they do with their dick, and she showed vaginal intercourse, using an anatomical girl and adult male doll, adding, "That can really hurt your pussy." When asked if they do anything else, she put the male doll's penis in the girl doll's mouth. She was asked if anything came out of the penis, and she nodded. As to what color it was, she said white. As to what it tasted like, she said salt.

She then went on to describe the specific acts her father committed and those his friend had engaged in.

In this case, Ellen demonstrates a great deal more sexual knowledge than one might expect of an 8-year-old. It is not too unusual that she is aware that the penis goes in the vagina during intercourse, but her knowledge of fellatio, ejaculation, and the color of semen are very concerning given her age. Moreover, her awareness that intercourse can hurt and that semen tastes like salt is information she could only acquire through direct experience and not from watching movies at her grandparents' house.

Sexual Statements

As will be discussed in detail in Chapter 5, the determination of sexual abuse is usually made on the basis of the child's verbal statements and/or behavioral demonstrations. Consequently, when a child makes a statement indicating she has been sexually abused, this requires careful investigation.

Sometimes these statements are made inadvertently: for example, in response to a particular situation or naively, because the child does not know anything is wrong with the sexual abuse. For example, while moving his bowels, a 4-year-old boy said to his baby-sitter that his bum hurt because his grandpa had put his wiener in it. In another case, a 3-year-old girl told her mother, who was assisting her in a bath, that when she visited her daddy, she helped him wash his dinky, and that he liked this.

In other instances, the child is more cognizant of the inappropriateness of the sexual maltreatment and may have been threatened with negative consequences for telling. When the child does tell, there may be a delay of weeks or years between the onset of the sexual abuse and the child's disclosure (Faller, 1988a; Sorenson & Snow, 1991; Summit, 1983). Often a crisis for the victim, such as the offender demanding to engage in more intrusive sexual behavior, the victimization of a younger sibling, or a change in family circumstances such as a parental separation, precipitates disclosure (Corwin, Berliner, Goodman, Goodwin, & White, 1987; Faller, 1991b). Some victims do not tell until they reach adolescence, a time when they may feel less dependent upon the offender and wish to engage in age-appropriate peer relationships, such as dating (e.g., Myers et al., 1989; Summit, 1983).

Even when children have decided they want to tell, they may be quite hesitant and tentative. In some cases, the information comes out slowly, the child revealing the least traumatic acts first. Furthermore, victims who have been sexually abused may retract their assertions because of pressure from the perpetrator or family, embarrassment and shame, or some of the other consequences of telling (Sorenson & Snow, 1991; Summit, 1983).

For a more extensive discussion of the process of disclosure of sexual abuse, see Chapter 6, and for a discussion of criteria for determining the likelihood of sexual abuse once disclosure has been made, see Chapter 7.

NONSEXUAL INDICATORS OF POSSIBLE SEXUAL ABUSE

Children may display a wide range of nonsexual symptoms when they are being or have been sexually abused. However, these symptoms can also be responses to other types of trauma, such as physical abuse, parental disharmony, parental divorce, alcoholism in the family, the birth of a sibling, the death of a family member, moving, or even a natural disaster. Nonsexual symptoms by themselves should never be considered conclusive of sexual abuse. Positive findings in any of these areas indicate only that the child is distressed and do not necessarily indicate the source of the distress. Unfortunately, some of the literature and training material on sexual abuse has cited these nonsexual indicators of stress as indicators of sexual abuse.

These nonsexual symptoms can be subdivided into the following categories: (a) disorders of functions, (b) emotional problems, (c) behavior problems, and (d) developmental lags/school problems.

Disorders of Functions

Disorders of functions include sleep problems, bowel and bladder problems, and eating problems. Children who are experiencing or have experienced sexual abuse may have nightmares, be unable to sleep, be afraid of the dark, walk in their sleep, or talk in their sleep. They may come into their parents' bed at night. Children who have been toilet trained may become enuretic, during the day or night or both, or encopretic, in reaction to sexual abuse. Encopresis is sometimes associated with anal penetration. Loss of appetite may be a response to the onset of sexual abuse. Children may also become picky eaters or refuse certain foods. The latter symptom is reported in cases of ritual abuse: for example, refusal to eat tomatoes or catsup, reportedly because they remind the child of blood. Adolescent female victims may become anorectic or bulimic. However, some eat excessively so as to be physically unattractive to potential abusers.

Emotional Problems

Some observers report personality change in children with the onset of sexual abuse. One mother described her daughter as a "motor mouth" prior to the onset of fondling and cunnilingus by her best friend's father. Afterward, she said her daughter was very quiet and would hardly talk to her.

Children may become depressed, preoccupied, hyperactive, or anxious as a consequence of sexual abuse. This anxiety is manifested in fears or phobias, the most common nonsexual sequelae found in victims of sexual abuse (Berliner & Saunders, 1996). These phobias may relate to the threats the offender uses to prevent disclosure. For example, in a day care center case, one perpetrator threatened to kill the children's parents if they told. A number of children became phobic about being separated from their parents. In other instances, phobias are long-standing and are associated with the sexual activities of the maltreatment. For example, a victim as an adolescent or adult may become overwhelmed and frightened when asked by a partner to engage in the sexual activities that were the ones inflicted by the abuser.

Behavior Problems

A wide range of behavior problems can result from sexual abuse. These may vary based on victim age and sex. Achenbach's Child Behavior Checklist is a standardized measure that can be used to gather information about these problems. It has versions for children aged 2 to 3 and 4 to 16. It is a widely used measure of children's behavior problems and yields a total score; two major subscales, internalizing problems and externalizing problems; and several other subscales, the number and nature of which vary depending upon the child's age.

Behavior problems include physical aggression toward younger children, peers, or even older persons, including parents, and other types of difficulties in getting along with others. As adolescents, female victims may run away, become suicidal, or become involved in drug or alcohol abuse. Victims may also act out by becoming incorrigible, violating curfew, and stealing. Male victims may engage in cruelty to animals and become fire setters, but some female victims will also harm animals and set fires.

Developmental Lags/School Problems

A possible effect of sexual maltreatment is interference with cognitive development. One of the outcomes of sexual abuse is an undermining of basic trust, a fundamental prerequisite for later development, including cognitive development. Thus, young children who experience sexual abuse, and usually other maltreatment, may suffer delays in speech, fine motor control, and even gross motor development. More common are problems in concentration and school performance in older victims of sexual abuse. Often lower grades are reported coincident with the onset of sexual abuse or the aftermath of disclosure. In addition, in adolescence, victims of sexual abuse, as part of their more pervasive acting out, may become truant from school or defiant in the school setting.

ASYMPTOMATIC CHILDREN

Some children currently experiencing sexual maltreatment or sexually victimized in the past do not manifest overt signs of the trauma. Conte and Berliner (1988) studied 369 victims of sexual maltreatment who resided in the community and found that 21% of the children were asymptomatic, according to their social workers. Research by Elliott and Briere (1994) compared children who had revealed sexual abuse, children who were thought to have been sexually abused on the basis of external evidence but had not reported it, and children who were determined not to have been sexually abused, using standardized self-report measures. They found that children who had recently reported sexual abuse were the most symptomatic but that children who had not reported but who were thought to have experienced sexual abuse were the least symptomatic. Furthermore, most mental health professionals have had the experience of working with children who were experiencing ongoing sexual abuse but who did not demonstrate any observable signs.

It is tempting to believe that asymptomatic children have not been harmed by their maltreatment. However, it is more likely that the effects are subtle or are delayed or that the child has been well socialized by the offender, and in some cases by the family, not to reveal signs of her or his distress. In addition, symptoms, particularly if they are mild, may be interpreted as consequences of other experiences (as they could be) or as developmentally normal. For example, many 3- and 4-year-olds have nightmares without having suffered any specific trauma. Therefore, nightmares that could be a consequence of sexual abuse may be judged to be characteristic 3- or 4-year-old reactions and behavior.

Finally, it is important to appreciate that there are children who are being sexually abused who do not disclose when asked or even when evaluated by a skilled mental health professional (e.g., DeVoe & Faller, 1999; Lawson & Chaffin, 1992).

Note

1   In addition to these indicators that mental health professionals are likely to note, there are, of course, medical indicators. For a discussion of medical indicators, see Bays and Chadwick (1993).

Part II

*Collaborating With Institutions
Having Mandatory and
Legal Obligations*

3

Working With Protective Services and the Police

Child sexual abuse is both a threat to child safety and well-being and a crime. Two separate social institutions are charged with investigating and handling these acts: Child Protective Services (CPS) and the police.

Moreover, beginning in the mid-1980s, virtually every state passed legislation resulting in collaboration between protective services and the police on child sexual abuse cases (National Center for the Prosecution of Child Abuse, 1997, Vol. 5). Thus, the roles of CPS and the police are more interrelated than they were when the first edition of this book was published, and some would argue that their alliance is an uneasy one (Pence & Wilson, 1994). A consequence of these legislative changes is increased priority on criminal prosecution of sexual abuse.

For professionals who encounter cases of sexual abuse, knowledge of the roles of CPS and the police is crucial to effective case management and treatment. The mandates of these two institutions, the roles of their personnel, how CPS and law enforcement differ and interrelate, and how other professionals are required to interact with them will be addressed in this chapter. The first section of this chapter will deal with collaborating with protective services and the second with law enforcement.

Collaborating With Protective Services

Professionals who work with children may be involved with protective services on sexual abuse cases in a variety of capacities. Probably most common is as a reporter of suspected sexual maltreatment, but additional roles are as an evaluator of a child and/or members of a child's family and as a therapist for individuals and families where sexual abuse has been documented. Issues that present dilemmas for mental health professionals, when and what to report, confidentiality and its abrogation, and the role of protective services will be covered in this section.

REPORTING REQUIREMENTS

For states to qualify for federal discretionary funds under the successive statutes that define requirements for state child abuse programs (e.g., Child Abuse Prevention and Treatment Act of 1974; Child Abuse Prevention, Adoption, and Family Services Act of 1988), they must have procedures for reporting child abuse and neglect. Most states require any mental health professional, any health care provider, and any person who works in an educational setting with children to report when they suspect child maltreatment by a caretaker. Other people, such as friends, neighbors, and relatives of the family, may report but are not required to do so. Currently nine states require all adults to report, professionals and nonprofessionals (Myers, 1998; National Center for the Prosecution of Child Abuse, 1997, Vol. 5). All states now specifically include sexual abuse among the reportable acts (Myers, 1998; National Center for the Prosecution of Child Abuse, 1997, Vol. 5).

Statutes do not assume that the reporter has absolutely determined that a child has been maltreated. Often a phrase such as "reasonable cause to suspect" or "reasonable cause to believe" is used to designate the standard of certainty the reporter must have (National Center for the Prosecution of Child Abuse, 1997, Vol. 5). Making reports sounds fairly straightforward, but it may not be.

The first issue is this: What is reasonable cause? A legal definition is what a reasonable person of the individual's profession would regard as reasonable cause. However, to some extent, this definition begs the question because professionals must then decide what is reasonable for persons with their training. Moreover, mandated reporters may not receive training as part of their professional education on the identification of sexual abuse. Nevertheless, it is clear that the professional need not have thoroughly investigated the case and proven sexual abuse before reporting. In fact, that is the role of protective services.

A second issue is that even though protective services agencies are mandated to investigate all reports of abuse and neglect, they may have their own standard for accepting a report of abuse or neglect. Virtually every state has a screening process that allows them to decline to investigate certain reports (Wells, 2000). Moreover, what is screened out can vary from community to community. For example, some agencies will reject referrals based upon third- or fourth-hand information. In some jurisdictions, a report by a social worker based upon information from an adult client who asserts her daughter has told her that a friend's father is sexually abusing the friend will be accepted and investigated. In other jurisdictions, the social worker will be told to get more direct information.

A third issue related to the obligation to report is how current the sexual maltreatment needs to be to require a report. Many professionals regard the propensity to sexually abuse as a chronic condition (e.g., Bench, Kramer, & Erickson, 1997; Carnes, 1984; Faller, 1988a; Groth, 1979; Leberg, 1997; Schwartz & Cellini, 1995; Steele, 1995). Moreover, most sex offenders are more likely to victimize multiple children than a single child (Abel & Rouleau, 1990; Becker, 1985; Faller, 1988a). Therefore, the fact that an incident occurred several years ago does not necessarily mean that the victim or others are not at risk. The following case example highlights this ambiguity.

Case Example: Mr. J. had sexually abused his daughter, Cecily, for about 4 years, from the time she was 6 to 10 years old. The abuse stopped when Cecily told her mother, who took the children, left him, and eventually obtained a divorce. Mr. J is now a grandfather and is frequently allowed to baby-sit for his grandchildren, both male and female. Cecily noted that these children, her nieces and nephews, had very advanced sexual knowledge and were engaging in oral sex with one another when she saw them at a family reunion. She wanted her therapist to make a report to protective services, but the therapist did not think she had sufficient information.

This is an example of a possible abuse situation that is falling through the cracks. Cecily's therapist made a determination based upon her experience with protective services. Cecily could make a report herself, but she may be fearful she will not seem credible.

A fourth issue is: Who is a caretaker? It is clear that a referral should be made when the alleged offender is a parent. Less clear is what to do about an uncle, a baby-sitter, or a neighbor. These persons may be reported to the police, but this action will not always protect children. A decision about a report to protective services should be based on the parental response to the alleged sexual abuse, assuming the mandated reporter has this information. If the parent takes steps to prevent further contact, then a referral may be legally unnecessary. Nevertheless, there may be other children who are at risk from this offender whom protective services could assist. Also, the involvement of protective services may be helpful to the victim and the parent in providing support, guidance, and access to therapy.

States vary in how they handle situations involving caretakers who are professionals acting *in loco parentis*. Examples of such caretakers are school personnel, day care staff, camp counselors, and staff at child care institutions such as residential treatment facilities, group homes, and psychiatric hospitals. Sexual abuse in these facilities is a licensing violation. Therefore, protective services may share responsibility for investigating these complaints with the agency that licenses these facilities, or the licensing agency may conduct the investigation alone. The police are usually involved in the investigation, but in some situations police are not brought in until after a preliminary investigation determines sexual abuse is likely. Finally, there will be different structures for investigating reports depending upon the institution involved, and the structures will vary not only from state to state but also by locality within a given state.

When a professional has a question about any of these issues—(a) what constitutes reasonable cause, (b) what level of knowledge and specificity is required, (c) how current the sexual victimization needs to be, or (d) who investigates various caretakers—the best practice is to consult protective services for guidance. Such a consultation will ensure that the report is handled in an appropriate and timely way.

CONFIDENTIALITY

Two types of confidentiality will be discussed in this section: protecting the reporter's identity and the reported client or family's confidentiality.

The reporting provisions in most states allow for keeping the identity of the reporting person confidential (National Center for the Prosecution of Child Abuse, 1997, Vol. 5). However, the intent of this provision is to facilitate reports by nonprofessionals whose well-being might be jeopardized should their identity become known to the parent or family who has been reported. In general, I think it is best for professionals to inform clients when they make a report to protective services. Informing the client allows for honest communication about the professional's concerns. When not informed, parents often figure out who reported anyway and are probably more upset than if the professional had told them. When the parent doesn't know who reported, he or she may focus on "Who reported me?" rather than on the abuse itself. Moreover, the professional may eventually have to testify about the sexual abuse (and other family problems) in court. It is better that the family be aware of the identity of the reporter than be confronted with this in court.

By state statute, any existing confidentiality between the reporting professional and involved parties (i.e., the victim, the offender, the nonoffending parent) is abrogated when the professional has reasonable cause to suspect child abuse or neglect.[1] Clients may be surprised and upset when information about child maltreatment they thought was privileged is reported by their therapist to protective services. Because of this potentiality, some advise informing clients before beginning treatment that any child maltreatment must be reported to protective services. Professionals should use their judgment in deciding the appropriateness of forewarning clients. Such a practice may not be needed and may unnecessarily alarm the client if the client has no access to children and comes to treatment for something entirely different. In contrast, if the client requests treatment for issues related to sexual abuse, the mental health professional should inform the client of reporting requirements. Finally, many of the services available to children and families involved in sexual abuse are services provided under contract with public child welfare agencies. These agencies will require periodic (monthly or quarterly) reports about clients' progress. In these situations, very little information is confidential.

Once a report is made, that information, as well as any other material in the protective services record of the reported family, is confidential (e.g., Child Abuse Prevention, Adoption, and Family Services Act, 1988). This provision has created problems in communication and understanding between protective services and reporters, as well as between protective services and other agencies involved with the family. States and communities have created procedures that do allow for sharing some information between CPS and reporters, but it is usually circumscribed.

THE ROLE OF PROTECTIVE SERVICES

CPS is the agency mandated by federal and state statute to investigate and intervene in cases of child maltreatment by caretakers.[2] Service is delivered by a county-level agency, usually the county department of social services (variously called human services, children's services, public welfare, and so on). Its goals are to protect children, which may involve temporary removal, and to ameliorate the home situation so that children will be safe. If the home situation does not improve as a consequence of intervention, then the agency is to find an alternate, safe, permanent living arrangement for the child. Temporary and permanent removal of children require court action. Protective services may also request court intervention to ensure the family's cooperation with their intervention.

The processes of investigation, decision making, and intervention will be described in this section. They are described as separate functions, but in actuality they may occur concurrently.

The Process of Investigation

Especially during the investigative phase of CPS intervention, statutes require cooperation with law enforcement. Both the actual requirements and how they are carried out will vary by state and locality, but professionals should expect protective services and law enforcement to work together. CPS may jointly interview family members with police, or there may be a division of labor, with, for example, CPS interviewing the child and the nonoffending parent and the police interrogating the suspect. Alternatively, each agency may conduct separate investigations and share information. This model of joint investigation is discussed further in Chapter 6.

In performing their investigative duty, protective services workers make home visits, interview children and other family members, contact other professionals who have been involved with the family, and, as already noted, work closely with law enforcement. Although protective services' primary role is child protection, because of statutory requirements of joint investigation with the police, CPS workers also collect information that may be used in the criminal case.

The expertise of CPS workers in sexual abuse investigative interviewing has been challenged. As a consequence, training CPS workers specifically in forensic interviewing has been undertaken. In addition, efforts have been made to standardize forensic interviews. Moreover, some communities have developed forensic interview services separate from CPS. Some of these services are hospital based, but the most prevalent model is the Children's Advocacy Center (e.g., Carnes, Gardell, & Wilson, 2000), a freestanding program providing forensic interviews and sometimes medical exams and treatment. However, even in communities with Children's Advocacy Centers and other forensic interview services, CPS workers usually conduct an initial child interview to determine if a specialized forensic interview is needed.

The Child Interview. As a rule, in responding to a complaint of sexual abuse, first the worker will try to interview the child. Whenever possible, this is done in a neutral setting, away from the influence of the suspect and sometimes the rest of the family, most frequently at the child's school. Tapes, including videotapes, may be made of the investigative interviews. For a discussion of documenting interviews, see Chapter 6.

Interview With the Nonoffending Parent. Next, the worker typically interviews the nonoffending parent, usually the child's mother. Issues in that interview will depend upon the tentative conclusion from the child interview—that is, whether the worker thinks it is likely the child has been abused, whether the worker thinks the child has not been abused, or whether the worker is uncertain.

If the worker has concluded that the child has been or may have been sexually abused, the worker will usually share that information with the mother. The worker will be interested in the mother's prior knowledge about the abuse and her ability to protect; thus, she will be assessing the mother's response to a discussion of the abuse. Is she angry at the perpetrator? Is she angry at the victim? Does she believe the child has been abused? What is her attitude toward the child? Maternal responses will help the worker assess the mother's relationship with the victim and her ability to perceive the child's needs, which may well be different from her own and the perpetrator's.

If, on the other hand, the worker believes the child has not been sexually abused, the interview agenda will be different. The agenda may merely be to inform the mother that there was a concern about sexual abuse but that the worker does not think the child has been abused. If the worker thinks there was a consciously made false allegation, the worker may use the mother's interview to try to determine its etiology.

Finally, if the worker is uncertain about abuse, the worker will use the interview with the nonoffending parent to gather additional information that may lead to a conclusion about the likelihood of abuse.

In practice, many initial conclusions are quite tentative and uncertain. Furthermore, agencies may have a more formal decision-making procedure that occurs when the investigation is complete. As a consequence, workers often collect information about all possible explanations for the allegation in the interview with the nonoffending parent.

Suspect Interview. The alleged offender is the next person typically interviewed. If the worker thinks this person has sexually abused the child, he or she will usually confront the alleged offender with that information. Sometimes the worker obtains a confession, but more frequently not. If the worker thinks the child has not been abused, this interview will be to so inform the accused. Finally, this may be a data-gathering interview if the worker is uncertain. As already noted, law enforcement may be responsible for this portion of the investigation.

Additional Data Gathering. Other children in the family should also be interviewed. Medical exams of the children may be sought, and the alleged victim and other family members may be sent to a mental health professional for an evaluation. As a rule, the worker seeks the family's voluntary cooperation with all of these procedures. However, if they resist, the worker has the ability to go to court and seek a court order to compel their compliance.

The Goals of Protective Services

The CPS worker's first task is to determine whether a child has been sexually abused. His or her second task is to determine whether the child is safe at home and, if not, to make provisions for the child's protection. Finally, the worker intervenes to ameliorate harm to the child and to improve family functioning so as to reduce the likelihood of subsequent sexual abuse. Each of these tasks will be discussed below.

Determining Whether Sexual Abuse Occurred. Child protection agencies use various terms to characterize this aspect of worker decision making (founding, substantiating, or accepting a case; unfounding, unsubstantiating, or denying a case) (Drake, 2000). Usually, but not always, this is a dichotomous decision. Founding or substantiating a case means the worker will open the case for services, and unfounding or denying means the case will not be opened and services will not be provided. Some states have an intermediate category, *indicated*, which allows the worker to provide services without actually determining there has been abuse, and a few states (e.g., Michigan) have a greater number of categories into which cases can be placed.

It is no easy task deciding whether a child has been sexually abused. Unlike physical abuse, sexual abuse usually has no physical evidence. In a large percentage of cases, it is the child's word against the alleged offender's and often the mother's as well. Moreover, a child's account is very likely to be less coherent and persuasive than the accused's. Although child protection workers may be aware of the literature that declares that children have little or no investment in making false allegations and may be aware that offenders have substantial investment in persuading others that the child is lying, fantasizing, emotionally disturbed, or mistaken (Faller, 1984, 1988a; McCarty, 1981; Sgroi, 1982), workers nevertheless are also subject to other influences. These include direct pressure from the accused and his or her supporters, literature asserting that children are suggestible and prone to make false allegations (e.g., Ceci & Bruck, 1993, 1995; Ceci, Huffman, Smith, & Loftus, 1994; Ceci, Loftus, Leichtman, & Bruck, 1994), and media showcasing of "false" cases.[3]

Cases in which the child is very young (under 4), the child is developmentally delayed or mentally ill, or the perpetrator is a prominent citizen or a person in a sensitive profession (e.g., education, medicine, mental health, law enforcement, or law) are very troubling for protective services and other professionals. Frequently, these cases are not substantiated.

Furthermore, in many cases, there is insufficient evidence to make a determination about whether sexual abuse occurred. The alleged victim may refuse to talk, may recant an earlier disclosure, or may make inconsistent statements about the abuse or who the perpetrator is. In addition, the family may refuse to cooperate, and the worker may be unable to obtain a court order. These clinical observations are borne out by a classic study of sexual abuse cases referred to CPS in Denver, Colorado. The researchers found that 22% were denied or not founded because there was insufficient information to make a determination (Jones & McGraw, 1987).

Protecting the Child. If the worker substantiates sexual abuse, the worker must next decide whether steps need to be taken to make the child safe. In many states, the worker will use formal risk and safety assessment tools in making this determination (Doueck, English, DePanfilis, & Moote, 1993; Dubowitz & DePanfilis, 2000; Holder, 2000).

If the worker decides the child is unsafe, he or she will have three general strategies to choose from as means for protecting the child: (a) leaving the child in the family with some safeguards, (b) removing the child, and (c) removing the alleged offender. There may be reservations about using the first strategy, not only because of concerns about the potency of safeguards to prevent further sexual abuse, but also because of concerns that the child will be blamed for reporting, pressured to change her story, or otherwise punished for her disclosure.

Historically, removal of the child has been the preferred strategy. The child may be placed with a relative, in foster care, or in a shelter. Although removal usually results in safety and may provide the child with a supportive and more appropriate living situation, it has some drawbacks. Often the child feels that she is the one being punished by separation from the family, her friends, and her school situation. In addition, the family may close ranks against the child, making her feel even more rejected and making it more difficult to treat the family.

Removal of the alleged offender may be the strategy of choice for protecting the child. This can be accomplished by a voluntary agreement with the family and the offender, a court order, or arrest and incarceration of the offender. Its advantages are that it communicates to the victim, the alleged offender, and the family that the offender is the wrongdoer, not the victim; it usually disrupts the family structure that facilitated the sexual abuse; and it allows the victim to stay within the family. Its potential disadvantages are that it may leave the victim vulnerable to family pressure and in an unhealthy living situation and that unless the offender is in jail he may violate the agreement or order. The decision about whether to remove the victim or the offender is based in large part on the mother's ability to be supportive to and protective of the victim, the compliance of the offender, and the level of family dysfunction.

Intervention to Ameliorate the Family Problems That Led to the Sexual Abuse. Although protective services' first duty is to protect the child, its second is to preserve families. The general assumption is that children are better off with their own families. Therefore, protective services usually works toward the goal of family rehabilitation and reunification. However, recent federal legislation (Adoption and Safe Families Act, 1997) allows states to designate certain classes of cases where attempts at family preservation are not required, citing sexual abuse among such cases. These federal guidelines, increased emphasis on criminal prosecution, and an expectation that the nonoffending parent will choose her children over the offender, have altered the role of protective services in sexual abuse cases. The family unit for rehabilitation and preservation is likely to be the nonoffending parent and the children.

The protective services worker faces a number of problems in trying to provide appropriate treatment to rehabilitate the family. Foremost is finding adequate treatment resources. In ideal circumstances, the community will have a comprehensive array of treatment resources for sexual abuse. Although an increasing number of communities do have specialized treatment for sexual abuse, these resources may be inadequate to meet the demand. It is not advisable to send a sexually abusive family to a treatment provider who does not have experience with this client population.

Second, because many families who come to the attention of the child protection system for sexual abuse have other problems in functioning, sexual abuse–specific treatment may be insufficient to meet the family's needs. These families may need additional intervention and services for longer time frames than most CPS cases are open.

Third, little is known about what constitutes successful treatment. To date, there have been few evaluations of sexual abuse treatment (Daro, 1988; Daro & Cohen, 1984; Kroth, 1979; Sgroi, 1982). In the last few years, cognitive behavioral interventions involving victims and sometimes the nonoffending parent have become the subject of evaluation (Berliner & Saunders, 1996; Cohen & Mannarino, 1996; Deblinger, Lippman, & Steer, 1996). However, more research is needed on these treatments, and many community-based programs use other treatment approaches.

Better evaluation and follow-up is found for treatment programs focusing on offenders than for those that provide family-oriented treatment for incest (e.g., Becker, 1985; Marshall, Laws, & Barbaree, 1990; Schwartz & Cellini, 1995). These studies suggest that incest offenders are at lower risk for reoffense than extrafamilial offenders but also that the number of reoffenders who actually are reconvicted is substantially smaller than the number who reoffend (Marshall et al., 1990; Steele, 1995).

LIMITATIONS OF CHILD PROTECTIVE SERVICES

The adequacy of the child protection system has been questioned by other professionals, the media, and politicians (Besharov, 1986; Duquette, Faller, & D'Aunno, 1988b; Faller, 1985; Hechler, 1988). CPS is criticized for both failure to identify and overidentifying of abuse, including sexual abuse, and its ability to help families has been challenged. These problems are real. They result from ever-increasing referrals—over 3 million per year since 1994 (Wang & Harding, 2000)—and inadequate staffing to respond to emergencies, do careful and sensitive investigations, and provide appropriate intervention. An additional problem is difficulty attracting and retaining qualified staff because of the stress of dealing with child maltreatment and difficult working conditions, such as having to make home visits to hostile families.

Moreover, because child protection workers often are not trained mental health practitioners and have a fairly narrow focus of concern (child maltreatment), mental health professionals may experience a degree of dissonance in trying to communicate with them. Workers may be perceived as unable to appreciate the complexities of family and intrapsychic dynamics and as unsophisticated in their approach. In addition, they may appear primarily concerned with their mandate, such as the adequacy of the evidence of abuse to open a case, whether CPS or another agency is required to provide service, or the need to close the case because the time limit for case activity has expired.

Because of the limitations of the child protection system, helping professionals may worry about the consequences to clients of CPS involvement and may be tempted not to report suspected sexual abuse (Kalichman, 1993; Zellman & Faller, 1995). Failing to report is not an appropriate solution to the problems of the child protection system. First, there are legal penalties for failure to report. In most states, practitioners opens themselves up to legal action. They may incur civil damages, based upon harm to the child because of professional negligence, or a misdemeanor charge, with conviction resulting in a fine and/or jail time (Mayhall & Norgard, 1983; National Center for the Prosecution of Child Abuse, 1997, Vol. 5). Second, most professionals who treat sexual abuse do not have the resources to remove children from dangerous situations and place them in a safe place. It is psychologically damaging to the victim, as well as ethically inexcusable, to act as if the sexual abuse is being alleviated by treatment when the abuse is ongoing. Third, the child protection system will not improve as long as professionals avoid it and do not confront its inadequacies. Helping professionals have a duty to address the system's shortcomings, both on a case level by advocating for a particular client and at the agency and community level by pressuring for improvements in service delivery.

Collaborating With Law Enforcement

In this section, the avenues that lead to collaboration between police and mental health workers, the role of law enforcement in sexual abuse cases, and issues related to the rights of suspects and confidentiality will be discussed.

HOW HELPING PROFESSIONALS
BECOME INVOLVED WITH LAW ENFORCEMENT

In most states, the legal obligation that professionals have to report suspected child maltreatment does not require that a referral be made to the police. Therefore, as a rule, collaboration with the police is undertaken when helping professionals feel an ethical duty to contact the police. These situations are likely to be ones where the offender poses a danger to the victim(s), the victim(s)' family, the professional making the report, and/or the community. Examples of offenders who fall into these categories are violent sex offenders; offenders who make specific threats of bodily harm to the victim(s), the family, or the professional; and pedophiles (persons with a history of sexually abusing many victims, who cannot control their behavior, and whose primary sexual orientation is to children). In addition, any case where it is in the victim's best interest to prosecute criminally and no other agency has involved the police (i.e., protective services) warrants a police report. By and large, these will be situations where the perpetrator is not related to the victim. An example is the following case.

> *Case Example*: Mr. and Mrs. I brought their 3½-year-old son, Kevin, for an evaluation because they thought he had been sexually abused by his baby-sitter. They had fired her before seeking the evaluation. Kevin demonstrated and described how the baby-sitter had repeatedly pulled down his pants and fondled his penis and his anus. In addition, he showed how she had spanked him very hard. He also reported to his parents that he had been induced to bite her nipple.
>
> The baby-sitter was unlicensed. Before coming to work for the family, she had baby-sat for another family for about 4 years, and, before that, she had provided unlicensed day care out of her home. Mr. and Mrs. I knew that she was looking for another baby-sitting job because she asked them for a reference. They were also somewhat afraid of her because she had interacted with them in a rather bizarre fashion on a number of occasions. Kevin showed that he was quite frightened of her.

The evaluator sent a copy of her findings to the relevant law enforcement agency. Included in the report was the name and address of the previous employer of the baby-sitter.

Because Mr. and Mrs. I reacted proactively to suspicions about the baby-sitter, it was not likely that protective services would pursue the case. In addition, because this baby-sitter was unlicensed, she did not come within the purview of social services or a licensing body. However, because this woman appeared to have committed a crime, law enforcement was the appropriate agency to involve. Although it was unlikely that Kevin would be able to testify against her in a criminal proceeding, both he and his family needed to know that someone was taking action. In addition, children might have been damaged by the sitter in the past, and she posed a threat to other children, should she continue providing child care. Moreover, the children for whom she had previously sat might be judged competent witnesses for a trial. Finally, the parents had some fears that this woman might harm them, and police involvement offered some protection.

Helping professionals may also collaborate with law enforcement when their assistance is sought in the investigation or prosecution of cases. For example, the police may ask for an assessment to determine whether an alleged victim has been sexually abused. An additional area in which mental health expertise may be sought is regarding a victim's competence or ability to testify. Finally, the police may also ask a child's therapist to prepare a child to testify.[4]

THE ROLE OF LAW ENFORCEMENT

The responsibility of the police is to catch criminals. Their role is to investigate alleged crime, obtain supportive evidence (or rule out criminal activity), arrest suspects, and provide evidence to the prosecutor that will result in successful criminal prosecution. Although they may also be concerned with protecting victims and doing what is in their best interest, and with the well-being of their families, these concerns are secondary to their mission. Thus, their goals differ from those of protective services. However, with statutory changes calling for CPS-police collaboration, the net effect has been that law enforcement's goal, criminal prosecution, has taken precedence.

Interrogating Suspects

The police may be involved in interviewing the victim, the nonoffending parent, and other witnesses. However, their unique role is interrogating the alleged offender. Their goal, assuming they think the individual committed a crime, is to obtain a confession. Other than informing the suspect of his rights (see the section below), there is no legal or ethical requirement that the police be honest with the alleged offender. It is quite acceptable to try to trick, cajole, or coerce a suspect into confession. However, many law enforcement personnel report greater success by appearing to care about the well-being of the offender and trying to appeal to the offender's concern for the welfare of the victim (Cage, 1988; Goldstein, 1987; Kleinheksel, 1988). Once a verbal confession is elicited, it is written and signed by the offender (Goldstein, 1987).

Because law enforcement's primary focus is on criminal prosecution, it is less concerned about such issues as the potential detrimental effect of having a child testify in court. Moreover, in cases where it is clear that the victim will not make a good witness, law enforcement may close its case because there is no chance of a successful criminal prosecution.

The Polygraph

If a suspect protests his innocence during the police interrogation, in many communities he will be offered a polygraph examination. The polygraph, or lie detector, is supposed to be able to determine whether the alleged offender is lying or telling the truth when he says that he did not sexually abuse the child.

It is important for helping professionals to understand that the polygraph is not a litmus test; it has both validity and reliability problems (Cross & Saxe, 1992, 2001). This is why it is inadmissible in most court proceedings[5] (Murphy & Murphy, 1997; Saxe, Dougherty, & Cross, 1987). In fact, in a comprehensive evaluation of research on the polygraph, the procedure was found to have a little better than chance probability of accurately distinguishing between subjects who were telling the truth and those who were lying and thus to have unacceptably high proportions of false negatives and false positives (Lykken, 1987).

Validity refers to whether a procedure measures what it is supposed to measure, in this instance whether the polygraph differentiates whether an individual is lying or telling the truth. What the polygraph actually measures is autonomic arousal as the interviewee answers questions. The autonomic responses most polygraph instruments measure are galvanic skin response (sweaty palms), pulse rate, blood pressure, and breathing rate. The assumption is that these will increase when a person is anxious and that lying makes people anxious.

Taking the last assumption first, although lying does make some people anxious, clinical findings suggest sexual abusers are less likely to become upset by their lying behavior than other people. Many of them lie habitually to conceal their sexually abusive behavior, and they may suffer from personality disorders (e.g., narcissistic personality disorder or antisocial personality disorder) and have little compunction about lying (e.g., Hare, 1991; Leberg, 1997). Moreover,

Reid and Inbau (1977), two advocates for the polygraph, stated that it is not useful with neurotics or psychopaths. This qualifier rules out its utility with most sex offenders.

It is also important to recognize that anxiety is not the only emotion that can lead to autonomic arousal. For example, anger or sexual excitement might also lead to increased rates of pulse, heart beat, and breathing. Both of these emotions are possible responses to the polygraph questions in a sexual abuse case. Moreover, when anxiety is the cause of arousal, it may not be related to lying but merely to the situation of being questioned about sexually abusive behavior.

Reliability refers to consistency in findings across uses. The polygraph is vulnerable to two types of reliability problems: interrater reliability and test-retest reliability. With regard to the former, two polygraphists may interpret the same polygraph printouts differently (Lykken, 1987; Saxe et al., 1987). The polygraph lacks test-retest reliability because a person may produce different printouts with different administrations. This can be the result of a desensitization effect—that is, the person becoming accustomed to being hooked up to the machine and answering difficult and upsetting questions, and experiencing progressively less autonomic arousal to the procedure. Persons accused of sexual offenses may take and pass a private polygraph prior to agreeing to take a police polygraph (Faller, 1997). Even proponents of the polygraph state that it loses its capacity to differentiate between those who are telling the truth and those who are not over successive trials (Abrams & Abrams, 1993). In addition, arousal responses can be controlled, both voluntarily and by the use of drugs and medication.

Finally, many proponents of the polygraph support its use, not because it can truly differentiate who is telling the truth and who is lying, but rather as an apparatus that compels the suspect to confess. Some suspects confess during the prepolygraph interview, in anticipation of flunking, and others confess when told that they have flunked. Cross and Saxe (2001) defined this as the "bogus pipeline effect." Indeed, research indicates that belief in the efficacy of the polygraph increases its capacity to differentiate truth tellers from liars (Saxe et al., 1987). In addition, the skill of the polygraph operator plays an important role in its utility, not unlike the skill of a mental health evaluator (Cross & Saxe, 2001; Saxe et al., 1987). An additional argument made for its use is that a refusal to take the polygraph is suggestive of guilt.

Law enforcement and other professionals feel a pressing need to know whether an individual has or has not committed a sex offense. This need probably explains police dependence on the polygraph. Of concern, however, are situations in which its results are flawed, especially when sexually victimized children are not believed or protected because the offender passes a polygraph (Faller, 1997).

Collecting Physical Evidence

In addition to interrogation responsibilities and administration of the polygraph, law enforcement is responsible for gathering physical evidence in sexual abuse cases. In some cases, there will be evidence from the scene of the crime. Examples of such evidence are bed or other clothing that might contain minute particles of physical evidence, such as body hairs, clothing fibers, or dirt. Clothing may also have traces of seminal fluid, blood, saliva, or other secretions. Both the victim's and the suspect's clothing may be confiscated. In addition, any instrument such as a vibrator or a weapon that might have been employed in the abuse is secured by the police. Likewise, law enforcement will document evidence supportive of any physical activity—for instance, signs of a scuffle.

Other types of physical evidence that may be collected by the police are letters written by the alleged offender to the victim, other written records or correspondence, suggestive or pornographic pictures taken of the victim or offender, other pornography, and cameras and other equipment for producing pornography (Cage, 1988; Moreau, 1987a, 1987b). Investigators may confiscate computers when they believe that evidence of sexual abuse, such as pornography, lists of victims, lists of other sex offenders, or other records related to the abuse, may be found on them.

The police are also responsible for seeing that a forensic medical exam is completed and that the evidence collected is conveyed to the police crime laboratory. The exam will be conducted on the victim by a physician. Specimens collected include smears that might contain evidence of sexual activity, samples of pubic and scalp hair, combings from the victim's pubic hair and hair on her head, and any other evidence of the sexual activity (Moreau 1987a, 1987b; Steinberg & Westhoff, 1988).

Physical evidence is more likely to be sought and found in situations of child rape or recent sexual assault. Such evidence is also more likely in cases where the alleged offender is thought to be a pedophile who has a lengthy history of sexual involvement with children.

Law enforcement has the capability of preserving the chain of evidence: That is, they have official procedures for seizing, labeling, and storing in a secure place any evidence that is obtained. Child protection workers and others who might be involved in an investigation of sexual abuse do not have this capability. Being able to establish a chain of custody for any physical evidence is a prerequisite for its admission in a court proceeding (Moreau, 1987a, 1987b).

LEGAL PROTECTIONS AND CONFIDENTIALITY

Police may interview an alleged offender without advising him of his rights if they have not taken him into custody. However, because of judicial concerns about coerced confessions, if the police arrest someone, they must inform him of his Miranda rights before they question him (*Miranda v. Arizona*, 1966). These are the right to remain silent (that any statement may be used as evidence against him in a court of law) and the right to the presence of an attorney, should the suspect choose to be interviewed. Neither protective services workers nor others involved in the investigation of alleged sexual abuse take people into custody or are required to give such warnings, and clearly these practices are likely to result in a very different interview than one conducted under less intimidating circumstances.

Police files are not necessarily confidential. The Freedom of Information Act of 1974 (e.g., Michigan Compiled Laws Annotated, 15.321) makes such records potentially available to the public. Law enforcement has discretionary power not to disclose information in investigative records under certain conditions, but it is wise not to expect confidentiality.[6]

Therefore, any information in police records may be available not only to the parties involved in the case but also to the public, including the press. It is important for mental health professionals and others involved to be aware of this. In writing reports, responding to questions by the police, and turning over written material to the police, it is necessary to bear in mind that this material could eventually be quoted in the newspaper.

Conclusion

Protective services and the police both play vital roles in the appropriate management of sexual abuse cases. To be effective, helping professionals must appreciate that they cannot act alone but must, in most instances, collaborate with these two key players. Nevertheless, it is important to understand that both their training and their responsibilities for a sexual abuse case differ from those of mental health professionals. Therefore, working together presents a challenge. However, this challenge must be met in order to assist victims of sexual abuse and their families.

Notes

1 States vary in their provisions for waiver of confidentiality: 20 states waive confidentiality for all persons except attorneys; 22 limit the waiver to physicians (Mayhall and Norgard, 1983).
2 Cases that do not involve caretakers are the responsibility of the police.
3 These high profile cases are not necessarily false but are portrayed as such by the media.

4   Court preparation may also be provided by a county-based victim-witness program or by the prosecutor.

5   However, in 20 states, results of the polygraph are admissible if both parties agree to their admission, and, in Massachusetts and New Mexico, they are admissible even if one party objects (Wrightsman et al., 1987).

6   Investigative records are exempt from disclosure if their release would (1) interfere with a law enforcement proceeding, (2) deprive a person of a fair trial, (3) constitute unwarranted invasion of privacy, (4) disclose law enforcement techniques, or (5) endanger the life or physical safety of a law enforcement officer (M.C.L.A. 15.321).

4

Collaborating With Attorneys and Working With the Courts

N onlawyer professionals often feel ill at ease in their interactions with the legal system, for at least two reasons. The first is that rules that govern interactions in the legal system differ from rules pertaining to other professional interactions. The second is that interactions are often adversarial. However, to be effective in cases of child sexual abuse, professionals must understand the legal aspects of child welfare and lawyers' roles and responsibilities. The following topics will be discussed in this chapter: (a) mental health professionals' roles in the legal system, (b) the courts involved in sexual maltreatment litigation, (c) the roles lawyers take in sexual abuse cases, and (d) testifying in court.

Mental Health Professionals' Roles in the Legal System

Mental health professionals involved in sexual abuse cases may have varied roles in the legal process: (a) as a reporter of suspected sexual abuse, (b) as an evaluator of one or more of the parties, (c) as a therapist for one or more of the parties, and (d) as a client. These roles and their challenges will be covered in this section.

Author's Note: I would like to thank Frank Vandervort, JD, Manager of the Child Welfare Legal Resource Center at the University of Michigan Law School, for his careful review and assistance with this chapter.

REPORTER

Reporting requirements are discussed in Chapter 3. However, after a report has been made, the professional making the report may become a witness in court. The lawyer for the child protection agency may subpoena the reporting professional to testify concerning the suspicions that led to the report. As noted in the previous chapter, when a person, including a professional, makes a report of suspected sexual abuse, the reporter's name can be held confidential but will be revealed if the reporter must testify.

Although testimony may be requested early in Child Protective Services (CPS) involvement, the lawyer is more likely to request it later, when temporary custody of the child is being adjudicated or even later, when termination of parental rights is being sought. As a consequence, the mental health professional may be providing testimony months and sometimes years after the referral was made. Initial observations and concerns may seem moot by then, and the reporter's memory may have faded. Professionals should take good notes at the time of the referral so that later they can provide accurate testimony. In addition, much may have transpired since the initial report. Professionals may be aware of these developments, but their testimony should be about their observations and concerns at the time of the report.

EVALUATOR

Mental health professionals are often involved in the legal process as persons who evaluate cases of alleged sexual abuse and address a range of issues. These include whether sexual abuse occurred and the dynamics that led to the victimization. There may be restrictions in the evaluator's ability to testify in court about the likelihood of sexual abuse, even though this issue is addressed in the evaluation. Restrictions on mental health testimony will be addressed later in this chapter. In addition, evaluators may address what sorts of treatment are necessary or what the treatment prognosis is for various parties. In addition, the evaluator may be asked whether it is safe to leave the child in the home, whether the child can return home if she has been removed, and whether it is appropriate to terminate parental rights.

The party requesting the evaluation may be the protective services worker, the guardian *ad litem* or attorney for the child, one or both parents or their lawyers, the prosecutor, or the court. Ethically, it is important to consider carefully the conditions of involvement as an evaluator. The central issue here is that the court arena fosters adversarial relationships: That is, persons involved must take sides (Saunders, 1997). Not only will many mental health professionals have questions about whether an adversarial confrontation is the best way to address a problem of sexual abuse, but it is unusual for a mental health professional to find that one side is all right and the other all wrong.

Generally, as the evaluator for protective services, the guardian *ad litem*, or the court, the mental health professional will not experience serious differences of opinion because each of these entities is primarily concerned with the child's best interest, albeit from varying perspectives. Difficulties arise when the professional is asked to act as an evaluator for the parents in a protection proceeding, for one parent against the other in a divorce matter, or for either the prosecutor or the defendant in a criminal trial.

The professional may do an evaluation, arrive at conclusions not supportive of the client, and then simply not be called to testify. Depending upon the court rules in the particular state, the lawyer may be under an obligation to disclose the evaluation findings.

Alternatively, more subtle problems may occur. Most mental health professionals want to help; therefore, if they are asked to be involved, they will want to support their client. This pressure may, without the evaluator intending it to, influence the findings. A related problem is that the attorney will, of course, be advocating for his or her client and therefore will describe the case from the client's viewpoint. The attorney may even selectively furnish written information and not supply material detrimental to his or her client. A final issue is money. The professional or his or her agency usually expects to be paid by the side asking for the evaluation. Most mental health professionals and their agencies cannot be bought, but the financial arrangement may subtly influence the evaluation results.

There are several ways of handling these problems. None of them successfully addresses all of the issues mentioned above, but sometimes these strategies can be used in combination. One is to make a prior agreement with the client that the report of the evaluation will be made available to all parties. That is, regardless of the findings, all sides will receive the results. This strategy ensures that results will be available not only to all parties but also to the court. In addition, such a disclosure agreement enhances the credibility of the findings and the evaluator.

A second strategy is to require an opportunity to review all documents, such as protective services reports, police investigations, and other evaluations, in order to make a preliminary determination of the efficacy of the case before agreeing to do the evaluation. So, for example, if an attorney describes his client as wrongly accused of rape but the records show that the client has been convicted previously of sex offenses against minors, the evaluator can decline to work on the case. Less obvious cases will be more problematic.

A third strategy is to require, as a condition for doing the evaluation, permission to contact and, if necessary, interview all parties and to obtain documents from all sides. This strategy is helpful in ensuring that the evaluator has access to all documents. One problem that can occur with this strategy is that persons on the other side may refuse to cooperate. Sometimes a court order can be obtained to compel their involvement. However, the evaluator must then appreciate the effect that being coerced in this manner is likely to have on the interviewees. Even more than in other evaluations, they are likely to perceive the evaluator as hostile and may be quite guarded or hostile themselves.

A fourth strategy is to require that all sides agree that the mental health professional be the sole evaluator for the case. This approach is most relevant to divorce situations and child protection proceedings. In addition to assisting the evaluator in being impartial, this strategy may have the added advantage of avoiding multiple assessments, which can be quite stressful on all parties but especially on the child.

THERAPIST

Probably more frequently, mental health professionals become involved in the legal system when they are therapists. Professionals should be wary of serving as both a therapist and an evaluator on the same case. These two roles differ. Therapists do and should take a role in support of their client. In contrast, evaluators should consider all aspects and all views of the case before arriving at conclusions. However, ethical guidelines regarding the separation of the roles of therapist and evaluator vary both by profession and by which guidelines the professional follows (American Academy of Child and Adolescent Psychiatry, 1997; American Professional Society on the Abuse of Children, 1996; American Psychological Association, 1994).

Nonetheless, therapists may have a great deal of useful information to offer the court. They may have the most current and in-depth relationships with clients, when compared, for example, to CPS workers. Nevertheless, the therapist-witness role can present challenges. These vary depending upon whose therapist the practitioner is—the child's, the family's, or the offender's.

As the victim's therapist, the professional will want to consider a number of issues. The first is the impact of the testimony upon the child. A second is what the child wants the therapist to say. A third is what is in the child's best interest for the therapist to say. Children may feel supported when there will be someone else there who is on their side. Yet they may have mixed feelings about the therapists telling everything about the sexual abuse to a room full of people. The child may also have said something against the parents or the offender in treatment that she does not want revealed to others. The child may also fear that the therapist's testimony will result in an undesired outcome, such as a criminal charge, conviction of the parent, or termination of parental rights. The therapist cannot refuse to answer any relevant questions and should not say anything in court that is untrue (i.e., perjury) but should nevertheless take into account the child's feelings. One way of moderating the impact of testimony on the child is for the therapist to talk to the child ahead of time and explain what he or she is likely to say and the reasons for saying it.

More challenging are situations where the therapist is working with the offender, the nonoffending parent, or the family and is called to testify. It is important for the therapist to provide balanced testimony reflecting the client's strengths and weaknesses. Such testimony not only is more accurate but is likely to have increased weight in court because it will be viewed as more credible. It also may be useful for the client to hear this testimony. Moreover, court oversight and the prospect of the therapists providing testimony about progress may motivate clients to change.

On the other hand, the therapist may make statements in court that the client perceives as very negative. This does not mean that the therapist is being dishonest with the client in treatment. Rather, therapy is a process of helping people change, and issues are dealt with one at a time and in an order that maximizes the likelihood for change. Testimony occurs at a particular point in time and usually requires the therapist to telescope either forward or backward. In addition, the therapist may have to address issues in testimony that have not yet been dealt with in treatment because the client is not yet able to handle them. Therefore, testimony can sometimes interfere with the therapeutic process. The example below illustrates how this can happen.

Case Example: Ms. G was providing therapy to the S family, where Mr. S had sexually abused his two daughters, Angela, 14, and Sally, 12. A third daughter, Lucy, age 2, was thought not to have been victimized. Angela and Sally had gone together to their school counselor to make a report. Mr. S had run away when his daughters disclosed the sexual abuse. His whereabouts were unknown, and there was a warrant out for his arrest. CPS and the court allowed the three girls to remain with their mother because the CPS worker concluded that the mother had acted appropriately when she discovered sexual abuse. Ms. G, the therapist, was seeing each of the girls separately and in a dyad and was providing individual therapy and parenting training to their mother.

In therapy, the girls described chronic and severe sexual abuse by their father and trying to tell their mother about it earlier. Angela said that when she had been about 8, she had told her mother that her father was "kissing her down there." Her mother's response had been "Oh, he wouldn't do anything like that." Sally said that when she had been 10, her father had had her in the bathroom abusing her and her mother had knocked on the door. After she and her father had come out, she had told her mother that her "daddy was doing bad things to my privacy." Her mother's response had been "He was just trying to help you go to the bathroom." The girls also said their mother had told them that she missed their dad and wanted him to get some help.

In treatment, Mrs. S was beginning to acknowledge that she had seen signs of sexual abuse before the girls made a report. She readily admitted that her husband had dominated her and verbally abused her. Mrs. S was also starting to address her own sexual abuse as a child and her mother's failure to protect her.

Although Ms. G thought Mrs. S had many issues to address in treatment, she thought she was making progress. She also felt the girls were making progress and was intending to have sessions in which the girls were allowed to confront their mother about previous attempts to tell her about their father's abuse. Ms. G felt that the best course was to continue therapy and to have Angela and Sally remain in their mother's care. The CPS worker was kept abreast of treatment progress through Ms. G's quarterly reports and agreed that the children should remain with their mother.

At this point in treatment, there was a statutory review hearing, at which there would be a decision whether to end court jurisdiction. Ms. G was subpoenaed to testify. She told the girls that she might be asked about their previous efforts to tell their mother and that she would recommend that the court continue its jurisdiction. She told them that the judge might also ask them questions about their disclosures in treatment. Ms. G told Mrs. S that she was going to tell the court that the family was making progress in treatment but that she thought the court should continue to be involved.

Although the prosecutor wanted to terminate court involvement, the guardian *ad litem* did not. In her cross-examination of Ms. G, the guardian *ad litem* elicited testimony about the girls' prior efforts to tell their mother and their mother's responses. Ms. G's testimony also included the children's disclosure that their mother said she missed their father. Although the mother's attorney attempted to prevent Ms. G from testifying to the girls' and the mother's hearsay statements in therapy, the judge allowed the testimony in.

Not only did the judge decide not to end court jurisdiction, but he also ordered that all three girls be removed from their mother's care and placed in foster care.

In this case, it is clear that treatment was at a very delicate stage when Ms. G had to testify. The judge obviously had a different view about what was in the children's best interest than Ms. G and CPS. It was fortunate that Ms. G informed the children and the mother ahead of time about what she might testify to because it allowed her to sustain her therapeutic relationship with the family. However, probably no one, including Ms. G, was prepared for the judge's decision to remove the children.

CLIENT

Because of both the contested nature of sexual abuse cases and the fact that case-related activity takes place in an adversarial arena, helping professionals may need legal advice and legal representation. In fact, it is probably inadvisable to work on sexual abuse cases without the capacity to seek a legal opinion when needed. Because attorneys work on behalf of their clients and must vigorously pursue their clients' interest, it is not good practice to rely on the advice of lawyers representing others (e.g., the prosecutor). A useful guideline is the following: When a communication is received from an attorney or a court, it may deserve a legal consultation.

Subpoenas for Court Appearances or Documents

One circumstance in which legal advice may be needed is the receipt of a subpoena that compels a court appearance or production of documents and videotapes or both. As a general rule, helping professionals should honor court orders. Nonetheless, sometimes either the appearance or release of information is inconsistent with the helping professionals' ethics or best-practice guidelines. However, because this request derives from the legal arena, the prudent course of action is to seek legal advice before responding.

There are also times when subpoenas requiring an appearance or documents have an undisclosed agenda. Examples of such agendas are gathering information for a different legal proceeding or harassment of the professional. An attorney who understands how other attorneys operate may be able to discern the agenda and assist the professional in making an appropriate response. The attorney can request that the court set aside the subpoena.

Deposition Request

Another circumstance in which legal advice is necessary is when the professional's appearance is requested for a deposition. This request is usually also made via subpoena. Depositions are often taken in civil damages cases. The goal is to find out what the professional knows and thinks about the case. At these legal proceedings, there will be no judge, only attorneys representing the various sides. It is appropriate for helping professionals to consult with an attorney before appearing for a deposition, and it may be appropriate to take an attorney to a deposition.

Request for a Court Appearance Without a Subpoena

A third circumstance is when the professional is asked to appear in court voluntarily, without a subpoena. Although requests for voluntary appearances are usually made by parties friendly to the professional, professionals are nevertheless advised to obtain a legal opinion about whether appearing in court is appropriate. Legal rules will apply. Sometimes these rules are inconsistent with the professional's best-practice guidelines. Rather than either complying with the request or defying it, obtain legal advice before deciding how to respond. Often it is appropriate to have the attorney respond on behalf of the professional.

Decisions With Legal Implications

There are other situations in which the decisions to be made are essentially mental health decisions, but with legal implications. Because of these implications, a legal opinion may be informative in making a mental health decision. Examples are when the professional is asked to do work on behalf of one party in a sexual abuse case or to provide a specific type of treatment.

A good illustration of the latter is when a mental health professional is asked to provide sex abuse–specific treatment to someone who is denying that he is a sex offender. Not only is providing such treatment an area of some disagreement among mental health professionals, but it has a number of legal implications. What if the person confesses in therapy? What about court testimony about treatment progress if the person continues to deny? Discussing these and related issues with an attorney before making a decision can be very helpful.

Challenges to Professional Competence

Finally, lawyers need to be consulted when the professionals or their agency's practices are being questioned. Sexual abuse cases are potentially highly litigious. As a consequence, virtually all professionals who work on them are vulnerable to challenges to their practice. These may be in the form of threats to one's life or well-being, agency grievances, complaints against one's license, complaints filed with one's professional organization, or civil lawsuits.

The Role of the Courts

The courts that may have jurisdiction in a sexual abuse case and the stages of the court process will be described in this section.

COURTS THAT MAY HAVE JURISDICTION

Several different courts may have jurisdiction in a sexual abuse case (Myers et al., 1989). First, the juvenile or family court that hears child protection matters may be involved. Second, there may be a criminal case against the offender, which would be heard in a state, district, or circuit court. Third, if the sexual abuse was revealed at the time of parental divorce or if it started after a divorce, the case may be heard in domestic relations court, which handles divorces. Fourth, there may be civil damages cases, which will be heard in the civil side of the circuit or state court. Damages may be sought both by those who have been sexually maltreated and their families and by those who are accused of sexual maltreatment and their families. To further complicate matters, when there is child sexual abuse litigation, frequently more than one court is involved.

Not only will the goal of court action vary depending upon the type of litigation, but so will the "standard of proof" or amount of evidence necessary to prove the case (Myers, 1998). In a protection case, the child welfare agency will be seeking to prove that the parents have been abusive or neglectful so that the court can take jurisdiction over the child. The standard of proof necessary for the child protection agency to get the court to take temporary jurisdiction over the child varies from state to state. Some states require a "preponderance of the evidence" (about 51% probability that the child has been sexually abused or allowed to be sexually abused by the parents), and others require "clear and convincing evidence" (about a 75% probability level) (National Center for the Prosecution of Child Abuse, 1997). If the court is to take permanent jurisdiction—that is, terminate parents' rights—in all states the public child welfare agency must prove the case with "clear and convincing evidence" (Duquette, 1981; Long, 1988; National Center for the Prosecution of Child Abuse, 1997).[1]

In a criminal case, the prosecution's goal is to have the court decide that the defendant sexually abused the child and impose a sentence that will limit his liberty (i.e., place him on probation, put him in jail, or send him to prison). The standard of proof is higher, "beyond a reasonable doubt" (about 95% probability that the defendant sexually abused the child) (Myers, 1998).

In a domestic relations or divorce case, relevant issues are custody of and visitation with the child. It is not always necessary to prove that sexual abuse occurred in order to ensure child safety. The court is interested in what is in the "child's best interest," which must meet the standard of "preponderance of the evidence" unless the child's best interest requires a change of custody, in which case the standard of proof may be "clear and convincing evidence" (Duquette, Faller, & D'Aunno, 1988a; Myers, 1998).

Finally, in a civil damages suit, the goal is to prove that the person or institution charged is responsible for harm resulting from sexual abuse or an allegation of sexual abuse when the complainant is asserting a false accusation. The standard of proof for a damages suit is "preponderance of the evidence" (Myers, 1998).

STAGES IN COURT PROCEEDINGS

A further confusion for those unfamiliar with courts is that there are several stages of court proceedings. The names of these will vary depending upon the court and the jurisdiction. However, there are generally three main stages: a preliminary hearing of some sort, a trial or adjudication, and a disposition or sentencing. The purpose of the preliminary hearing is for the court to determine if there is sufficient evidence (or some credible evidence) to litigate or try the case. The trial is the hearing where the case is either proven or not (e.g., the court finds the offender guilty of sexual abuse or the parents negligent, resulting in their child being sexually abused). At the trial, usually there is strict adherence to the "rules of evidence." For the nonlawyer, this means that admission of hearsay evidence[2] will be quite circumscribed. The dispositional hearing is where the court decides what to do about it (e.g., send the offender to prison, take the children away from the parents). There may also be review hearings, and termination of parental rights in child protection cases is usually a separate hearing. In domestic relations cases, there may be numerous "show cause" hearings when one parent or the other is charged with having violated an existing court order—for example, an order for visitation or payment of child support. In addition, there may be hearings to litigate alleged changes in circumstances, such as claims that the child has been sexually abused.

Mental health professionals may be called to testify at many different stages of the court process. In child protection cases, they are likely to offer testimony at trials for temporary jurisdiction, at disposition, at review hearings, and at termination of parental rights hearings. In domestic relations cases, they may be witnesses at the custody and visitation proceedings and at subsequent show cause and change of circumstances hearings. Mental health professionals infrequently testify in criminal trials, and when they do their testimony is fairly circumscribed, especially with regard to the "ultimate issue," which is whether a particular individual sexually abused a particular child. In civil damages cases, when they have relevant knowledge, they may be called at the adjudication as either fact witnesses or expert witnesses.

Attorney Roles

In each type of court proceeding, there will be several attorneys, each having a distinct role. The roles of attorneys in protection, criminal, divorce, and damages cases and some of their structural and practical challenges will be described.

LAWYER ROLES IN CHILD PROTECTION PROCEEDINGS

Protective services goes to court on behalf of sexually abused children when a parent is the offender or a parent fails to protect a child from sexual abuse and court intervention is deemed necessary to ensure the child's safety. Usually this entails the child's removal from the parental home. There are three different attorney roles: the attorney for protective services, the attorney for the child, and the attorney for the parents.

Attorney for Protective Services

This attorney brings the case to court on behalf of protective services. The protective services lawyer is usually the initiator of the court proceedings, although other attorneys may request hearings later on in the court process.

In most communities, protective services will be represented by an attorney from the prosecutor's office. In many jurisdictions, there is a consistent prosecutor who handles child protection cases and thus gains expertise in child welfare law. However, in some jurisdictions, a variety of different attorneys are assigned to child protection cases. The problem with the latter procedure is that the prosecutor may not gain sufficient expertise and may not have an opportunity to develop a good working relationship with child protection staff. Furthermore, in some jurisdictions, the most inexperienced attorneys are assigned to juvenile work and, as they gain experience, are promoted to more prestigious work. (Juvenile cases are not regarded as high status.)

Another potential problem in child protection litigation is that some prosecutors feel that they are to represent "the people" in child protection proceedings, as they do, for example, in a criminal case. The prosecutor could decide that the remedies sought by CPS are not in "the people's" interest and could decline to pursue them in court. For these reasons, some child protection agencies have their own attorneys. This is more likely to be the case in communities with large child protection caseloads.

The attorney and the child protection worker should work closely in preparing a case for court. The attorney ascertains whether legal grounds exist for intervening as the worker wishes. The worker suggests who might be appropriate witnesses for proving the case. The attorney usually contacts and prepares the witnesses and/or subpoenas them. Usually the worker will sit with the attorney during the court proceedings to advise him or her.

Attorney for the Child

The federal Child Abuse Prevention and Treatment Act (CAPTA, 1974) requires that all state child protection laws provide for a guardian *ad litem* in child protection legal proceedings if the states are to qualify for federal discretionary funds. A guardian *ad litem*, or guardian for the matter being litigated, is usually an attorney. He or she is supposed to represent the child's best interest (Haralambie, 1993).

Sometimes conflicts arise between what the child says she wants and what the lawyer deems is in the child's best interest. For example, the child may want to go home, but the attorney believes this is not in the victim's best interest because the alleged offender is there and has persuaded the mother that he did not sexually abuse the child. This conflict may be resolved by the attorney communicating to the court what the child's wishes are, as well as his or her opinion about the child's best interest. In other instances, separate attorneys or one attorney and a guardian *ad litem*, who is not an attorney but acts in the child's best interest, may be appointed, one to represent the child's wishes and the other the child's best interest.

The guardian *ad litem* is supposed to conduct an independent investigation to determine the child's best interest. When CAPTA passed in 1974, there was little guidance for guardians *ad litem* on how to carry out their role. Professional organizations such as the American Bar Association Section on Family Law (Haralambie, 1993), the National Association of Counsel for Children (2001a, 2001b), child advocates (e.g., Duquette, 1990; Haralambie, 1993; Juvenile Defenders' Office of Wayne County; F. Vandervort, personal communication, January 2000), and specialized professional education programs such as the Loyola University Child Law Program and the University of Michigan Child Advocacy Clinic have done a great deal to define the role of the child's attorney and improve the advocacy for abused children. Also, some state laws now provide a more specific definition of the duties of the child's counsel (Duquette, 2000; Michigan Court Rules, Mich. Comp. Laws Ann. 712a to 712d, 2002; Vandervort, 2000). In addition, there have been some creative experiments in representation for children. For example, a team of a mental health professional and an attorney or a volunteer who works with an attorney may act as guardian *ad litem* (Duquette & Ramsey, 1987).

Nonetheless, in some instances, guardians *ad litem* are appointed for the hearing and paid only for their appearance in court, rather than being the child's counsel for the entire time the child is under court jurisdiction. Such a structure does not encourage an extended and careful investigation. As a consequence, the guardian may merely discuss the case with the child protection worker or read the record to arrive at an opinion. He or she may not ever see or talk to the child.

Parents' Attorney

The parents' attorney represents the parents' wishes and seeks outcomes parents want in court, regardless of his or her belief about their guilt or innocence. Outside of the hearing, the parents' attorney can attempt to persuade or counsel them toward a different position. However, if unsuccessful, the attorney should vigorously pursue the parents' goals.

In many cases of sexual abuse in child protection proceedings, the mother and father have different interests because the father is the abuser and the mother is not. She may have reacted protectively when she discovered the sexual abuse. This situation usually requires separate attorneys for mother and father. When the mental health professional testifies in court, she or he will face examination by two attorneys representing the parents rather than one.

Although legal representation for parents is not a federal requirement, as it is for children, in most jurisdictions parents receive court-appointed attorneys when they are indigent. Frequently, there is roster of attorneys from which the judge appoints parents' attorneys. However, like the child's attorney, he or she may be paid for the hearing rather than the amount of time he spends on the case, a situation that may discourage investment of time. In addition, the desire for subsequent court appointments and a belief that cooperation with the court will ensure positive outcomes for parents may discourage vigorous advocacy by these court-appointed attorneys.

LAWYER ROLES IN CRIMINAL PROCEEDINGS

Usually, just two attorneys are involved in a criminal case, the prosecutor and the defense attorney. The victim has no counsel, except in very rare cases where a guardian *ad litem* is appointed (Toth & Whalen, 1987). Sometimes, however, there is a support person who assists in the child's preparation for court. This person is usually employed by a victim-witness assistance program, which is associated with the prosecutor's office (Victims of Child Abuse Act of 1990).

The Prosecutor

As noted earlier, in a criminal case, the prosecutor represents "the people." As the police are completing their investigation, they bring their findings to the prosecutor. He or she then makes a decision about whether to pursue criminal prosecution. The prosecutor may also ask the police to investigate further. The decision about whether to try the case will usually turn on whether the prosecutor thinks he or she will be able to persuade the fact finder (judge or jury) that the child has been sexually abused, rather than whether the prosecutor believes the child has been sexually abused. Although there may be corroborating evidence, the most important factor is the persuasiveness of the victim as a witness. Because many children who are sexually abused are young, hesitant in describing their maltreatment, and easily intimidated, criminal prosecution occurs in only a small percentage of cases (Cross, De Vos, & Whitcomb, 1994; Cross, Whitcomb, & De Vos, 1995; Gray, 1993). In virtually all criminal proceedings, the child must testify, whereas testimony may not be required in juvenile court; when it is required, there may be ways to protect the child witness.

Often what prosecutors do instead of criminal prosecution is attempt to obtain a plea from the offender (Faller & Henry, 2000). Usually this involves an admission to lesser crimes than are in the original complaint. Pleas ensure a criminal record for the accused, spare the child the ordeal of testimony (Goodman et al., 1992; Myers et al., 1989), and decrease the time and expense to the legal system. However, sometimes the actual crimes the offenders plead to are not sex crimes (Gray, 1993), and the sentence may not entail any jail or prison time (Faller & Henry, 2000).

The Defense Attorney

The role of the defense attorney is to gain acquittal for his or her client. However, like the prosecutor, the defense attorney may want a negotiated settlement. If the defense attorney feels that he or she is going to be unsuccessful at trial, he or she may try to negotiate an outcome that is less onerous than the anticipated trial outcome. Thus, the attorney may have the client plead to a lesser charge that has a lesser penalty. For example, a sexual act that does not involve penetration will usually carry a mild sentence, sometimes merely probation (National Center for the Prosecution of Child Abuse, 1997, Vol. 5).

Anyone accused of a crime such as sexual abuse has a legal right to representation. If the defendant cannot afford counsel, the court will appoint one. The quality of the defense provided may vary depending upon whether the accused has a court-appointed or retained attorney. Court-appointed attorneys may have less experience and fewer resources to invest in their client's defense.

ATTORNEY ROLES IN DIVORCE OR DOMESTIC RELATIONS PROCEEDINGS

Issues related to child sexual abuse in a divorce court are custody and visitation. Custody and visitation are usually decided when the parents divorce but may be relitigated later—for example, if sexual abuse is alleged after the divorce settlement. An attorney for a parent who thinks her or his child has been sexually abused, either by the other parent or when in the custody of the other parent, might seek change of custody, change of visitation so that it is less frequent or of shorter duration, supervised visits, or no visits. Although these solutions may be sought against the parent who is the alleged abuser, sometimes they will be sought against the parent raising concerns about sexual abuse. The latter strategy may be used by an attorney who is asserting that his or her client has been wrongfully and maliciously accused. (See Chapter 10 for additional discussion for allegations of abuse in divorce.) In these cases, parents will have attorneys, but children usually do not.

Parents' Attorneys

In most instances, each of the parents will have legal representation. But in divorce or domestic relations proceedings, unlike child protection and criminal proceedings, there are no legal guarantees of representation. Parents may have to rely upon legal aid, they may bankrupt themselves to pay attorneys' fees, or they may act on their own behalf.

More so than in the legal proceedings described so far, lawyers are likely to seek a settlement that is acceptable to both parents. In fact, many divorce courts have mediation services to facilitate settlements (Bienenfeld, 1988). Because of the emphasis on mutually agreed-upon settlements, matters often are resolved without a formal hearing and without presentation of evidence about the sexual abuse (Duquette et al., 1988a; Haralambie, 1999).

Guardian ad Litem

In hotly disputed or unusual cases where the judge feels the child needs someone other than her parents to represent her best interest, he may appoint a guardian *ad litem* (Duquette et al., 1988a; Haralambie, 1999). Because appointing a guardian *ad litem* in a divorce proceeding is the exception rather than the rule, this role is less well defined than in a protection proceeding. In addition, there are no statutory provisions for payment for the guardian *ad litem*. As a rule, the judge decides who will pay him or her, and usually this is one or both parents. This arrangement can potentially compromise the independence of the guardian *ad litem*.

ATTORNEY ROLES IN CIVIL DAMAGES CASES

Civil litigation related to sexual maltreatment may be configured in many ways (Stein, 1991). Adult survivors and guardians on behalf of child victims may sue sexual abusers, institutions where they were abused, and, indirectly, insurance companies who provide coverage for these individuals or institutions for money damages. This money is frequently sought to pay for treatment for the victims. Victims or their guardians also may file lawsuits against professionals who fail to report sexual abuse.

Also suits by those alleging harm because of an accusation, including accused sex offenders, families of the accused, and even victims, appear to be on the rise (Dallam, 2001; see also the *False Memory Syndrome Foundation Newsletter* for the period 1995–1998, Vols. 5–7). Sometimes those accused of sex offenses file lawsuits against their accusers, who may be victims, victims' families, mandatory reporters (even though they are protected by child abuse reporting laws), and therapists. Of particular concern is the emergence of lawsuits in which parents are suing their adult children's therapists after their adult children have accused them of sexual and other abuse (e.g., False Memory Syndrome Foundation, 1998).

Attorneys who specialize in this type of personal injury litigation may seek out clients: for example, in multivictim cases. The attorneys involved in civil damages cases are those for the complainant, for individuals being sued, for institutions, and for their insurance companies.

Attorney for Complainants in Damages Cases

Often lawyers who handle personal injury cases, including those involving sexual abuse, do not request a retainer (money before beginning work on the case) from the client. Their pay will be a proportion of the damages money from the other side, usually one third. Any expenses, such as payment for expert witnesses and attorney's hours, are subtracted before the compensation is divided. The attorney for the complainant will argue that she or he has been harmed by the abuse or the allegation and deserves compensation.

When the complainant is asserting sexual abuse, issues that must be proved are that the sexual abuse took place; that the person being charged is responsible for either the abuse, failure to protect from abuse, or failure to report abuse; and that current problems are a result of the sexual abuse. A mental health professional might be called to testify on any of these issues.

The issues are parallel if the complainant claims that he was falsely accused of sexual abuse or was affected by the false accusation. First, the attorney must very likely prove that the accused individual did not commit sexual maltreatment. In addition, the attorney must persuade a jury that the person making the accusation acted inappropriately and that the complainant was harmed as a consequence of the false accusation. Inappropriate acts vary somewhat depending upon whether the person being sued is a professional or not. Both a professional and a nonprofessional could be accused of knowingly making a false report of sexual abuse. Professionals might be accused of using inappropriate assessment techniques to determine sexual abuse or providing unproven therapy for sexual abuse.

For example, the complainant might charge that an evaluator or a CPS investigator used leading questions when interviewing the child. Typical charges against therapists treating adult survivors of sexual abuse are they "had an agenda to find sexual abuse" in order to make business for themselves and that they had the client read *Courage to Heal,* which caused the adult survivor to believe falsely that she had been sexually abused. In fact, there is a national effort underway, supported by the False Memory Syndrome Foundation (Barden, 1995), to pass legislation, known as the Mental Health Consumer Protection Act and the Truth and Responsibility in Mental Health Practices Act, that would severely limit the treatment techniques considered acceptable for trauma treatment (American Psychological Association, 1995); passage of the act would pave the way for many more of these lawsuits.

Attorneys for Defendants in Damages Cases

As noted, defendants may be on either side of the sexual abuse allegation—accused of sex offenses (or allowing them to occur) or accused of falsely claiming sex offenses.

On the sex offender side, defense attorneys may represent individuals who are the alleged offenders, individuals in authority positions in facilities where the offense took place, the facility or the facility's board of directors, or the insurance company for the individual or facility. Because these parties' interests may differ and conflict, often there are several defense attorneys with different clients in such a case. In situations where there have been several victims and the potential costs to the defense are very high, they may spend a lot of money hiring witnesses to support their side, undertaking extensive investigation of the complainant and his or her witnesses, and resorting to procedural maneuvers to prevent resolution and, for them, a negative outcome in the case.

On the other side, defense attorneys may represent victims of sexual abuse and their supporters, CPS workers and their agencies, law enforcement officers and agencies, schools and school personnel (because they are the most common reporters), and medical facilities and staff (who conduct medical exams on sexual abuse cases), as well as mental health professionals, their employers, and their insurance companies. These lawsuits may also involve multiple defense attorneys because they are often filed against several individuals and their employers. Moreover, they may involve conflicts of interest among defendants. For instance, the different defendants may be protected by different statutory provisions (of the state Child Protection Law or another statute), and they may perceive themselves as having different levels of liability.

For mental health professionals, a potential conflict is that their employer may want to negotiate a money settlement with the alleged sex offender because it is cheaper than going to trial. However, the professional does not want to settle because it is an indirect admission of unprofessional practice and it will mean giving money to a sex offender. A settlement may also open the door for a complaint with the professional's licensing agency and a grievance in his or her professional organization. To avoid having no options in such dilemmas, it is probably advisable for mental health professionals to carry their own malpractice insurance and not merely to rely on that of their employer.

Testifying in Court

The most stressful aspect of a mental health professional's involvement with lawyers is testifying in court (Pruett & Solnit, 1998). This is because the norms for behavior are very different from those to which mental health professionals ordinarily adhere. First, as noted at the beginning of this chapter, the process is an adversarial one; second, the courtroom is a stage, and it is the performance that counts. Each of these issues will be discussed below, and suggestions will be offered for maximizing effectiveness and maintaining professional integrity.

THE ADVERSARIAL NATURE OF THE COURT PROCESS

A court of law is supposed to be an arena in which equal parties compete, presenting their various perspectives to be examined by an impartial arbiter, judge or jury, who then makes findings of fact and ultimately decides what the remedy should be.[3] It is assumed that a process in which parties can, by question and answer, develop their own case and challenge that of their adversaries maximizes the presentation of the facts. Although many mental health professionals may question whether a court of law is the optimal arena for getting at the truth and resolving problems, the issue of concern here is how mental health experts should conduct themselves as witnesses. The issues of impartiality, communicating in court, and dealing with hostile questions will be addressed.

Should the Mental Health Professional Try to Be Impartial?

A fundamental dilemma for the mental health witness is that she or he may feel caught in the middle of the adversarial process. That is, each party has a particular theory of the case, or viewpoint, and, as already noted, the mental health professional may not entirely agree with any of these. Exacerbating this problem is the fact that often the professional has been called to testify by one of the sides, and that that side will expect the witness's testimony to support its case.

To counter this pressure and maintain some degree of impartiality, some mental health professionals take a passive stance. They leave it to the attorney to discover what they might have to say, both favorable and unfavorable, for the attorney's client's case. They avoid having contact with the attorneys outside of the courtroom. They may even avoid forming an opinion about the case or the various parties. One problem with this stance is that very important information related to the case and the well-being of the people involved, especially the child, may never be heard in court.

I favor a different and partisan stance, but not necessarily one supporting any side in the dispute. Regardless of the mental health professional's role in the case, she or he will have gathered some information (from the case records, the child, the alleged offender, or others) and usually will have arrived at impressions, formed an opinion, and/or developed some recommendations for intervention. These findings are usually relevant to the questions being considered by the court, and it is these findings that the mental health witness wants to support with testimony in court. The mental health professional is partisan toward his or her findings and opinion, but not necessarily to any particular side in the case.

Approaching the court process with this stance is quite liberating. It allows the witness to feel comfortable revealing any information that has been considered in coming to an opinion about the case. Typically, the professional will have examined material that is both supportive and damaging to the various parties concerned and, having weighed the material, will have formed certain conclusions. Thus, sharing information that might appear damaging to one side will not damage the professional's credibility because, in fact, it is part of the basis for the conclusions toward which she or he is partisan.

For example, suppose the witness has concluded that an adolescent has been sexually abused by her stepfather but also that the child is sexually active with her boyfriend. The witness should not hesitate to reveal the sexual activity with the boyfriend because it is a matter already considered and judged not to be a basis for invalidating the assertion of sexual abuse by the stepfather.

An additional advantage of this approach to testifying is that it probably adds to the credibility of the testimony and the witness. Astute fact finders realize that it is the rare situation that is either all black or all white and the unusual individual who is all good or all bad. To provide such one-sided testimony is to damage one's credibility.

In the example that follows, the evaluator for protective services provided testimony that was balanced.

Case Example: Dr. X was asked to evaluate the H family, where two children, Betina, 7, and Kathy, 4, were saying Mr. H had sexually abused them. Mr. H was Kathy's father and Betina's stepfather.

Mr. and Mrs. H had separate attorneys, the children had an attorney, and the prosecutor represented protective services. Mr. H's attorney wanted testimony supportive of his client's strengths, Mrs. H's weaknesses, the children's emotional disturbance, and his client's innocence. Mrs. H's attorney intended to elicit confirmation of Mr. H's guilt, Mrs. H's protective reaction to discovery of the sexual abuse, and her ability to parent the children with the assistance of her new partner. The children's attorney wanted recommendations for termination of parental rights and no visits with either parent. The prosecutor wanted to elicit information that would substantiate sexual abuse by Mr. H and neglect by Mrs. H but also a recommendation for intervention that would keep the children with Mrs. H and work toward improving her functioning.

A summary of Dr. X's testimony is as follows: Mr. H had sexually abused the girls but appeared to feel quite guilty about what he had done. Contributing factors were that his wife bossed him around and refused to have sex with him. She appeared to be an alcoholic, to have neglected Betina before she married Mr. H, and to be neglecting both children now that he was out of the home. Mr. H seemed to be the more nurturing and appropriate parent despite his sexually abusive behavior. Both children reported that they had repeatedly told their mother about the sexual abuse but that she did not do anything until she got a boyfriend and wanted Mr. H out of the house. The children missed their father and wanted him to come back home so their mom wouldn't be so mean to them. They said she hit them with a belt and left them alone while she went to Happy Joe's, a neighborhood bar, with Ronnie, her boyfriend. They did not like Ronnie because he also hit with a belt, but not just on the butt, sometimes on the head.

Dr. X's recommendations to the court were for removal of the children from Mrs. H's care to a potentially long-term placement. If an appropriate relative could be found, such a placement would be the first choice. Treatment should be provided to the children with the involvement of their substitute caretakers. Because neither child was capable of testifying and because being a witness against Mr. H would be detrimental to their functioning, criminal prosecution was not recommended. There should be supervised visits with both parents. Both Mr. and Mrs. H should receive a 6-month trial of treatment to assess their potential for change. However,

Mr. H would not be an appropriate caretaker for the children in the future. Further intervention plans should be made after the 6 months.

In the H case, the viewpoints of the various parties are more divergent than they are in most. Nevertheless, the case illustrates how a mental health expert can evaluate the totality of the situation and arrive at a position that does not entirely support that of any of the parties in the adversarial process.

How to State One's Findings and Conclusions in Court

Testifying to represent one's position accurately in an adversarial process is easier said than done. As noted earlier, each party in the court proceeding will be interested in eliciting findings, opinions, and recommendations supportive of his or her client (e.g., Holden, 1989; Pruett & Solnit, 1998). The following strategies may be helpful.

First, the mental health professional should decide exactly what essential points she or he wants to be sure to make. Some experts put these on an index card and refer to them during testimony; others memorize these essential points.[4] As will be described later, it may be possible to get one of the attorneys to ask questions that will allow the witness to make these points. However, the witness should also look for opportunities to respond to questions by making these points.

Sometimes this requires going beyond a simple answer to a question. For example, taking the H case above, the mother's attorney asked Dr. X if, "on Oct. 22, 1988, when Betina told Mrs. H that her daddy stuck his finger in her wee-wee, didn't Mrs. H throw him out of the house?" Dr. X might merely have answered, "Yes, she did." However, what Dr. X did was to add, "But the children say they informed their mother on previous occasions of the sexual abuse."

Attorneys will sometimes object to this more balanced testimony or will ask the expert to merely answer the question posed and not elaborate. The expert should look to the fact finder, judge or jury, to determine whether to continue to testify, emphasizing essential points, or to revert to giving the kinds of answers the attorneys want. The fact finder is the person whose opinion the expert wants to influence, not the attorneys.

Another issue to be sensitive to is whether these essential points, even though they have been made, are becoming obscured. If the testimony goes on for several hours or days, or if other testimony is emphasized, the essential points may not have their impact. An example of the latter can be taken from the H case. Dr. X stated on direct examination by the prosecutor that, in her opinion, the two girls had been sexually abused but that the father had some strengths and the mother was very dysfunctional. Mr. H's attorney asked numerous questions about Mr. H's strengths: "Didn't he support the family, even though not all the children were his?" "Didn't he keep Mrs. H from being a neglectful parent?" "Didn't the kids miss him?" "Didn't they want him to come home?" "Wasn't he the more nurturing parent?" "Didn't he love the kids?" "Hadn't he made lots of sacrifices for the children?" "Hadn't he endured lots of verbal abuse from Mrs. H to stay with the children?" The attorney also asked comparable questions about Mrs. H's dysfunction. Dr. X responded affirmatively to the attorney's questions but from time to time added, "It's important to remember that Mr. H also seems to have sexually abused these girls."

Another strategy for making essential points is to use the opportunity at the end of all the direct and cross-examination, when the judge asks questions, as an occasion for getting those points across. The judge's questions may provide the opening, or the expert may merely add, "Your Honor, there is one more point I want to make." The advantage of waiting till the end of testimony is that the statement will be a "parting shot" and possibly carry more weight. The potential disadvantage is that the judge may not choose to ask any questions or may not be amenable to allowing the expert to make one or more last points.

The Adversarial Process

One of the most difficult aspects of court testimony for mental health professionals is how they may be treated by the attorneys. As already noted, attorneys may distort the professional's findings to support their client or theory of the case, but attorneys may also challenge the professional's techniques, assumptions, competence, and conclusions. Sometimes this treatment violates expectations mental health practitioners have for civility and professional courtesy. Examples include suggesting bias, implying that the professional has been bought, alluding to malpractice that has no support in fact, and asserting that the professional's personal life disqualifies him or her. Especially vulnerable to the last challenge are professionals who have a history of sexual abuse. Moreover, both the tone of voice and the way questions are asked may be quite offensive.

Illustrative are the strategies of an attorney for an alleged offender. This attorney demeaned the therapist witness because she had only a master's degree in social work; because she believed the victim, whom he asserted was a slut; and because she was unmarried and had no children. He punctuated his remarks by throwing his pencil at her and declaring he wouldn't trust her to give him the right time of day.

There are no simple rules of thumb for dealing with these various challenges and occasional insults. However, if there are likely to be challenges to expertise, experience, or bias, it is important to anticipate them and have a considered response.

For example, because most graduate education does not deal in depth with child sexual abuse, the professional should be prepared to respond to this challenge. The witness can simply point out that most advanced degree programs give scant or no coverage to sexual abuse and present a list of the continuing education conferences, workshops, and other training programs related to sexual abuse that he or she has attended. The witness might also prepare a list of books and articles on sexual abuse that he or she has read.

Mental health professionals who testify in court should also maintain an up-to-date resumé or curriculum vitae that includes all continuing education. This should be provided to attorneys when called to testify. It is very important that it be scrupulously accurate because the professional will be cross-examined on it.

Similarly, if the professional can reasonably anticipate being challenged for either always finding sexual abuse or never finding sexual abuse, it is important to have relevant statistics in mind. It also may be important to point out any artifacts of the case-referral process that might cause findings in a particular direction. For example, if the professional deals only with allegations involving very young children, the substantiation rate may be lower than that for professionals dealing with older children.

It is also probably a good strategy not to show anger, although there are times when righteous indignation is an appropriate response. Nevertheless, becoming angry may make the witness appear defensive and may give the impression that the expert is engaged in a battle with the attorney.

Sometimes the attorney who has subpoenaed the witness will object and interrupt an inappropriate or abusive line of questioning. However, the witness should not rely on that possibility. When an attorney begins to inquire about the professional's personal life, an appropriate response is "How is that relevant to the issue before the court?"

Another possible strategy is appealing to the judge, stating that the line of questioning seems abusive or irrelevant. However, because a witness's credibility is always open to challenge, courts will often allow attorneys a good deal of latitude in cross-examining the witness. This is not an excuse for lawyers to raise entirely irrelevant issues.

Finally, it may be helpful to recognize that harassing a witness may ultimately damage an attorney's case. Particularly if a jury is the fact finder, an overall impression that the attorney is "a bad guy" may obscure any points he has scored in his cross-examination.

THE COURTROOM AS A STAGE

Mental health witnesses must appreciate the importance of their performance in court. Although the judge and/or jury may also receive the professional's written report and curriculum vitae and refer to these while making decisions, testimony is an opportunity to infuse the written word with the professional's competence, conviction, and integrity. Preparation, dress and demeanor, knowing the fact finder, and admissible evidence will be discussed in this section.

Preparation

Like any performance, court testimony requires a great deal of preparation. Depending on the complexity of the case, the expert should expect to spend three to five times as much time in preparation as on the witness stand. The expert should review his or her written report (assuming there is one) so that the material in it is thoroughly familiar. Case characteristics need to be memorized: for example, names, ages, and educational levels of family members, marriage and divorce dates, number of and reasons for protective services referrals, length of time the children have been in placement and names of substitute caretakers, interventions tried with the family, and other professionals involved. If the witness has read other reports or records in coming to conclusions about the case, these need to be reviewed as well. Notes other than the expert's report should also be reread. If there are audio- or videotapes, it is advisable to review these. Finally, because time may have passed and family circumstances may have changed, it is important to ascertain the current status of the family.

The importance of this final point is illustrated by a case in which a mental health expert was subpoenaed to provide testimony about a child whom she had seen a year earlier and determined to have been sexually abused by her stepfather. The mother had divorced the man and left the state with the victim and her younger sister, the offender's biological child. The expert assumed she was to testify about the man's fitness to have unsupervised access to the children. It was not until she had completed her direct examination that she learned that the mother had abandoned both children and the court was deciding about their custody. The expert's just-delivered testimony about the fitness of the mother and her appropriate reaction to the discovery of the sexual abuse was irrelevant to the case.

Having reviewed all the documents cited above, the witness decides on the essential points she or he wants to make during testimony and, as noted in the previous section, either commits them to memory or makes notes. Thorough review of the material will enhance the expert's capability to respond accurately to questions and to evaluate critically questions and the attorney's theory of the case before responding. Committing case characteristics to memory will avoid factual mistakes that can damage the witness's performance. It will also eliminate the need for the witness to shuffle through records to ascertain case facts. Such shuffling may interrupt the pace of the testimony and make the witness appear unprepared, indecisive, or lacking knowledge.

Mental health professionals should appreciate that there is no such thing as a perfect case. This means that regardless of how well they have done their job, someone, usually one of the attorneys, will find fault in their work. This is simply part of the attorney's job in representing his or her client. For example, if the professional has interviewed a child only once, for fear of contaminating the child's account with too many interviews, he or she may be challenged for concluding that the child has been sexually abused after only one interview. In contrast, if the professional has seen the child several times, the challenge may be that the professional has programmed the child.

In addition, sometimes there are genuine weaknesses in the case or the professional's work on the case. An example of a case weakness is the following: The child initially made a coherent disclosure of sexual abuse, later recanted, and then reaffirmed sexual abuse. An example of a weakness in the professional's work would be a situation in which the suspect was supposed to be interviewed but failed to show up for his appointment, and the professional had to form an opinion without the suspect interview. It is important for experts to consider these weaknesses and prepare responses that take them into account before going to court.

A preparatory interview with the attorney who has issued the subpoena before the court date can be extremely useful, and, if the attorney fails to contact the expert, the expert should seek the attorney out. Sometimes this interview does not occur until just before the hearing, and it may be conducted in the hallway at the courthouse. Regardless of when the meeting occurs, it is important to have determined essential points of testimony beforehand. These can then be communicated to the attorney, and some negotiation can take place so that appropriate questions are asked. Sometimes it is wise to prepare a list of questions related to the essential points for the attorney. In addition, this meeting is an opportunity to communicate the weaknesses in the case. It is often a good strategy to have these brought out on direct examination, rather than waiting and having them exposed on cross-examination. Tact needs to be used in offering advice to attorneys on courtroom strategies, for they may regard this as the witness telling them how to do their job.

Dress and Demeanor

The mental health professional should dress in a manner that shows respect for the court and reflects his or her professional status. A good rule of thumb is to dress as the attorneys do, which usually means wearing a suit.

Sit up straight, speak clearly, and try to portray conviction about the points you are making. One of the somewhat awkward aspects of the court process is that the person who asks the questions is not the person to whom the answers are directed. Attorneys ask the questions, but it is the judge and/or jury the witness wants to communicate with. To further complicate matters, usually the expert must also speak into a microphone. The expert may look to the attorney as the question is being asked but then turn to the fact finder to respond. The witness does well to keep in mind that testimony is not a contest in which she or he is trying to beat the attorney but an opportunity to educate the judge and/or jury.

Finally, professionals should remember that although their role in the litigation is important, they are not responsible for the outcome of the case. They are responsible only for their testimony. The fact finder, judge or jury, is the decision maker.

Know the Fact Finder

Judges are individuals, each with a unique view of his or her role, with more or less substantive knowledge about sexual abuse, with greater or lesser experience, and with personal opinions that may affect how he or she performs the role. Some judges may be skeptical about the performance of protective services workers; others may not believe in rehabilitation for sex offenders; still others may regard children as incompetent witnesses; and some may have no use for mental health testimony.

Whenever possible, the mental health witness should try to find out about the judge's background and experience and take this information into account in testimony. For instance, if the witness discovers that this is the judge's first sexual abuse case, he or she should try to assume more of an educative role, providing empirical and substantive information about the prevalence of sexual abuse, its characteristics, its treatability, and so forth. Similarly, if the judge thinks children's statements are very unreliable, the expert should be prepared to cite the research that supports their competence and explains their limitations as witnesses. When the mental health professional meets with the lawyer who has called him or her, questions to elicit appropriate testimony can be arranged.

Juries are more of an unknown quantity than judges. However, in general, they will have less information about sexual abuse and less mental health knowledge than a judge. Therefore, the educative role of the witness will be more prominent in testimony. Some jurors will have very little education. Consequently, if the trial is by jury, the expert should give careful consideration about what concepts are absolutely necessary for the jury to understand and then develop explanations of them in lay language, using concrete illustrations.

For example, expert witnesses are frequently relied upon to explain children's delay in disclosure of sexual abuse. For the judge's benefit, the witness may refer to the "child sexual abuse accommodation syndrome" (Summit, 1983) and may cite relevant and supportive research (e.g., Faller, 1988a; Lyon, 2002; Sas & Cunningham, 1995; Sorenson & Snow, 1991). However, for the jury the expert should say something like this: "Children may not understand what sex and sexual abuse are when they are abused. They may be afraid of what will happen if they tell: For example, they may fear that they will be blamed or considered 'gay.' Or they may love and/or fear the person who sexually abuses them. These factors can cause children to wait a very long time before telling anyone."

Moreover, a jury's emotional reactions are likely to play a more prominent role in their decision making than a judge's. In sexual abuse, this may be disbelief: "How could anyone do such a thing to a little child or his own daughter, especially a man who looks so respectable?" Alternatively, jurors may be incensed that someone could harm a child in this way and may take a vengeful attitude. In the first instance, the mental health professional needs to focus testimony on the prevalence of sexual abuse and the fact that people who are normal in other respects may, under certain circumstances, sexually abuse a child. In the latter case, it may be important to emphasize the offender's potential for rehabilitation and the fact that the victim wants him to get help.

Admissible Evidence

There will be limitations on what mental health professionals will be able to say in court, even when they have been qualified as experts. These limitations will be more strictly adhered to at the trial or adjudication than at other stages in the court process. Constraints on testimony will be much greater in criminal cases than in civil cases. In fact, in a criminal trial, the mental health expert's testimony will be very circumscribed. These testimonial limitations relate to the professional's conclusions and the basis for those conclusions.

Limitations on Testimony About Conclusions. Regarding conclusions, it is fairly clear that the mental health professional will not be allowed to testify that the child, or anyone else, is telling the truth or is credible, regardless of the type of court procedure (Berliner, 1998; Myers et al., 1989). Mental health professionals are not human lie detectors. Decisions about credibility are the province of the fact finder, not the expert witness.

In addition, experts should expect challenges to testimony that indirectly addresses issues of credibility. Examples of such testimony include that (a) the child's statements are consistent with those of other children with a known history of sexual abuse, (b) the child's account of sexual abuse contains the criteria used to determine the likelihood of sexual abuse, and (c) the child's behavior is consistent with being sexually abused (Faller, 1994a; Stern, 1997). The judge may allow this testimony, especially in child protection proceedings and other civil proceedings, but historically courts have been divided about this kind of testimony (Berliner, 1998; Myers et al., 1989).

Similarly, the professional will not be allowed to testify to a conclusion that the defendant is an abuser based on his or her opinion that he has characteristics commonly found among sex offenders (Berliner, 1998; Melton, 1987). In fact, current research suggests that there are many types of sex offenders and that a substantial proportion cannot be differentiated from people without a sex offense history (e.g., Leberg, 1997; Marshall et al., 1990; Schwartz & Cellini, 1995). On the other hand, if the offender has confessed to the mental health professional, the confession is admissible if the professional has told the offender that their relationship is not confidential or if the legal proceeding is one of child protection. This kind of evidence will be discussed further in the next section.

Finally, the professional may be able to testify as a rebuttal witness: that is, to refute assertions made by the accused or his witnesses about the child or about other witnesses who are claiming that the offender is guilty of sexual abuse. Typically, this testimony will be to rehabilitate the child witness when her credibility has been impeached. Testimony related to research and clinical knowledge about victims of sexual abuse as a class, rather than about the child who has testified, will be allowable (Myers et al., 1989).

Limitations on the Testimony About Bases for Conclusions. In court, witnesses may testify to information and events they have perceived directly—things they have observed, tasted, smelled, or felt. It is rare in a sexual abuse case for a mental health professional, or any other witness, to actually observe the sexual abuse.

What this means is that mental health professionals rely heavily on second-hand information or hearsay. Hearsay is "an out of court statement offered to prove the truth of the matter asserted" (Federal Court Rules, 192-278, FRE 801(c) West, 2002). As a general rule, hearsay is inadmissible in court (Myers, 1998). Common examples of the kind of hearsay mental health professionals rely on in sexual abuse cases are what the child told the professional regarding the sexual abuse and what the mother observed and related to the mental health professional regarding the child's sexual behavior. The reason hearsay may not be admissible is that it does not allow the opponent to confront and cross-examine the real witness and expose weaknesses in his or her testimony (Lilly, 1978, p. 57).

As already noted, court rules, including rules making hearsay inadmissible, will be more closely observed at the trial or adjudication stage of a court proceeding. There is more informality at the preliminary, dispositional, review, and the termination of parental rights hearings. Moreover, at any hearing other than a trial, a mental health professional may merely be asked to submit a written report or an affidavit and may not be required to testify. The written word is hearsay because the professional is not there to be cross-examined. Similarly, at hearings other than the adjudication, if the practitioner does appear, the rules of evidence will usually be relaxed, and the witness will be able to include hearsay or rely on hearsay in testimony. However, a termination-of-parental-rights hearing may be considered a new trial, and if so, rules regarding hearsay will be applied more strictly.

In all state and federal court rules, there are exceptions to the hearsay rule. These exceptions involve information that is hearsay but has been obtained in select and clearly defined circumstances that cause it to be regarded as inherently reliable. Hearsay exceptions vary from state to state. However, there are some common exceptions used in sexual abuse cases. These are (a) statements made during the course of medical diagnosis and treatment (e.g., the child's assertions about sexual abuse to a medical or sometimes a mental health professional) (Myers, 1998; Stein, 1991) and (b) excited utterance (e.g., the child's distressed, spontaneous account of the sexual victimization to a parent or other adult, usually occurring soon after the abuse) (Myers, 1998; Stein, 1991). States may also have a child witness or "tender years exception" that allows an adult to testify to what a child has said under certain circumstances (Myers, 1998). In a child protection proceeding, the tender years exception may be used to allow a mental health professional to testify to the child's statements about sexual abuse.

In addition, "party admissions" or statements made to the witness by one of the parties to the court proceeding (e.g., the alleged sex offender in a criminal case or the mother of the victim in a protection proceeding) are admissible (Stein, 1991). Business records (agency records) are allowed in as exhibits and can also be relied on in testimony (Stein, 1991). Finally, the opinion of an expert witness, which may be based in part or wholly on hearsay, will usually be admissible, except the opinions noted in the section just above. However, the general admonition made earlier also applies here: Mental health professionals need to consult with the appropriate attorney regarding what hearsay will be admissible.

Conclusion

Collaboration with attorneys and working in the legal system are perhaps the most challenging tasks for mental health professionals working with sexually abused children and their families. The purpose of this chapter is to assist the practitioner in understanding the various courts that may be involved, the court process, the orientations of the range of attorneys who may be encountered, court rules, and how to be both effective and ethical in the legal environment.

Notes

1   Standards for intervention to protect Native American children are higher. Under the Indian Child Welfare Act (1978), the standard for temporary placement of an Indian child (as defined by the statute) is clear and convincing evidence, and the standard for permanent custody or termination of parental rights is beyond a reasonable doubt (U.S.C.A. 25, sec. 1912 [e] and [f]). See Jones (1995).

2   Hearsay is an out-of-court statement used to prove the matter at hand.

3   When there is a jury, it will typically be charged with making findings of fact (e.g., in a protection proceeding, whether the parent has neglected the child; in a criminal proceeding, whether the offender is guilty of criminal sexual conduct), but the judge will decide what should be done (e.g., in a protection proceeding, to remove the child from the home; in a criminal case, that the offender should serve 5–15 years in prison). When there is no jury, but only a judge, he or she will decide questions of both fact and disposition.

4   These notes are discoverable: That is, any of the parties may ask to see them, and they may be admitted into evidence. However, this will not harm the case or the testimony.

PART III

Data Collection and Decision Making

5

Child Interviews When Sexual Abuse Is Suspected

C entral to assessment of and decision making about sexual abuse is an interview or interviews with the child. This chapter will deal with the "nuts and bolts" of the child interview. In the years intervening since the first edition of this book, quite a lot of change has taken place in the forensic interview field. The following topics will be addressed: (a) flexibility in interview structure and strategies; (b) interview structure; (c) general principles for interviewing children who may have been sexually abused; (d) questioning techniques; (e) the use of media as communication aids; and (f) the scope of the child interview.

A Flexible, Child-Focused Interview

Various approaches have been suggested for interviewing children who may have been maltreated sexually (e.g., Bourg et al., 1999; Davies, Cole, Albertella, McCulloch, Allen, & Kekevian, 1996; McDermott-Steinmetz, 1997; Morgan, 1995; Poole & Lamb, 1998; Saywitz, Geiselman, & Bornstein, 1992). Although some approaches rely on research, most of the studies relied upon involve preschool children without a history of sexual abuse who participate in analogue or laboratory research. As a consequence, the relevance of the research and therefore the ecological validity of approaches based upon it are open to some question. This research is discussed in some detail in Chapter 6.

Table 5.1   Interview Structure

Initial Phase
Interviewer explains his or her role.
Interviewer builds rapport.
Interviewer provides ground rules.
Interviewer assesses overall functioning.
Interviewer assesses the child's developmental level.

Abuse-Focused Phase
Open-ended inquiry.
Follow-up regarding disclosures.
Specific questioning.

Closure Phase
Interviewer explains what will happen next.
Interviewer calms the child, if needed.

Children requiring interviews for possible sexual abuse vary in age, gender, ethnicity, and cultural background. In addition, the abuse experience, the relationship to their offender, the child's reaction to the abuse, and the reaction of people close to the child may vary. Moreover, cases vary in the likelihood of sexual abuse.

Because of the dearth of empirical data supporting a particular interview approach, the fact that children differ in characteristics, and the fact that situations related to the abuse allegations vary, it is advisable for professionals conducting child interviews to have a range of approaches in their repertoires and the capacity to be flexible.

Interview Structure or Protocol

Quite a number of writers have proposed structures or protocols for interviews of children who may have been sexually abused (Boychuk & Stellar, 1992; Bull, 1995; Cantlon, Payne, & Erbaugh, 1996; Faller, 1998a; Michigan Governor's Task Force, 1998; Saywitz et al., 1992; Sternberg et al., 1997, Yuille, n.d.), and in England there is even a model that is agreed upon for law enforcement for the whole country (Home Office, 1992). The outline in Table 5.1 is the current guideline for interviewing children who may have been sexually abused in the program I direct at the University of Michigan. It contains elements common to many of these protocols, but it is not very prescriptive so that interviewers can be flexible and provide an interview that meets the needs of the child being interviewed.

In this section, I discuss phases of the interview, describe advice from various sources about these phases, and offer cautionary advice about protocols. The general interview structure will be described in this section, but specific components of the second or abuse-focused phase will be discussed in later sections. These are (a) questioning strategies, (b) the use of media during the interview, and (c) the scope of the interview.

INITIAL PHASE

The initial phase involves assessing the child's overall functioning, ascertaining the child's developmental level, and building rapport. Some writers suggest inquiring about a neutral event during this phase in order to ascertain the child's ability to recall past events and provide a narrative. Lamb and Sternberg (1999) advised interviewers to ask children open-ended questions about their families, their school, and a recent holiday in order to socialize children to providing narrative responses to evaluators' questions. These researchers demonstrated that using these three questions during the beginning stage of the interview increases the number of words in children's responses to later abuse-focused open-ended questions (Sternberg et al., 1997). That is, this approach will increase the likelihood that the interviewer will obtain a narrative from the child. (Narrative accounts will be discussed in the next section of this chapter.) Even when these opportunities to practice providing a narrative do not result in narratives, they allow the interviewer an opportunity to assess the child's ability to respond to open-ended questions. This assessment information can be used to structure inquiry in the abuse-focused phase of the interview.

During the beginning phase, some interviewers try to determine the child's ability to differentiate between the truth and a lie and obtain from the child a promise to tell the truth during the interview (Yuille, n.d.). Because there is no evidence that this exercise will affect the accuracy of children's reports positively (e.g., Goodman, Aman, & Hirschman, 1987; Poole & Lamb, 1998) and because of concerns about the tone such an exercise sets for the interview, some protocols do not recommend it (e.g., Davies et al., 1996). If the interviewer is concerned about the accuracy of the child's account, an alternative is to ask the child afterward if what the child has said is "something that really happened or pretend."

In addition, some interviewers try to assess the child's suggestibility by asking them misleading questions (e.g., Reed, 1996). (The use of misleading questions will be discussed in greater detail in the section of this chapter on questioning.)

Finally, interviewers usually provide rules for the interview, such as

- "I'll be asking lots of questions."
- "Only tell what really happened."
- "If I ask a question you don't know the answer to, just say 'I don't know,' but if you do know the answer to the question, tell me the answer."
- "If you don't understand a question, say so, and I'll try and ask it in a better way."

Rules provide the child with a set of expectations for the interview. The interviewer needs to take into account the child's level of development when giving rules. The younger the child, the fewer the rules. In any case, it is not clear that children either remember or abide by the rules later in the interview. Finally, children with histories of sexual abuse have control issues.[1] Rules imply adult control over the child and may be counterproductive—that is, they may lead to fear of, resistance to, and avoidance of the interview tasks.

ABUSE-FOCUSED PHASE

The second phase usually begins with open-ended inquiry about possible sexual abuse. The transition from the initial phase to the abuse-focused phase is undertaken in various ways. Some writers advise asking a question such as "I heard something might have happened to you. Tell me about it as best you can" (Boychuk & Stellar, 1992). Some writers, myself included, prefer to begin the abuse-focused phase by general, then more focused inquiry, about people in the child's life, including the possible offender, rather than by beginning with the assumption something has happened to the child (Faller, 1990). Some interviewers begin this phase by conducting a body parts inventory and then asking about body touch (e.g., Davies et al., 1996).

Regardless of whether the child makes a disclosure during open-ended inquiry, the interviewer will need to ask more specific questions. If the child has not described sexual abuse, the child will be asked more directly about possible abuse. If the child has described sexual abuse, in most cases additional questions are needed to gather information about details. As noted, specific techniques to be employed in this phase of the interview will be described in later sections in this chapter.

CLOSURE PHASE

The third phase is closure. It may consist of reiterating the child's prior disclosures (Home Office, 1992), letting the child know what will happen next, helping the child reestablish a sense of equilibrium, and giving an older child information about whom to contact if difficulties arise. Some interviewers thank children for their participation in the interview.

ADDITIONAL COMMENTS ON INTERVIEW STRUCTURE

Most writers advise a several-phase interview. The outline above divides the interview structure into three phases, but the majority of writers suggest more phases, as many as nine, including some optional steps (Boychuk & Stellar, 1992; Michigan Governor's Task Force, 1998; Poole & Lamb, 1998; Yuille, n.d.). My practice experience indicates that with multiphase interviews, the child's attention and capacity to tolerate stress may be exhausted before the interviewer can get to the abuse-focused phases. In addition, the more prescriptive the protocol, the more difficult it will be to tailor the interview to the individual child. If the interviewer nonetheless tailors the interview to the child, the interviewer will be vulnerable to challenge.

Although most interview structures advise assessing the child's developmental level and overall functioning during the beginning phase, most interview structures do not take these into account in subsequent phases. This makes it difficult to conduct an interview that takes into account the child's development, strengths, and weaknesses.

Moreover, interview structures assume that the interviewer will be able to proceed in an orderly and linear fashion through the phases. In fact, many interviews are not linear. During the abuse-focused phase, interviewers must "do a dance" between the task of obtaining information from the child and maintaining rapport. Rapport is not static; it is not something that is established during the first 10 minutes of the interview and present thereafter. It is likely to be undermined as the child has to reveal difficult material. So interviewers must be prepared to mediate the impact of talking about abuse-related material by backing off and discussing less stressful material or engaging in a neutral activity. Similarly, because most interviewers ask about any other events and additional offenders during closure or toward the end of the abuse-focused phase, abuse-related questioning may occur during closure.

Also, most interview structures rely primarily on verbal communication with the child. As will be discussed later in this chapter, there are many reasons for not relying solely on verbal communication when interviewing a child.

Finally, most protocols assume that children are willing to tell about sexual abuse and that the main challenge for the interviewer is avoiding false allegations and contamination of children's accounts through faulty interview techniques. As is discussed in Chapter 6, research on both actual cases and analogue studies suggests that a much more common challenge is getting avoidant children to talk about sexual abuse.

PRINCIPLES OF THE INTERVIEW

A number of general principles can serve as useful guidelines for evaluators assessing children for possible sexual abuse.

- Interviewers need to take into account individual differences in children when they interview them. This includes being sensitive to the child's reactions to the interview situation. Interviewers need to follow the child's lead.
- An important interview goal is to elicit information from the child rather than to ask the child to confirm information the interviewer already knows or to support the interviewer's beliefs about what happened.
- The interviewer should attempt to elicit a narrative account from the child.
- The interviewer should use as many open-ended questions and techniques as possible: for example, the open-ended "What happened when you were at Mr. Smith's cabin?" as opposed to the close-ended "Did Mr. Smith sexually abuse you at his cabin?"
- If the interviewer must use more close-ended questions or techniques, he or she should place less confidence in the information obtained from them.
- A close-ended question should be followed by a more open-ended one. For example:

Interviewer: "Was your dad the person who did the 'bad things'?"
Child: "Yeah."
Interviewer: "Tell me everything you can remember about the 'bad things' your dad did."

- Interviewers should consider and explore alternative hypotheses or reasons for the allegation of abuse. The nature and amount of information the interviewer possesses as he or she begins the interview process will influence what hypotheses the interviewer considers and the extent to which they are pursued. Nonetheless, interviewers should guard against pursuing selective explanations for the allegation. A hypothesis-testing and "rule-out" approach is discussed in some detail in Chapter 7.

Questions Used in Interviewing
Children Who May Have Been Sexually Maltreated

Professionals differ in their definitions and terms for types of questions that may be used in questioning children (e.g., Bourg et al., 1999; Graffam-Walker, 1994; Sternberg, Lamb, Davies, & Wescott, 2001). They also differ somewhat in what types of questions they consider acceptable and unacceptable in child interviews (e.g., Boychuk & Stellar, 1992; Graffam-Walker, 1994; Yuille, n.d.). Table 5.2 provides a designation of 12 types of questions. They are divided into most preferred, preferred, less preferred, and least preferred

Table 5.2   Questioning Typology

Type of Question	Definition	Example
MOST PREFERRED QUESTIONS		
General Question	Open-ended inquiry about the child's well-being or salient issues that does not assume an event or experience	How can I help you? How are you doing today? Is there something I can help you with?
Invitational Question	Open-ended inquiry that assumes there may be an event or experience	I heard something may have happened to you. Do you know why you came to see me today? Tell me about it as best you can. (Boychuk & Stellar, 1992)
PREFERRED QUESTIONS		
Facilitative Cue	Interviewer gesture or utterance aimed at encouraging more narration	Uh huh (affirmative) Anything else? And then what happened?
Follow-up Question	Follow-up inquiry to gather details about the child's experience	Do you remember where it happened? What were you wearing? Where was your mom?
Focused Question	One that focuses the child on a particular topic, place, or person but refrains from providing information about the subject (Myers, Goodman, & Saywitz, 1996)	Can you tell me all about day care? Tell me about your dad. (Are there things you like about him? Are there things you don't like about him?) Can you tell me about penises? (Who has one? What are they for? Did you ever see one? Whose did you see?)
LESS PREFERRED QUESTIONS		
Multiple-Choice Question	A question that presents the child with a number of alternative responses from which to choose	Did he do it one time or more than one time? Did it happen in the daytime or night or both?
Externally Derived Question	A question that relies on information not disclosed in the child interview	Do you remember anything about a camera? Did John say anything about telling?

(*Continued*)

Table 5.2 (Continued)

Type of Question	Definition	Example
Direct Question	A direct inquiry into whether a person committed a specific act	Did John hurt your peepee? Was your father the one who poked your butt?
Repeated Questioning	Asking the same question two or more times	Did anything happen to your pecker? Do you remember if anything happened to your pecker?

LEAST PREFERRED QUESTIONS

Leading Question	A statement the child is asked to affirm	Isn't it true that your brother put his penis in your mouth? Chester was really cleaning, wasn't he?
Misleading Question	A question that assumes a fact that is not true and that the child is explicitly or implicitly asked to confirm	What color scarf was the nurse wearing? (when she wasn't wearing one). Show me where the doctor touched you (when he didn't touch).
Coercion	Use of inappropriate inducements to get cooperation or information	If you tell me what your father did, we can go for ice cream. Don't tell my boss that I was playing (interviewer gives child a piece of candy).

on the basis of existing literature and practice. Definitions and examples of each type of question are provided. There is some overlap among question types, and interviewers might use probes that cannot be classified using this typology.

The types of questions can be viewed as representing a continuum from most open-ended to least open-ended. As a rule the more open-ended the question, the greater the confidence the interviewer should have in the child's answer. However, the appropriateness of a particular type of question depends a great deal upon its context in the interview, especially what disclosures and types of questions have preceded the question. As a consequence, there may be a place for virtually all the questions on the continuum.

The types of questions in Table 5.2 and some of the controversies related to them will be discussed.

MOST PREFERRED QUESTIONS: GENERAL AND INVITATIONAL QUESTIONS

As Table 5.2 indicates, professionals include two types of questions in the most preferred category: *general,* which do not imply that the child has experienced abuse, and *invitational,* which imply that something has happened. Although adults may respond to general questions, some research indicates that children, even those who have previously disclosed sexual abuse, will not respond to these questions (DeVoe & Faller, 2002).

Lamb and Sternberg (1999) are doing important work using a semiscripted protocol. They have proposed ten probes, which I have tried to classify according to the questioning typology in Table 5.2. They are listed in their order of preference and from more open-ended to more close-ended.

1. Tell me why you came to talk to me. (invitational probe)
2. Tell me everything about that from the beginning to the end. (invitational probe)
3. It is important that I understand why you came. (invitational probe)
4. I hear you saw (professional). Tell me what you talked about. (focused probe)
5. Tell me why you think (transporter) brought you here today. (invitational probe)
6. Is (caretaker) worried that something may have happened to you? (focused question)
7. I heard someone has been bothering you. (focused probe)
8. I heard someone may have done something to you that wasn't right. (focused probe)
9. I heard something may have happened to you at (location, time). (focused probe)
10. I heard someone may have (allegation). (direct probe)

Lamb and Sternberg (1999) reported that most children in their studies who disclosed did so to the first probe. They also described the last probe as a last resort. Although a number of the above probes are invitational, only one is a question. The probes are either overt or implied commands.

There is disagreement among professionals about whether the interviewer should use a request (e.g., "Can you tell me everything you remember about day care?") or a command (e.g., "Tell me everything you remember about day care.") Similarly, professionals disagree about whether the child should be given an opportunity to say they don't remember by being asked "Do you remember where this happened?" rather than being asked "Where did this happen?" Queries about whether the child *remembers*, *knows*, or *can tell* about events avoid demand characteristics, which communicate to children that they should provide information whether they know it or not. In addition, asking rather than commanding eliminates an element of coercion. However, asking for rather than requiring responses also gives the child a way out of talking about difficult material.

Child and case characteristics probably should determine how the invitation is phrased. An oppositional child may require a "Tell me" probe, whereas a compliant child may need a "Can you?" query. In terms of case characteristics, if case material indicates that the child should know the response, a command is probably more appropriate. On the other hand, if it is questionable that the child possesses the information, a "Do you remember?" is probably more appropriate.

The context of the interview and the role of the interviewer will influence what invitational questions are appropriate. Other invitational questions that may be useful are:

- "Do you know what kind of place this is?"
- "This is a place where we help children when things may have happened to them. Has anything happened to you?"
- "Did (caretaker) tell you why you were coming to see me? What did he/she say?"
- "My job is to help kids when things are worrying them. Is anything worrying you?"
- "I talk to kids when something may have happened to them. Has anything happened to you?"

PREFERRED QUESTIONS

Facilitative Cues

Many writers (e.g., Home Office, 1992; Yuille, n.d.) advise interviewers not to follow up invitational questions and probes with reactions, responses, and additional questions until the child stops talking. Although this strategy minimizes the potential for interviewer contamination of the child's account, it is antithetical to normal discourse, which is interactive. A concern is that a nonresponsive interviewer may be interpreted by the child as uncaring or uninterested. I recommend that interviewers be attentive to children's behavior and respond accordingly. This may require judicious use of facilitative cues, such as a nod or "Umhum." Such responses will communicate to the child that the interviewer is listening.

Repeating what the child has just stated is another sort of facilitative cue. It is more appropriate when the child has stopped talking. It communicates to the child that the interviewer is attending and is interested in what the child is saying and encourages more information. In addition, it serves as a check on whether the interviewer has understood what the child has said correctly. If the interviewer has made an error, the child can correct the interviewer. That correction also serves as an indicator that the child is not suggestible.

There are other types of facilitative cues. After the child has exhausted initial recall, the interviewer can probe by asking, "Anything else you can remember?" or "Then what happened?" or "Can you tell me more about that?"

Follow-Up Questions

After the child has exhausted initial recall is also an appropriate time for the questions of who, what, where, when, and how: for example "Where were you?" "Where was your mom?" "When did this happen?" "What were you wearing?" "How did you get into the room?" However, the interviewer may want to attempt focused questions, described in the next section, first.

Evaluators should be careful to follow up on all leads the child provides. It is easy to pursue only information that conforms with the evaluator's ideas about what happened. This may result in incomplete or inaccurate information gathering, and it also will leave the evaluator open to challenges in court.

Focused Questions

In my experience, many and perhaps most children fail to provide narrative accounts to general and invitational questions. Moreover, children who have been admonished not to tell and children who are fearful of the consequences of disclosure may deny that anything has happened or not respond when asked invitational questions. Focused questions are needed. In addition, for some children invitational questions do not trigger their memories. Such may be the case for young children, for children who do not appreciate the inappropriateness of the sexual activity, and for children whose lives are filled with chaos and many types of mistreatment. In such cases, focused questions may be indicated for resolving concerns about sexual abuse. Four types of focused questions will be discussed:

1. Person-focused questions

2. Circumstances of abuse–focused questions

3. Body parts–focused questions

4. Questions about the source of concern

Although these questions are more closed than general and invitational questions, they can be varied in their degree of openness. Evaluators are advised to begin with open-ended focused questions and to resort to more close-ended ones when open-ended questions don't resolve the issue of sexual abuse. If the evaluator elicits material indicative of sexual abuse, he or she will pursue the allegation further using invitational questions such as "Can you tell me all about that?", additional focused questions, and other types of questions to be described below.

Questions Focused on the Person. Focused questions may be directed toward significant persons in the child's life, including the alleged offender. Usually the evaluator begins by asking about persons with whom the child has positive and/or neutral relationships and delays questions about the possible offender until toward the end of this line of questioning. If there is more than one possible offender, or if someone is likely to suggest that the offender is some-one else (e.g., an older brother rather than the father, or the stepfather rather than the biological father), the evaluator should ask focused questions about all of these people. The child can be asked questions such as the following:

- "Does your mom/dad have another name besides mom or dad?" (If yes) "What is it?"
- "Tell me all about your mom/dad."
- "How do you get along with your mom/dad?"
- "What sorts of things do you do with your mom/dad?"
- "Does mom/dad do things with you that she/he doesn't do with anyone else?" (If yes) "What?"
- "What sorts of things do you do with your mom/dad that you like?"
- "Is there anything she/he does that you don't like?" (If yes) "What don't you like?" (If the child gives a response unrelated to sexual abuse, the interviewer may ask if there is anything else the parent does that the child doesn't like.)
- "Do you have any worries about things your mom/dad does?" (If yes) "What?"

As the reader can see, the initial questions are neutral and open-ended. Because open-ended focused questions like "Tell me all about your mom" are not usual in adult-child discourse, they may elicit a blank look or "What do you mean?" from an older child. More concrete questions such as "What do you like to do with your mom?" may be required.

Questions Focused on the Circumstances of the Sexual Abuse. For many professionals, the preferred type of focused question is one related to circumstances of possible abuse. Focused questions about circumstances can relate to environmental circumstances, including child care; how the offender characterizes the abuse; or how the offender induces the child not to tell. Possible questions are as follows:

- "What do you do when Georgie lets you stay up late at night?"
- "What do you do when you go over to grandpa's?"
- "Do you ever play games with your dad?" (If yes) "What kind of games?"
- "Do you have any secrets in your family?" (If yes) "Tell me all about the secrets."
- "What does your mom get mad at your dad about?"
- "Does anyone help you take a bath?" (If yes) "Who helps?" "How do they help you?"
- "Where do you sleep at your house?" (If the child responds she or he sleeps with someone, the evaluator should ask what this is like or if anything happens when she or he sleeps with that person.)
- "Do you go to the bathroom by yourself?" (If no) "Who helps you?" "What do they do to help?"
- "What does your dad do when he drinks?"
- "Does your mom have parties?" (If yes) "Can you tell me about the parties?"

Some of these circumstances-focused questions call for a yes/no response; an affirmative response is followed by an invitational or a follow-up question, querying "what". Focused questions that may call for a yes/no response should not be confused with direct questions, which also call for a yes/no response but ask the child if an individual has committed a specific act. However, some children will provide details in response to a focused question without the evaluator asking the invitational or "what" question.

As noted, some questions are about child care tasks: for example, who puts the child to bed and helps the child with a bath. These questions may be asked during the initial phase of the interview. If so, follow-up questions that may elicit information about abuse should probably be delayed until the abuse-focused portion of the interview. In the abuse-focused portion, the evaluator might say, "You remember you told me before that your dad gives you a bath, can you tell me more about that?" "Or what is it like when your dad gives you a bath?" perhaps followed by "How does your dad help you with your bath?" and "What do you think about him helping you?"

Questions Focused on the Body Parts. Another type of focused question relates to the child's experience with or knowledge about body parts. Such questions usually follow a body parts inventory in which the child's terms for body parts, including private parts, are ascertained. A body parts inventory can be conducted using anatomical dolls, drawings, or free drawings of body outlines. If the body parts inventory is conducted during the abuse-focused portion of the interview, a body parts–focused question may immediately follow a body parts inventory. If the body parts inventory is conducted during the initial phase of the interview, the question may be delayed until later in the interview. The following are examples of focused questions that might elicit relevant information:

1. Questions related to penises

   - "Who has a (child's name for penis)? (If the child responds, "My brother," the interviewer may ask if anyone else has one.)
   - "What is (child's name for penis) for?" (If the child answers that it's for going pee, the interviewer may ask if it does anything else.)
   - "Did you ever see (child's name for penis)?" (If the child responds yes, the evaluator can ask the child to tell about seeing [child's name for penis].)
   - "What do men do with (child's name for penis)?"
   - "Does (child's name for penis) ever do things you don't like? (If yes) "What?"
   - "Does anything ever come out of (child's name for penis)?" (If yes), "What?"
   - "What is (child's name for semen) like?"

2. Questions related to vaginas

   - "Who has a (child's name for vagina)?"
   - "What are (child's name for vagina) for?" (If the child responds, "Going pee") "Do (child's name for vagina) ever get used for anything else?"
   - "What do you do with your (child's name for vagina)?"
   - "Has anything ever happened to your (child's name for vagina)?" (If yes) "What?"
   - "Did your (child's name for vagina) ever get hurt?" (If yes) "Tell me all about your (child's name for vagina) getting hurt."
   - "Has anyone ever done anything to your (child's name for vagina)?" (If the child says yes, she should be asked who did this and what the person did it with.)
   - "Has anyone ever touched your (child's name for vagina)?" (If the child says yes, she should be asked who did this and what the person did it with.)
   - "Has anyone ever tried to touch your (child's name for vagina)?" (If yes) "Tell me about that."

Questions about body parts should, of course, be varied according to the sex of the alleged perpetrator and victim. However, it is a good idea to ask the child questions about both male and female private parts. This provides a more balanced interview. Often the contrast between the child's responses related to the alleged offender's genitalia and a nonoffending parent can be enlightening. In addition, a substantial percentage of children are sexually abused by more than one person and sometimes adults of both sexes (Faller, 1995). Thus, it is prudent to ask about all private parts.

Questions Focused on the Source of Concern. If the evaluator has tried other questioning strategies without resolving the allegation of sexual abuse, it may be appropriate to ask questions that direct the child's attention to the cause for concern about sexual abuse. This may be a disclosure by the child, revelation by someone else, sexualized behavior, advanced sexual knowledge, physical evidence, or some other sign.

- "Did you have to go to the doctor? (If yes) "Do you know why?"
- "Do you know how your butt got hurt?"
- "Did you tell your foster care worker about something that happened to you?" (If yes) "What was that?"
- "Do you remember telling your teacher about humping?" (If yes) "What exactly is humping?" "How did you learn about humping?" "Who does humping?" "Has anything like humping ever happened to you?"
- "Your mom said you did something to your new puppy." "Can you tell me about that?" "What made you decide to suck the doggie's peepee?"

I suggest asking about the child's sexualized behavior in the most nonaccusatory way possible. If these inquiries are accusatory, children may perceive themselves as the wrongdoers or deny the sexualized behavior altogether.

LESS PREFERRED QUESTIONS

Multiple-choice, externally derived, and direct questions fall in the less preferred category because they are inconsistent with the interview principle of gathering information from the child. Instead, these less preferred questions present information to the child to be confirmed or denied. Therefore, if interviewers need to use them, the information they yield should be viewed with less confidence.

Multiple-Choice Questions

Multiple-choice questions are less preferred because of their demand characteristics—that is, they may compel a response. If the child does not know the answer or is too young to process the alternative choices, she may choose the first or last choice, the response that sticks in her mind.

It is advisable to follow several principles if using multiple-choice questions. First, they should usually be preceded by a focused question to which the child fails to respond or says "I don't know" or "I don't remember." For example, after a child has said the offender "poked me in the butt," the evaluator might ask, "Do you remember where you were when Joe poked your butt?" If the child does not answer, the interviewer might ask, "Were you indoors or outdoors?"

Second, the interviewer should be sure the correct answer is included among the alternatives. Thus, instead of saying, "Did he poke you in the butt in the bathroom or the bedroom or the kitchen?" it is better to say, "Did he poke you in the butt in the bathroom or the bedroom or the kitchen, or someplace else?" in case the correct response is not one of the rooms named.

Finally, it is advisable to limit multiple-choice questions to the context of the abuse or "where" and "when" and not to use them when inquiring about "who" did it and "what" sexual acts were performed.

Externally Derived Questions

In some instances, interviewers may decide to ask questions based upon externally derived information, or information obtained from a source other than the child interview. Some professionals oppose their use altogether (e.g., Yuille, n.d.), but others think they can be used (Boychuk & Stellar, 1992; D. Corwin, personal communication, 1998). Such questions may be necessary to avoid a situation of *prior inconsistent statement* (i.e., the child alleging certain acts at an earlier time but not mentioning them in the interview), a situation that could result in impeachment of the child. Alternatively, the information not mentioned may seem crucial to establishing the likelihood of abuse or protecting the child. However, externally derived questions can vary in their degree of open-endedness. The following example is illustrative:

> *Case Example*: John, age 7, had told a road officer that his mother, father, and two men whom he called "Uncle" had sexually abused him. Among the acts he attributed to his father were sodomy and oral sex.
>
> When the forensic interviewer asked John about his father, he said his father "stuck his penis in my butt." When asked what that was like, he replied, "It hurt." He indicated this happened in the parental bedroom and that his mother was there. His two brothers were at a friend's.
>
> The interviewer then asked if there was anything else his dad did, and John said, "No." The interviewer then asked if there was anything with mouths. John said, "Yuck!" The interviewer then said, "What's yuck?" John said, "Suck." The interviewer said, "Suck what?" and John replied, "He stuck his dick in my mouth and made me suck it. It was yuck!"

In this example, John apparently did not recall sucking his father's penis when first asked an open-ended question about "anything else." The forensic interviewer made judicious use of the information by selecting a word, *mouths*, that she thought might trigger John's memory. She didn't ask, "Did you ever have to suck your father's penis?" which would have been a more close-ended use of the externally derived information.

Direct Questions

The term *direct question* is used for questions that contain the identity of the alleged offender and the sexual act. For example, if the question is "Did your daddy hurt your peepee?" the answer is yes or no. Generally, interviewers trying to determine sexual abuse avoid direct questions because they are regarded as too closed ended. However, analogue studies of nonabused children who experience medical exams indicate that such questions are needed when asking children about sensitive material, such as private parts touch (Saywitz, Goodman, Nicholas, & Moan, 1991; Steward et al., 1996). In analogue studies, such questions overcome apparent reluctance to reveal private parts touch for a substantial majority of children. However, they also result in a slight increase in false positives: that is, cases in which children who have not experienced private parts touch indicate that they have. See Chapter 6 for additional discussion of analogue studies.

In forensic interviews, the concern is that direct questions may elicit false positives in the following circumstances. Children who want to please the interviewer and think the interviewer desires a "yes" response may give a "social desirability response." Young children who don't understand the question may reply "yes." Finally, children who don't know the answer and do not want to show their ignorance may say "yes." Because of the concern about false positives, direct questions will likely be challenged in court. Moreover, from a practical standpoint, a child who fails to respond to a focused question because she doesn't want to talk about the topic is not likely to be moved to be more forthcoming by a direct question.

However, as with other types of questions, when interviewers decide to use direct questions, they can vary their degree of open-endedness. The following contrasts are illustrative.

Close-Ended	More Open-Ended
Did your grandpa tickle your peepee with his tongue?	Did grandpa do anything with his mouth?
Did Mr. Jones put his finger in your butt hole?	Did any of the men do something to your butt hole?

Regardless of the degree of openness, a direct question can be followed by a more open-ended one, such as "Can you tell me everything you remember about that?" which reverts to eliciting information from the child rather than providing information to the child for a response. Nevertheless, interviewers are advised to avoid direct questions when possible.

Repeated Questions

Evaluators may be challenged in the legal arena for asking repeated questions. The implication is that they have programmed or browbeaten the child. Table 5.2 defines repeated questions as asking the same question more than once and classifies them as "less preferred." Nevertheless, there are three legitimate reasons an interviewer might repeat a question: to check for consistency in the child's response, to obtain a response when the child has not initially answered the question, and to check for the accuracy of the child's response (because the interviewer thinks the child's initial response was inaccurate). A fourth reason an interviewer may repeat the question is that he or she does not remember the child's answer or that the question has already been asked, but both of these are situations that interviewers try to avoid.

A concern about repeating questions is that children will think their correct initial responses were incorrect and will change their answers. There is some analogue research indicating that when a yes/no question is repeated, children are more likely than adults to change a correct response (Warren & Lane, 1995). However, the general research findings from analogue studies are that repeated, neutral questions do not increase inaccuracy, may elicit more information about the event, and may enhance recollection (Poole & White, 1991, 1993, 1995). These benefits are stronger in within-session repeated questions. In addition, some practitioners and analogue researchers inoculate children against changing their responses by telling them that the same question may be asked more than once but that this does not mean the child's answer is wrong (e.g., Saywitz et al., 1992).

On the other hand, when interviewers want to repeat a question the child has not answered or a question thought to have been answered incorrectly, they are advised not to ask exactly the same question but to ask about the issue in a somewhat different way. Initial failure to respond may be because the interviewer's question did not trigger the child's memory. Children may not conceptualize events in the same way as adults. Alternatively, the child may have been unwilling to answer a particular question.

There is a difference between repeating a question and asking numerous questions. Although it may be optimal to have the abuse-related phase consist of general or invitational questions with a few follow-up questions to gather details (Lamb, 1994), in both analogue studies and research on actual cases this does not happen. It is usually necessary to ask lots of questions simply because lots of information is sought.

In the analogue study involving medical exams mentioned earlier, Saywitz et al. (1991) asked 215 questions in order to gather information about a single medical checkup. Similarly, Steward et al. (1996) employed about 100 questions to gather information about body touch during a single medical exam. In actual cases, the interviewer may be gathering information about more than one event, and in some cases about sexual abuse that has persisted for years. Thus, one would anticipate needing more questions in real-world cases. In the study by Faller and DeVoe (1995b) cited earlier, we found that, on average, disclosing children were asked 95 questions before they revealed sexual abuse. Similarly, in research on interviews using the Memorandum of Good Practice, the English forensic interview protocol, Sternberg et al. (2001) found that interviewers made on average 207 "utterances," of which 145 were substantive.

LEAST PREFERRED QUESTIONS

Leading and misleading questions and coercion fall into the general category of least-preferred questions.

Leading Questions

Because leading questions are those in which the respondent is asked to confirm an assertion by the interviewer (Graffam-Walker, 1994), they are generally not appropriate. However, sometimes they can be used to confirm information the child has already provided. For example, suppose the interviewer is reviewing and recapitulating statements the child made at the end of an interview. The interviewer might say, "You said your cousin, Joey, grabbed you and pulled your pants down, didn't you?"

Another circumstance in which a leading question might be acceptable is one in which the child contradicts her previous statement. Suppose the child has told the interviewer that the man who molested her had black hair and a beard but then states it was a boy who molested her. The interviewer might respond, "Now, before, didn't you say it was a man with black hair and a beard?"

Misleading Questions

Misleading questions are ones in which the interviewer asks the child to support or accept incorrect information. They are used extensively in analogue studies to determine children's suggestibility. Some professionals also advise their use in interviews of suspected victims to assess suggestibility (e.g., Reed, 1996). For example, the interviewer might state, "You told me that you live with your Aunt Minnie, didn't you?" (when in fact the child said she lived with her grandmother). A suggestible child might affirm the interviewer's question, but a nonsuggestible child might resist and correct the interviewer. Although the child's resistance might indicate a lack of suggestibility in response to this incorrect assertion, there is no empirical basis for concluding that the child would also resist a misleading question about actual abuse. And of course, a potential cost is undermining the abuse-related statements of a child who doesn't correct the interviewer. If interviewers use these questions to assess suggestibility, they are advised to ask them about non-abuse-related issues.

An additional consideration is that misleading questions may be confusing to children, and if the offender has used subterfuge, misleading questions may parallel the offender's behavior. That is, if the interviewer also tries to trick the child, he or she may reinforce the child's bewilderment with adults and inability to trust them.

Coercion

At the other end of the continuum is coercion or coercive questions. Coercion involves the use of inappropriate inducements, such as positive activities, material rewards, privileges, threats, and escape from stress (e.g., the interview) to obtain cooperation or elicit information during the interview. Most interviewers are confident that they do not coerce children. Thus, they would never say, "You can only have the candy bar if you tell me what happened" or "You can't go to the bathroom until you talk." However, the structure of the interview is inherently coercive. By that, I mean that the interviewer wants the child to talk or otherwise communicate about events the child usually does not even want to think about. In addition, the interviewer is a big person and the child is smaller. Children may avoid the topic by stating they are not going to talk, by saying they want to play, by asking to leave to see their caretaker, or by announcing they want to end the interview. Interviewers may use inducements to keep the child on task, such as "We'll play once we've finished talking," or "You can't leave until we're all done here."

There is no way to eliminate the conflict between the interviewer's needs and the child's wishes. However, sometimes the conflict can be mediated by allowing the child breaks, allowing some play before talking, or allowing the child to engage in an undemanding activity, like coloring, while talking. The interview room can also be structured in such a way as to be comfortable but absent numerous distractions and temptations, such as games and toys, thereby decreasing stimuli that may result in avoidance.

Media to Be Used for Communication in Interviews

In this section, several reasons for using media to communicate with children will be discussed, and appropriate use of several media (anatomical dolls, anatomical drawings, and free drawings) will be described. Although media for communication are discussed separately from questioning techniques, usually the two go hand in hand, with the interviewer asking questions and the child providing both demonstrations and verbal communication. In fact, evaluators should be cautious about interpreting the child's demonstrations without some verbal checking about their meaning. For example, suppose an 8-year-old girl inserts the penis of an anatomical doll into her mouth. The evaluator should not assume automatically that the girl has been involved in fellatio. Rather, the evaluator should ask, "Who does that?" in order to gather more information.

WHY USE NONVERBAL MEANS OF COMMUNICATION DURING CHILD INTERVIEWS?

When interviewed, adults generally communicate through the medium of language, which may be supplemented by body language, such as facial expressions, hand gestures, and body posture. Children, especially young ones, are not as accomplished as adults in verbal communication.

Moreover, children are likely to be socialized by adults to provide "short and sweet" verbal responses, often both at school and at home. Thus, when the teacher asks: "What is two times four?" he or she is looking for the answer "Eight," not a narrative. Similarly, when a mother asks, "Did you take out the garbage?" she wants a yes or no and no excuses, and if Dad asks, "Do you know it's bedtime?" he hopes for a yes and no protests.

Although evaluators interviewing for sexual abuse may encourage children to provide narratives of their experiences, encountering an adult who wants a lot of talk may be anomalous, and the child may not talk a lot. Thus, the information children provide is likely to be sparse. Some writers (e.g., Poole & Lamb, 1998) suggest repeatedly asking the child to provide verbal information, and there are analogue studies that support the efficacy of this strategy (Poole & White, 1991, 1993, 1995). Nevertheless, clinical experience suggests that there are potential demand characteristics to asking the same question repeatedly. As already pointed out, the child may think her first response was incorrect and change it. A related point is that the child may think she should know more and may generate additional but inaccurate responses in an effort to please. A slightly different dynamic may operate with some children who will take repeated requests for verbal information as an opportunity to embellish, providing inaccurate information.

Perhaps a better strategy to overcome the paucity of verbal information is to allow the child to communicate through additional means, such as demonstrating with dolls or drawing a picture of the event. The information thus provided may lead the interviewer to ask additional questions about the event.

A second rationale for employing means of communication other than mere words is that it can allow the interviewer to check for consistency in information across media. Assuming the information is consistent across media, the evaluator should have greater confidence in its accuracy. If it is inconsistent, evaluators should ask the child to clarify.

A third rationale for using nonverbal media to communicate is that in certain circumstances nonverbal communication eliminates the need for numerous close-ended questions. For example, suppose the child says, "Daddy did the dirty to me." The interviewer can ask the child to show with anatomical dolls what that means. A demonstration may eliminate the need for a lot of specific questions about "the dirty."

Fourth, certain media provide children cues needed to trigger their memories. For example, a body map or anatomical drawing may be needed to trigger the child's recollection of details of an experience (American Professional Society on the Abuse of Children [APSAC], 1995).

Fifth, media may overcome children's reluctance to disclose. This reluctance may derive from distress associated with speaking about the abuse, admonitions not to say "dirty words" needed to explain the abuse, or specific threats of consequences of telling. Some children take literally an instruction by the offender or others not to tell what happened but may not interpret this instruction as preventing them from showing or writing responses. The following case illustrates this phenomenon.

> *Case Example*: Lucy, age 10, had been sexually and physically abused by several adults who were members of a nontraditional church. They said they would kill her if she told. She used anatomical drawings, drew pictures herself, and wrote responses on the drawings to the questions posed by the evaluator. Occasionally she whispered something into the evaluator's ear. Altogether she employed 22 drawings with writing on them to communicate her experiences at the church. Lucy appeared to have taken literally the offenders' threats but seemed to have felt she was safe if she used drawings and whispered.

Finally, nonverbal media may be useful if there are concerns about programming by adults. If programming has occurred, it is likely to be verbal. For example, suppose a 7-year-old child has been told by her mother to say that grandma's boyfriend hurt her peepee because the mother does not like her mother's boyfriend. A 7-year-old can probably repeat what her mother has told her to say, but she may have difficulty demonstrating with anatomical dolls the specifics of an event because her mother has not shown her how to do this.

CAUTIONS ABOUT MEDIA

Media also have disadvantages: They can serve as distractions and may elicit fantasy, a reason for having few toys and other child-focused materials in forensic interview rooms. Some analogue studies indicate that props, such as doctor tools, can serve as distractions for children (e.g., Steward et al., 1996).

Interviewers who use anatomical dolls are admonished to tell the children they are not for play. This admonition may not prevent play or fantasy, however. In my clinical experience, I have found that male victims of sexual abuse often inject fantasy that allows them mastery over the abuse situation. For example, after showing abuse with anatomical dolls, more than one male victim has then made the child doll prevail.

Another important caution is that children 3 years old and younger may not understand the concept of having a drawing or a doll represent themselves (DeLoache, 1995). However, they may be capable of using a doll or drawing to represent the offender, and they may be able to demonstrate on their own bodies. The following example is illustrative of the limitations of young children.

> *Case Example*: Tommy was 2½ and allegedly had been anally penetrated by his mother on an unsupervised visit. He had physical findings. The interviewer obtained a verbal disclosure, "Her hurted my butt." When asked what with, Tommy said, "A butt tool." In an attempt to clarify, interviewer presented Tommy with anatomical dolls to represent himself and his mother. When asked to show where his mother had hurt, he first pointed to his own anus. When presented with the boy doll, he ignored it and pulled down his own pants, and placed his finger on his anus. The interviewer gave Tommy the mother doll and asked him to show what his mother had done. He replied, "Her didn't do it with a doll; her did it with a butt tool."

In this case, Tommy was too young either to have the doll represent himself or to have a doll represent his mother.

Finally, as will be discussed in the next section, media, especially anatomical dolls, may increase attacks on the interview in the legal arena. This appears to be the primary reason many forensic interviewers are reluctant to use media.

TYPES OF MEDIA EMPLOYED IN INTERVIEWING CHILDREN WHO MAY HAVE BEEN SEXUALLY ABUSED

Many media can be useful in interviewing children who may have been sexually abused, and evaluators are encouraged to think creatively about media that might be useful with the particular children they are interviewing. The child's age, gender, ethnicity, and any unique skills or dislikes should be taken into account. Media to be discussed here are ones that have been employed fairly widely and for which there are some guidelines.

Anatomical Dolls

Evaluators for child sexual abuse have found anatomical dolls very useful. As a consequence they have been widely employed. In a study conducted a decade ago, the most commonly employed medium was anatomical dolls, employed by 92% of the 212 sexual abuse evaluators who participated in a national study (Conte, Sorenson, Fogarty, & Dalla Rosa, 1991). At the same time, the dolls have been an easy target for those who are skeptical about sexual abuse and children's accuracy.

Perhaps because of both their appeal for interviewers and the attacks leveled against them by critics, dolls have been subjected to more research than other media employed in child interviews. Studies of free play and instructed interaction with anatomical dolls by children without a reported history of sexual abuse find that the dolls do not elicit sexualized behavior from sexually naive children but may serve as a stimulus for sexual interaction for sexually knowledgeable children (Boat & Everson, 1994; Everson & Boat, 1994; Sivan, Schor, Koeppl, & Noble, 1988). These differentiated responses are useful in evaluating children who may have been sexually abused. However, sexual interactions only indicate sexual knowledge; they do not tell the interviewer the source of that knowledge. Although advanced sexual knowledge may derive from having been sexually abused, it can also derive from other sources, such as observing people engaged in sexual behavior, watching pornographic videos, or viewing sexual material on the Internet. As material about sex becomes more available, the likelihood that sexually knowledgeable children have learned about sex in ways that do not involve abusive sexual contact increases.

In addition, several studies have compared the reactions of children with and without a history of sexual abuse to anatomical dolls (August & Foreman, 1989; Britton & O'Keefe, 1991; Cohn, 1991; Jampole & Webber, 1987; White, Strom, Santilli, & Halpin, 1986). The findings of these studies are consistent with those just cited: Most results indicate that children with a history of sexual abuse are significantly more likely than children without that history to demonstrate sexual behavior with the dolls but that not all children with an abuse history do so and a few children without an abuse history do. What these studies tell us is that sexualized behavior with anatomical dolls during free play is a red flag; the source of the child's knowledge about sexual behavior should be explored.

However, observations of children's interaction with the dolls, described below as using the dolls as a memory stimulus and diagnostic screen, are but one use of the dolls, and not the most common one. In Table 5.3, five different potential uses of the dolls are defined. Table 5.3 is based upon a review of 20 anatomical doll guidelines undertaken by Everson and Boat (1994).

Boat and Everson (1994) found that the most frequently endorsed use of anatomical dolls is as a demonstration aid: that is, to show an event rather than merely to describe it verbally. There is disagreement in the field about whether the interviewer should exhaust the child's ability to communicate verbally

Table 5.3   Uses of Anatomical Dolls

1. **Demonstration Aid** (Endorsed in 18 guidelines)
   A. Subcategories of use
      1. To facilitate disclosure
      2. To clarify disclosure
      3. To corroborate disclosure
   B. Choose and use as many dolls as are needed to show the child's abuse circumstance.
   C. Do not stop the discussion of abuse to name all body parts.

2. **Anatomical Model** (Endorsed in 16 guidelines)
   A. Introduce dolls independent of any statements.
   B. Use two, three, or four dolls.
   C. Identify nonsexual and sexual body parts.
   D. Ask the child questions about body parts.

3. **Memory Stimulus and Diagnostic Screen** (Endorsed in 9 guidelines)
   A. Dolls usually serve both functions simultaneously.
   B. Allow the child time in free play with the dolls.
   C. Make observations and/or ask questions about material in play.

4. **Icebreaker**
   A. Employ as many dolls as you have.
   B. Identify sexual and nonsexual body parts.
   C. Discuss body parts functions.

5. **Comforter**
   A. Choose a doll with whom the child can identify.
   B. Allow the child to hold the doll.
   C. Talk about the doll's feelings.

SOURCE: Adapted from the work of Boat and Everson (1988a, 1988b, 1994).

before presenting the anatomical dolls for use as a demonstration aid (APSAC, 1995; Everson & Boat, 1996; Faller, 1999; Yuille, n.d.). Anatomical dolls may be used to facilitate, clarify, or corroborate verbal disclosures as a demonstration aid.

The second most frequently endorsed use is as an anatomical model: The interviewer employs the dolls to conduct a "body parts inventory," gathering information from the child about the names, characteristics, and functions of various body parts. Interviewers may then ask focused questions about private body parts. However, interviewers who conduct a body parts inventory during the initial phase of the interview may delay body parts–focused questions until a later phase of the interview (M. Everson, personal communication, January 24, 1996).

The third most frequently endorsed use is as a diagnostic screen and memory stimulus, a technique that grew out of the research on children's responses to anatomical dolls described above. Children are given an opportunity to interact with the dolls, and their behavior is observed by the interviewer. Observation of behavior that gives cause for concern, such as making the dolls engage in sexual activity, is then followed up with verbal probes.

Much less frequently suggested uses of the dolls are as an icebreaker and a comforter. Significantly, none of the guidelines recommend using anatomical dolls as a psychological test: that is, making determinations that children have or have not been sexually abused solely on the basis of how they interact with anatomical dolls. A conclusion that the dolls are not appropriate as a psychological test is consistent with the research findings.

Anatomical Drawings

Anatomical drawings are fairly widely used by interviewers but have been less criticized than anatomical dolls (Conte et al., 1991). Hence, they represent a viable alternative to anatomical dolls. However, unlike the dolls, they have not been the subject of much research—only one study (Steward et al., 1996). The first and most widely available version was developed by Groth and Stevenson (1990). Although the authors described them as useful in the investigation and treatment of child sexual abuse, in reality they have been employed mostly in forensic interviews.

The Groth and Stevenson (1990) drawings come in five developmental stages: (a) preschooler, (b) school-aged, (c) adolescent, (d) adult, and (e) elder. The drawings are of both males and females, with front and back views, and are both African American and white. Like anatomical dolls, they can be used as an anatomical model and as a demonstration aid. It is also possible to use them as an icebreaker. Table 5.4 describes a method for using the drawings as an anatomical model and then as a demonstration aid. As a demonstration aid, the drawings can be used to facilitate, clarify, or corroborate disclosure about abuse.

The drawing in Figure 5.1, attached to the evaluator's written report, is illustrative. It has both the child's and the interviewer's writing on it.

Children's Drawings

Drawings may be a useful medium of communication with any child who is old enough to draw. Conte et al. (1991) found that 87% of the sexual abuse experts in their study used free drawings when evaluating sexual abuse allegations.

Table 5.4   Uses of Anatomical Drawings

1. The interviewer makes copies of the drawings from the manual.
2. The interviewer and child choose appropriate drawings.
3. The child identifies the body parts, including the private parts, on all drawings.
4. If the child has already disclosed, the interviewer can ask the child to mark the parts on the drawing where something happened to her.
5. If the child has not disclosed, the interviewer may ask the child if anything has ever happened to any parts of the child's body. If the child responds "yes," the interviewer then asks the child to mark on the drawing those body parts.
6. The interviewer then asks the child what happened to each body part marked and writes the child's responses on the drawing. If the child is able, she can write the responses.
7. It is also a good idea for the interviewer to write on the drawing the exact wording of the question used to elicit information about what happened.
8. The interviewer uses a drawing representing the alleged offender in a similar manner, in this case asking the child to mark the body parts the offender used.
9. The interviewer then asks the child to describe what the alleged offender did with each part.
10. As with the child drawing, questions used and responses given by the child are written on the drawing.
11. The reason for writing directly on the drawing, rather than merely including the questions and answers in the interviewer's report, is that this produces a more coherent illustration of the child's account.
12. These drawings may also be admissible as evidence in court under the "business records" exception to the hearsay rule.
13. The interviewer may choose to attach some or all of the anatomical drawings used directly to his or her report.

Most of the research on free drawings involves the researchers' assigning drawing tasks to children with and without an abuse history and then examining the drawings for characteristics thought to be indicative of abuse, such as the portrayal of genitals (Friedrich, 1993; Hibbard & Hartman, 1990; Hibbard, Roghmann, & Hoekelman, 1987). Although this research usually demonstrates that children with a history of sexual abuse are more likely than those without to draw private body parts on their pictures, drawing private body parts is a low-frequency occurrence. What this means is that a finding of private parts on a child's drawings should raise concern and lead to further exploration. However, because such drawings are found in such a small percentage of cases, looking for private parts on drawings is not very useful clinically. However, clinicians assessing for possible sexual abuses usually do not use drawings in this way; instead, they use them as demonstration and communication aids.

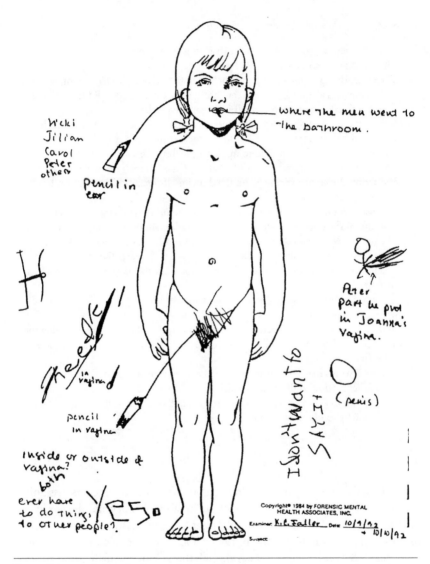

Figure 5.1   A Sample Anatomical Drawing

Having the child draw pictures can also mediate the child's stress. First, draw-ing gives the child a task that, unlike an interview, is likely to be familiar to the child. Second, the task may be experienced as less stressful than responding to questions, especially if, as in some instances, the drawing is not directly related to the abuse allegations. Third, having the child draw slows down the interview. This may not only calm the child, but, as with other media, may allow the

Table 5.5   Drawing Tasks for Children Who May Have Been Sexually Abused

Generic drawing tasks
1. Draw a picture of anything.
2. Draw a picture of a person.
3. Draw a picture of yourself.
   a. What are you thinking, feeling in this picture?
   b. What makes you happy, sad, mad, scared?
4. Draw a picture of your family.
5. Draw a picture of your family doing something (Kinetic Family Drawing).

Abuse-specific drawing tasks
1. Draw a picture of the offender.
   a. What is he thinking, feeling in this picture?
   b. What makes him happy, sad, mad, scared?
   c. Is there anything else you can tell me about this person?
2. Draw a picture of the place where the abuse occurred.
   a. Where were you?
   b. Where were other people?
   c. What happened? Then what?
3. Draw a picture of the abuse.
   a. Did (the offender) say anything?
   b. What were you thinking?
4. Draw a picture of the instrument used to abuse you.

---

interviewer to gather more information than would be obtained by relying only on language. Fourth, drawing gives the child some control. The interviewer observes, expresses interest in, and asks questions about the child's picture.

There are two general types of drawing tasks evaluators may employ: generic drawing tasks and abuse-specific drawing tasks. Table 5.5 above provides a nonexhaustive list of possible drawing tasks. Generic drawing tasks are used in various mental health contexts. Abuse-specific drawing tasks focus more directly on the sexual abuse or its context.

There are several approaches to the use of drawings. In rare instances, children will draw an abuse-specific drawing in response to a request for a generic drawing.

For example, a 5-year-old girl was asked, "Draw a picture of anything." She gave the evaluator a strange look and, while drawing, covered the paper with her arm, exclaiming, "Don't look!" She drew a picture of her father (the offender) with his genitals enlarged and exposed. Questions about the drawing elicited an account of her sexual abuse by her father.

Although an abuse-specific drawing produced in response to a generic drawing request is rare, such a drawing can be very compelling.

A second approach is to ask the child to draw one or more generic drawings before asking the child to draw an abuse-specific one. For example, the child might be asked to draw a picture of her family doing something and then be asked to draw the suspected offender. With both drawings, the interviewer can ask the child to tell about the people in the drawing and to tell what the people are thinking or doing in the drawing.

A third approach is to ask the child, "Do you think you could draw me a picture of that?" after a child's verbal statement about abuse. This approach may be useful when the interviewer has doubts of the veracity of the allegation or needs to clarify the child's verbal communication. For example, I had a case in which the child said the offender put a knife in her vagina. I wasn't sure whether that was literally what happened or whether it felt like a knife when the offender abused her. So I asked the girl if she could draw me a picture of what he used. She drew a knife. I then asked her to draw me a picture of what the offender did with the knife and she drew herself lying on her back and the offender putting a knife in her vagina.

A drawing of the place where the abuse occurred is especially useful. Such a picture can serve several purposes. It can help the evaluator check the accuracy of the child's account because the drawing may yield information that can be corroborated. A drawing may assist the interviewer in understanding the abuse better because the picture contextually embeds the event. Drawing may also help the child who is hesitant to disclose the abuse because she doesn't have to talk so much. Finally, a picture may elicit details, especially about the context but also about the abuse.

Like anatomical drawings, various aspects of the drawings can be identified, and questions and responses can be documented by writing directly on the drawing. Drawings can also be attached to the evaluator's report and should become part of the child's file.

In the picture shown in Figure 5.2, the child depicts her mother fondling her. She had given a detailed and vivid description of neglect by her mother, who was a cocaine user. In contrast, her verbal account of the sexual abuse had been sparse and without affect. The drawing task produced tears in both the child and the child's representation of herself in the drawing. The interviewer used the drawing as an opportunity to elicit more detail about the fondling and its context.

The Scope of Information Gathering

Generally, interviewers are advised to gather as much detail about the suspected abuse as the child can provide. The specifics of the allegations and child's

Figure 5.2   A Sample Child's Drawing of Abuse

characteristics will guide the type of information the evaluator will seek from the child. If the child indicates that she has been abused, the interviewer will want to gather information about the scope of the abuse and then will usually direct the child to describe individual instances. Scope includes when the abuse began, when it ended, and the approximate number of times or approximate frequency.

In terms of the individual instances, the evaluator will be interested in both the context of the abuse and the specific sexual acts. Context includes *where* and *when*. *Where* may involve the general location (inside or outside, vehicle or building) as well as the room and the location in the room. *When* can be the year, month, day, and time of day. Young children can be cued regarding *when* by asking their age at the time, where they were living, or what grade they were in. Similarly, asking them about seasons, weather, and holidays can assist in establishing the month. Time of day may be established by querying when the event occurred in relation to important events in the child's day, such as meals, bedtime, and school. Even with these cues, locating the event in time is much harder for children than locating the place. However, establishing time is important if the offender is to be charged criminally.

Other types of information to be elicited include where other people were at the time of the abuse, what the offender did to get the child involved, clothing worn and/or removed, and any inducements not to tell.

With regard to the abuse, that is the *who* and *what*, the interviewer will want to know the specific sexual acts, the positions of the child and the offender during the acts, and any other details, particularly sensorimotor details, that the child can provide.

If there have been multiple incidents, it may be useful to begin by inquiring about the last time the child was abused because she should remember the most about that incident. This may be followed by a query about a time the child remembers well and then perhaps the first time it happened. For each event the child can recall, the interviewer may need to ask about the details of the context and the abusive acts.

Gathering all this specific information can be very stressful for a child. The interviewer should be guided by the child's response to the inquiry and how much the interviewer actually needs to know in order to provide the appropriate intervention. Several interviews may be required. The younger the child, the fewer details she will be able to give. Also, children who have experienced multiple instances of abuse may not be able to differentiate one event from another. Children whose lives have been fraught with turmoil and trauma may also have difficulty providing specifics, especially about context.

Finally, there are additional areas of information the interviewer should usually cover. These include whether anyone else has sexually abused the child, whether the offender has abused anyone else, whether there were other sexual acts, and how adults came to be concerned about sexual abuse.

Table 5.6 is a checklist of important topic areas and acceptable questions for gathering needed information, the purpose of which is to offer guidance. The interviewer need not cover every area on the list, and there may be other, more appropriate ways to pose the questions depending on the characteristics of the case. Finally, the question examples are given for specific aspects of the abuse, but comparable questions are appropriate for other aspects as well.

Conclusion

In this chapter, the "nuts and bolts" of the child interview have been described and discussed. Chapter 6 will cover how the child interview fits into the larger

Table 5.6   Checklist for Areas of Inquiry and Appropriate Sample Questions

If the child indicates that she has been sexually abused, here are some general areas of inquiry:

—— Frequency
"How many times?"
"One time or more than one time?" (younger children)
"About how many times a week, month, year?" (older children)

—— Onset
"When did (child's words for the abuse) start?"
"How old were you the first time?"
"What grade were you in the first time?"
"Where were you living when (child's words for the abuse) started?"

(It may be useful to gather detailed information about the last time first because it is the most recent and the child may remember more details.)

—— Last abuse
"When was the last time (child's words for the abuse)?"
"Tell me everything you can remember about the last time."

—— Another salient time
"Can you tell me about another time you remember well?"
"Tell me everything, starting at the beginning, then the middle, then the end."

—— First time
"Can you tell me about the first time (child's words for the abuse)?"
"Only tell me what you remember, don't guess."

Context information

(To be gathered about each incident)
—— Where
"Where were you?"
"Were you indoors or outdoors?"
"What place?"
"What room did (child's words for the abuse) happen in?"
"Where in the room?"
"Can you draw me a picture of the place?"
"Where was (the offender)?"

—— Whereabouts of others
"Where were other people?"
"Was anyone else there?"

(Continued)

Table 5.6 (Continued)

_____ When (time of day)
"What time in the day did it happen?"
"Before or after bedtime, supper, school?"

_____ Clothing (victim)
"Do you remember what you were wearing?"
"Were any of your clothes taken off?"
"How did they get off?"
"Which clothes?"

_____ Clothing (offender)
"Do you remember what (the offender) was wearing?"
"Were any of (the offender's) clothes taken off?"
"How did they get off?"
"Which clothes?"

_____ Inducements
"Did (the offender) say anything before?"
"How did (the offender) explain (the abuse) to you?"

_____ Admonitions not to tell
"Did (the offender) say anything about telling or not telling?"
"What would happen if you told?"

_____ Substance use
"Were there any drugs or alcohol?"
"Who drank/used them?"
"How did the drugs/alcohol make the person act?"

———— Idiosyncratic event

Abuse-specific information

———— Body parts involved
"What body part did (the offender) use?"
"What part of your body was involved?"
"Point to the part on you that (child's words for the abuse)."

———— Skin contact
"Was the touching inside or outside your clothes?"
"Was there any touching on bare skin?"

———— Child and offender position.
"Can you show me how you were (with dolls)?"
"Were you standing up, sitting down, or lying down?"
"Was (the offender) standing up, sitting down, or lying down?"

——— Sensorimotor details
"What did (child's words for the abuse) feel like?"
"Do you remember any smells?"
"What did (child's word for semen) taste like?"
"Were there any sounds?"
"Was there any moving?"
"Can you show me what (the offender) did (with dolls)?"

——— Penetration
"Did anything go inside?"
"Was it on the inside or the outside?"

——— Ejaculation
"Did anything come out of (child's word for penis)?"
"What color was it?"
"Where did it go?"

——— Force
"Did you get hurt?"
"Did it leave a mark?"
"Where was the mark?"

Concluding questions

(The following are questions it is useful to ask to complete inquiry about sexual abuse.)
——— Other sexual acts
"Are there any other (sexual acts) (the offender) did to you?"
"Did (offender) do anything else like that?"

——— Other victims
"Do you know if (the offender) ever did (sexual acts) to anyone else?"
"Who?"
"Tell me everything you know about that."

——— Other offenders
"Did anyone else ever do (sexual acts) to you?"
"Who?"
"Tell me everything you can remember about that."

——— Disclosure information
"How did people find out about what happened?"
"Did you tell anyone? Who?"

picture of assessment and related issues. Chapter 7 will present a framework for using this information to determine likelihood of sexual abuse.

Note

1   Sexual abuse is a form of adult control over the child's body. Sexually abused children may come to fear, resist, and avoid any situation in which an adult tries to control them, including a forensic interview.

6

The Context of Child Interviewing

Professional concerns about child sexual abuse assessment have focused on the child interview, the topic of the previous chapter. However, this interview occurs in a larger context. Salient aspects of that larger context will be covered in this chapter. These are (a) models for assessing child sexual abuse allegations and the role of the child interview or interviews in the overall investigation, (b) strategies for documenting the child interview, (c) children's memory and suggestibility, and (d) the process of disclosure of sexual abuse.

Models for Assessing Child Sexual Abuse Allegations

As the child protective system in the United States was developed and expanded, child sexual abuse was added as a type of maltreatment that needed to be reported by professionals whose employment involved working with children (Faller, 1981; Mayhall & Norgard, 1983).[1] Models for investigating and assessing physical abuse and neglect are not very useful in the realm of sexual abuse. Generally, physical abuse and neglect are determined based upon the child's physical condition and/or the child's living condition (Faller, 1996a). Sexual abuse rarely leaves physical findings, and if there are injuries, they usually resolve quickly (Bays & Chadwick, 1993; Finkel, 1989; Jenny, 1996; McCann, Voris, & Simon, 1992). Early experience with asking the alleged abuser and sometimes the nonabusive parent about allegations of sexual abuse usually yielded denials (Faller, 1984). Essentially as a result of trial and error, professionals such as child protection workers, police officers, mental health specialists, and medical staff came to rely upon interviews with alleged victims to determine whether these children had been sexually abused.

In this section, four different models for evaluating allegations of sexual abuse and the role of the child interview in each of them will be described. These models are (a) the child interview model, (b) the joint investigation model, (c) the multimodal model, and (d) the parent-child interaction model.

THE CHILD INTERVIEW MODEL

A model for assessing the probability of child sexual abuse whose core component is an interview with the child is the dominant strategy for assessing the likelihood of sexual abuse. This model is employed by child protective services, is found in specialized programs that assess sexual abuse, such as children's advocacy centers, and is used in high-volume programs found in medical facilities (e.g., Bourg et al., 1999; Carnes & LeDuc, 1994; Davies et al., 1996; McDermott-Steinmetz, 1997; Morgan, 1995).

Originally, interviewers were advised to allow the child to have a support person, usually a parent, with her during the interview. However, that practice has gradually died out and been replaced by a preference for interviewing the child alone. There were concerns about the supportive adult's influence on the child when this person was a parent. The parent might inhibit the child's willingness to talk about sexual abuse, and more recently some professionals have been concerned that the parent might coach the child to make a false allegation.

Even though these concerned adults are not in the room with the child during her interview, they are usually interviewed by those using the child interview model. However, the primary purpose of their interviews is to gather information that will facilitate the child interview. Thus, they are asked what behavior, statements, or physical findings have led to suspicions of sexual abuse, and sometimes the names the child uses for private body parts. In children's advocacy centers and hospital-based programs, the adult who brings the child to be interviewed may be a child protection worker or law enforcement officer. When this model is employed in medical facilities, in addition to interviewing the child, the child also receives a medical exam (Davies et al., 1996). Some children's advocacy centers also conduct a medical exam on site.

A core assumption of the child interview model is that children's statements should be taken at face value (Everson, 1996). If children state they have been sexually abused, they are assumed to be telling the truth. Conversely, if they deny sexual abuse or are nonresponsive in the interview, the assumption is they have not been sexually abused.

The child interview model has been criticized because it does not take into account all the information that might be available. For example, as a rule those using this model limit themselves to the child's current account. They do not ordinarily delve into past history or past accounts. In addition, the model puts little weight on accounts by the alleged offender and by the nonoffending parent and does not address the psychosocial functioning of these individuals. Critics of the child interview model are concerned about both false positives and false negatives, as well as other potential errors (Faller, 1999).

THE JOINT INVESTIGATION MODEL

The joint investigation model emerged in large part because of lack of successful criminal court outcomes. Sexual abuse is not merely a child protection issue; it is also a crime. Beginning in the mid-1980s, most states passed or amended statutes to require greater collaboration between Child Protective Services (CPS) and law enforcement (National Center for the Prosecution of Child Abuse, 1997, Vol. 3). These statutory changes are both the cause and the effect of a shift in social policy to criminalization of child abuse, especially sexual abuse, and, in many communities, these changes have resulted in joint investigation by CPS and law enforcement of child sexual abuse cases (Pence & Wilson, 1994).

Joint investigation can be implemented in various ways. Sometimes law enforcement and CPS interview the child together. Sometimes the practice is to have one professional behind the one-way mirror or in the room, but silent, while the other interviews the child. And in some instances, a forensic interviewer talks to the child while both CPS and law enforcement, and, in some communities, the prosecutor, are behind the one-way mirror. The goal of this collaboration is to gather information necessary for both protection and prosecution in the same interview.

However, in joint investigation, data gathering is not limited to the child interview. Other parties, including the suspect, the nonsuspected parent, and other potential witnesses, need to be interviewed. How these responsibilities are divided between law enforcement and CPS varies by local practice, but a common division of labor is to have the police interview the suspect and CPS interview the nonsuspected caretaker. Law enforcement also has responsibility for collecting and preserving physical evidence. This evidence might be obtained from the crime scene, or it might be collected by the physician during the physical exam. In the latter instance, the physician collects and preserves specimens using a rape kit, which is then turned over to state police for analysis at the crime lab.

Although joint investigation can minimize the number of child interviews and prevent redundancy in the investigation, it also has a number of challenges. Law enforcement and CPS have different missions. The goal of law enforcement is to gather evidence to determine whether a crime has been committed. In contrast, the goal of CPS is first to ensure child safety and second to preserve the family. These goals may not be entirely compatible, and in practice the goal of seeking information for successful criminal prosecution usually takes precedence.

Another challenge, in part deriving from different missions, is that CPS and law enforcement may not be entirely satisfied with one another's work. This may result in parallel, rather than joint, investigations (Pence & Wilson, 1994).

Finally, in many communities law enforcement relies on the polygraph as a screening device to make decisions about whether to prosecute criminally, despite the lack of validity and reliability of the polygraph, and despite the fact that polygraph results are inadmissible in most court proceedings (Cross & Saxe, 1992; Faller, 1997; Saxe et al., 1987).[2] Thus, in part because the law enforcement agenda tends to prevail, if a suspect passes a polygraph, the criminal case is likely to be dismissed, and if a suspect fails a polygraph, that is a signal to proceed with the criminal prosecution.

Thus, an assumption of the joint investigation model is that the most positive case outcome is successful criminal prosecution. When evidence will not support criminal prosecution, not only does law enforcement drop its case, but often the child protection case is in jeopardy. CPS may doubt the other confirming evidence and may not substantiate the case (Faller, 1997).

MULTIMODAL MODEL

Largely because of shortcomings of other models, more complex models have evolved, including a multimodal model (e.g., Hoorwitz, 1992; Kuenhle, 1996). This model is generally not available in mandated agencies, such as CPS, but may be purchased by CPS or the court from other social agencies. This is not a "quick response" model, like the two described above. It is time consuming and expensive. Often assessments require as many as 100 professional hours, and two or more evaluators are needed (Faller & DeVoe, 1995a). Because of these characteristics, the best policy is selective use. This model is generally not necessary for cases involving extrafamilial sexual abuse and single-instance abuse. It is more suitable for complex intrafamilial cases where other problems coexist with allegations of sexual abuse and for cases where there have been prior investigations and/or assessments with competing findings. Competing findings may include competing case facts—for example, the suspect passes a polygraph, but there is definitive medical evidence of child sexual abuse, or competing conclusions by different professionals who have been involved in the case.

Most programs employing a multimodal model will interview the child more than once and engage in direct inquiry of the child about sexual abuse at some point during these interviews. However, the multimodal model also involves interviews with others—nonoffending parents, the alleged offender, and others who have relevant information, such as other children, stepparents, grandparents, and day care providers. Practitioners employing this model endeavor to gather a detailed history of past and current family functioning and of the history of concerns about sexual abuse. This process involves a review of past records and collateral contacts, as well as information gathered from family members. In addition, abuse-specific standardized tests and generic psychological tests may be employed. Finally, there is usually a medical exam or a review of the medical records (Faller, 1999).

This model can address questions in addition to whether the child has been sexually abused. For example, data gathered in the assessment process can inform individual and family treatment recommendations and treatment prognosis. Practitioners using this model consider a range of possible hypotheses that might explain an allegation of sexual abuse, cognizant of the varying vested interests in a case where allegations of sexual abuse have been made. Decision making using this model may be collaborative, involving several professionals who are part of a team and community professionals working with the family.

An assumption of this model is that the more information the professionals have, the more accurate their decision will be. However, different types of information are likely to receive different weight, with the child's statements and behavior receiving the greatest weight.

PARENT-CHILD INTERACTION MODEL

The parent-child interaction model also derives from a dissatisfaction with the child interview and joint investigation models. Although this model usually involves separate parent and child interviews, its distinguishing feature is an observation of the interaction between the child and the alleged offender and a comparable observation of the interaction between the child and the nonoffending parent (Haynes-Seman & Baumgarten, 1994). Some practitioners using this model ask the child to repeat the accusation to the alleged offender (Gardner, 1992b). Some allow the alleged offender to confront the child about the accusation (Gardner, 1992b), and some practitioners share information the child has related to them with the alleged offender in the child's presence (Benedek & Schetky, 1987; Faller, Froning, & Lipovsky, 1991).

This model has two origins. First, early efforts to assess the causes of infants' physical injuries and failure to thrive used observation of the parent-child interaction as an approach, the assumption being that a good interaction would indicate that the infant's condition was not caused by the parent. Second and more recently, mental health professionals evaluating custody issues in divorce have relied on observing the child with each parent to determine their respective parenting abilities. In cases of alleged sexual abuse, the parent-child interaction model may be employed in cases where one parent is accused and the other parent is siding with the child. However, there is one author, Gardner (1991), who advocates broader use, asserting that the best way to get to the bottom of an allegation of sexual abuse is to allow the accused to question the child, regardless of this person's relationship to the child.

Assumptions that underlie this model are that children's accounts are unreliable and easily contaminated (Everson, 1996) and that it is not harmful to the child for the practitioner to require an interaction and/or confrontation with the alleged offender. In part, these assumptions derive from a conclusion that false allegations occur frequently. Finally, this model assumes that practitioners can readily determine from observing an adult-child interaction whether a child has been sexually abused by the adult. The assumptions of the parent-child interaction model have been challenged (Corwin et al., 1987; Faller et al., 1991). The first assumption, that children are highly suggestible and false allegations are frequent, will be addressed later in this chapter.

The assumption that parent-child interactions that allow a confrontation of the child by the suspected abuser in the course of evaluations are not traumatic has been questioned. In fact, some forensic interviewers have ethical concerns about this practice (e.g., Faller et al., 1991). How does it affect a child to disclose sexual abuse to an adult (the forensic interviewer) and then be required to have a session with the adult the child has accused? Children who have been sexually abused already have difficulty trusting adults, and the interviewer who facilitates an interview with the accused, regardless of whether it involves a confrontation, may be perceived as another adult who cannot be trusted. Children who actually have been sexually abused but do not tell the interviewer may be reinforced in their silence by a parent-child interview. On the other hand, for the child who has not been sexually abused and truthfully denies abuse, there is nothing inherently detrimental about a parent-child interview. It is difficult to hypothesize about the impact of a parent-child interview on a child who has not been sexually abused but falsely says she has been abused during a forensic interview.

Finally, there are questions about the assumption that evaluators can identify an abusive relationship by observing the parent with the child. Thus, the practical utility of a parent-child interview with the accused and a comparable interview with the nonaccused parent is uncertain. The minimal research available indicates that professionals are not very good at differentiating interactions between abusive and nonabusive parents and their children (Deitrich-MacLean & Walden, 1988; Starr, 1987).

Sexual abuse usually occurs in private rather than during the course of a parent-child interaction. Most offenders are able to control their behavior while others are observing them, and children, who are rarely the initiators, will be unlikely to engage in sexualized behavior while being observed by an evaluator.

In the absence of overt sexual acts during the evaluation, some practitioners have relied on more subtle behaviors, such as physical contact between parents and children (e.g., Haynes-Seman & Baumgarten, 1994), but these behaviors are open to a variety of interpretations. For example, it may be difficult to differentiate between affectionate hugging and hugging that provides an adult with sexual stimulation. Similarly, an adult may demonstrate an ability to play on a child's level because he or she is a sensitive and good parent or because he or she is more comfortable functioning at an immature level, a characteristic of some sex offenders.

Likewise, interview behaviors involving nonaccused parents and children may be variously construed. When a child looks to a parent before answering a question, that behavior may indicate the child's need for reassurance in order to talk about difficult experiences, or it may signal that the child's responses have been programmed. There is no empirically demonstrated method to determine the motivation of the child's behavior. Thus, evaluators are on shaky ground when they interpret such behavior.

Documentation of the Interview

It is generally acknowledged that interviews about possible sexual abuse must be documented accurately, which may involve note taking, audiotaping, or video-taping. The method of documentation, however, is the subject of hot debate. The principal debate is to videotape or not to videotape. The American Academy of Child and Adolescent Psychiatry (1997) has develop guidelines that support videotaping. In contrast, after several years of work, the American Professional Society on the Abuse of Children has failed to arrive at a consensus on the issue of videotaping (B. Boat & W. Walsh, personal communication, 1999).

In the mid-1980s, videotaping child interviews was thought to be the answer to proof problems in child sexual abuse (e.g., Colby & Colby, 1987a, 1987b). However, it soon became apparent that videotaping did not satisfy Sixth Amendment protections of the accused[3] and that it brought on some unantici-pated problems. The main argument against videotaping child interviews is that the existence of videos may provide opportunities to attack the child and to attack the interviewer (Myers, 1998).

Videotapes of child interviews may provide ammunition that can be used to impeach the child's credibility on the basis of "prior inconsistent statement." Examples can include the contrast between what the child says when first asked about sexual abuse and when asked later, or alternatively the contrast between the child's videotaped statement and what the child says on the witness stand. Many reasons other than that the child is a liar may explain inconsistencies in the child's statements, some of which will be discussed later in this chapter. However, inconsistent statements can substantially weaken a child protection or a criminal case. Inconsistencies can be demonstrated when other methods of documentation are used but are often more striking when on videotape.

Other material in videotapes can be used to undermine children: for example, the child laughing or being silly, evidence that the child likes the accused, or indications the child lacks developmentally expected knowledge. As with inconsistencies, these may appear in other types of documentation but may not be recorded, especially if the method of documentation is notes.

Videotaping usually records both the child and the interviewer. As a consequence, interviewer questioning techniques and behavior can be challenged using the videotape (Myers, 1998). Sometimes interviewers use techniques that should be challenged. However, because segments of the videotape can be taken out of context and because indeed there is no empirically demonstrated best way to interview, interviewers may be wrongly accused of inappropriate interview techniques. Similarly, the interviewer's body language, tone of voice, use of media, and other activities and statements may be characterized as leading or unprofessional. The strategy of attacking the interviewer shifts the focus of the case from what the child said or demonstrated about sexual abuse to how the interviewer elicited information about sexual abuse, which can undermine the case. Challenges to language and questions can also occur when audiotaping is used but again may be less compelling than when the interview is on videotape.

There are also secondary drawbacks of videotaping. The video may not be of ideal quality, or there may be other technical glitches. The video may not capture the child's demonstrations that are out of camera range or disclosures that occur at other times, such as on the way to the bathroom. In addition, children may find the videotaping intrusive. Videotapes can be misused when copies have to be given to the defense (Myers, 1998). Sometimes unscrupulous defense attorneys or their expert witnesses use them unlawfully or share them with the press.

With all these drawbacks of videotaping, readers might be wondering what would recommend videotaping. The fact of the matter is that videotaping provides the best record of all documentation methods of what takes place in the interview. It is my view that if professionals are going to make decisions that affect issues related to a child's custody and an adult's liberty, as well as other potentially life-altering issues, the basis of those decisions should be made available to individuals affected. In addition, videos can reduce the number of different people who have to interview the child, can be used to persuade professionals and family members that the child has been abused, can be employed to induce offenders' confessions, can serve as a means to prepare a child and professionals for court, and can, in some parts of the legal process, substitute for child testimony. Videos may also be useful in producing accurate reports and for supervision. Finally, failure to videotape may leave interviewers open to all kinds of challenges: for example, that they wanted to conceal their techniques, their techniques did not meet the standard of practice, or the child did not say what the interviewer asserts she said.

Given the current controversy about videotaping, it is advisable that professionals and, in some cases, communities decide what method of documentation best suits their needs. However, professionals working with and on behalf of sexually abused children should be cognizant that the issue may soon be addressed by the courts, with case law determining how professionals practice.

Children's Memory and Suggestibility

A crucial question related to allegations of sexual abuse is: Can children's accounts be trusted?[4] Of specific concern is how accurate children's memories of past experiences are, including their experiences of sexual victimization. A related issue is whether and how easily their recollections or reports can be contaminated by others, whether perpetrators, nonoffending parents, or professionals.

SOURCES OF KNOWLEDGE ABOUT CHILDREN'S MEMORY AND SUGGESTIBILITY

Two main categories of research inform opinions about the memory and suggestibility of children where sexual abuse is a concern: laboratory or analogue studies involving children without a history of possible sexual abuse and studies of children where sexual abuse is suspected. The volume of the former type of study is much larger than that of the latter. There are also a very small number of analogue studies involving children with a possible history of maltreatment (Eisen, Goodman, Qin, & Davis, 1998; Katz, Schoenfeld, Levanthal, & Cicchetti, 1995; Lyon & Saywitz, 1999).

Analogue Studies

Analogue studies usually involve middle-class, nonabused children whose parents voluntarily allow them to participate. These studies either involve staged events, such as encountering a stranger in a classroom (Poole & Lindsay, 2001; Thompson, Clarke-Stewart, & Lapore, 1997), or take advantage of naturally occurring events in children's lives, such as a medical procedure (Bruck, Ceci, Francoeur, & Renick, 1995; Goodman, Quas, Batterman-Faunce, Riddlesberger, & Kuhn, 1997; Saywitz et al., 1991).

After the event, children are questioned using various types of questions, from free recall to leading and misleading questions. Some analogue studies using staged events employ manipulations, such as misinforming children that their parents have verified the occurrence of childhood experiences that never happened (Ceci, Huffman, et al., 1994), and pre-event programming—for example, telling the child that the adult is a clumsy, oafish person before the child meets him (Leichtman & Ceci, 1995). Postevent contamination—for example, trying to confuse a child's memory of the genus of stuffed animals in a slide show—is included in some research paradigms (Zaragoza, 1991), and postevent programming may be employed by the use of suggestive questioning (e.g., Leichtman & Ceci, 1995) and interrogation (e.g., Clarke-Stewart, Thompson, & Lapore, 1989).

Questions must be raised about the relevance or ecological validity of the analogue research (Faller, 1996a). That is, to what extent do the studies actually replicate a sexually abusive event and questioning techniques employed by child protection workers, police, forensic interviewers, mental health professionals, and others who talk to children about suspected sexual abuse? The most useful studies are the ones that are based upon participatory experiences rather than observed ones; that ask about core rather than peripheral aspects of an experience; that derive from naturally occurring events rather than staged ones; that include body touch, especially intrusions into private parts; that involve admonitions to maintain secrecy; and that include a power differential between the child and an adult. However, researchers cannot replicate some aspects of sexual abuse, such as coercion, exploitation, transgressions of sexual taboos, and the stigma associated with sexual abuse.

Similarly, the ecological validity of the questioning techniques of some of the research is not established. In fact, in some studies, it is hard to discern the analogy for the programming and questioning (e.g., Ceci, Huffman, et al., 1994; Ceci, Loftus, et al., 1994). Although analogue studies include invitational probes and questions, such as "Tell me everything that happened when you went to the doctor" (Saywitz et al., 1991), they rarely include focused questions, such as "How do you know about Big Birds (penises)?" Rather, the analogue studies tend to go from invitational questions ("Tell me what happened when you went to the doctor") immediately to direct substantive questions ("Did the doctor touch you here?") (e.g., Saywitz et al., 1991; Steward et al., 1996).

Moreover, although forensic interviewers may ask direct substantive questions, such as "Did Uncle George touch your weewee (vagina)?" (e.g., Warren, Woodall, Hunt, & Perry, 1996; Wood, Orsak, Murphy, & Cross, 1996), there is scant evidence that professionals program children during interviews. It is possible that perpetrators and relatives coerce and program, but in the case of perpetrators and in some cases of relatives, the programming would probably be in the direction of nondisclosure, the subject of few analogue studies.

Real-World Research

Turning to research on cases of suspected sexual abuse, there are a few studies of children with independently corroborated histories of sexual abuse. The corroboration is usually offender confession, but, in some studies, medical evidence, criminal conviction, or a composite of several quasi-independent factors corroborates the abuse (DeVoe & Faller, 1999). However, corroboration may provide, not a detailed account of the victimization, but only an indication that the abuse has occurred (e.g., Bradley & Wood, 1996; Faller, 1988c; Lawson & Chaffin, 1992; Sorenson & Snow, 1991; Terry, 1991).

It is virtually impossible to identify a cohort of "real-world" false allegations because of obstacles to independent corroboration. As a consequence, studies of false allegations rely on researcher opinion or a consensus of a group of researchers about the characteristics of false allegations. These studies do not rely on independent criteria of falseness. Although most of these are important efforts, they are methodologically problematic (e.g., Goodwin, Sahd, & Rada, 1980; Jones & McGraw, 1987; Sink, 1988b) because they are tautological: That is, the researchers determine the children's accounts to be false because they contain criteria researchers say are in false accounts.

Analogue Studies Involving Children With a History of Abuse

To my knowledge, there are just four analogue studies conducted on children with a maltreatment history, three involving medical exams (Eisen, Goodman, Davis, & Qin, 1999; Eisen et al., 1998; Katz et al., 1995; Steward et al., 1996) and one exploring the ability of children, whose cases were pending in dependency court, to tell the difference between the truth and a lie (Lyon & Saywitz, 1999). This is an extremely important line of research because it allows researchers to examine the memory and suggestibility of maltreated children. At the same time, these studies overcome the weakness of studies using interviews about abuse because the researchers know "ground truth." However, because the researchers do not study the child's capacities to describe their maltreatment, we must assume these capacities translate to interviews about the maltreatment itself.

MEMORY FINDINGS

Neither adults nor children have total recall of past events. Memory does not function like a sensorimotor video camera with a wide-angle lens. The ability to recall, for both adults and children, is a complex set of phenomena: memory acquisition, storage, interpretation, and retrieval. Analogue studies suggest some aspects of memory that may pose difficulties in interviewing children about sexual abuse.

Aspects of events and experiences that are salient for adults may not seem important to children. As a consequence, children may not attend to and encode this material in their memories. Inattention to events important to adults is likely the source of some memory errors in children (Brainerd & Ornstein, 1991). For example, a child who suffers sodomy at the hands of her father may not pay attention to what her mother is doing at the time or what subsequently happens to her brother.

In addition, researchers have noted, especially with young children, that reporting ability is better for central than peripheral events (e.g., Goodman, Hirschman, Hepps, & Rudy, 1991). In a situation of sexual abuse, such attention failures may involve key details about the victimization, such as what the penis looked like. The absence of details in the child's account may lead to challenges to the veracity of the abuse.

Analogue studies indicate that preschoolers have memory storage capacity as good as adults' (Brainerd & Ornstein, 1991; Fivush, 1993). However, some memories originally stored fairly completely may deteriorate over time (Goodman & Clarke-Stewart, 1991). With few exceptions (e.g., Goodman & Clarke-Stewart, 1991; Hudson & Fivush, 1987; Huffman, Crossman, & Ceci, 1997; Steward et al., 1996), analogue studies test recall over a few days or weeks. In cases of possible sexual abuse, interviewers may be asking children to report experiences that happened months or years earlier. Based upon knowledge about memory deterioration, questions have been raised about the accuracy and completeness of children's reports. However, memory over time is an issue where concerns about ecological validity are relevant. To what extent is a visit for a few minutes with a stranger in a trailer, an outpatient medical appointment, or a trip to an amusement park, like an experience of sexual abuse?

Moreover, some researchers and clinicians interested in adult memory of sexual abuse have countered that traumatic memory is fundamentally different from narrative memory, as represented in analogue studies. Traumatic memory is more likely to be sensorimotor than verbal. As such, it is less susceptible to forgetting, although it may be dissociated (e.g., Bremner, Krystal, Southwick, & Cahrney, 1995; Van der Kolk, 1994; Van der Kolk & Fisler, 1995). Understanding the issue of memory deterioration versus dissociation, as it relates to child sexual abuse, is further complicated by an appreciation that not all sexual abuse is experienced as traumatic (Conte & Berliner, 1986).

In fact, the issue of memory over time may be very complex indeed. In a longitudinal study of preschoolers, Fivush and Shukat (1995) found that children's reports of a memorable event, a visit to an amusement park, were quite accurate and increased in sophistication as they grew older. However, the details they recalled at different ages were very inconsistent, with very little overlap in recollections from one interview to the next. A likely interpretation of the latter finding is that salient aspects of the visit to the amusement park varied depending on age and other experiences in the child's life.

Children's interpretation of experiences of sexual abuse may be another obstacle for memory retrieval. The more a person knows about a topic, the more accurately he or she interprets a related experience. Children may have encoding problems with experiences they don't understand (Brainerd & Ornstein, 1991), such as sexual abuse. Thus, children may idiosyncratically interpret sexual abuse because they don't usually have background knowledge about sex and sexual abuse. Children may also have trouble with interpretation and communication of their experiences because they don't have the language for it. This may particularly be a problem with sexual activity because children may have no names for the private body parts or words for sexual acts.

Moreover, children may fail to retrieve information in their memories. As noted above, some researchers and clinicians may attribute this problem to dissociation, as well as other dynamics. Analogue studies and research on actual cases (DeVoe & Faller, 2002; Sorenson & Snow, 1991) suggest that young children have difficulty providing narrative accounts. Moreover, they may not understand what information or event the interviewer is asking about. In response to open-ended questions, the information young children provide is sparse but accurate (Steward et al., 1996). They require direct questions to access past experiences (e.g., Goodman & Clarke-Stewart, 1991; Steward et al., 1996). However, accuracy may decrease somewhat with direct questions (e.g., Goodman & Clarke-Stewart, 1991; Saywitz et al., 1991; Steward et al., 1996).

CHILDREN'S SUGGESTIBILITY

Concerns that children are suggestible are central to the controversy about children's capacities to report sexual abuse. These concerns are not only that children might be vulnerable to suggestive interviewing by professionals but that they could potentially be programmed by others, such as offenders or parents, before they are interviewed. Present concerns center on children being persuaded to say they have been sexually abused when they have not, rather than on what seems to be a more common occurrence, children being persuaded to say they have not been sexually abused when they have (e.g., Everson, 2000; Lawson & Chaffin, 1992).

Analogue studies indicate that children are more suggestible than adults (Ceci & Bruck, 1993). Nevertheless, a fairly universal finding from such studies is that children are quite accurate in accounts of their experiences when they are not asked leading questions (Ceci & Bruck, 1993; Leichtman & Ceci, 1995; Clarke-Stewart et al., 1989). The implication for professionals interviewing children who may have been sexually abused is to ask as many open-ended questions as possible.

Interrogation with leading techniques can elicit false positives from preschoolers, however. Young children can be cajoled into endorsing an adult interpretation of an ambiguous event: for example, whether a janitor touched some toys, including a doll, to clean them or to play with them (Clarke-Stewart et al., 1989). Apparently the analogy would be that a child can be induced to reinterpret an experience of benign body touch, such as putting medicine on the child's genitals, as sexual abuse. But the analogy could also be to the opposite situation, in which a child could be persuaded that sexual touch was child care behavior.

In one study, 10 sessions of pre- and postevent programming and suggestion got a minority of preschoolers (less than 20%) to affirm, when gently challenged, that they had seen an adult engage in negative behaviors when they had not. The behaviors were specifically tearing a book or soiling a teddy bear (Leichtman & Ceci, 1995). Thus, the analogue research does not involve private parts or even body touching.

In addition, children 4 years and under are more vulnerable to suggestion than those over 4 (Ceci, Loftus, et al., 1994; Eisen et al., 1998, 1999; Leichtman & Ceci, 1995). Children age 3 and under are especially problematic because a substantial minority may provide false positives to direct questions, such as "Did the doctor touch your (child's term for penis)?" (Bruck et al., 1995; Gordon et al., 1993). However, a substantial minority will also provide false negatives to such a direct question. Thus, a serious dilemma faced by interviewers is that children who are the most vulnerable have the least developed communication skills and are the most suggestible.

To Talk or Not to Talk:
Patterns of Disclosure of Sexual Abuse

Another important issue in forensic interviewing is the number and structure of interviews. Opinions about appropriate practice in many respects depend on how professionals conceptualize disclosure of sexual abuse. Conceptualization of disclosures is both a topic of debate and one about which research findings are discrepant. To assist professionals in understanding this issue, I will first talk about why children might not report sexual abuse. I will then present a framework that dichotomizes the conceptualizations of disclosure. Finally, I will describe how research and practice can inform professionals about disclosures of sexual abuse.

CAUSES OF REPORTING FAILURE

Forensic interviewers need to appreciate that there are a number of causes for failure to talk about sexual abuse when asked. First, the child may not have been abused. With increased public and professional knowledge about child sexual abuse comes a greater likelihood that sexual abuse will be considered as a possibility when children are symptomatic. Individuals may jump to the conclusion that a child has been sexually abused when, in reality, some other experience is making the child appear traumatized.

Second, the child may have been sexually abused but may not know the incident was abusive. If the child lacks sexual knowledge, he or she may not appreciate that a taboo has been violated. In their follow-up interviews of children who had been through the court process, Sas and Cunningham (1995) found that about 40% did not know what sexual abuse was and thus did not understand that they were being sexually abused when the abuse first took place.

Third, children may not disclose when they have been sexually abused because they don't know what the interviewer wants them to talk about. This null response may derive from the nature of the interviewer's questions. The questions may be so open-ended the child doesn't have any idea what the interviewer is talking about. For example, a question like "Do you have any worries?", the invitation "This is a place where we talk about feelings," or a probe such as "Do you know why you came to see me today?" may be too vague for the child to know what to report. Often when asked these open-ended questions, children report experiences not remotely related to sexual abuse. For example, one 6-year-old boy responded to the feelings question by talking about his dog dying. A 10-year-old girl responded to the worry question by saying she was worried she wasn't going to Heaven.

In other instances, children do not know what to talk about and fail to disclose because the abuse is not memorable or salient for the child. This may be the case when the child has experienced many other traumatic or disorienting events (e.g., other abuse or sexual abuse, death of a loved one, or divorce), as in the case described below.

Case Example: Sally, a 7-year-old girl, was removed from the care of her mother, who was chronically neglectful. She was being questioned by a forensic interviewer about two instances of sexual abuse by her father, which she had previously disclosed to her foster care worker. The interviewer asked her focused questions about her father:

I: Tell me all about your daddy.

S: He's nice. Sometimes I stayed at his house. He gives me money.

I: What do you like about your daddy?

S: Oh, he's really nice. He gives me money.

I: What kinds of things do you do with your daddy?

S: We play games sometimes. He lets me steer when I ride in his car.

I: Are there any things you don't like about your daddy?

S: No, I like everything about him. There's nothing I don't like. He gives me money.

Finally, the interviewer said, "Did you tell Miss Jones about something your daddy did?" to which Sally replied, "Oh yeah. But that was my Uncle James; he did more." She then responded to the interviewer's questions first about what Uncle James did and next about what her father did, describing different types of sexual abuse. She had already testified in criminal court against her uncle.

Sally was in foster care because her house had burnt down. Another uncle, Alan, had caught Uncle James sexually abusing Sally and had taken her from her house. Uncle James, apparently in order to distract attention from the sexual abuse, had set the house on fire.

In describing the scene of the fire, Sally said Uncle Alan took her back to see the house afterward, and "all the burnt animals were there, my doggy, two kitties, and the hamster, and the chickens." But she said, "My baby brother wasn't there. They took him somewhere else." Not only all the family pets but also her 1-year-old brother had been killed in the fire.

In this case example, the sexual abuse by Sally's father, about which the forensic interviewer wanted to gather information, was probably one of Sally's less traumatic experiences and was not salient to Sally in her current circumstances.

Fourth, in a number of situations children don't disclose sexual abuse because they don't want to disclose it. That is, they fully understand what the interviewer is asking about, but they avoid answering the interviewer's questions. In these instances, the failure to disclose is not caused by a memory retrieval problem. In Sas and Cunningham's research (1995), 12% of children reported that they had made up their minds not to tell. Parenthetically, it is unlikely in these situations that asking more direct questions will change the child's mind. Sometimes offering reasons for disclosure will be persuasive. Reasons for avoidance of talking are multiple.

Children may be traumatized by talking about the abuse and therefore avoid the topic or deny the abuse. Young children who wish to avoid distress may simply fail to respond to the question or may change the subject. If asked directly about why they are not answering questions, they may say they don't want to answer them. Older children are more likely to say, "I don't like talking about this; it makes me really upset."

Children may fail to disclose because they feel shame about or responsibility for the experience. Young children, who initially may have been naïve about the inappropriateness of the abuse, often think they are bad because they participated in the abuse, which they may have enjoyed. Older children often blame themselves for failure to resist, failure to report, and any pleasure, attention, or material gain associated with the abuse.

Children may also fail to report because they have been bribed, admonished, or threatened with negative consequences should they tell. Half of the children interviewed after litigation in the Sas and Cunningham study (1995) had been told by the offender not to tell. Methods that offenders employ to ensure silence vary with the age of the child, the role relationship to the child, and the personality of the offender. An offender with a close relationship to the victim may admonish the child by saying, "If you tell, I won't love you anymore" or "I won't be able to see you anymore." An offender who is an authority figure, such as a priest, may warn the child that "God won't love you if you tell." Older children who are abused by a pedophile who has befriended children may be told that disclosure will mean he can't help other children or continue to help the victim. Some offenders threaten to kill the victim, harm the victim, harm the victim's pets, destroy the victim's valued property, or injure or kill the child's parents. An example of the latter involved a deacon of a church who took a 7-year-old boy out into the graveyard after he had sodomized him in the basement of the church. He pointed out to the boy the spot where he would bury him if he told.

Table 6.1   Patterns of Disclosure

An Event?	A Process?
1. Like a crime report	1. Like a confession—embarrassing, shameful
2. Narrative account	2. Gradual unfolding
3. Child very straightforward	3. Child hesitant, avoidant, retracts
4. Requires a single interview	4. Requires multiple interviews
a. A few open-ended questions	a. Many questions
b. Follow-up questions to clarify	b. A continuum of questions
5. Standard protocol	5. Flexible use of modules
6. Forensic skills	6. Clinical skills
a. Introduction	a. Rapport building
b. Competency	b. Support
c. Elicit disclosure	c. Pacing
d. Nonleading questions	d. Vary questions by child
e. Avoid media; rely on verbal communication	e. Use media and vary use depending upon child's needs

Finally, children may not know the outcome of disclosure, and the fear of the unknown results in failure to report. Questions such as "Will I be believed?" "What will happen to the offender?" "Where will I live?" and "What will happen to my family?" all may inhibit telling. In a study of children who disclosed sexual abuse, Petronio, Reeder, Hecht, and Ros-Mendoza (1998) found that children are often anxious about the consequences of disclosure and "test the waters" before revealing sexual abuse. These researchers found that disclosure was incremental and a process, even in a group of 38 children in treatment for sexual abuse and willing to be interviewed about their disclosure.

A CONCEPTUAL FRAMEWORK FOR EXAMINING THE DEBATE

Everson (1996) has defined the issue as "Is disclosure of sexual abuse an event or a process?" In part, the issue is whether the child is willing to disclose. As Table 6.1 indicates, whether disclosure is perceived as an event or a process has implications for both professional expectations and interview practice.

Table 6.1 provides two very discrepant perspectives of disclosure of sexual abuse. The conception of disclosure as an *event,* during which the child straightforwardly makes a report of her abuse, implies that a single session should be adequate and that the child will provide information if asked. The child does not feel a personal sense of stigma or responsibility; instead, she feels that the offender is the one who did wrong. The interviewer merely has to trigger the child's recollection in a way that is not leading. Perhaps leading or suggestive questions will lead to affirmation of events or details that did not happen, and use of media may elicit fantasies or play instead of facts.

In contrast, the conception of disclosure as a *process*, during which children have to overcome fears, shame, and embarrassment, would suggest that information emerges over time. Interviewers will need more than a single session and will need to pace their data gathering, deciding when to continue and when to back off. In addition, the interviewer may need to use strategies to address the child's thoughts and feelings about the abuse and disclosure in order to persuade the child to tell. If disclosure is a process, the challenge to the interviewer is to overcome denial and minimization. Many questions and a variety of approaches, including the use of media, may be required to gather all the data. Because the child may feel guilty or fearful, she is unlikely to endorse experiences she has not had. Moreover, because of these feelings, recantation of actual experiences may occur during the course of revelation.

RESEARCH AND PRACTICE KNOWLEDGE
RELATED TO THE DISCLOSURE PROCESS

Findings from the research and practice suggest there are numerous patterns of response to experiences of child sexual abuse. *Child, abuse, family, interviewer,* and *system* factors can affect the pattern of disclosure. As will be seen in the discussion that follows, these categories are overlapping.

Child Factors

Some child factors are the child's age, whether the child has previously told, and whether the child intends to tell. Research on real-world cases involving young children indicates that it is very difficult for children age 4 and younger to disclose sexual abuse in a structured forensic interview (Cantlon, Payne, & Erbaugh, 1996; DeVoe & Faller, 1999; Keary & Fitzpatrick, 1994), even after a prior disclosure (DeVoe & Faller, 1999; Keary & Fitzpatrick, 1994). Older children have better communication skills and thus can provide a more coherent description of the abuse if they want to tell. They also have better free recall than younger children and are therefore more capable of providing a narrative account of their experiences.

Studies with the perspective that disclosure is an event are conducted on cases in which children have made a prior disclosure (Bradley & Wood, 1996; Sternberg et al., 1997) or include only children who make a disclosure (Bradley & Wood, 1996). In contrast, studies with the perspective that disclosure is a process involve children who have not made a prior disclosure (Keary & Fitzpatrick, 1994; Lawson & Chaffin, 1992; Sorenson & Snow, 1991).

Abuse Characteristics

Abuse factors that influence disclosure include the relationship the child has to the abuser, the strategies the offender uses to involve the child, the nature of the abuse, the child's perception of the abuse, and the strategies the offender uses to inhibit disclosure. It is likely that the closer the relationship the offender has to the victim, the less likely the child will be to tell (Faller, 1988a). Similarly, children may have more difficulty disclosing abuse by offenders whom they hold in high esteem, such as a priest or a mentor. And, as already pointed out, some children do not know the behavior is inappropriate (Sas & Cunningham, 1995), and this may impede reporting. Or they may feel responsible or guilty. Interviewers may need to explain to children that the abuse is not their fault. Moreover, again as already noted, if victims have been threatened with dire consequences, it may be more difficult to gather information from them should they tell. The just-described characteristics may lead to denial of actual abuse, a delay in disclosure, and possibly more interview time before disclosure.

Family Factors

Family factors that affect the pattern of disclosure include support (Everson, Hunter, & Runyan, 1989; Heriot, 1996; Hunter, Coulter, Runyan, & Everson, 1990), culture, and other trauma the child has experienced in the family. With regard to support, Lawson and Chaffin (1992) found that the predictor of disclosure of 28 children with sexually transmitted disease was parental support. On the basis of interviews with children who disclosed, Petronio et al. (1998) found that the trustworthiness of the person the child told and the child's reciprocity with him or her were critical factors. Confidants could be both family members and friends.

Cultural differences regarding sex and sexual abuse may also affect the disclosure pattern (Fontes, 1995). Although most cultures have prohibitions against discussion of sex, cultures vary in the degree to and circumstances under which sex is a taboo topic. Similarly, regardless of culture, at least some people will blame the victim, but the tendency to blame the victim may vary by culture. Finally, in most cultures, there is some stigma associated with sexual victimization. This may vary from little to a belief the victim is utterly ruined and not marriageable.

With regard to other trauma, clinical experience suggests that children who have endured multiple traumas may report sexual abuse more readily because they are desensitized to the trauma. However, as already noted, paradoxically, such children may not think to mention sexual abuse because it does not register as a notable event in their memories when compared to other traumatic experiences.

Interviewer Characteristics

Interviewer characteristics that can influence patterns of disclosure include gender, age, race, class, and interview style. It is hard to predict exactly how these factors will have an impact because their effect depends upon child and abuse factors. However, there is some research indicating that children of color will have greater difficulty disclosing bad acts committed by a Caucasian adult to a Caucasian questioner than disclosing bad acts by a person of their own color to an interviewer of their color (Dunkerley & Dalenberg, 2000).

System Factors

System impacts on patterns of disclosure include what agency the interviewer comes from and where in the process the interview occurs. Professionals are usually, but not always, strangers to the children whom they assess, a characteristic that is likely to impede disclosure. In addition, they may also come from agencies about which children and families have preconceived notions. Children may perceive police as either friends or foes. For some children, the fact that a police officer wants to talk them indicates they have done something wrong. Similarly, if children have prior knowledge of CPS, that may affect their response. They may have been removed from their family previously, or the offender may have threatened them with being taken away by protective services should they disclose. The child's reaction to an evaluation by someone from a treatment agency may be very different if the child has been prepared with information that the clinician will try to help the child.

Timing of the assessment may affect disclosure in several ways. Professionals are advised to interview the child as soon as possible after the abuse because the child's memory will be the freshest at this time and to gather data before any contamination of the child's account (e.g., Lamb, 1994). This may be advantageous if the child is motivated to disclose. However, if the child is avoiding disclosure or is "testing the waters"—that is, disclosing a little bit to see how adults respond to the information—this strategy may not be optimal. The interview may yield nothing or only part of the information. On the other hand, if the assessment takes place later and several interviews are scheduled, more information may be revealed. Still another possible scenario is that a delayed interview may come after the child is tired of talking about the abuse or may have experienced some of the consequences of disclosure and may be in recantation. In such circumstances, the interviewer may encounter an angry or resistant child who discloses little or refuses to talk.

In summary, what practice-based knowledge and research indicate is that how the child responds to queries about possible sexual abuse is subject to a great deal of variation. As a consequence, each case requires careful consideration as the interviewer decides what will best enable the child to describe events, if any, that she has experienced. The factors to be considered include what the level of suspicion is about abuse, who should conduct the child assessment, when the assessment should be undertaken, how many interviews should occur before a decision is made, and what methods the evaluator should employ in the assessment process.

Conclusion

Child interviews about possible sexual abuse do not take place in a vacuum. Mental health professionals need to consider the larger context of the child interview, both when they are responsible for conducting an assessment of a child and when they are evaluating an assessment conducted by someone else. Appropriate assessment processes need to take into account the specifics of the case, practice knowledge, and research findings.

Notes

1   The ideas in this section draw in considerable part upon the conceptualization of the state of practice by my colleague Mark Everson, PhD.

2   The polygraph is of questionable validity. What it measures is physiological reactions—changes in heart rate, breathing rate, and galvanic skin response (sweaty palms). The hypothesis is that these responses increase when an individual lies; there is no research, however, to support this hypothesis. In fact, experts have noted that the mere asking of questions about sex may lead to these arousal reactions. They have also noted that the personality of the accused may influence his physiological reactions to questions about sexual abuse. In addition to validity problems, there are reliability problems. These include both test-retest reliability (because there is a desensitization effect to being asked questions about sexual abuse) and interrater reliability. That is, two polygraphists may differ in how they score the same polygraph output.

3   The Sixth Amendment to the Constitution allows persons accused of a crime the right to confront witnesses against them. This means that persons accused of sex crimes must be afforded the opportunity to cross-examine those accusing them, including children. This constitutional provision substantially limits use of videotapes at the trial stage of a prosecution.

4   This was adapted from a section on children's memory and suggestibility that appears in Faller (1998b).

7

Decision Making in Child
Sexual Abuse

Professionals may be asked to address a number of questions related to an allegation of sexual abuse. These include whether the professional thinks the child has been sexually abused, the degree of certainty the professional attributes to that opinion, whether the child can be protected in her current living situation or needs to be removed from the home, what treatment is needed for the child and/or family, and whether the offender is treatable.

Perhaps the most challenging of these decisions, and the one that will be the focus of this chapter, is whether sexual abuse has occurred. The reasons why this is a very difficult decision will be described. A protocol for collecting data to be used in the decision about the probability of sexual abuse will be discussed in detail. Finally, a strategy for making the decision itself will be offered.

Why Deciding About the
Probability of Sexual Abuse Is Difficult

First, in the decision about the likelihood of sexual abuse, the stakes are very high for the child, the accused, the family, and the professional him- or herself. An incorrect conclusion that either the child has or has not been sexually abused can have grave consequences for all involved. However, even a correct conclusion that the child has been sexually abused carries life-changing and sometimes devastating consequences.

Second, professionals may be trained extensively in how to interview children and collect information in forensic interviews. But typically they have little training in how to make decisions about the probability of sexual abuse based upon forensic data gathering.

Third, in general, education in the mental health professions usually does not address how to decide whether an event (such as sexual abuse) has occurred. Mental health training is more likely to focus on assessing individual, family, or group functioning, designing and delivering interventions to ameliorate problems identified during the assessment, and evaluating the effect of the interventions.

Fourth, most current forensic interview guidelines and protocols do not address the decision-making aspect of the investigation/assessment. They guide the professional in interview structure and offer advice about appropriate questioning techniques and other data-gathering strategies (e.g., Bourg et al., 1999; Davies et al., 1996; Michigan Governor's Task Force, 1998; Morgan, 1995). These newer protocols contrast with a number of older, practice-focused works that address the decision-making process (Benedek & Schetky, 1987; Berliner & Conte, 1993; Conte et al., 1991; Corwin, 1988; De Young, 1986; Faller, 1993a, 1994a; Gardner, 1991, 1992b; Green, 1986; Heiman, 1992; Hoorwitz, 1992; Sgroi, Porter, & Blick, 1982; Sink, 1988a; Undeutch, 1989; Wehrspann, Steinhauer, & Klajner-Diamond, 1987; Yuille, 1988). Recent work by Kuehnle (1996) and McDermott-Steinmetz (1997) offers advice about deciding likelihood. However, both the older and newer guidelines are practice rather than research based. On the other hand, the empirical studies of decision making about abuse that do exist are methodologically problematic (Horner, Guyer, & Kalter, 1993; Leichtman & Ceci, 1995).

Despite these challenges, because decision making about the likelihood of sexual abuse is such a crucial question, it is very important that professionals have an articulated strategy for making these determinations. All too frequently, professionals examining the same set of facts arrive at different conclusions. Although there are a variety of causes for these differences of opinion, often they derive from subjective decision-making processes. There are many sources of potential subjectivity and bias, including gender, age, beliefs about the probability of sexual abuse and the probability of false allegations, professional discipline, past professional experience with cases of sexual abuse, and personal experiences with sexual abuse. In addition, subjective impressions of the parties involved in the case (e.g., the child, the alleged offender, nonoffending family members), personal impressions of the other professionals involved in the case, the professional role on the case in point, and who is paying for the professional's services may affect decisions about the likelihood of abuse. Thus, there is a wide spectrum of sources of bias in sexual abuse decision making.

The Protocol

The strategy to be suggested in this chapter attempts to counter unarticulated subjectivity in decisions and is embodied in a protocol composed of several components. Originally designed as an exercise for the individual decision maker, this protocol has also been employed successfully by several professionals collaborating in the decision process, with each individual contributing information. The substantive and procedural components of the protocol will be described in this section.

A FRAMEWORK FOR DATA COLLECTION

First, the protocol provides a framework for gathering and recording information systematically on a range of topics from a variety of sources (see the protocol in Figure 7.1). The information is organized under two general categories: (a) child interview–derived data and (b) data from other sources. However, these are not entirely discrete categories. For example, one category of child interview–derived information is "recantations." These may occur during the child interview but may also occur elsewhere and be reported by others. The categories of information designated in the protocol will be discussed in greater detail below.

EXPLORING COMPETING HYPOTHESES

Second, the framework guides the forensic interviewer to consider a range of interpretations for individual pieces of information and decide which interpretation is the most likely.

Recently, forensic interviewers have been admonished to use a hypothesis-testing approach to their assessments/investigations (American Professional Society on the Abuse of Children [APSAC], 1996). This means that instead of focusing the investigation on gathering information to confirm (or disconfirm) sexual abuse, the interviewer gathers information with a range of possible explanations for the allegation in mind. Thus, the interviewer checks children's information during the interview: for example, by asking the child if an event the child describes "really happened or is pretend." Similarly, the interviewer considers the possibility that benign experiences can be misinterpreted as sexual abuse (e.g., APSAC, 1996; McDermott-Steinmetz, 1997).

Although the hypothesis-testing approach is good advice, each piece of information about the allegation may in fact be subject to alternative interpretations. For example, medical findings consistent with anal penetration might

(Text continues on page 172)

PROTOCOL FOR ASSESSING THE LIKELIHOOD OF SEXUAL ABUSE

Child's name   Child's age   Date   Clinician(s)

Alleged event or events covered (e.g., last incident, most serious incident)

PIECES OF INFORMATION	INTERPRETATIONS		IMPORTANCE
	List of Interpretations	Likely Interpretation	
I. CHILD INTERVIEW–DERIVED DATA			
A. Sexual abuse reported			
1. Types of sexual acts Frequency/duration			
a.			
b.			
c.			
d.			
2. Verbal description Y N			
Specify:			
a. Child's perspective Y N			
Specify:			
b. Explicit sexual acts Y N			
Specify:			
3. Demonstrations Y N			
a. Medium (e.g., dolls, drawings)			

Figure 7.1 (*Continued*)

b. Explicit demonstrations	Y	N
4. Advanced sexual knowledge	Y	N
Specify:		
B. Other types of abuse		
Specify:		
C. Context of the sexual abuse		
1. Where it happened	Y	N	NA*
Specify:		
2. When it happened	Y	N	NA*
Specify:		
3. Grooming or inducements	Y	N	NA*
Specify:		
4. Whereabouts of others	Y	N	NA*
Specify:		
5. Child's clothing	Y	N	NA*
Specify:		
6. Suspect's clothing	Y	N	NA*
Specify:		

Figure 7.1 (*Continued*)

7. Idiosyncratic event	Y	N	NA*
Specify:			
8. Child's emotional state	Y	N	NA*
Specify:			
9. Strategies to discourage telling	Y	N	NA*
Specify:			
10. Disclosures by child	Y	N	NA*
Specify:			
11. Reactions of persons told	Y	N	NA*
Specify:			
12. Other			
Specify:			
D. Child's affect during direct inquiry/disclosure			
1. Reluctance to disclose	Y	N	
Specify:			
2. Other affects (e.g., embarrassment, guilt, anxiety, disgust, anger, fear)	Y	N	
Specify:			

Figure 7.1 (*Continued*)

E. Child's functioning				
1. Child's sexualized behavior	Y	N		
Specify:				
2. Child's externalizing behavior	Y	N		
Specify:				
3. Child's internalizing behavior	Y	N		
Specify:				
4. Child's competence	Y	N		
Specify:				
5. Child's developmental level	Y	N		
Specify:				
6. Cultural issues	Y	N		
Specify:				
7. Other	Y	N		
Specify:				
F. Child's statements in other contexts	Y	N		
Specify:				

Figure 7.1 (*Continued*)

169

PIECES OF INFORMATION	INTERPRETATIONS List of Interpretations	Likely Interpretation	IMPORTANCE
G. Recantations Specify:			
II. INFORMATION FROM OTHER SOURCES			
A. Medical findings Y N Specify:			
B. Police evidence Y N Specify:			
C. Explanation of suspect Y N Specify:			
D. Any witnesses Y N Specify:			
E. Other alleged victims Y N Specify:			
F. Relevant observations by others (e.g., parents) Y N Specify:			

Figure 7.1 (*Continued*)

G. Evidence from other professionals Y N						
Specify:						
H. Other information Y N						
Specify:						

*NA = not asked

INSTRUCTIONS

Complete protocol, using information from all sources (background material, testing, interviews, collateral contacts, standardized measures). For each type of information, consider alternative explanations for its presence, absence, and/or significance. If the child describes multiple incidents of sexual abuse, focus on most recent or best remembered.

Findings related to sexual abuse allegations can be open to a variety of interpretations, for example:

A. Actual report of sexual abuse
B. Misinterpretation of benign activity by child
C. Misinterpretation of benign activity by adult
D. Communication problem
E. Coaching/programming by others
F. Sexual knowledge from other source
G. Different offender
H. Lying
I. Fantasizing by child
J. Attention seeking
K. Exaggeration
L. Minimization

Select the interpretation that seems most likely and indicate in the appropriate column.

Indicate on a 5-point scale how important the particular piece of information is to the decision about the likelihood of sexual abuse in the appropriate column.

5 = very important; 4 = important; 3 = slightly important; 2 = unimportant; 1 = very unimportant.

Figure 7.1   Protocol for Assessing the Likelihood of Sexual Abuse

have been caused by the alleged abuser or by someone else. In that same case, a child's statement that "Uncle Jack touched my bootie" could be a description of sexual behavior, child care behavior, or accidental touching. So forensic interviewers need to consider alternative explanations for all pieces of information they gather in assessing for sexual abuse. And, as noted earlier, this protocol asks the forensic interviewer to determine the most likely interpretation, another important aspect of the decision-making process.

In addition, although interviewers should always consider hypotheses that can "explain away" sexual abuse allegations—that is, provide an understanding of the data that eliminates sexual abuse—interviewers also need to bear in mind not only that the data might support abuse but also that the actual abuse might be much more serious than the data indicate.

Possible Alternative Explanations

Alternative explanations may relate to information from the child and information from other sources, including professionals and nonprofessionals. Below are 12 possible explanations for allegations of sexual abuse that have been identified by forensic interviewers.

1. *The child is providing a description of an actual experience of sexual abuse.* When the procedure of identifying child sexual abuse by listening to children first began, their accounts were taken at face value. Because of the life-altering consequences of believing children, their accounts have been subject to increasing scrutiny. Nevertheless, the reality is that children rarely have a vested interest in falsely stating they have been sexually abused (Faller, 1984). Indeed although a child's disclosure of sexual abuse may result in its cessation, the child may also experience many negative sequelae for reporting actual sexual abuse. The best estimates are that false assertions of sexual abuse are uncommon (Jones & McGraw, 1987; Oates et al., 2000). The number of false negatives (i.e., children failing to report actual abuse) appears much greater than the number of false positives (i.e., children stating they have been sexually abused when they have not). This conclusion is supported by both studies of high-certainty cases of sexual abuse and analogue studies (Faller, 1988c; Lawson & Chaffin, 1992; Saywitz et al., 1991; Sorenson & Snow, 1991).

Nevertheless, neither the perceptions of children nor those of adults are 100% accurate. Human beings do not possess the capacity to attend to and store all information they are exposed to. In addition, they may forget or make errors in their recall, and these are reflected in their accounts of past experiences.

2. *The child has misinterpreted benign activity*—for example, child care behavior, such as assistance in bathing or toileting. If children have been exposed to sexual abuse prevention material or have been told about "good touch/bad touch," they may misinterpret appropriate touch as sexual touch.

Moreover, if they have prior experiences with sexual victimization, they may assume that any private parts touch is sexual abuse.

In other instances, erroneous interpretations of appropriate touch are communicated to children, and they then perceive themselves as having been sexually abused. For example, a 5-year-old girl was told that her mother's putting A&D ointment on her sore vagina was sexual abuse, and she came to view herself as a victim of sexual abuse. A complicating aspect of interpretation of private parts touching is that adults may disguise sexual abuse as child care. Moreover, independent of the adult's intent, the child can experience an act of private parts touching as either abusive or caring.

3. The child's statements and/or behavior have been misinterpreted by adults. Probably the most common false positive derives from misinterpretations (Bala et al., 2001; Faller & DeVoe, 1995a; Thoennes & Tjaden, 1990). The misinterpretation could be made by a professional or by a nonprofessional, such as a parent or grandparent. For example, a child's fear of or avoidant responses to an individual or a situation may be assumed automatically to indicate sexual abuse when the source of the child's reaction is something else.

4. Communication problems are another possible explanation and represent a serious challenge to forensic interviewers. They can result in false positives or false negatives. Communication errors generally involve misunderstanding or not understanding children's statements, especially those of young children, and sometimes their demonstrations. Frequently forensic interviewers attempt to question children concerning topics about which the children have little knowledge and sometimes for which they have no words. In contrast, the forensic interviewer knows a lot about sexual abuse and has an extensive vocabulary. This type of problem is best understood with illustrative examples. The first is a false positive.

Case Example: A 6-year-old girl told her child care provider that "Daddy touched me down there (pointing generally to the genital area) with his buzzer. He touches me lots with his buzzer. He touches me all over with his buzzer." These buzzer touching episodes were reported to happen in the father's bedroom when the mother was downstairs cooking supper. The child care provider, assuming that the "buzzer" was a vibrator and "down there" meant the genitals, made a report to Child Protective Services (CPS). In fact, the buzzer turned out to be a tuning fork, which the father used in his work. He said he touched the child in various places on her body to show how this made the tuning fork "buzz" louder and to tickle her. The child provided an account to a forensic evaluator that was similar to the one she had given to her child care provider but did not repeat the child care provider's report that the touching involved the genitals.

Here is a false negative.

Case Example: Great-Uncle Larry lived with his niece, her husband, and his great nephew, Henry, who was 4 years old. Larry has his own bedroom, bathroom, and sitting room on the third floor. He paid rent and paid for his meals with the family. Uncle Larry was allowed to have his friends over and to keep his pet parakeets in his quarters. The parakeets fascinated Henry, and he often visited his great-uncle to admire them. Uncle Larry would also sometimes baby-sit for Henry when his parents went out. Henry went to preschool and one day told his teacher about his Uncle Larry. He said Uncle Larry had a big bird and he had to play with Uncle Larry's big bird. The teacher was concerned because Henry seemed somewhat upset about this, and she reported her concerns to Henry's mother. The mother explained to the teacher that Henry was referring to Uncle Larry's parakeets. It wasn't until a year later, when Henry forcibly fondled a 3-year-old boy in the neighborhood, that it was learned that the big bird was Uncle Larry's penis and not his parakeet.

5. *The child has been coached/programmed by others.* The alternative explanation that the child has been programmed has received a good deal of attention (e.g., Ceci & Bruck, 1995). Although the programming explanation should be considered, there is no empirical support for an assumption that children are routinely programmed to make false allegations of sexual abuse (Bala et al., 2001; Faller & Corwin, 1995; Faller & DeVoe, 1995a; Jones & McGraw, 1987; Oates et al., 2000; Thoennes & Tjaden, 1990). Some have accused professionals, such as child protection workers, law enforcement officers, and therapists, of programming children because they "have an agenda" (Gardner, 1992b; Underwager & Wakefield, 1988). Nevertheless, when programming does occur, it appears more likely at the hands of a parent or caretaker.

6. *The child has obtained sexual knowledge from another source.* Advanced sexual knowledge is a hallmark of sexual abuse in young children. Nevertheless, it is important for forensic interviewers to explore alternative information sources. Illustrative of the importance of considering this hypothesis are Boat and Everson's (1994) findings that about a quarter of 5-year-old boys of lower socioeconomic status had acquired knowledge about intercourse from a source other than sexual abuse. To address this possibility, Friedrich (1993), beginning with Version 2 of the Child Sexual Behavior Inventory, a standardized instrument for data gathering about signs of sexual abuse, added questions regarding nonabusive exposure to sexual information.

Forensic interviewers should explore whether knowledge was obtained from watching people involved in sexual acts or from observing sexual activity on videos, television, or the Internet. In addition, older children may simply read or be told about sexual activity and try it, which can result in concerns about sexual abuse. However, the fact that children know about sex from a nonabusive source does not rule out sexual abuse, especially when they report a situation of sexual abuse.

7. *The child has been sexually abused but is attributing the activity to the wrong offender.* It is possible for children to identify the wrong offender both accidentally and purposefully. Children, especially preschoolers, are not as good at eyewitness identification of people they see briefly as adults (Goodman et al., 1987). But they are not usually confused about the identity of an abuser with whom they have an ongoing relationship. There is anecdotal clinical evidence, however, that children may blame someone less valued or less feared than the actual offender for the abuse (Faller, 1988a). This person may be another child rather than an adult.

In addition, professionals frequently come in contact with cases in which "daddy" is named as the abuser, but the child calls more than one person "daddy." It is important to determine which "daddy" is the alleged abuser because sometimes the wrong one is blamed. The latter type of misidentification usually originates in the suggestion or insistence of an adult who has a vested interest in protecting the real perpetrator.

8. *Lying—that is, the child knowingly makes a false allegation.* Although calculated false allegations should always be considered, as already noted, the best evidence to date is that such situations are quite uncommon, representing between 1% and 6% of reports (Bala et al., 2001; Jones & McGraw, 1987; Oates et al., 2000). In one study that examined their characteristics, the majority involved older children who were girls with a prior history of sexual abuse (Jones & McGraw, 1987). Calculated false cases are more likely to be reported by adults than children, although they are uncommon among adults as well (Faller & DeVoe, 1995a; Jones & McGraw, 1987).

9. *Fantasizing by the child* is a possible explanation, but fantasizing about having been sexually abused when one has not appears to be quite rare, especially among children. The etiology of concerns that children will have fantasies about sexual activities lies in Freud's Oedipal theory. The explanation is that allegations of sexual abuse are based upon a child's wish to have sex with an adult, which then results in the child fantasizing about such acts and confusing fantasy with reality. This is a largely discredited theory (Herman, 2000; Masson, 1984), although it still has some supporters (e.g., Gardner, 1991, 1992b).

10. *The child is seeking attention.* An alternative explanation for an allegation is that the child is making it in order to receive solicitous attention. Although this argument is often made by those supporting the accused, there is no empirical evidence that children make false allegations of sexual abuse to this

end. In fact, being a victim of sexual abuse is regarded as stigmatizing (e.g., Faller, 1988a; Sgroi, 1982), and the consequences of disclosure do more to discourage reporting than to foster false reports (Faller, 1984, 1988a).

Nevertheless, attention seeking can be the source of an allegation in children with a past history of sexual abuse and marked psychological impairment. At the same time, children with a prior history appear at increased risk for subsequent sexual abuse.

11. Exaggeration of actual abuse may be done by child victims and adults. Little empirical information exists about exaggeration. There are a few case studies in which an adult admits to exaggerating events to make sure that the abuse is taken seriously (Faller, 1988a). Situations of actual abuse in which adults imagine that much worse events have taken place are more common. The following case example is illustrative.

Case Example: A father had a history of domestic violence and admitted to touching his son's and daughter's genitals, but said he did this only when bathing them. The mother, who was estranged from him, and her new boyfriend characterized the father as a dangerous pedophile. They wrote a letter to his place of employment stating he was a risk to children and posted signs in the father's neighborhood indicating that he was a child molester.

In addition, sometimes lawyers who are in an adversarial role to the accused will try to enhance their position by suggesting or asserting additional sexual acts than those for which there is any evidence.

Professionals must also be aware that they can perceive a child or adult to be exaggerating when they simply have difficulty believing part of the allegations. For example, whereas professionals may believe an individual has sexually abused a child, they may have much more difficulty imagining the possibility that two or more adults, especially if one of them is a woman, have collaboratively sexually abused a child or children.

12. The child or an adult acknowledges the sexual abuse but minimizes it. It is important for professionals to appreciate that the knowledge they gain about sexual abuse in the course of the forensic assessment process may be a very small part of the acts the offender has actually committed. There are many reasons, both emotional and practical, that the offender will minimize and deny. Shame, guilt, and fear of rejection may motivate minimization. From a practical standpoint, offenders may admit to fondling and deny penetration because the criminal consequences are lighter in the former. Similarly, offenders may admit to more recent acts but deny remote ones because acts perpetrated when the child was quite young warrant a more severe sentence.

Moreover, children may reveal only a small amount of what they have actually experienced because of obstacles to communication, incomplete assessment, or affective reactions to the abuse and disclosure. There is a fair amount of research on actual cases indicating that for most children disclosure of sexual abuse is a process rather than something they tell about all at once (Petronio et al., 1998; Sas & Cunningham, 1995; Sorenson & Snow, 1991) and that there are many obstacles to disclosure for children. For a discussion of the disclosure process, see Chapter 6.

Most Likely Explanation

Despite the importance of generating and considering a range of possible hypotheses to explain the pieces of information gathered by the forensic inter-viewer and the allegation itself, most forensic interviewers must make a deter-mination as to the most likely interpretation. This is done by considering each piece of information in the larger context of the other pieces of information about the case. The following case example is illustrative.

Case Example: Tara, age 7, comes from a single-parent family and is on welfare. She accused the father of two school friends of sexually abusing her and his two daughters. Both of the friends deny their father sexually abused them and deny he sexually abused Tara.

The father says Tara has never even been in his house. His daughters only associate with Tara at school. He does not think Tara is an appropriate playmate for his daughters because she comes from a broken family and her father is a drug dealer. If Tara has been sexually abused, it was probably when she visited her father.

Tara had medical evidence of penetration. She gave a detailed descrip-tion of the room in which she was abused, saying there was a green dresser in the room. There was a double bed. There were sex toys and dirty maga-zines in the bottom drawer of the dresser.

Given the detail of Tara's description, police obtained a search warrant. They found the room Tara described with the double bed and the green dresser beside it. No sex toys were found in the bottom drawer, but there was a pornographic magazine.

The medical evidence tells the professional that Tara has been sexually abused. The professional will consider the possibility that Tara was sexually abused when visiting her father or somewhere else. However, the fact that she provides a detailed description of sexual abuse by her friends' father and pro-vides an accurate description of the room indicate the most likely explanation is that the friends' father is the abuser. The most likely explanation is that he is lying when he states Tara has never been in his house because she can describe accurately the room in which he abused her. With regard to his daughters, the most likely explanation is that they are not disclosing abuse because they are still in their father's custody.

WEIGHTING THE INFORMATION

Third, the framework instructs decision makers to consider what weight to give pieces of information. As a rule, professionals place a fair amount of weight on children's detailed disclosures. They place less weight on suspects' denials.

Interestingly, there is evidence that professionals without medical training place great weight on the presence or absence of medical evidence (Faller, 1994a), even though medical findings are present in only 10% to 30% of cases, with the variation being based upon the source of cases being studied (Bays & Chadwick, 1993).

There are other pieces of information whose weight is more disputed. For example, law enforcement professionals and sometimes child protection workers may place considerable weight on polygraph findings, especially when the accused passes the polygraph. In most communities, local practice is not to criminally prosecute if the suspect takes and passes the polygraph. In contrast, most mental health professionals, familiar with the research on the polygraph, place little or no weight on its results (Cross & Saxe, 1992; Faller, 1997; Saxe et al., 1987; Williams, 1995). See Chapter 3 for a discussion of use of the polygraph.

It is important that professionals articulate the weight being given to pieces of information as well as their interpretations so that differences of opinion can be objectively discussed. This protocol suggests using a 5-point scale for weighting information: 1:very unimportant; 2:unimportant; 3:slightly important; 4:important; 5:very important.

COMPLETING THE PROTOCOL

The protocol can be found in Figure 7.1. The decision maker should indicate demographic data and who is completing the form at the top of the protocol. It also may be advisable, in cases with multiple allegations, to designate the specific events to be covered. In most instances, the most recent instances will provide the level of detail that will afford the decision maker the best opportunity to determine likelihood of abuse.

As the protocol indicates, the first source of information is the child interview. The fact that the child does not reveal sexual abuse during a forensic interview should not be regarded *prima facie* as evidence that there was no sexual abuse. Rather, the conclusion should be that no evidence of sexual abuse was elicited during the interview. There may have been disclosures or demonstrations in other contexts. In such instances, the forensic evaluator has to rely on them.

SEXUAL ABUSE REPORTED (SECTION IA)

The first type of information to be recorded is the specific sexual acts, including their frequency/duration. The interviewer notes whether the description is verbal, involves demonstrations, or both. He or she should record on the protocol the child's exact words and, if there were demonstrations, in what medium and specifically what the child demonstrated. Further, the interviewer should note whether the child's description suggests advanced sexual knowledge for the child's age and whether the description reflects a child's perspective. Obviously, these latter characteristics are most relevant to young children.

OTHER FORMS OF ABUSE (SECTION IB)

Often offenders engage in other types of maltreatment, both in conjunction with and separate from the sexual abuse. In some instances, they are kind and cajoling when they sexually abuse but coercive when committing other acts of abuse.

Case Example: A case involving an 11-year-old learning-disabled boy, Jeremy, is illustrative. Jeremy attended a Catholic school and received tutoring from Father James, who taught his class. Father James had a terrible temper and would paddle the boys with little provocation. Once he got angry at Jeremy and kicked him in the shin and spit in his face. However, he had a "caring side" and bought Jeremy clothing so he would not stand out as poorly dressed when compared to the rest of the boys. He had Jeremy try on his new clothing in the basement of the church and fondled him when he tried on these clothes.

CONTEXT OF SEXUAL ABUSE (SECTION IC)

The protocol guides the interviewer in the documentation of the particulars of the context of the sexual abuse and asks the interviewer to indicate *yes, no,* or *not asked* about each piece of contextual information and then to specify the particulars. Obviously, *yes* means the child has provided some information in the contextual category. *No* is recorded when the child was asked and provided no information. For example, the interviewer asks the child, "Did Mr. Jones say anything about telling or not telling?" and the child replies, "No." The *not asked* category is included because circumstances of the allegation might indicate that an inquiry into a contextual detail is inappropriate. Indeed, there is no requirement that information be sought about all of these contextual details.

The protocol cues the interviewer to inquire into a number of contextual details, including where the abuse occurred, when it occurred, any grooming or inducements employed by the offender, where other people were, what clothing the child was wearing and what was removed, and what clothing the offender was wearing and what was removed. The interviewer is cued to record any "idiosyncratic event" in the child's account (Faller, 1984; Jones & McQuiston, 1985). The rationale for tracking idiosyncratic events is that a child would be unlikely to fabricate an allegation and include an idiosyncratic event in the false report. Similarly, an adult programming a child would not be likely to have the ingenuity to include such an event. Below is an example.

> *Case Example*: Sally, age 10, reported sexual abuse by her father. In describing the last time it happened, she said that she and her father had been sitting on the couch watching TV. She was wearing her nightgown, and he began to fondle her. She said, "But then I tricked him and told him I needed to go to the bathroom." She went into the bathroom and stayed from a long time. After a while, she snuck up into her bedroom in an attempt to avoid her father's molestation. But he came into the bedroom and continued his abuse.

The idiosyncratic event in this account is Sally's statement that she tricked her father and said she needed to go to the bathroom.

Contextual material can also include any recollection the child has of her emotional state at the time. Again, the rationale of ascertaining this is that it would be unlikely that children could fabricate this piece of information. Emotional state is usually elicited by the interviewer asking, "Do you remember how you felt when he did that?" or "What did you think when that happened?"

Finally, items regarding disclosure are in the context section—whether the suspect employed any strategies to prevent disclosure, whether the child has previously disclosed, and the reactions of those individuals to disclosure. Although strategies to prevent disclosure are not universal, they are very common. These strategies may involve appeals to the relationship. When the offender and victim are close, the offender may try to manipulate the child by saying, "If you tell, I won't love you anymore," or "If you tell, I'll have to leave the family." Strategies to prevent disclosure may also involve bribes, including providing material possessions, money, and privileges. Or the strategies may consist of threats of blaming the victim, of causing bodily harm or death, or of injuring people the child cares about. An example of the latter is a case involving a 4-year-old boy whose mother was mentally ill and hospitalized. The boy resided with his grandmother and siblings in a trailer park, and the offender, who was an uncle, knew where they lived. The offender warned the boy that if he told, the offender would set fire to the trailer and kill them all.

Whom the child has told about the abuse and the reactions of these individuals are important pieces of information. In some instances, the forensic interviewer is hearing about the allegation some time after the alleged abuse and after a number of prior disclosures. It can be important to trace the chain of disclosure to discern the circumstances of initial disclosure and to find out if there are marked differences in the initial report and the current one. The circumstances of initial disclosure may indicate more or less certainty regarding the veracity and accuracy of the allegation. Differences in the current account and past accounts may reflect contamination, incremental disclosure, or recantation.

The reactions of those to whom the child reported the abuse can help the forensic interviewer make determinations about child safety and gather information that might support or rule out a hypothesis that the child received solicitous attention for alleging sexual abuse.

THE CHILD'S AFFECT DURING
INQUIRY/DISCLOSURE (SECTION ID)

The protocol has a section on the child's emotional reaction to being asked to recount sexual abuse. Most children are reluctant to disclose, but children who receive emotional support from a primary caretaker may do so more readily (Sas & Cunningham, 1995). Other potential affects include embarrassment, guilt, anxiety, disgust, anger, and sexual arousal. In determining the likelihood, the forensic interviewer will be interested in the extent to which the child's emotional response is consistent with the abuse reported and the circumstances of the abuse (Faller, 1988c).

However, these emotional reactions are open to a variety of interpretations. The apparent absence of emotion is no longer regarded as a marker of a false allegation. Children may not appreciate the enormity of the normative transgression and therefore may not display much affect. Children may also emotionally dissociate, and there is a desensitization effect for children who have described the abuse numerous times. Boys, because of their socialization, may describe their abuse in a matter-of-fact manner (Faller, 1988c). Also some children, when nervous, become silly, which may be regarded as inappropriate affect for a situation of actual abuse.

CHILD'S FUNCTIONING (SECTION IE)

In this section, the interviewer documents the child's behavior and functioning—including any sexual and other acting out, competency, development, and cultural issues. Findings or absence of findings in these areas do not rule in or rule out sexual abuse but are important nonetheless, and the first three categories may provide direction for treatment.

Sexualized behavior is the most common marker of sexual victimization, although it is found in only about 40% of children with a history of sexual abuse (Friedrich, 1999). This information can be obtained by using the Child Sexual Behavior Inventory (also called the Child Behavior Survey) (Friedrich, 1993) or by anecdotal reports. Certain behaviors, such as inviting others to engage in sexual acts, are very low frequency for children without a history of sexual abuse and thus very concerning and suggestive of sexual abuse (Friedrich, 1999). Sexualized behavior is discussed in greater detail in Chapter 2.

Information about both *externalizing and internalizing behavior* can be obtained by having the child's caretaker complete the Child Behavior Checklist (Achenbach, Edelbrock, & Howell, 1987; Faller, 1996b; Friedrich, 1993), by collecting social history information, and by observing the child's behavior during the interview. Externalizing or acting-out behaviors, such as blaming others, showing hostility and aggression, fighting, stealing, and destroying property, may be sequelae of sexual abuse or other experiences. Internalizing behaviors involve acts against the self, such as self-blame, self-harm, suicidal thoughts, gestures, and attempts, and behaviors such as phobias, nightmares, enuresis, encopresis, and eating problems. Like externalizing behaviors, they may reflect the impact of sexual abuse or other experiences. See Chapter 2 for a discussion of these nonsexual indicators of stress.

Many forensic interviewers focus on legal issues associated with *competency*—the child's knowledge of the difference between the truth and a lie and the child's promise to tell the truth during the forensic interview. In fact, many forensic protocols require the inclusion of a competency assessment.

Nevertheless, it is important that forensic interviewers appreciate that the child's knowledge of definitions of truth and lies and even the child's promise to tell the truth may bear no relationship to the veracity or accuracy of the abuse-related information in the interview (Poole & Lamb, 1998). Children may lack knowledge about concepts of truth and lies and nevertheless provide accurate information. Similarly, children may understand these concepts and even agree to tell the truth but nevertheless not tell the truth.

Probably more important are other indicators of competency: (a) the child's capacity to recount past events, (b) the child's awareness of her surroundings and living circumstances, and (c) the child's capacity to communicate with the interviewer. Other child characteristics, such as evidence of the child's suggestibility or lack thereof, can be documented here in the protocol.

In this section, the forensic interviewer also documents the *child's developmental level*. This information may derive from an informal developmental assessment during the forensic interview, including data gathering about concepts key to describing sexual abuse and its context, or from formal testing.

Any *cultural issues* should be noted. Not only is the child population in the United States becoming more diverse, but children of color are overrepresented in reports to child welfare agencies. Culture can influence sexual practices, responses to sexual abuse, and reactions to questioning about such issues. Moreover, cultural differences between the interviewer and the child may impede the interview process (e.g., Dunkerley & Dalenberg, 2000). These issues are also discussed in Chapter 6.

CHILD'S STATEMENTS IN OTHER CONTEXTS (SECTION IF)

As noted earlier, tracking how the child has described the victimization previously is useful in establishing likelihood. If the child has described the abuse in the same fashion consistently, then prior inconsistent accounts cannot be used to challenge the child's current account. However, many children lack the sexual knowledge to know what is happening when they first experience abuse (Sas & Cunningham, 1995). In addition, this absence of knowledge may result in children's failure to categorize in their minds all the abuse events as under the same general rubric—to wit, "my sexual abuse." Moreover, as already noted, there is a fair amount of evidence that disclosure is often delayed and incremental (e.g., Petronio et al., 1998; Sas & Cunningham, 1995; Sorenson & Snow, 1991; Summit, 1983). Finally, children may recant true allegations of sexual abuse. Although inconsistent accounts make it more difficult to decide what, if anything, has happened, inconsistent accounts should be considered in light of the possible explanations just described.

RECANTATIONS (SECTION IG)

Research on high-certainty cases suggests that about a fifth of actually sexually abused children recant (Sorenson & Snow, 1991). They may recant because of admonitions by the offender or others, because of the practical consequences of disclosure, or because of emotional consequences of being defined as a sexual abuse victim. However, recantation can also occur because the allegation is false. There are no clear-cut strategies for differentiating a recantation of a true allegation from the retraction of a false one, although in some cases one explanation will seem more likely than the other.

INFORMATION FROM OTHER SOURCES (SECTION II)

In this part of the protocol, the interviewer documents information that does not derive from the child's interview statements or behavior but comes from other sources. Among these sources are the *medical exam* (Section IIA) and any *law enforcement investigation* (Section IIB). Although most sexual abuse does not result in physical findings (Bays & Chadwick, 1993), and although physical signs, when they are present, may quickly resolve (McCann et al., 1992), nevertheless most children will have had a medical exam. Currently, physicians categorize their findings into four levels based upon how supportive and nonsupportive findings are of sexual abuse (Bays & Chadwick, 1993).

Because sexual abuse is a crime, law enforcement will be involved in many, and in some communities most, investigations. Moreover, most state child protection statutes call for some level of cooperation between CPS and law enforcement on cases that fall within the CPS mandate. Law enforcement evidence may consist of information from child and suspect interviews, including a confession or a plea, forensic physical evidence (e.g., hairs, fibers, semen, blood, saliva) from crime scenes or from the child's body, and polygraph findings. Police may also provide corroboration of the child's description of the crime scene (e.g., there was a poster on the wall in the room where the child was raped) or the suspect (e.g., the suspect had a birthmark on his left buttock). The polygraph does not warrant a specific category because of its lack of validity (Cross & Saxe, 1992; Faller, 1997). Law enforcement's role in sexual abuse investigation is discussed in detail in Chapter 3.

The protocol has a place for *any explanation offered by the suspect* (Section IIC). Depending upon the structure of the forensic interview program, this information may be obtained directly through an interview with the suspect or from other sources. Sometimes the suspect can provide a sensible alternative explanation, in which case the forensic interviewer may conclude there has been no sexual abuse. The interviewer should attend to whether the alleged offender's explanation fits with the other facts of the case. In the following example, the suspect's explanation did not fit the facts very well.

Case Example: Grandpa Roy was accused of digital penetration of his 4-year-old granddaughter. She began screaming as he was bathing her. Grandma Roy came into the bathroom and noted blood in the bath water. Grandma Roy took her granddaughter to the doctor, who noted a hymeneal tear. Grandpa Roy said it was an accident. As he was bathing his grand-daughter, his finger accidentally slipped and went into her vaginal opening.

The protocol also allows space for accounts from *any witnesses* (Section IID) and information related to *other alleged victims* (Section IIE). Because sexual abuse is usually something that happens in private, there are not likely to be witnesses. But in the example above, although Grandma Roy was not an actual eyewitness, she arrived shortly after the abuse and provided compelling evidence. On the other hand, because multiple victims are the rule, rather than the exception, there may be other victims. In most cases, if the suspect has unsupervised access to other children, they also should be interviewed.

The protocol also allows for the inclusion of *relevant observations from others* (Section IIF). Persons who know the child and have opportunities to observe the child may be excellent sources of information. They may be parents, other relatives, partners of the accused or the nonoffending parent, baby-sitters, neighbors, or friends. They have much more extensive contact with the child and sometimes other people involved in the allegation than forensic interviewers. They may observe patterns of behavior and may be present when the child first discloses sexual abuse. It is appropriate to contact them in the course of the assessment to gather information. However, some-times these individuals have particular predispositions to believe or not believe that the child has been sexually abused.

Finally, *evidence from other professionals* (Section IIG) can be documented. Some cases have a long history of concerns that precede the forensic interview. It is appropriate for forensic interviewers to gather and review information, reports, and any conclusions rendered by these individuals. As with other infor-mation, the forensic interviewer should review these findings critically and not feel bound to support them. Issues that need to be considered are the age of the child at the time, any indications of where in the process of disclosure the child might have been, the completeness of the information gathered, and the exper-tise of the other professional. For example, although child protection workers are dedicated to investigation of child maltreatment, they have a high turnover rate, may have inadequate training, and usually have high caseloads, which means they may not have time to do a thorough investigation. With regard to specific expertise, a mental health professional may be very competent to assess adults but not have expertise to assess children. Similarly, a professional may know a great deal about substance abuse but little about sexual abuse assessment.

In addition, forensic interviewers should be alert for professionals with regular contact with children and family members and seek them out as sources of information. Young children may attend day care, and school-aged children have teachers who see them every day. If children are in foster care when the allegation is being evaluated, their foster parents may be important sources of information. Therapists who have provided services to children and family may also be important resources in understanding the allegation and coming to a decision about its likelihood.

Forming an Opinion

Once all the information has been documented in the protocol, the possible explanations considered, the most likely one selected, and the information weighted, the professional or group of professionals needs to form a conclusion about the most likely explanation for the allegation.

A "RULE-OUT" STRATEGY

Making a decision about probability of sexual abuse usually begins by ruling out certain explanations for the allegation because they are inconsistent with the evidence. For example, a "no sexual abuse" explanation should usually be ruled out when there is conclusive medical evidence. Then, considering the weighted information, the professional or group of professionals usually rank-orders the alternative explanations, with the most likely being ranked highest.

DEGREE OF CERTAINTY

Not only should forensic interviewers form an opinion about the most likely explanation for the sexual abuse allegation, but it is helpful to decide the degree of certainty regarding the opinion. Jones and McGraw (1987) have developed a useful framework for addressing this issue. They speak of a continuum of certainty (see Figure 7.2). In very few cases, the interviewer will be 100% certain sexual abuse *did* or *did not* occur, and in most instances it is probably inadvisable to make an absolute statement. Although professionals may wish for a high degree of certainty in concluding that sexual abuse either did or did not occur, it should be remembered that even in criminal prosecution, the requirement to prove the case is 95% certainty, and child protection agencies usually intervene when there is a preponderance of evidence (51% probability). See Chapter 4 for additional discussion of standards of proof.

100% certain child was sexually abused				100% certain child was not sexually abused
Very likely	Likely	50–50	Unlikely	Very unlikely
95% beyond a reasonable doubt for criminal conviction	CPS substantiation	51% preponderance of the evidence for court jurisdiction to protect.	Inconclusive	CPS denial

Figure 7.2   Continuum of Certainty

SOURCE: Adapted from Jones and McGraw (1987).

Sometimes the interview and assessment are inconclusive. Both APSAC (1996) and the American Academy of Child and Adolescent Psychiatry (AACAP, 1997) guidelines point out that the forensic interviewer may not be able to form a conclusion and should so state and document the reasons why.

The language employed by the forensic interviewer should reflect the degree of certainty that he or she has about the likelihood of sexual abuse in the case (Faller, 1993a). Moreover, interviewers must keep in mind research demonstrating the substantial proportion of false negatives (Faller, 1988c; Lawson & Chaffin, 1992; Saywitz et al., 1991; Sorenson & Snow, 1991) and the cautionary comments of Conte et al. (1991) regarding indicators of sexual abuse when they write their conclusions. When no information supporting abuse is elicited during the assessment, forensic interviewers are advised to use language such as "sexual abuse could not be substantiated" or "no evidence of sexual abuse was found" rather than "sexual abuse did not occur."

REPORTING THE BASES OF THE DECISION

The protocol in Figure 7.1 assists the forensic interviewer in meeting current standards of practice, which are to state not only conclusions but also the evidence employed in reaching them (AACAP, 1997; APSAC, 1996; Faller, 1993a). Current standards also advise professionals to include information from all sources, not merely the child interview(s).

It is useful to chronicle the information gathered and state the conclusions or opinion in a separate section of the report, referring back to supporting evidence. Professionals should avoid interspersing opinion with the data.

Conclusion

Forming a conclusion about the likelihood of sexual abuse is a difficult and demanding task. Often this task is overlooked in graduate training, in continuing education, and by agencies conducting forensic interviews. The goal of this chapter was to provide the interviewer with some guidance about how to make this decision.

PART IV

Sexual Abuse in Special Contexts

8

Sexual Abuse in Family Foster Care

Family foster care used to be regarded as a living arrangement of unmitigated superiority for children who had been maltreated by their parents and, at one time, even as a better alternative than living with a biological family without financial resources (Kadushin, 1980; Kline & Overstreet, 1972). Times have changed, and child welfare and mental health professionals are now concerned with structural aspects of foster care that can have potentially detrimental effects on children (e.g., Barth, Courtney, Berrick, & Albert, 1994; Fahlberg, 1997; Gil, 1982; Kadushin & Martin, 1988). First, the child's attachment capability can be damaged as a consequence of separation from parents and, later, as a result of removal from foster parents and return home (Fahlberg, 1997; Gil, 1982). Second, a foster family living arrangement is likely to be less stable than a biological one because the commitment of foster parents to the child is often not as lasting as that of biological parents. Third, once children are placed, they are prone to being allowed to languish in foster care for a variety of reasons (Barth, Yeaton, & Winterfelt, 1994). The most important of these is the fact that the foster care worker, who usually has a large caseload with continually erupting emergencies, just does not get around to serving children who are in safe and satisfactory living situations in foster care (Faller, 1986).

In recent years, mental health professionals and others have become aware that, for many children, foster care is not safe and satisfactory. In fact, there are

Author's Note: I wish to express my appreciation to my colleague Patricia Ryan, PhD, who shared unpublished findings from the study she conducted with Jean McFadden regarding maltreatment of children in foster care.

detrimental effects other than attachment problems, foster care instability, and foster care drift that children in placement can experience. Professionals have raised concerns about victimization in foster care and also in other out-of-home care settings (Benedict, Zuravin, Somerfield, & Brandt, 1996; Cavanaugh-Johnson, 1997; Gallagher, 1999; Gil, 1982; Hobbs, Hobbs, & Wynne, 1999; McFadden & Ryan, 1991; Nunno & Motz, 1988; Nunno & Rindfleisch, 1991; Rosenthal, Motz, Edmondson, & Groze, 1991; Zuravin, Benedict, & Somerfield, 1993). Cases of physical, sexual, and emotional abuse of children in care have been identified, with some researchers finding sexual abuse more common (Benedict et al., 1996; Gallagher, 1999; Hobbs et al., 1999; Nunno & Motz, 1988), and others physical abuse (McFadden & Ryan, 1991; Rosenthal et al., 1991). Although there are some similarities between abuse in foster care and in other out-of-home care situations, there are sufficient differences that sexual abuse in foster care deserves separate treatment.

This chapter will discuss why maltreated children might be at greater risk for sexual abuse in foster care, will present some research findings on characteristics of sexual abuse in foster care, will describe three types of sexual abuse in foster care, and will make suggestions for ways of preventing foster care sexual victimization.

Characteristics of Children in Care That May Increase Risk

It is important not to blame the victim for the abuse the child experiences. Nevertheless, if the goal is to understand sexual abuse in foster care and intervene effectively, one must not overlook aspects of the child's functioning and behavior that may play a role in her victimization. The characteristics to be described may increase risk of victimization not only in foster care but in other contexts as well. Although other child factors also can enhance vulnerability to sexual maltreatment, the impact of having been physically and emotionally maltreated and sexually abused will be the focus of the discussion here.

THE IMPACT OF PHYSICAL AND EMOTIONAL MALTREATMENT

Physically and emotionally abused and neglected children may be at greater risk than other children for sexual abuse in foster care. In their home situations, their physical and emotional needs have not been met. Therefore, they may not have an understanding of appropriate nurturance and care. In addition, they are likely to have unmet dependency and affective needs. Both of these characteristics may place them at increased risk for sexual abuse. The case example that follows is illustrative.

Case Example: Evelyn, age 8, was placed in foster care because of long-standing physical and emotional neglect. Her mother was mentally ill and in and out of the hospital. Her father was extremely obese, had a bad back, and spent most of his time in bed. The house was filthy, with bags of garbage in every room. The family had six dogs that lived in the house and were not housebroken.

Evelyn was the youngest of three children, but the older children had been placed in care earlier. Evelyn was expected to look after herself: She had to get up, dress herself, feed herself, and catch the bus for school. After school she came home, fed the dogs, and watched television. Sometimes her father fixed dinner, but often Evelyn had to prepare her meal and his.

When Evelyn came into care, she had developmental delays that appeared to have been caused by her family situation. At times, she engaged in self-stimulating behaviors, including rocking and masturbating. However, there was no evidence that she had been sexually abused. She appeared excessively friendly and quite childlike.

She adjusted well to foster care and attached quickly to her foster parents. They described her as needing lots of affection and attention but said she was very good-natured and compliant.

She soon began to explore the neighborhood and made friends with some children who lived down the street. Because the foster parents knew and liked the parents of these children, they were happy to have Evelyn play with them after school.

About 2 months after Evelyn came, they became concerned because Evelyn called Tommy, the 13-year-old boy in the neighbor family, her lover. They investigated the situation and found that Tommy and two of his friends were having sexual intercourse with Evelyn. Evelyn found this to be a positive experience. She said the boys did not make fun of her the way the other kids did, they gave her candy, and it felt good to do loving.

In this case, the child's developmental delays and lack of social skills probably caused her to be rejected by peers. Her naivete and emotional deprivation made her an easy and willing target for adolescent boys.

THE IMPACT OF BEING SEXUALLY ABUSED ON FUTURE VULNERABILITY TO SEXUAL ABUSE

Sexually abused children may be at even greater risk than those mistreated in other ways for sexual abuse in foster care. I found that 24% of a clinical sample of close to 300 sexually abused children had been victimized by more than one person. Although half had been victimized in contexts where there was more than one offender, the remainder were subjected to serial sexual abuse by different offenders (Faller, 1988b). This finding and those of other writers (e.g., De Young, 1984; Russell, 1986) support clinical assumptions regarding effects of sexual abuse on future vulnerability. Furthermore, the research of Ryan and her colleagues (McFadden & Ryan, 1986, 1991; Ryan, McFadden, & Wiencek, 1988), which examined predictors of child maltreatment in foster care, including predictors of sexual abuse, found that having been sexually abused or exploited previously rendered children at risk for sexual abuse in foster care involving penetration. (However, there was no comparable relationship between prior victimization and sexual abuse without penetration.)

Five ways in which sexual victimization can contribute to subsequent sexual abuse and activity will be described here. Chapter 2, which describes some of these vulnerabilities as indicators of sexual abuse, is relevant.

First, children who have experienced sexual abuse may have been socialized by their offenders to behave in ways that can be interpreted as invitations to sexual activity. The example that follows is one involving very young children.

Case Example: Nancy, 4, and Denise, 3, were sexually exploited by their mother and her boyfriend. In addition to having been sexually abused by them, they were made to undress and have their pictures taken in sexual poses with numerous men. Their foster mother described them as both avoidant of and provocative with her husband. When they were having their baths, they would run out of the bathroom naked and "moon" him, then retreat again to the bathroom. They engaged in a comparable pattern when church elders came to visit. First they hid; then they came and sat on the laps of the male elders, stroking their faces and chests and calling them "my man."

This is the kind of behavior that may be seen with very young children. Older children may wear tight clothing, clothing more suitable to adult women, or makeup. Or they may behave in ways that seem seductive (McFadden & Ryan, 1986). It is important to appreciate that such behavior is a product of socialization and not a spontaneous expression of sexual desire.

Second, sexually abused children may have expectations that adults will be sexual with them. Often they learn to equate sexual behavior with affectionate behavior. They therefore expect adults to be sexual when showing affection. When these children fail to resist sexual overtures, it is often because they need the nurturance for which sex has become a substitute.

Third, victims' early introduction to sexual behavior results in precocious sexual awareness. Victimized children may experience sexual pleasure at a much younger age than most children. Physical pleasure is more likely to be associated with sexual abuse if the offender has gradually introduced the child to sex and has not employed force. Especially if the victim's life is devoid of other normal childhood pleasures, the attraction of sexual behavior is enhanced.

Fourth, repeated involvement in sexual abuse may represent counterphobic behavior. De Young (1984) has described four young girls who were traumatically sexually abused and who initially evidenced marked negative reactions to these experiences and phobic responses. Nevertheless, they all were later involved in sexual interactions with older people in which they played an initiating or participating role and did not display the evidence of trauma noted earlier. She hypothesized that the reinvolvement was a form of counterphobic behavior. That is, they achieved a sense of mastery over their previous traumas by seeking out sexually abusive situations where they could be in control.

Fifth, a related dynamic that is sometimes present is identification with the aggressor. Victims overcome their feelings of vulnerability and helplessness by becoming like their abusers and sexually victimizing other, usually younger, children. Boys seem to be more likely than girls to cope with the trauma of sexual abuse by identification with the aggressor. This is probably so because offenders against boys are more often of the same sex, making such identification easier, and because boys are socialized to seek sexual gratification whereas girls, as a rule, are not.

SUMMARY OF FINDINGS REGARDING CHILD VULNERABILITY

What the discussion of the role of the victim suggests is that child maltreatment of all types may increase a child's vulnerability to sexual abuse. Moreover, sexually abused children are probably at greater risk than children who have suffered physical and emotional maltreatment. In part, this increased risk is a consequence of the particular impacts of sexual abuse, but it may also derive from the compounding of the insults of the sexual abuse with those of physical and emotional maltreatment. The general outcome of physical and emotional abuse and neglect is to create deficits that may result in a propensity to tolerate sexual abuse. Moreover, because of their anomalous socialization and early exposure to sex, sexually abused children may expect, accept, and/or experience some pleasure from sexual interactions with older persons. In addition, children who have been quite traumatized by sexual abuse may nevertheless be drawn into subsequent sexual relationships with adults in order to work through their trauma. Making these sexual encounters even more difficult to understand is the fact that more than one dynamic may operate in an incident of sexual abuse in foster care and that different dynamics may operate at different times with the same victim. Nevertheless, the contribution of the child should never be viewed as the primary cause of sexual abuse.

Research on Characteristics
of Sexual Abuse in Foster Care

In this section, I draw on cases seen at the University of Michigan over the last 20 years, a group of 40 children who were substantiated for sexual abuse in 21 foster homes.[1] Findings from these cases will be supplemented with some from other studies. These studies include one by Ryan, McFadden, and colleagues (McFadden & Ryan, 1991; Ryan et al., 1988), who surveyed all types of maltreatment by foster parents and drew their cases from five states. Their data source was agency records. They found 14 cases of sexual abuse not involving penetration and 13 involving penetration. In addition, Zuravin and colleagues (Benedict et al., 1996; Zuravin, Benedict, & Somerfield, 1993) have published several articles on a sample of 62 inner-city foster homes in which there was a documented case of child maltreatment during a 5-year period. Finally, there is a more recent English study by Hobbs et al. (1999) of children in residential and foster care who came to the attention of physicians during a 6-year period because of child maltreatment. Ninety-one children had been sexually abused in foster care.

Of the children in our clinical sample, 40% were male and 60% were female. Similar proportions are found in other reports of children sexually abused in care (e.g., Benedict et al., 1996; Hobbs et al., 1999). McFadden and Ryan (1986) reported that more than 80% were females, but they did not include child-child encounters, defining those as neglect on the part of the foster parents (P. Ryan, personal communication, 1989).

The mean age of the children was 7.6 to 8.3 years for boys and 7.1 for girls (nonsignificant difference). Other studies report victims to be somewhat older, about 12 years (Hobbs et al., 1999; McFadden & Ryan, 1991). Twenty-nine (72.5%) children in our cases had been sexually victimized prior to placement in foster care. Hobbs et al. (1999) reported that about one third of children had a prior history of sexual abuse.

Researchers have described risk factors for sexual abuse in foster care that derive from case characteristics. These findings often come from case record reviews (e.g., McFadden & Ryan, 1991; Zuravin et al., 1993). Research findings differ with regard to whether kinship placements (Faller, 1990) or nonrelative foster homes (Hobbs et al., 1999; Zuravin et al., 1993) present a greater risk for sexual abuse. Researchers have found that female children (Faller, 1990; Hobbs et al., 1999), children whose foster mothers are younger (Zuravin et al., 1993), and children in foster homes that caseworkers have worried about (Zuravin et al., 1993) are more likely to be reported for sexual abuse. Although this information is useful from a policy perspective, such findings are not so helpful in understanding the dynamics of sexual abuse in foster care.

Investigations of sexual abuse in foster care have noted the seriousness of this abuse (e.g., Rosenthal et al., 1991). The most serious sexual abuse for our cases was coded for each child. Eighteen of the children (45%) were involved in some form of penetration; for 9 (22.5%), oral sex was the most serious form of abuse; and for 13 (32.5%), the most severe form of molestation was fondling. None of the children experienced only noncontact sexual abuse, and none in the sample were involved in exploitation, although other children in some of the homes were. McFadden and Ryan (1991) included oral sex in the category of sexual abuse involving penetration and found their cases almost evenly split between sexual abuse with penetration and without. Hobbs et al. (1999) reported that 39 (43%) of their cases had abnormal genital findings, 19 of which were consistent with genital penetration, and that 53 (58%) children had abnormal anal findings, 34 of which were consistent with anal penetration.

Types of Sexual Abuse in Foster Care

From our cases, three different types of sexual abuse in foster care were identified: sexual abuse by other children, opportunistic sexual abuse by a foster parent, and planned sexual abuse by a foster parent. These will be described and illustrated with data from the clinical sample of 40 children and from other studies.

SEXUAL ABUSE BY OTHER CHILDREN

Foster children may become sexually involved with one another or with biological children in the foster home (Hobbs et al., 1999). In our cases, 19 (47.5%) were involved in child-child encounters in foster care; 8 of these children were offenders. All of the latter had been sexually abused before they became perpetrators, two in foster care and the remainder in their biological families. Five were male and three female. Victims were as likely to be boys as girls. Hobbs et al. (1999) described a similar proportion of victims of other children. It is less common to find the biological children initiating sexual contact with foster children (Hobbs et al., 1999; P. Ryan, personal communication, 1989). Sometimes the sexual activity in child-child encounters is mutual sexual exploration, but in other instances it involves older or more sophisticated children taking sexual advantage of younger or more naive children.

A common predisposing situation is the presence of one or more sexually abused children in the same foster home. In addition, risk may be increased for child-child sexual abuse by the scarcity of foster homes. Sometimes foster families are asked to take more children than they can feasibly care for well.

Consequently, supervision is inadequate, and the foster parents cannot meet children's needs for nurturance. The scarcity of placements may be an even greater problem where sexually abused children are concerned. Many foster families are not willing to care for sexually victimized children. However, sexually abused children constitute a considerable percentage of the children coming into care (e.g., 42% in Michigan; S. Kelly, personal communication, 1988). Therefore, it is not uncommon for those families willing to foster these children to have more than one placed with them.

Because of the increased likelihood that sexual abuse victims will act out sexually and allow themselves to be revictimized, as described above, the presence of one or more victims of sexual maltreatment in a foster home can present considerable risk. Moreover, as already pointed out, even those children who were victims of other types of maltreatment may be at risk because of their unmet dependency and affective needs and the anomie of foster care.

The case example described below illustrates the complexity, good intentions, and unanticipated consequences of cases where children abuse children in foster care.

Case Example: Mrs. P. and her husband had been regarded as model foster parents. They had eight children living with them: an 18-year-old adopted daughter; two foster sisters, aged 16 and 15; 12-year-old Johnny, who had been at the Ps for a year and a half; 10-year-old Vincent, the new boy, who had been at the Ps for only 8 weeks; 6-year-old James, who had been with the Ps since birth and had been adopted; and Sally, 5, and her brother, Gregory, 3, who had been at the Ps since Gregory was an infant, and whom the Ps planned to adopt. The 15- and 16-year-old foster sisters had been sexually involved with older boys in a previous foster home; Johnny's father was in prison for sodomizing him and an older brother; and James had been sodomized at age 3 by a very disturbed foster brother who had also plotted to kill the Ps and steal their money.

Two very disruptive events preceded the sexual abuse in the P home. First, Mr. P's mother, who had Alzheimer's disease, was moved in. She was put into one of two downstairs bedrooms, the other being the P's bedroom. Prior to her arrival, Sally and Gregory had slept there. On the second floor there were two large bedrooms, one for boys and one for girls.

Second, Mr. P died suddenly of a heart attack. Despite the tragic loss of her husband, Mrs. P did not want to give up fostering. Because all of the children except perhaps Vincent appeared attached to the Ps, the Department of Social Services decided not to move any of them and tried to give Mrs. P as much support as they could to sustain her through her grief.

Gregory told Mrs. P and then his foster care worker that James had "poked him in the butt with his wiener." Sally corroborated his statement. When James was confronted, he vehemently denied that he had done anything to Gregory. However, he said that Johnny had poked him in the butt and was teaching them all to play with wieners. They would rub themselves and each other to see whose could get the biggest. James said Johnny also initiated contests to see who could pee the farthest. In addition, James said Johnny was doing sexual things with the girls. Later James denied that Johnny had sodomized him. Although Johnny denied any sexual activities, Vincent corroborated James's assertions regarding the masturbation and urination. No further information could be obtained regarding any sexual activity between Johnny and the girls or the sodomizing of James.

In this case, it is likely that the sexual abuse was precipitated by the sudden death of Mr. P. Mrs. P could not handle her own grief and the needs of grieving children. It is also clear that trying to handle eight children, all of whom had been maltreated, and a woman with Alzheimer's disease is too much for any foster parent. The risk was increased by the sleeping arrangements, which precluded adequate supervision. The dynamics of the sexual abuse of Gregory by James probably involved identification with the aggressor. It is noteworthy that Gregory was the same age as James when he was first sodomized. It is very likely that Johnny sodomized James, and the dynamics of this abuse would be similar. Although Johnny's initiation of the other boys into masturbation and his involvement with the girls may have stemmed from sexual precocity, sexual activity by 12-year-old boys is common. Its occurrence in foster care is nevertheless worrisome.

OPPORTUNISTIC SEXUAL ABUSE BY FOSTER PARENTS

The term *opportunistic sexual abuse* refers to victimization by an adult who in other circumstances would be unlikely to be sexual with a child. The term *circumstantial* is also used for this type of abuse. In most situations of this sort of abuse in foster care, the offender seems to be the foster father. Fifteen children (37.5%) in our cases were sexually abused by adults involved in opportunistic sexual abuse. Most victims were girls. Hobbs et al. (1999) reported that only about a quarter of the children in their study were sexually abused by a foster parent.

From what can be determined in these cases, the foster father does not have a history of sexual abuse and has raised or may be raising his own children without any sexual involvement. However, once he sexually abuses one child, he may repeat the pattern with other children.

Three characteristics of the fostering situation generally may play a role, and additional ones are found when sexually victimized children are reabused in foster care. One of the general factors that may increase risk is the fact that the "incest taboo" does not operate to inhibit sexual involvement between the foster parent and foster child. What this means is that the foster father does not have the same relationship or level of investment that he may have with biological children. Alternatively, he may use the absence of a biologic relationship as a rationalization for his attraction to and/or behavior toward the child. If the child is an adolescent, the prohibitions against sexual contact may be even weaker, and the foster father may regard this as an adulterous rather than abusive sexual liaison (P. Ryan, personal communication, 1989).

Regardless of the child's age, the foster father may rather abruptly find himself in a situation where he is having daily, close contact with someone else's child. He may have responsibility for such activities as bathing, disciplining, or putting the child to bed. Because the child is not his, this intimacy may be more likely to stimulate sexual arousal, and/or he may be more likely to act on these feelings. Furthermore, the fairly frequent changes in family composition, which regularly require development of new parent-child relationships, may exacerbate these dynamics. Related findings, such as unclear sexual boundaries (McFadden & Ryan, 1991) and foster children sharing bedrooms with family members (Zuravin et al., 1993), are noted in other studies.

The second characteristic found generally in the foster care context relates to husband-wife dynamics and fostering. Clinical observations suggest that often the woman gains more from fostering than the man. In many cases, she is the one who wants to become the foster parent, and the foster father agrees to it. The foster mother usually has greater responsibility and gains more in self-worth and a purpose for her life from fostering. The rewards she receives from being a foster parent may be greater than those she receives from being a wife. The demands may be great as well, so great that the foster mother has little time or energy left to meet her husband's needs, including his needs for nurturance and sex. He may be "left out in the cold." His use of the children for sex may reflect not only a need for emotional and sexual gratification but his anger at his wife for deserting him in favor of someone else's children.

A third and related characteristic of foster care is that, by its very nature, it results in a great deal of stress and numerous crises for the families involved. The foster parents may feel overwhelmed and unsupported, as often worker caseloads are so high that families have little contact with the professionals who are supposed to supervise them. In these emotionally draining circumstances, family members may regress and look to get their needs met by the foster children. These high-stress situations can play a role in sexual abuse by foster fathers (P. Ryan, personal communication, 1989). In addition, such tensions can be a factor in child-child sexual encounters. Children may react to the turmoil by being sexual with one another, and lack of adult supervision, because of preoccupation with other crises, may contribute to child-child sexual encounters.

As already noted, children who have been sexually abused already may be at greater risk than other children for sexual maltreatment in foster care. This heightened vulnerability arises not only from victims' behavior and attitudes but also from perceptions of the foster parent (usually the foster father). The presence of a sexually abused child in the home may lead a foster parent to consider the possibility of engaging in sex with a child when he had not considered doing so before. In fact, he may be titillated by thoughts of having sex with a child. These reactions may be enhanced by behaviors of the child, which he interprets as sexual invitations. Furthermore, because the child has already been sexually abused, the foster father may rationalize his behavior by reminding himself that he is not the first adult to have sex with the victim. He may therefore convince himself that the abuse will not be particularly harmful. In the following case example, a number of the predisposing factors are present.

Case Example: Carrie, 5, and Yvonne, 6, were placed in foster care following their reports that they were involved in group sex with their mother and father. Their first foster family asked that they be moved after 2 months because the foster parents could not tolerate their sexual play with each other. After supervised visits with their parents, they were usually caught in bed together engaging in mutual fondling.

Their second set of foster parents, Mr. and Mrs. T, were forewarned about their sexual acting out. The T home was a potential adoptive home for Carrie and Yvonne. Mrs. T, an "earth mother" type, appeared more eager to adopt than Mr. T. Mrs. T had been married previously and had a teenaged son. The Ts had not been able to conceive. Mrs. T was also licensed to do day care and took in several preschool-aged children.

The Ts lived in a large, old farmhouse. Carrie and Yvonne decided there were ghosts in the house and used their fear of ghosts as a reason for getting into bed with the Ts. No limits were set on this behavior. The children would wiggle down between the Ts and rub up against them. On these occasions, they would also sometimes describe their sexual abuse.

Mr. T later admitted that he found these revelations both disgusting and fascinating. He also confessed that on two occasions he was sexually aroused by the combination of their wiggly, warm bodies and their statements about sex with their parents. He said he found this to be a frustrating experience, stating he would have had sex with his wife if the children had not been there.

His first sexual interaction was to allow the girls to watch him urinate and then have them touch his penis. He said that initially when he did this, he thought it was a way to teach them not to be afraid of penises. Soon he was having them come into the bathroom with him when he had no intention of urinating. He would sit on the edge of the bathtub, take out his penis, and have them fondle him. He said that he never ejaculated during these encounters but would later masturbate while reliving the incidents or would think of them when he was having sex with Mrs. T.

In this case, it appears that Mrs. T is the one who is more invested in children. Mr. T probably felt he was the one responsible for their not having children of their own, adding to his sense of inadequacy and isolation. Moreover, the children were allowed to come physically between the Ts in bed. Mr. T's frustrated desire to have intercourse with his wife after having been aroused by the children is an interesting illustration of his needs not being met. His admission to being fascinated yet disgusted by the children's statements is a clear example of titillation. The children's behavior in bed may well have been a reflection of activities related to group sex with their parents.

PLANNED SEXUAL ABUSE OF FOSTER CHILDREN

Foster care, like other child-caring institutions, can be vulnerable to exploitation by those who are sexually attracted to children or desire to use them sexually for profit. Examples of other facilities that may be similarly at risk are day care centers (discussed in Chapter 8), camps, schools, and group care facilities. On the basis of our limited data, planned sexual abuse in foster care was found in two instances. Ryan and colleagues (P. Ryan, personal communication, 1989) found two or three possible cases. Other researchers do not report this type of abuse, but failure to identify such cases may be an artifact of the information available to them rather than the absence of planned sexual abuse. Six victims in our sample were sexually abused in planned sexual abuse; all were boys. There were other victims from the two sites where planned sexual abuse was identified who were not interviewed. One of the foster homes was reportedly part of a ring of sexually abusive foster parents that exploited over 100 children.

Persons whose primary sexual orientation is to children (pedophiles), individuals who are polymorphously perverse and whose perversions include sex with children, and people intending to use children in pornography or prostitution may seek licenses as foster parents. Fortunately, this kind of misuse of foster care seems to be rare. However, it may go on for years without detection.

Pedophiles are likely to be single male foster parents. In the polymorphous situation, there may be a couple involved, as well as others outside the family. Group sex may be practiced. An individual or a couple may be the foster parents when exploitation is the primary motive for becoming a foster parent. Our findings suggest that sometimes a sexually abusive foster parent will encourage other like-minded people to become foster parents. Similarly, occasionally a foster parent may develop a sex ring with current and former foster children and their friends.

An important issue is why an adult would choose foster care as the context for finding child sexual partners. First, foster care affords the adult a great deal of unsupervised access to the child, more, for example, than a school setting or an institutional placement. Illustrative of the role lack of supervision can play is the finding of Ryan et al. (1988) that sexual penetration while in foster care was associated with lack of contact between the worker and the child and lack of visitation between the child and the biological family. A second reason exploitative adults might choose foster care is that the child is more dependent upon the offender than in other contexts where the child goes home at night to parents. Third, the offender is likely to be aware of the unmet dependency and affective needs of abused and neglected children, which can be manipulated by the abuser to gain the victim's compliance and participation. The case example that follows illustrates some of the characteristics of this type of foster care sexual abuse.

Case Example: Mr. R was an X-ray technician. He had been married for 3 years to a woman who had had a 4-year-old son when they married. Ultimately it was learned that Mr. R's wife had divorced him after she found him fondling her son's penis. However, when this sexual abuse happened, she made no report.

Mr. R's first involvement with the Department of Social Services was after his divorce. He was a volunteer driver, taking children to various appointments, when he was not working. He then applied to be a foster parent. He faithfully attended the six orientation sessions and was regarded as a very good candidate for foster parenting. He asked that he be given only boys who were 6 years or older, stating that his single-parent status might present problems for girl children and that he did not know how to care for very young children. The Department of Social Services found these requests to be eminently sensible.

Initially, he would take only one boy at a time, and usually these placements lasted a long time because he also asked for children who were not likely to return home. After 5 years as a foster parent, he had his attic finished so he could accommodate more children. He then was licensed to take as many as five boys.

He sexually abused all the boys who were placed with him. He decided to expand from one boy to several after he met a pedophile, Mr. X, who ran a child sex ring. Mr. R found Mr. X through an ad in a pedophile magazine. Mr. X persuaded Mr. R to develop his own sex ring of foster children. Mr. X then got Mr. R to take pictures of some of his boys and sell the pictures to him. As time went on, Mr. R began to make a considerable profit from the sale of these pictures. He was also persuaded by Mr. X to share his boys with him.

Mr. R was caught when one of the boys refused to return to foster care after a visit to his grandparents. When Mr. R was interviewed, he confessed and asked for help. He also described how he got involved in sexual abuse of boys. He said that he had had a couple of sexual experiences with his nephews when he was in his 20s. When he married, he did not intend to molest his wife'sson but "fell into it naturally." He was very upset when she divorced him and felt quite deprived. However, he admitted that he missed the stepson more than the wife.

He said he decided to become a foster parent so he could find a boy to replace the stepson he had lost. Nevertheless, he said that the companionship was more important to him than the sex. He described himself as shy with the first boy, waiting several months before he started to stroke the boy's body. He declared that all of the boys enjoyed their sexual activities. He also said that he gave them a lot of individual attention and that he was sure that he "gave them much more than I took away." He was quite surprised at Kevin, the boy who told, because he said that he really loved Kevin and had just bought him a new 10-speed bicycle.

In this case, although Mr. R protests that he was looking for companionship more than sex from his victims, it was clear that the motivation for becoming a foster parent was to have access to young boys. He was also involved in a progression of sexual activity beginning with single victims, then multiple victims, and finally pornography. Although he does not appear to have become involved in picture taking for financial reasons, as time went on his financial status improved markedly because of it, so much so that he could afford a 10-speed bicycle for Kevin. In addition, like many pedophiles, Mr. R has cognitive distortions that allow him to believe that his abuse was not that harmful and that the boys benefited greatly from their relationships with him.

LIMITATIONS OF THE INFORMATION AND FINDINGS

It is important to conclude the discussion of types of sexual abuse in foster care with a cautionary note. The number of studies of sexual abuse in foster care is quite modest, and studies examined different variables. Our sample is relatively small and consists of clinical cases; the other research relies primarily on case record review. Thus, the findings are quite preliminary and probably do not cover the full spectrum of types of sexual abuse in foster care. Nevertheless, these preliminary findings may assist professionals in identifying sexual abuse in foster care and understanding its etiology.

What Can Be Done About the Problem?

When children are placed in foster care, it is to provide them with a living arrangement that is superior to the one from which they have been removed. The burden is on the professionals to ensure that children are not harmed further in foster care. Strategies that involve training, screening, case management, and intervention that might reduce the risk of sexual abuse in foster care will be described.

TRAINING AND GUIDANCE FOR FOSTER PARENTS

First, foster parents who care for sexually abused children require special training and guidance so they can address the unique needs of these children (Barth et al., 1994; Cavanaugh-Johnson, 1997; McFadden, 1989). Because sexual abuse is often not discovered until after a child has been placed, and because many parents who do not volunteer to care for sexually abused children end up doing so, all foster parents should receive this training (P. Ryan, personal communication, 1989). Ideally, they should receive both preparatory training and ongoing support when caring for a sexually abused child to address problems as they arise (Barth et al., 1994).

Training for foster parents can be delivered in a variety of formats. It might be part of a more general program for foster parents (McFadden, 1989; Ryan, 1984), or it might consist of classes focused specifically on fostering sexually abused children (Barth et al., 1994; Cavanaugh-Johnson, 1997; McFadden, 1989). Finally, preparation and support may be provided informally to individual foster families.

There are some psychoeducational training programs developed specifically for persons providing substitute care for children who have been sexually abused and children who may be at risk for sexual abuse or sexual acting out in care (Barth et al., 1994; Braga & Schimmer, 1993; Cavanaugh-Johnson, 1997; McFadden, 1989). For example, McFadden has prepared a very thoughtful training program and manual for foster parents caring for sexually abused children that consists of four sessions and supporting documents: (a) the world of the sexually abused child, (b) behaviors of the child who has been sexually abused, (c) protecting the child and our (the foster) family, and (d) the foster parents' therapeutic role (McFadden, 1984a, 1984b, 1989).

More recently, Barth et al. (1997) described a study of the use of psycho-educational groups with foster parents who had sexually abused children in their care. The program is well crafted and positively evaluated by participants. However, foster parents who received the intervention rated children in their care as more symptomatic upon completion of the intervention than before. In addition, participating foster parents rated their foster children significantly more symptomatic than foster parents who did not receive the intervention.

The following outline of a psychoeducational program is based upon our clinical experience with sexually victimized children and sexual abuse in foster care. Topics suggested are the following:

1. An exploration of attitudes and feelings about sexuality and sexual abuse

2. Normal childhood gender identification and sexual development

3. Normal adolescent gender identification and sexual development

4. Sexual sequelae of sexual abuse

5. Behavioral sequelae of sexual abuse

6. Strategies for management of sexual sequelae

7. Strategies for management of behavioral sequelae

8. Variations in victim attitudes and emotional reactions to the sexual abuse, the mother, and the offender

9. The causes of sexual abuse

10. Variations in the reactions of nonabusive parents to sexual abuse

11. The dynamics of relationships between sexually abused and nonabused siblings

12. How to handle visitation with the sexually abusive family

These sorts of training programs are what is hoped for, but because resources in child welfare are limited many communities will not be able to offer this level of support. However, in the absence of specialized training programs, the worker can provide individual families with guidance that can minimize the risk for sexual abuse in foster care and provide therapeutic intervention for sexually abused children. Families need, at minimum, information about the effects and sequelae of sexual abuse. Most important, they need to be made aware of the sexual behaviors of victimized children. Sexually abused children are likely to engage in excessive masturbation, consensual sexual interaction with other children, and behaviors that might be perceived as being seductive. In addition, sexual abuse victims are vulnerable to revictimization and becoming offenders.

Foster parents can be taught how to set limits when children engage in inappropriate sexual behavior (tell them to stop; a second infraction leads to a time-out; no unsupervised interaction with other children) and to make rules that will reduce the risk of child-child and other sexual abuse. An example is the following set of rules foster parents might make related to "privates":

1. It's okay to touch your privates, but do it in private—that is, in bed at night or in the bathroom.

2. Although you can touch your privates, you should not touch anyone else's privates.

3. No one else should touch your privates.

4. You do not show anyone else your privates (except the doctor, etc.).

5. No one else should show you his or her privates.

Though rules like these might seem to make children unduly self-conscious and inhibited about their bodies, such an outcome is preferable to sexual abuse in foster care.

Other rules may also be necessary, such as restrictions related to bathing, toileting, sleeping arrangements, and nudity around the house. These might be as follows:

1. One child at a time in the bathroom for bathing.

2. You must wear your bathrobe to and from the bathroom.

3. Only one child in the bathroom while toileting.

4. Only the foster mother can assist in wiping after toileting.

5. Only one child to a bed.

Foster parents should be encouraged to have family meetings in which the rules regarding these daily activities are discussed. As new children enter the home, the rules should be again discussed at a meeting involving all children.

Some provocative behaviors may not be appropriate for rules but are better handled by the foster parents when they arise. When children engage in inappropriate hugging, kissing, or lap sitting, the foster parent should be instructed to interrupt the behavior and either demonstrate or describe more appropriate interaction to the child. For example, a child might be told, "Kids don't put their tongues in people's mouths when they kiss. They kiss on the cheek." Similarly, a 10-year-old lap sitter might be told that she is too old to sit on the foster father's lap but that she can sit beside him on the couch when watching television.

Sometimes it will be appropriate to assist foster parents in developing behavioral child management interventions to extinguish inappropriate sexual interaction and foster appropriate interactions. The case example illustrates foster parent management of some of these sexual behaviors.

Case Example: The Gs were new foster parents. They had two children of their own. They were asked to care for Sally, 6, who had been sexually abused by her father and her grandfather. Prior to that abuse, her mother had viciously physically abused her, and custody had been given to her father.

The first problem the Gs had with Sally was her open discussion of her abuse with school staff, classmates, neighbors, and their children. They were concerned about the effect of these disclosures on Sally's ability to make friends, on their relationships in the community, and on their children. With the assistance of their caseworker and Sally's therapist, they praised Sally for being brave and telling about the abuse but advised her that she should limit her discussion about it to them, the caseworker, and her therapist. As far as they were able to tell, Sally stopped telling everyone she met about the sexual abuse.

However, they began to notice that Sally was unusually attentive to the toileting habits of their 2-year-old son, Jason. She would follow him into the bathroom and want to help him. She also expressed a great deal of interest in his "rootie" and wanted to know why it was so small. The foster parents explained to Sally that Jason was learning to go peepee by himself and that it was important that he do this alone. If he needed help, Mrs. G would help him. At the suggestion of the therapist, the Gs made a general rule that only one person should be in the bathroom at a time.

In addition, Mr. G expressed discomfort with the way Sally wiggled around when she sat on his lap. He felt that she was trying to locate his penis and rub her crotch on it. Initially he was instructed that he should tell her that she had to sit still if she wanted to stay on his lap. This appeared to work for a few minutes, but then she seemed to forget and start wiggling. He then was told to remove her from his lap when she resumed wiggling and tell her that she had to sit beside him if she was going to wiggle. Eventually the combination of instruction not to wiggle and removal if she started again extinguished her wiggling. She was able to sit on his lap without masturbating.

In this case, the child had a number of hypersexual behaviors that were very concerning to the foster parents. These were dealt with fairly successfully so that Sally was not involved in reabuse and the placement was not disrupted. However, ideally, the Gs should have received prior instruction on how to care for a sexually abused child, and probably their first foster child should not have been a sexually abused one with Sally's level of disturbance.

SCREENING OF FOSTER PARENTS

A question that is sometimes asked is whether it is possible to screen foster parent applicants for potential or actual sexual abusers. It appears that some sexually abusive situations could be avoided by screening, but most cannot. One problem that makes screening difficult is that there are very few predictors of sexually abusive behavior. A second problem is that family dynamics as well as individual characteristics may play a role in sexual abuse. In an attempt to understand how foster family characteristics might play a role in sexual abuse in foster care, Ryan et al. (1988) examined a number of factors (e.g., whether the home was in compliance with licensing standards, the total number of children in the home, prior substantiated maltreatment allegations against the family, and the foster parent holding strong religious views about discipline). They found that none of the factors they examined were related to sexual abuse of children in foster care.

There is really only one characteristic that is clearly indicative of risk of sexual abuse as a foster parent: having sexually abused a child in the past. Sexual abuse is regarded as a chronic condition for which there is no real cure but only enhanced capability to control (e.g., Faller, 1988a; Groth, 1979; Quinsey, 1993; Ward, Hudson, & Marshall, 1995). Therefore, if a person has a history of sex offenses, he or she should not be licensed as a foster parent.

Unfortunately, most applicants will not disclose such a history readily. However, it is worthwhile asking about possible sexual offenses within the larger context of an extensive personal history. In asking about intimate rela-tionships and sexual activity, the worker can indirectly ask about sexual abuse. Revealing information may be obtained by inquiring about the oldest and the youngest sexual partner he or she has had (Faller, 1988a). Depending upon the age of the respondent, an age gap of 5 or more years is cause for further inves-tigation. Ryan (personal communication, 1989) suggests that letting applicants know that sexual abuse (as well as other types of maltreatment) are issues case-workers monitor may discourage potential abusers, especially pedophiles, from pursuing licenses as foster parents. In addition, although the majority of sex offenders are male, past sexual activity should be explored with potential foster mothers as well.

Because it is very unlikely that sexual abusers will be candid about their victimizing, other sources of information must be sought. Police and protective services records need to be examined. It is important not to rely merely on state abuse registers or state police records because frequently these are incomplete. An allegation of sexual abuse that has been denied will not be in the state register, but the county may have a record. Similarly, a local law enforcement agency may have records that the state police do not have. In addition, if the person has lived previously in another state, information from that location should be sought. Pedophiles who have lost their licenses as child care providers or who have been investigated by the police have been known to move to another state and again attempt to gain access to children. Moreover, it is often important to investigate records in addition to those of protective services and the police—for example, records of licensing agencies and employment records.

Another way a past history of sexual abuse may be uncovered is by taking a careful history of the potential foster parent's past activities with children. Persons in responsible positions related to these activities should be contacted. If these persons are not listed as references by the applicant, the licensing worker should ask for permission to contact them.

As part of screening, other possible correlates of sexually abusive behavior, described below, should also be explored. However, positive findings are certainly not conclusive of risk for sexual abuse. Rather, they should lead to further exploration and be weighed along with other factors in making licensing decisions.

It is important to ask if the potential foster parent was sexually abused as a child. A foster father with such a history may be more vulnerable to becoming an abuser, whereas a foster mother may be at greater risk for allowing children in her care to be victimized sexually. As with information about adult sexual activity with children, any history of childhood sexual abuse should be ascertained as the interviewer collects information about the person's general history. However, a finding of sexual abuse in childhood should not rule out foster parenthood, for many excellent and very sensitive foster parents were sexually abused as children. Nevertheless, if an applicant has been sexually abused, the licensing worker needs to explore this experience in some detail and to determine its effects. Sometimes a potential foster parent will need additional assistance to cope with this abuse, and other times it will be a contraindication for foster parenthood.

McCormack and Selvaggio (1989) have devised an instrument for detecting pedophiles who apply to be Big Brothers. It includes several questions about sexual victimization during childhood, questions that probe for social isolation, and questions that might reveal attitudes indicative of sexual attraction to children (e.g., a belief that children are innocent, a preference for the company of children). This is not a validated instrument but nevertheless an important first step in developing a method for systematically screening out pedophiles applying for child care positions.

A second possible correlate of risk for sexual abuse may be having been maltreated physically or otherwise emotionally deprived as a child. Sometimes adults with such a history will lack the skills for showing affection and may manifest their caring for children in a sexual way. These adults may also be at risk for being physically abusive. However, as with a history of sexual victimization, such a finding should not automatically disqualify the applicant. Rather, it should lead the worker to explore the applicant's relationships, both with children and adults, for evidence that he or she has the ability to show affection appropriately and, with children, to set limits.

A third possible correlate of risk for sexual abuse is sexual dysfunction. Again, sexual problems should not automatically result in rejection as a foster parent. Nevertheless, the worker should bear in mind possible patterns in the sexuality of offenders and their families. The first is evidence of the offender having discomfort with adult sexual relationships. The second is hypersexuality on the part of the parent or the family. The latter is evidenced by a description of sexual activity several times a day and having several sexual partners. These are red flags both because they may signal a risk of sexual abuse and because children may observe adult sexual activities. Licensing workers should also ask about aberrant sexual activities (e.g., group sex, voyeurism, sadomasochism, cross-dressing, and exposure). Persons with these habits should not be foster parents.

Other characteristics that might indicate a risk of sexual abuse, as well as being contraindications for foster parenthood, are substance abuse, criminal activity, violent behavior, and mental illness. Though none of these is as directly related to sexual abuse as the factors just discussed, they all suggest deficits in the ability to foster.

THE FOSTER CHILD'S CASEWORKER

Ongoing support is also needed for abused children in foster care. Some public child welfare agencies recognize the special needs of the child in care and structure service delivery so there is a caseworker whose role is dedicated to the child. Among other issues, this worker is alert to the possibility of abuse and adjustment difficulties in foster care. However, in many public child welfare systems, the foster care worker has too many and conflicting roles. He or she is the worker for the biological parents, assisting them toward reunification; the worker for the foster parents, helping them handle foster children; and finally the worker for the child. Foster children who were maltreated by their biological parents and are being abused in their foster families may not see this worker as a confidant but rather as someone aligned with the adults in the child's life.

When the public agency caseworker has too many responsibilities, someone else, who may be a therapist or a caseworker in a voluntary agency, should be assigned to the child. This professional should be alert to signs of abuse in care and also careful to structure his or her role so that the child perceives this professional as a safe person to talk to about problems in foster care as well as with biological parents.

Exit Interviews for Foster Children

Ryan (personal communication, 1989) suggests a client satisfaction survey for children who are being moved from one foster home to another, who are being returned home, or who are going to some other living arrangement. This practice would not prevent sexual abuse of the children being interviewed, but it could prevent future victimization. Of course, caseworkers have responsibility for ongoing assessment of children's functioning in foster care, but, for a variety of reasons, victims might be more reluctant to disclose sexual abuse while they are still residents of the foster home. A postplacement interview could focus on a range of aspects of the foster home, not merely sexual practices.

THE IMPACT OF FUNDING ISSUES ON SAFETY IN FOSTER CARE

The absence of sufficient funding prevents the assurance of child safety in foster care. Without adequate resources, foster parents do not receive a decent wage. In fact, they barely receive enough to meet the child's basic needs—and sometimes they do not receive even that. This limits both the number and the types of people willing and able to be foster parents. Another consequence is that professionals cannot really expect the time commitment from foster parents that is necessary if they are to be part of the therapeutic process for the child. For example, it is unreasonable to expect a foster father to come to meetings if he is the sole wage earner in the family and the family is not compensated adequately for fostering. Licensing as a therapeutic foster home and differential compensation based upon difficulty of care are appropriate solutions to this problem.

However, a second impact of inadequate funding relates to the capability of supporting foster parents. Frequently, the child welfare worker caseloads are very large, and caseworkers do not have the time to provide the needed supervision and support for foster parents trying to deal with the special needs of sexually abused children. In addition, without funding, there can be no parenting classes, and it will be impossible to provide the resources to integrate foster parents into the treatment of the child. Smaller foster care caseloads, respite care, special classes in handling sexually abused children, and ongoing supports (Hobbs et al., 1999) are good financial investments.

Ironically, paying foster parents for their services and providing adequate support for them is much cheaper than institutional care, which is often what sexually abused children who are retraumatized in foster care ultimately receive. Currently, however, many foster parents are left with 24-hour-a-day, 7-day-a-week responsibility often for quite damaged children without adequate compensation and support. Mental health professionals must look beyond the individual sexually abused child in their advocacy and advocate for foster children in general. Taking the broader view is essential if foster care is to make a difference for children rather than being an institution with potential iatrogenic effects.

Conclusion

Foster care and other substitute care arrangements may possess characteristics that increase risk for sexual abuse. First, children requiring foster care may be more vulnerable to sexual exploitation because of past physical and emotional maltreatment and past sexual abuse. However, the victim should not be viewed as the major contributor to maltreatment in foster care. Structural characteristics of foster care and attributes of the foster parent and family play a greater role. These include the nature of foster care as a familylike living arrangement in which the incest taboo is not present; the relative lack of supervision of the adult-child relationship when compared with other substitute care; possible differential gratification that husband and wife receive from fostering; and the high level of stress inherent in foster care.

Three different types of sexual abuse in foster care have been described. The first is *child-child sexual abuse*, which usually entails children who were sexually victimized previously becoming perpetrators in the foster care context. The second is *opportunistic sexual abuse*, in which an adult, usually a foster father, who does not have a previous history of sexually abusing children becomes involved in sexual activity with a foster child. Structural factors, noted above, and child behavior may lead to sexual arousal in the foster parent and then to abuse. Finally, there is *planned sexual abuse* in foster care, in which persons seek to be foster parents with the intention of sexually abusing the children for whom they are given responsibility. These persons may be pedophiles or persons who intend to exploit children sexually for money.

Mental health professionals and others must do whatever is possible to prevent children who have been traumatized already from being further maltreated in foster care. This can be done by providing support and guidance to foster parents who are caring for sexually abused children, by screening foster care applicants for potential sexual abusers, and through advocacy for adequate funding and support for foster parents dealing with sexually abused children.

Note

1 For a description of the procedures employed to substantiate allegations of sexual abuse, see Faller (1988a).

9

Sexual Abuse in Day Care

In the intervening years since the publication of the first edition of this book, the public perception and, to some extent, the professional perception of allegations of sexual abuse in day care have been transformed. Whereas 10 years ago the issue was the danger of day care because of its potential as a context for sexual abuse, today allegations of sexual abuse in day care elicit a skeptical response. Currently, the first reactions to a report of sexual abuse in day care are often concerns for the accused; considerations of the suggestibility of young children (Ceci & Bruck, 1995); consideration of the possibility that parents have overreacted to their children's behavior or statements and asked leading questions; and a query about whether the children have been interviewed inexpertly by professionals (Raskin & Yuille, 1989). Thus, the typical response may be to protect the accused adult rather than the children in day care.

This shift in reaction derives from a number of factors. First, those accused have mounted vigorous defenses, sometimes funded by day care centers' insurers (Faller, 1988d). Second, in recent years, the number of analogue studies structured to demonstrate preschool-aged children's suggestibility has grown, as has the readily available group of expert witnesses who will testify to vulnerabilities of young children as witnesses (e.g., Bruck, Ceci, & Hembrooke, 1998; Ceci & Bruck, 1993). Third, this skepticism is also related to the allegations themselves. Many reports of sexual abuse in day care involve collaboration among several perpetrators, scores and occasionally a hundred or more victims, and sometimes extreme and sadistic abuse (Finkelhor et al., 1988). Some of this abuse is described as ritualistic and satanic. Moreover, some convictions of individuals incarcerated for sex crimes against children in day care in the 1980s have been reversed on appeal (e.g., *New Jersey v. Kelly Michaels*, 1993; *North Carolina v. Robert Kelly*, 1992). Finally, the media, evidently having exhausted the potential of portraying the horrors of sexual victimization in day care, now have turned to exposés of allegedly false accusations involving day care (e.g., Bikel, 1993; Pfeiffer, 1999; Rabinowitz, 1999).

Though others' perceptions of the problems of sexual abuse in day care have changed, mine essentially have not. I still regard sexual abuse in day care as a genuine phenomenon and think all reports need to be investigated carefully. Day care abuse, on the basis of the available information, shares characteristics of other types of sexual abuse but is also unique because of the young age and vulnerable developmental stage of its victims, the severity of the abuse described, and the relatively high proportion of female offenders (Finkelhor et al., 1988; Kelley, Brandt, & Waterman, 1993; Schumacher & Carlson, 1999).

In this chapter, the issue that was paramount 10 years ago, the risk of sexual abuse in day care, will be addressed. In addition, causes of day care sexual abuse, variations of patterns of sexual abuse in day care, the immediate and longer-term effects of day care sexual victimization, and interventions, both preventative and therapeutic, will be covered. The literature to be drawn upon includes studies of day care sexual abuse (e.g., Bybee & Mowbray, 1993; Faller, 1988d; Finkelhor et al., 1988; Kelley, 1989, 1990, 1994, 1996; Waterman et al., 1993), journalistic books that recount day care abuse (Crewdson, 1988; Hechler, 1988; Hollingsworth, 1986; Mansell, 1990), and reviews of the abuse in day care literature (Kelley et al., 1993; Schumacher & Carlson, 1999).

More specifically, I will draw upon a number of important pieces of research. The first is a national study conducted by Finkelhor et al. (1988) that involves case findings, use of multiple sources, and key informant interviews of substantiated cases from 270 day care centers identified over a 3-year period from 1983 to 1985. A second important study is that of Kelley (1989, 1990, 1994, 1996), whose cases are composed of samples of ritually abused (N:35), sexually abused (N:32), and nonabused (N:67) children attending day care. Data were collected on types of abuse and the impact of the abuse on both the children (Achenbach's Child Behavior Checklist [CBCL]) and their parents (Parenting Stress Index). A third important source of information is a 6-year federally funded study using 42 data collection measures. The sample consists of alleged sexual abuse victims from Manhattan Beach, California (including the McMartin Preschool) (N:82), where children were allegedly sexually abused by multiple abusers and experienced ritualistic abuse, and from a day care center in Reno, Nevada (N:15), involving one perpetrator, who admitted to the abuse. This study has a comparison group of Manhattan Beach children in day care (N:37) (Waterman, Kelly, McCord, & Oliveri, 1989a, 1989b; Waterman et al., 1993). Fourth, another federally funded study of one center in western Michigan with approximately 100 reported victims will be referenced (Bybee & Mowbray, 1993; Valliere et al., 1988). Finally, I will draw on my clinical and research experience at the University of Michigan with 61 day care cases, which is in part reflected in an article (Faller, 1988d), and on my knowledge gained as a consultant on other day care cases.[1]

How Dangerous Is Day Care?

In their pioneering national study of sexual abuse in day care, Finkelhor et al. (1988) arrived at an estimate of the incidence of sexual victimization in day care, as well as a comparison of the risk of being sexually abused in day care contrasted to risk of sexual abuse at home. Taking their data from 1985, these researchers projected that sexual abuse occurred in 267 centers that year and involved 1,300 children. Although the figure seems high, it is important to appreciate that there were 229,000 licensed day care programs in the country at that time (Finkelhor et al., 1988). Comparing these findings to other reports of sexual abuse is also instructive. In 1985, there were 120,000 cases of sexual abuse substantiated by child protection agencies (American Association for the Protection of Children, 1987).

On the basis of a calculation of the relative risk of sexual abuse in day care and at home, Finkelhor et al. (1988) concluded that 5.5 children per 10,000 enrolled in day care centers were sexually abused but that 8.9 children per 10,000 under the age of 6 were sexually abused at home. Although these figures indicate that risk is greater at home, it must be remembered that children in day care are also at home. What these statistics indicate is that although sexual abuse in day care is not rampant, it poses a significant problem for young children.

Causes of Sexual Abuse in Day Care

Although there are some theories about why adults choose to sexually abuse children in day care, any understanding of the motivation for this sort of abuse is still speculative because few offenders allow Child Protective Services (CPS) or police to interview them, and fewer still confess (Waterman et al., 1993). Many deny vehemently that they have abused children years into their prison sentences (Mansell, 1990). Even those who do confess may later recant (Hollingsworth, 1986).

In the Country Walk case (Hollingsworth, 1986), where a husband and wife sexually abused children in their baby-sitting service, the wife confessed. Her testimony indicated that the decision to open the business was in order to procure children for her husband to molest. Nevertheless, after she discovered she would receive a prison sentence herself, she recanted her earlier confession.

Alarmed by the apparent explosion of sexual abuse in day care in the 1980s, professionals have proposed that pedophiles conferred and determined to target children in day care because, given their young age, they would not be able to provide persuasive accounts of their abuse. The argument continues that, with the increasing awareness of the problem of sexual abuse and the increasing willingness to believe children's allegations, older children were risky targets. Therefore, pedophiles were choosing younger victims, perhaps not out of preference but out of prudence. Similarly, the rather sudden discovery of ritual and satanic abuse in day care has led to theories that preschool children are viewed as uncorrupted and therefore as desirable targets for satanists, who particularly relish harming and defiling the innocent. I know of no source other than speculation to support either of these theories.

Although the emergence of sexual abuse in day care invites such concerns, perhaps more mundane explanations can suffice. Day care is a recent phenomenon because, before World War II, women remained at home to care for preschool children. Thus, until recently there were no reports of sexual abuse in day care centers or homes because there were few such institutions.

Institutions that allow adults and adolescents ready access to children, especially unsupervised access, may be at risk for being settings for sexual abuse. These institutions include the family, the stepfamily, the Boy Scouts, Big Brothers, overnight and day camp, residential treatment, and programs for delinquent youth. Settings such as these may be likely places for circumstantial sexual abuse and may be selected as places of work and volunteer activities by pedophiles, individuals whose preferred sexual object is a child.

Finkelhor et al. (1988) reported that 29% of the abusers in their sample were attributed pedophilic motives; however, they regarded this as an overestimate because it was based upon the reports of professionals involved, some of whom had quite broad definitions of the term *pedophile*. About a third of the children in day care cases seen in the program I direct at the University of Michigan appeared to have been sexually maltreated by at least one person who would be defined as a pedophile.

There may be characteristics specific to day care that result in sexual abuse. It is possible that disturbed individuals who desire to inflict harm on children choose day care as a context to do so because these children will not be able to resist. Cases in which the abuse is sadistic and accompanied by physical abuse suggest such a dynamic. Although coercion may be designed either to gain cooperation with the sexual acts or to prevent children from telling, in some instances it seems to be gratuitous cruelty or terrorizing. When referring to the circumstances of alleged victimization at Manhattan Beach preschools,

Waterman et al. (1993) described these abusers as intent on terrorizing the children.

Case Example: In one multivictim case, a child described the abuser pulling a rug out from under his friend as he was standing on it. The offender then laughed when his friend fell on his face and got a bloody nose. Another victim of the same offender said the man threw him across the room against the wall and then made him crawl on his knees to the man's penis and kiss it.

The offender in this case example is described not only as sexually abusing children but also as apparently taking delight in hurting and humiliating them.

Finally, in a small percentage of day care cases, children report being used in pornography and for prostitution (Faller, 1988d; Finkelhor et al., 1988; Kelley et al., 1993). These would be cases in which the motive for sexual abuse in day care is profit. One reason that unscrupulous day care providers might be tempted into the production of pornography and offering children as prostitutes is that day care is a financially marginal institution. It is hard to make a living in day care because of the high cost of providing quality care and the low income of the clientele: that is, the adults who must use day care. By exploiting children in one's care, one could turn a shaky business into a lucrative one. However, to my knowledge, there is no report in the literature of this set of circumstances being documented.

In about 10% of the cases seen at the University of Michigan, children described picture taking or being required to have sex with someone other than a child or a worker at the center. It was not possible to substantiate that the pictures were actually sold, and in some cases pictures were reportedly used for other purposes. For example, at one center, several children reported that the offender took pictures and threatened to show them to the parents or the police should the children disclose the sexual abuse. Finkelhor et al. (1988) also reported numerous cases where the children said pictures were taken, but there was a similar difficulty in determining whether these were actually sold. However, the authors noted that in one case a parent reported seeing copies of photos in Mexico. Similarly, in their review of literature on sexual abuse in day care, Kelley et al. (1993) noted that although children describe pictures being taken of them engaged in sexual acts, these pictures are rarely found.

In cases seen at the University of Michigan, a few children have described both people coming to the center to have sex with children and being taken themselves to other places to have sex with strangers. In one instance, two 4-year-old girls said they were taken to a place where they had to fellate three men. In addition, they stated that men gave the teacher money and that afterward the teacher bought them candy with some of the money.

Patterns of Sexual Abuse in Day Care

Researchers and practitioners have identified variations in patterns of sexual abuse in day care. In describing these, some writers have focused solely on day care centers, whereas others have also included day care homes, both licensed and unlicensed. In her research using a state database of registered sex offenders, Margolin (1991) found day care homes to pose greater risk for sexual abuse than day care centers and preschools. Although standards and licensing vary by state and indeed by community, generally a day care home not only is in a person's home but is limited to caring for about six children.

The variations of sexual abuse in child care settings to be described in this section reflect the literature on sexual abuse in day care and my practice experience but are preliminary. The variations are as follows: (a) single offender/single victim, (b) single offender/multiple victims, and (c) multiple offenders/multiple victims.[2]

SINGLE OFFENDER/SINGLE VICTIM

Cases that fall into this category by definition involve one adult and one child when they are discovered. Information in the literature (e.g., Margolin, 1991; Schumacher & Carlson, 1999) and my experience suggest that the cases appear dyadic because this is the offender's first victim (as may be the case with an adolescent offender), because other cases are not detected at the time, or because the individual is a serial offender. In the latter instance, the offender may develop a special relationship involving sexual abuse with one child that may continue as long as the child is willing to cooperate and is at day care. When that child is no longer accessible, another may be groomed and recruited.

Offenders who are classified as single offenders with single victims are often peripheral to or not directly involved in the running of the day care program (Faller, 1988d; Schumacher & Carlson, 1999). They include the following types of people: janitors who work at the center; bus drivers; volunteers spending a limited time there; relatives of the staff, including adolescent sons, husbands, and grandfathers; and friends of the staff, including boyfriends and neighbors. Finkelhor et al. (1988) found less trauma associated with having been abused by an offender whose was peripheral to the day care program.

In the cases I have seen, most of these abusers were male and most of their victims were female (close to 90%). Such offenders did not seem to have chosen to associate themselves with day care in order to have access to children for sexual purposes. Thus, they fall into the classification of "circumstantial offenders." Moreover, most of the cases involving single offenders and single victims were in family day care homes or centers run out of or attached to the director's home. These abusers obtained access to children by virtue of their relationship to the day care staff. However, as Finkelhor et al. (1988) pointed out, sometimes people peripheral to the running of the center who abuse children are given responsibilities for which they are unqualified because of staff shortages.

> *Case Example*: Mrs. J had three adolescent children, two boys and a girl, and ran a day care home. She cared for some children of relatives and some children from the neighborhood. Both her daughter and her sons helped out with the day care. Sometimes they were left in charge of the children because Mrs. J was also a substitute bus driver for the school district. Her oldest son, Jake, seemed to enjoy helping out, as did her daughter. But Leroy, her youngest child, resented being asked to help out. He preferred to "run with his friends."
>
> When Jake was 15, a single mother withdrew her 7-year-old daughter, Angela, from Mrs. J's day care home because she said Jake was too interested in Angela. When Mrs. J asked specifically what the mother's concerns were, she said she couldn't say. When Mrs. J asked Jake, he laughed and said Angela used to try to watch him when he went to the bathroom to "take a piss." Mrs. J dropped the issue, feeling satisfied her son had done nothing inappropriate.
>
> A year later, Jake was caught in the back seat of a car with an 8-year-old-girl from the neighborhood. He had taken her dress off and was rubbing his penis all over her body.
>
> When police interviewed family members, Leroy told them of the earlier case of Angela. Police then interviewed Angela. She described Jake following her into the bathroom, when Mrs. J left him in charge, and making her take off her clothes. He then touched her private parts and rubbed his penis against her bare skin until he ejaculated. He told her he wouldn't put his penis inside her because she was a virgin.

In the J case, Jake had ready access to young children because his mother provided day care. He selected one child as his victim. Later, after he no longer had access to her, he engaged in comparable activity with a child who was not in his mother's day care home but lived in his neighborhood. It is instructive that the case was not discovered until Jake abused outside the day care situation.

SINGLE OFFENDER/MULTIPLE VICTIMS

Although not the most sensational, the most widely identified type of day care center case involves a single offender who sexually abuses multiple victims (e.g., Faller, 1988d; Finkelhor et al., 1988; Margolin, 1991). Of cases reported, these abusers are most likely to have a regular role in day care provision. They may be teachers, sometimes directors, or teacher's aides who work regular hours at the center. Such cases are characteristic of day care centers rather than day care homes. The offenders operate solo and, therefore, are concerned about keeping their abusive behavior secret from other staff. They are likely to victimize children when taking them to the bathroom, at nap time, and early or late in the day, when there are fewer staff around (Finkelhor et al., 1988; Schumacher & Carlson, 1999).

In cases seen at the University of Michigan, most of these offenders are male. Finkelhor et al. (1988) reported some women in this role, and the Wee Care case in New Jersey involved allegations against a single female (Mansell, 1990). In these cases, there are multiple victims. They may be male or female or both, evidently depending upon the offender's preference. In my sample, the proportions of male and female victims were equal, but in some cases the offender abused only boys, in others only girls, and in still others children of both sexes (Faller, 1988d).

Cases seen at the University of Michigan that fell into this category involved, not extreme threats to prevent children from disclosing, but rather reliance on the relationship. Two threats reported by children were "Don't tell or I'll get in trouble" and "Don't tell, or your mom and dad won't let you come back here anymore." In yet another case, the child was given a toy soldier as a bribe to prevent disclosure, which aroused the parents' suspicion and caused them to question their child. He disclosed the abuse.

These perpetrators appear to be pedophiles, either naive or calculating ones. Their sexual maltreatment is not usually characterized by other harm to their victims. Although some cases involve group sex, most consist of dyadic encounters. The latter pattern may be a consequence of the need to maintain secrecy.

Case Example: Mr. T had two special-needs children and a developmentally delayed wife. The family was on public assistance, and Mr. T had to satisfy a work requirement to receive the public assistance. He was hired by a day care center run by a women's advocacy center to fix some broken playground equipment. He did a very competent job and then was asked to do more repairs. He interacted warmly with the children in the day care center and appeared quite comfortable around them.

Because of his experience as a parent and his evident ability to relate to children, Mr. T was hired as a day care aide by the women's advocacy center. His responsibilities included taking children to the bathroom, which was in the women's advocacy center and not directly in the day care center, supervising the 3-year-olds at naptime, and caring for children who couldn't participate in activities planned for the whole group. For example, if a child wasn't feeling well, or a parent was to pick a child up early, the child was left with Mr. T while the other children were on outings.

Mr. T was reported to have sexually abused more than 20 children over an 11-month period. These children were both boys and girls. Most of the reports involved fondling. In addition, however, with some boys he played the "baby game," which consisted of picking the boy up during naptime, rocking him in his arms, and sucking his penis. However, he also reportedly sodomized three boys, and he required at least two girls to suck his penis.

The abuse by Mr. T was reported by a boy who had just turned 5. During the course of the investigation, it was discovered that Mr. T had an open protective services case for neglect and a conviction of statutory rape as an adolescent. He was tried and convicted on the testimony of the 5-year-old boy and sentenced to 20 years in the state prison.

It appears that the women's advocacy center relied upon their observations and judgment about Mr. T instead of following normal procedure, which would have been to conduct a records check before hiring him in a child-caring capacity. The fact that he molested so many children in such a short period of time suggests that he has a fixation on children as sexual objects.

MULTIPLE ABUSERS/MULTIPLE VICTIMS

Multiple-abuser/multiple-victim cases are the ones that have received extensive media attention, initially highlighting the horrors of the abuse and later challenging the veracity of the allegations. The McMartin Preschool (Crewdson, 1988; Hechler, 1988; Waterman et al., 1989a, 1989b, 1993), Fells Acres, Small World (Bybee & Mowbray, 1993), the Presidio case (Ehrensaft, 1992), Little Rascals (Bikel, 1993), and Country Walk (Crewdson, 1988; Hollingsworth, 1986) are all instances in which several children described abuse by several perpetrators. For the most part, this type of abuse appears limited to day care centers, although Burgess, Baker, and Hartman (1996) described a case in which husband, wife, and their two teenaged children sexually abused preschoolers and school-aged children in a day care home.

In centers where multiple abusers are identified, the issue of secrecy seems less pronounced because many staff may be involved. Nevertheless, there are still concerns about parents encountering adults involved in sexual activities with children. Children report special alerts used by staff when a parent approaches or enters the center. Investigators report identifying secluded places in centers where abuse would not be observed easily.

These are the contexts in which women are likely to be reported as sexually maltreating children (Faller, 1988d; Finkelhor et al., 1988; Kelley et al., 1993; Waterman et al., 1989a, 1989b, 1993), although there may be men in these situations as well, sometimes taking leadership roles.

Victims are usually both male and female. However, in multiple-abuser/ multiple-victim cases, unlike single-perpetrator/multiple-victim cases, the sex of the victim does not seem to depend upon the proclivities of an individual perpetrator. All such cases in my sample (Faller, 1988d), those on which consultation was provided, and most multiple-perpetrator reports in the literature involve victims of both sexes. These are the situations in which group sex and coercion of children to have sex with one another are reported (Bybee & Mowbray, 1993; Faller, 1988d; Kelley et al., 1993). These are also the cases in which group sex games may be played (Faller, 1988d; Schumacher & Carlson, 1999).

Multiple-abuser centers are ones where there seems to be a plan by the offenders to sexually abuse children. Possible motivations include sexual attraction to children, profit, a desire to harm children, or an ideology that supports ritualistic abuse. It is these cases that raise questions about offenders opening centers in order to sexually abuse children. Most cases where allegations of picture taking and child prostitution are alleged are multiple perpetrator/ multiple victim (Faller, 1988d; Kelley et al., 1993).

Finally, most of the situations where children are threatened sadistically and where ritual abuse is alleged occur in these centers. Not surprisingly, children sexually maltreated in multiple-perpetrator/multiple-victim sites evidence the most psychological trauma and symptomatology (Kelley, 1994; Waterman et al., 1989a, 1989b, 1993).

Case Example: The Little People day care center was started by a licensed teacher, Miss Nancy, and her husband, Mr. George, in a small, middle-class community. The families who used the center were grateful for the service and assisted Miss Nancy and Mr. George in building a purpose-built center to replace the older building in which Little People was housed initially. In addition to Miss Nancy, the director, and Mr. George, a day care aide, there were four young single women serving as day care aides. To address the needs of dual-career families in the community, Little People developed an after-school program for school-aged children. The public school bus dropped off the school-aged children at the center instead of taking them home.

About 3 years after Little People opened, there was a report that a 6-year-old boy who had attended the center had sexually molested a 4-year-old girl. When police interviewed the boy, he said he had learned about "wieners in baginas" at Little People from Mr. George. However, the victim's mother thought the boy had learned it at home. He came from a single-parent family and his mother had had a series of boyfriends. Law enforcement referred the case to CPS, which could not substantiate sexual abuse because the boy recanted his story about Mr. George.

A year later Little People was reported to day care licensing because a parent had observed Miss Nancy kissing children on their mouths; the parent didn't think this was appropriate. When licensing investigated, they discovered some code violations related to the qualifications of the staff and staff/student ratio and put the center on probation. Miss Nancy was told not to kiss the children on their mouths.

Six months later, there was another police investigation involving six children who reported that Mr. George had been mean to them and had sucked their privates. Eventually more than 100 children were interviewed, and more than 60 made disclosures. Over the next 5 years, 10 of the children who had originally denied sexual victimization made disclosures.

There were allegations involving both Mr. George and Miss Nancy as well as the coercive inclusion of other teachers in group sexual activities. The children reported physical, psychological, and sexual abuse. Older children were required to engage in sexual activities with younger ones. Pictures of the sexual activities were taken, and the children were told that the pictures would be shown to the police or their parents if they disclosed.

Two specific case situations will be described, one of early disclosure and one of delayed disclosure. Alice was a 2½-year-old girl who attended Little People. She told about abuse in her second interview. She was 3 at the time. Her 5- and 6-year-old brothers also attended Little People. Her brothers were coerced consecutively to have intercourse with Alice, and their pictures were taken. They were told that if they told, they would be sent to jail, especially once their parents were shown the pictures of them having sex with Alice. Mr. George treated Alice as his favorite and told her that he loved her. However, he also digitally penetrated her.

In addition, Alice reported the following incident. Mr. George told her he had killed the center's pet rabbit and then made it into rabbit stew. She said she was required to eat the rabbit stew, declaring that it had bones and fur in it and tasted awful. Mr. George then assured her that if she told about sexual activities at the center he would make her into stew like the rabbit.

The next specific case situation involved delayed disclosure. David was a 6-year-old boy whose father was hospitalized with leukemia when David entered the center. To obtain David's involvement in intercourse with his 4-year-old sister, Mr. George told him that if he didn't participate, Mr. George would follow the boy's mother to the hospital and kill his father.

Sometime later, the father did in fact die, and Mr. George used the event to manipulate David so he would not tell. Mr. George declared that he had killed David's father by shooting him through the heart and that because of the manner of death his father would not go to heaven. Mr. George threatened David that if he told, Mr. George would shoot David, his little sister, and his mother, all through the heart so that none of them would go to heaven. David kept silent for 3 years.

In this case, there was a criminal trial, and, on the basis of the testimony of one 5-year-old boy, Mr. George was convicted. None of the other accused adults were prosecuted. Mr. George appealed his case, and 5 years after he was incarcerated, his conviction was reversed on a technicality. The case was remanded for retrial. Because so much time had passed, the prosecutor entered into a plea bargain with Mr. George, which he accepted. Shortly thereafter, Mr. George appeared on a talk show representing himself as falsely accused of sexual abuse in a day care center.

Many of the characteristics of the Little People case are found in multiple-offender/multiple-victim day care center cases. These include scores of victims, some collaboration among perpetrators, group sexual activities, apparent killing of animals, and terrifying threats. Although it is possible that these acts were dictated by some belief system, that is not evident from the acts themselves. Rather, the motivation of the offenders appears to be sexual gratification and a desire to undermine children's sense of order in the world, to humiliate the children, and to prevent disclosure of the abuse.

Experiences of Victims

The experiences of victims of sexual abuse in day care are in some respects unique when compared with those of other victims of sexual maltreatment. Three aspects of these experiences will be discussed: (a) the sexual abuse itself, (b) other types of abuse, and (c) threats employed by the offenders. The findings are based upon a review of the existing literature (e.g., Faller, 1988d; Finkelhor et al., 1988; Kelley, 1994; Waterman et al., 1993) and my practice experience.

THE SEXUAL ABUSE

One of the distinguishing features of sexual abuse reported in day care is the severity of the sexual abuse (Kelley et al., 1993; Schumacher & Carlson, 1999). Thus, despite the young age of victims, a large proportion of them experience some form of sexual penetration. This may be digital penetration of the vagina or anus, penetration with objects, or genital or anal intercourse. Consequently, there may be physical evidence. More than a third of victims I have evaluated had some physical evidence, either documented by a physician or noted by the parents. In the cases investigated by Finkelhor et al. (1988), 62% of victims were injured physically during the sexual maltreatment, a very high percentage.

In addition, one of the characteristics that appears to differentiate sexual abuse in day care is that there is proportionately more sexual activity that occurs in a group context (Kelley et al., 1993). This includes group sex involving adults and children, children being required to have sex with one another while adults observe, and children being made to watch adults (and sometimes other children) having sex with one another. In one case I have seen, an animal was also involved (a 4-year-old girl stated that she had to fellate a dog).

As well, there are reports of sexual games involving children and adults (Faller, 1988d; Waterman et al., 1993). For example, several boys who attended the same center described being taken to a barn by three teachers. Then everyone, including the teachers, took off their clothes, and the boys were chased around the barn by one of the teachers. When they were caught, they were molested in some way. For example, one boy said the teacher poured orange pop on his penis and then licked it off. After that, the children became "it" and chased the teachers. Waterman et al. (1989b) had a category of sexual abuse involving sexual games and stories. Seventy-two percent of children at Manhattan Beach and 21.4% of those at the Reno center reported such experiences.

Findings of sexual exploitation (i.e., prostitution, pornography, ritualistic abuse) are another distinguishing characteristic of sexual abuse in day care. Each of these types of maltreatment constitutes only about 10% of the kinds of abuse experienced by victims in cases I have seen, but the findings are very concerning nevertheless. Finkelhor et al. (1988) reported 14% as the proportion of their cases with pornography. Furthermore, 66% of their multiple-perpetrator and 5% of their single-perpetrator cases contained some ritualistic elements. Similarly, Waterman et al. (1989b) reported that 87.7% of the children from Manhattan Beach had alleged ritualistic abuse. They contrasted these findings with those from the day care center in Reno, where only 7.1% of victims were subjected to ritualistic abuse.

OTHER ABUSE

In addition to sexual maltreatment, children abused in day care may be otherwise harmed. A surprising 60% of my sample (Faller, 1988d) reported being abused in ways other than sexual abuse. This is surprising because the investigations focused on sexual abuse. None of these assaults resulted in severe injury, but children reported sustaining bruises and red marks, some of which were corroborated by their parents. The acts reported included physical abuse; confinement; being given drugs, poison, or medicine; and being required to engage in delinquent acts. These kinds of insults were inflicted primarily by offenders who were sadistic. Similarly, Waterman et al. (1989b) reported that 78.5% of Manhattan Beach victims allegedly were subjected to other abusive acts.

THREATS TO VICTIMS

Finally, one of the striking characteristics of sexual abuse in day care is the extent to which offenders threaten their victims (Faller, 1988d; Waterman et al., 1993). In sexual abuse cases, coercion may be used to induce children to cooperate in the sexual acts and to keep them from telling. Because little coercion may be required to gain the compliance of such young children in sexual acts, most of the threats appear to be to prevent disclosure.

The most common sort of threat found in my practice experience was a threat to kill either the victim or the victim's parents, younger siblings, or, in a few cases, grandparents. In a small number of cases in my sample, a weapon, usually a gun or knife, was used, but Finkelhor et al. (1988) reported that in 10% of their cases a weapon was used in the sexual abuse, and in 20% the children were threatened with one. A striking 80% of the victims that Waterman et al. (1989b) evaluated reported being threatened with death to themselves and/or others.

The next most common was a threat to do bodily harm. This was most likely to be to the victim but could also be to loved ones. Finkelhor et al. (1988) found instances of threats to the children's pets as well. Another fairly frequent threat in my sample was to implicate the victim (Faller, 1988d). This kind of coercion is sometimes found in other cases of sexual abuse, but in the day care center cases some of the characteristics of the abuse and the young age of victims seemed to add to the potency of these threats. Specifically, because children were required to do things with other children and because pictures were taken, threats that blamed the victims were very compelling. For example, children were told that the pictures would be shown to the police and that the children would go to jail. In addition, the offender said he would tell victims' parents about sexual acts with other children and that the parents wouldn't love the children any more.

A final unique kind of threat involved killing animals, with the implication that the same would happen to the child if she failed to cooperate with or disclose the sexual abuse. Reported killings occurred in only 4% of my cases (Faller, 1988d). However, they were found in 14% of cases surveyed by Finkelhor et al. (1988), and Waterman et al. (1989b) reported that 80% of

Manhattan Beach victims stated that they had endured such experiences. Moreover, in some cases killing of babies was reported (Waterman et al., 1993).

A pressing question is this: Why do offenders engage in these dramatic threats? As was noted in an earlier discussion, some perpetrators wish to do serious psychological harm to their victims. However, perhaps there is a further explanation. In sexual abuse cases involving very young but unrelated children, offenders are less likely to be able to rely on subtle manipulations or ones based upon the special relationship between adult and child. As a consequence, they may need to resort to extreme threats to obtain cooperation and silence. At the same time, these threats are likely to be believed by very young children.

Impact of Sexual Abuse in Day Care

Of concern to both professionals and parents is the impact of sexual abuse in day care. The following issues will be addressed: (a) the impact of the special circumstances of day care sexual abuse, (b) initial effects of sexual abuse in day care, and (c) longer-term effects.

IMPACT OF THE SPECIAL CIRCUMSTANCES OF SEXUAL ABUSE IN DAY CARE

The fact that the offenders involved in day care sexual abuse are not within the family would suggest that the trauma would be less severe. However, the young age of the children, combined with the circumstances of the abuse, can make it very harmful. That is, the abuse occurs in a situation that may be traumatic anyway—separation of very young children from their parents for a substantial portion of their day. For many victims, this is their first experience in the world away from their parents. Moreover, although the abusers are not the parents, they are people to whom the parents have entrusted the children. Often the parents have described the day care providers in glowing terms and have admonished their children to obey them (Faller, 1988d; Schumacher & Carlson, 1999).

However, as with other types of sexual abuse, the impact is variable. The effects of this type of sexual abuse appear to be mediated by the nature of the sexual abuse, including the number and kinds of sexual acts, the number of perpetrators, whether the child was required to have sex with other children, and the presence of other maltreatment or threats (Kelley et al., 1993; Waterman et al., 1993). These characteristics are ones commonly found in situations of ritual sexual abuse. Studies that compare children who report ritual abuse in day care, sexual abuse in day care, and children who attend day care but have no history of abuse demonstrate the severity of the effects of ritual abuse on children's functioning (Kelley, 1989, 1990, 1994; Waterman et al., 1993).

Finkelhor et al. (1988) noted comparable findings. They reported that, where force was used and there was ritualistic abuse, victims had more sequelae. In addition, when the offender was peripheral to the running of the center and the perpetrator was a woman, children had fewer symptoms. Finally, maternal impairment was a predictor of more symptoms.

In addition, there is a counterintuitive finding that children and families that experience sexual abuse in day care may appear more traumatized than children and families in other sexual abuse situations. Families whose children are sexually abused in day care may differ from those referred to child protection agencies in other situations of sexual abuse. The former tend to be better functioning and of higher income. Although these characteristics mean the family is likely to have more material and psychological resources for coping, the immediate and long-term impact of sexual abuse on both the family and the child may be more marked because the experience of sexual abuse is so alien. This is in contrast to many families reported to protective services. Parents and children in CPS families are likely to have experienced many disasters, and children may have endured pervasive failures to have their needs met. It is important for professionals to be sensitive to the special impact that sexual abuse in day care is likely to have.

IMPACT OF SEXUAL ABUSE IN DAY CARE
NOTED AROUND THE TIME OF DISCLOSURE

One of the very painful issues for parents is that often there were indicators that their children were being sexually maltreated preceding the actual disclosure, but the parents ignored them or attributed them to something else (Burgess et al., 1996; Faller, 1988d). A very common assumption is that reluctance to go to day care and regressive behavior, such as bed-wetting and nightmares, are merely a result of the child's not wanting to be separated from her parents. Moreover, symptoms that with hindsight seem obvious indicators of sexual abuse are simply explained away. In a case seen at the University of Michigan, one mother, who was a nurse, said that her daughter had repeated urinary tract infections, pain on urination, and a red vagina, possible indicators of sexual abuse. Yet the mother attributed these symptoms to poor hygiene. Parents may need help in dealing with guilt associated with their failure to appreciate the significance of symptoms as well as guilt related to putting their children in the hands of abusers.

In cases seen at the University of Michigan, sequelae of sexual abuse were categorized into sexual acting out, sleep disturbances, physical problems (enuresis, encopresis, headaches, stomachaches, eating problems), emotional problems, behavior problems, and phobias. The average number of symptoms per child was 3.7, a very worrisome finding. However, more than half of the children had two or fewer symptoms. A comparable categorization was employed by Finkelhor et al. (1988). Other researchers have used standardized measures to assess impact of sexual abuse, usually the CBCL[3] (Kelley, 1990; Waterman et al., 1993).

One of the distinguishing features of the impact of day care sexual abuse is its generation of phobias (Faller, 1988d; Finkelhor et al., 1988; Waterman et al., 1993). In my sample, almost 40% of victims were reported to be phobic. Finkelhor et al. (1988) reported an even larger proportion having fears (arguably a broader category than phobias), 69%. Kelly and Ben-Meir (cited in Waterman et al., 1993), using the Louisville Fear Survey, noted that children reporting ritual abuse in day care scored higher than the norm for phobic children.

Most of the phobias of children seen at the University of Michigan could be related to the circumstances of the sexual abuse or the threats used against the children. For example, twin brothers became phobic about bugs and spiders. Later it was ascertained that they had been sexually abused in a basement full of bugs and spiders. A number of children were terribly afraid of being separated from their parents. These fears were explained by two children as a consequence of threats to kill their parents. Kelly and Ben-Meir (cited in Waterman et al., 1993) reported that fear of the devil was the most common fear among their ritually abused children. Also the large proportion of children with phobias may relate not only to the special abuse experiences but also to their age. Preschool and young school-aged children are prone to have unreasoned fears.

Other sequelae, like the sleep disturbances, bowel and bladder problems, and sexual acting out found in substantial proportions of cases, probably also reflect the victims' ages. Young children are more likely to demonstrate distress by enuresis and encopresis than older ones because they may have uncertain control over these bodily functions. Similarly, their naivete regarding the inappropriateness of sexual behavior is likely to result in a greater propensity to demonstrate the effects of sexual abuse by engaging in sexual activity than would be seen with older and/or more sophisticated children (Friedrich, 1997).

LONGER-TERM EFFECTS OF SEXUAL ABUSE IN DAY CARE

Of concern to parents and professionals involved with children sexually abused in day care is the ultimate impact of the experience. Although the accumulated body of research on this issue is modest, findings to date suggest a lasting impact on many children, especially children from multiple-perpetrator/ multiple-victim sites.

Bybee and colleagues (Bybee & Mowbray, 1993; Valliere et al., 1988) reported follow-up findings from a multiple-victim/multiple-perpetrator day care situation in southwestern Michigan. Children who were victimized at the Michigan center were compared with children in the local school system 1 and 2 years after the abuse ended, and these subjects' scores were compared with normative scores of nonclinical and clinical samples using the CBCL (Achenbach & Edelbrock, 1983). General findings were that, at 1 year, the victims of sexual abuse looked similar to the normative clinical sample and were significantly more symptomatic than the normative nonclinical sample and the comparison children from local schools. At 2 years after the abuse, boy victims continued to be described as having significantly more symptoms than the two normal groups, but the girls' symptoms lessened (Valliere et al., 1988).

As described above, the research design of Waterman et al. (1989a, 1989b, 1993) involved two groups of victims with different experiences as well as a comparison group. Data were collected at two time intervals, the second a year or two after the first. Ratings came from the parents, the children, and their therapists. The Manhattan Beach (ritually abused) group continued to experience significant difficulties 4 to 5 years after disclosure of the alleged sexual abuse and after extended treatment. The comparison group was functioning the best, and the Reno group (children sexually abused by a single perpetrator) fell between these two groups.

Burgess et al. (1996) conducted a follow-up study of children sexually abused at three different multi-offender centers. The follow-up occurred 5 to 10 years after the abuse disclosure, and effects were measured with the CBCL. Approximately one third of the children were very symptomatic, one third had milder symptoms, and one third were asymptomatic.

My clinical experience suggests that sequelae of sexual abuse in day care, like sequelae of sexual abuse in other contexts, may emerge intermittently. These symptoms are triggered by developmental challenges, such as going to a new school; by development of sexual awareness, such as learning where babies come from; and by crises in the child's life, such as a parental divorce. The long-term impact of sexual abuse in day care should be a topic for continued research.

Intervention

Two aspects of intervention that are unique to day care sexual abuse will be discussed. They are (a) special treatment needs for children and families and (b) how to differentiate a high-risk center from an adequate one.

TREATMENT NEEDS

In this section, the treatment needs of children and parental needs for support will be covered.

Victim Treatment Needs

Most victims of sexual abuse in day care need some treatment. In cases with the following characteristics, treatment will probably be brief: There was a single incident; the behavior was not intrusive or accompanied by coercion or threats; the child disclosed soon after the incident; the child evinces no significant symptomatology; and the family responded appropriately and is not severely traumatized. The treatment should focus on helping the child express her feelings about the victimization, including any anger toward the parents for entrusting the child to the abuser; what is wrong with sex between adults and children; why the abuser did it; and what to do in the future if someone attempts sexual abuse.

The importance of parental involvement in the child's treatment cannot be stressed enough. The younger the child, the less central the therapeutic role of the clinician and the more central that of the child's caretakers. This is because young children are much less individuated from their parents than older ones.

Furthermore, young children don't understand therapy and are not very cooperative with the treatment process. Often they do not want to deal with their problems when they come to therapy. They want to play. When they do need help is, for instance, in the middle of the night when they wake up because they have had a nightmare about the perpetrator or when they become frightened because their parents are going to leave them with a baby-sitter. Most therapists do not make themselves available for such occasions.

It is important to successful treatment outcome, in day care center and other cases involving young children, that parents become surrogate therapists. They need to be taught how to deal with the children's symptomatology. This includes not only phobias and sleep disturbances, mentioned above, but sexual acting out and anger at the parents for allowing them to be sexually abused.

Often the most appropriate structuring of the therapy session is to begin by allowing the child to play in the playroom while the parent is interviewed nearby. Ideally, there should be someone with the child. The discussion with the parent should center on issues that have come up since the last session and how the parent has handled them. Advice for more appropriate handling may be in order or, in some cases, role play. The material from the parent will assist the therapist in developing the content of therapy with the child, which may be covered verbally or in activities. Then at the end of the individual session with the child, the parent may be seen again, or there may be a conjoint session with parent and child, or both. A conjoint session is a context for the therapist to model appropriate responses to the child's issues as well as to facilitate three-way communication among therapist, child, and parent.

Although initial needs for treatment should be addressed at the time the sexual abuse is discovered, parents should also be told that issues related to the sexual abuse may emerge later in life. If parents, and indeed children, are fore-warned about the possibility of needing treatment in the future, they are likely to seek treatment more promptly. As noted above, developmental challenges, acquiring sexual knowledge, and individual crises may result in the need for additional treatment. Thus, treatment is likely to be intermittent.

Supporting the Parents

Parents of children sexually abused in day care need support (Burgess et al., 1996; Kelley, 1990, 1996). As Finkelhor et al. (1988) pointed out, often their treatment needs are ignored by the professionals and the parents themselves, and this can result in family dysfunction as well as individual problems for the victim and the parents. Waterman et al. (1993) found that parents were deeply affected by discovering their children had been sexually abused. Results were more marked for women and for parents whose children reported ritual abuse.

When the case involves multiple victims, parents of these victims usually have shared issues, including feelings of guilt, disbelief related to the allegations, questions about how to help their children, concerns about how the case is being handled, and, most important, the need for mutual support. Support groups for parents whose children have been sexually abused in multiple-victim contexts are the most effective way to provide services for their needs.

Groups for parents can be short term or open ended, depending upon the specific needs. Professional group leaders should be involved, even though parents can assist one another greatly. An appropriate structure may be to have relevant professionals come to meetings, depending upon the issues that need to be addressed. For example, as the case moves toward criminal prosecution, the prosecutor might be invited to the group meeting.

Sometimes professionals whose primary responsibility is criminal prosecution object to parental support groups because they are concerned that the group will contaminate the case (i.e., parents will discuss with one another the various allegations and then question their children inappropriately about a particular sexual activity the child has not previously alleged, or such a claim will be made by the defense). In my experience, most parents do not engage in contamination and will take direction offered by professionals. In addition, the benefits of such groups usually outweigh any challenges they may elicit from the defense. For example, this kind of support can play a key role in convincing individual parents of the importance of having their children testify, despite the hazards involved.

ARE THERE WAYS OF IDENTIFYING HIGH-RISK CENTERS?

Obviously, a pressing question for parents who must put their children in substitute care is how to know when a setting is safe. Unfortunately, few guidelines can be offered. Finkelhor et al. (1988) found that only 8% of offenders had histories of sex offenses. They also found that sexual abuse occurs at all kinds of centers, including those that are licensed and have never had licensing violations previously, as well as unlicensed centers and programs that have a history of complaints against them. In cases seen at the University of Michigan, a number of the centers where sexual abuse occurred were regarded as model programs. In contrast, Burgess et al. (1996) described a center in which there were multiple offenders that had a policy of hiring staff without any formal training.

Finkelhor et al. (1988) and Margolin (1991) pointed out that both centers and day care homes are vulnerable. However, some parents have turned to using baby-sitters and day care homes rather than sending their children to centers because they think the children will be safer.

The only guideline that I can offer has to do with parental access and participation. Parents should choose a center that has an open-door policy that will let the parent come to the center at any time, despite the disruption it may cause to the program. When it is feasible, a parent should pick a program that has a parental participation requirement, where parents must spend some time, usually on a weekly basis, contributing in kind to the running of the center. This affords the parent more information about what goes on in the program and usually more say about what goes on.

Conclusion

Children are sometimes sexually abused in day care. Despite the skepticism in some circles about day care cases, the number of reports and number of studies demonstrate the phenomenon exists. Moreover, its impact on the children and their families is considerable.

The more informed professionals are about this problem, the more astute they will be at detecting it and providing treatment to victims and support to their families. In addition, knowledge about the problem will enable professionals to advise parents on how to avoid situations where their children might be at risk for sexual abuse in substitute care.

Notes

1 The 61 cases I have evaluated or treated personally come from 24 centers and involve 36 perpetrators.

2 A more differentiated typology, which specifies seven categories of sexual abuse, has been developed by Wilson and Steppe (1986). However, some of their categories are not really sexual abuse in day care.

3 The CBCL is the most widely used instrument to assess the child's behavior, including the effects of maltreatment on children. It has two parent-completed versions, one for children aged 2 to 3 years and another for children aged 4 to 18 years; a teacher-completed version; and a version completed by children 10 and older. The CBCL provides a total score; two major subscales, internality and externality; and nine more specific-symptom subscales—depression, social withdrawal, somatic complaints, schizoid-obsessive behavior, hyperactivity, sexual problems, delinquent activity, aggressive behavior, and cruelty.

10

Sexual Abuse
Allegations in Divorce

Allegations of sexual abuse in divorce and custody/visitation disputes present serious challenges for all professionals involved and require extraordinary care to effect judicious intervention. A child-centered approach is particularly difficult to achieve in these cases. Unfortunately, the needs of children, the alleged victims, are often ignored or become secondary in the turmoil that surrounds allegations of abuse in divorce. This turmoil is in part a reflection of the emotionally fraught dynamics of divorce. They seem to fuel the intensity of behavior and responses of family members and others who are involved. Professionals often are drawn into this turmoil (Faller, 2000b).

When sexual abuse allegations are raised in divorce cases, accusations may be brought against fathers, stepfathers, mothers, their boyfriends, or others but most often are made against fathers (Bala et al., 2001; Faller & DeVoe, 1995a; Thoennes & Tjaden, 1990). The accusers may have a variety of roles: mothers, fathers, grandparents, professionals, or victims themselves (Bala et al., 2001; Faller & DeVoe, 1995a; Jones & Seig, 1988; Thoennes & Tjaden, 1990). However, in about half of these cases, the person raising the issue is the child's mother, who usually bases her concern on statements or behavior of the child (Thoennes & Tjaden, 1990).[1]

Children in these cases may be subjected not only to interviews by protective services, the police, and medical personnel, as happens in other cases of alleged sexual abuse, but also to multiple evaluations by mental health experts for the divorce litigation. In some cases, there is litigation in three separate courts: the juvenile or family court, which addresses the issue of protection; the domestic relations court, which has jurisdiction over the divorce; and the criminal court, which has responsibility for prosecuting the alleged offender (Faller, 2000b). Involvement in these proceedings is psychologically and economically extremely taxing for the parents, but it is even more traumatic for the children. The child may be the key witness in any of these proceedings. Moreover, even when parents attempt to shield the child, she is likely to feel responsible for the tremendous disruption in the lives of both of her parents.

As a rule, the alleged offenders and their attorneys forcefully assert that the accusations are false and may go to extraordinary lengths and expense to prove this is so. Further, there are mental health professionals who hold the view that virtually all allegations in divorce are false and believe that mothers cold-bloodedly make up allegations of sexual abuse in custody disputes in order to gain exclusive rights to their children (Blush & Ross, 1986; Gardner, 1987, 1991, 1992a, 1992b, 1995; Guyer, 1983). Alternatively, they assert that these mothers have distorted perceptions of events at the time of divorce (Benedek & Schetky, 1985) or are hysterics or psychotic (Benedek & Schetky, 1985; Blush & Ross, 1986; Gardner, 1992b, 1995).

On the other side are the parents who believe their children have been sexually abused. They plead that they are only trying to protect their children and are not receiving a fair hearing in court. They may come with medical, protective services, or mental health evidence that supports the abuse allegation. In many cases, the court carefully considers the evidence and makes a decision that is in the child's best interest. But in a substantial number of cases, information supportive of sexual abuse is not taken seriously or is dismissed out of hand by the court (Ducote, 2000; Kaufman, 2000; Myers, 1997; Neustein & Goetting, 1999). This may result in the nonaccused parent's allowing the child to be exposed to further sexual abuse. Alternatively, that parent may, in effect, take the law into her own hands and violate court orders. Then the nonaccused parent is at risk of being found in contempt of court for not allowing unsupervised visitation with the alleged offender or for taking the children out of the court's jurisdiction without obtaining the court's permission. As a consequence, she may be jailed until she agrees to comply with the court, or she may lose custody of her children (Neustein & Goetting, 1999). Sometimes the children are given to the alleged offender, other times they are placed with relatives, and in still others they are put in foster care (Faller & DeVoe, 1995a; Neustein & Goetting, 1999).

In the 1980s, parents who believed that their children had been sexually abused by an ex-spouse and were dissatisfied with the court's actions began taking their children and hiding. The prevalence of the problems of sexual abuse in the context of divorce and the dissatisfaction of nonaccused parents with the court's response are illustrated dramatically by the fact that an underground network of people developed, often persons who had themselves been sexually victimized or who had had loved ones who were. The network provided sanctuary, financial support, and a chance for a new life to parents and their children on the run (Galtney, 1988). Known as the Underground and the Sanctuary Movement (Detrich & Carpenter, 1997), this network has variously been estimated as having 1,500 and 2,000 members.

It is important to appreciate the effects of this radical solution on both the parents involved and the children. The alleged offender may become entirely consumed with finding the child. He often appeals to the press and the public to assist in this effort. He may hire a private detective or pursue his ex-spouse and the child, incurring large debts or leaving behind his other responsibilities. For the fleeing parent, life is filled with uncertainty, instability, economic privation, and fear of being discovered. Such experiences are bound to have an impact on parenting ability. However, it is probably the child who suffers the most from being on the run. A young child will not comprehend fully the parent's decision to flee. She may well still be attached to the alleged offender but cannot express these feelings. She learns to fear the police, to conceal her identity or change her name, and to be suspicious of people who may turn her in. She has left behind familiar people and places and the comforts of life. She may sleep in a different place each night in crowded conditions with little privacy. Yet she is told that all of this is for her own good and is occurring because of something that happened to her.

The existence of the Underground has occasioned retaliatory responses both by parents who have lost contact with their children and by legal authorities (Children of the Underground Watch, 2001; Detrich & Carpenter, 1997; St. Charles & Crook, 2000). Efforts to dismantle the Underground were highlighted in the trial of Faye Yager in Atlanta, a pioneer in the Underground and a woman who had lost custody of her daughter to the child's father when she accused him of sexual abuse. At age 18, her daughter came forward and described a childhood of sexual abuse at the hands of her father and was believed. In 1992, Faye Yager was prosecuted criminally for kidnapping two children, one for 2 hours and the other overnight. These were children whose mother stated they had been sexually abused. Because of repeated efforts to sabotage the Underground, it had become Ms. Yager's practice to talk to children separately from their caretakers regarding their sexual victimization before taking family members into the Underground. Ms. Yager's trial was widely publicized and broadcast on Court TV. She was acquitted of the kidnapping charges (MSNBC, 2002).

The case example that follows is characteristic of the course of disputed custody and visitation cases. It illustrates how children can be harmed in these situations but certainly does not represent the worst of these situations.

Case Example: Mr. and Mrs. D separated when their daughters were ages 3 and 6. The reasons for the separation were Mr. D's alleged violence and Mrs. D's alleged inability to cope with household responsibilities and her headaches that led to refusal of sex. Mrs. D was awarded custody of the children and Mr. D weekend visits. These visits went fairly smoothly for the first 9 months.

Then Mrs. D and her mother reported that the children were saying their father licked their vaginas, engaged in digital penetration, and fondled them. Initial protective services investigation yielded no definitive evidence. The father took and passed a polygraph. The police case was closed, and the protective services case was denied.

However, the children continued to make these allegations. The two children and their parents were then evaluated by an expert in sexual abuse, who substantiated the allegations. In response, the father hired his own expert, who interviewed him and, on the basis of that interview, asserted that Mr. D was not a sexual abuser. Mrs. D then took the children out of the state for an evaluation by a nationally known team of experts, who confirmed the sexual abuse. She was in contempt of court for taking the children out of state and refusing the father unsupervised visitation. The judge issued orders *ex parte* for her arrest and for change of custody to the father.

Upon her return to the state, the mother was arrested and spent 10 days in the county jail. She was released with the agreement that there would be yet another evaluation of the children and that in the meantime she would retain custody. The proposed evaluators refused to assess the case, as they said the issue of sexual abuse had already been determined. There was no litigation for the next 3 years, and the father had no visitation.

Five years after the original allegations, the youngest child, then 8, was in the hospital having an emergency appendectomy. Mr. D alerted the police to the mother's whereabouts, in the hospital with her daughter. She was arrested on the old contempt-of-court warrant. Mr. D, with the assistance of the police, took custody of his 8-year-old daughter upon her discharge from the hospital. Mrs. D remained in jail because she would not disclose the whereabouts of her other daughter. After the mother had been in jail 45 days, the father discovered the other child at school and went there with the police and received custody of her.

The judge consistently refused to hear any testimony regarding the sexual abuse and gave permanent custody to the father. The children are unhappy and frightened there. Mr. D's new wife does not want these children, and her children do not like the D children. The mother and her parents, who had sheltered the children when their mother was in jail, are in agony.

It seems quite probable that these children were sexually abused, and it appears that the mother most certainly thought they had been. Nevertheless, the judge refused to address the issue and seems to have punished the mother for her violation of his orders by putting her in jail and by taking her children away from her. In doing so, he punished not only the mother but also the children. Finally, he rewarded the father, who may have sexually abused the children, by giving him custody.

It is crucial that allegations of sexual abuse be handled in a way that places children's best interests paramount. To assist professionals in doing so, in this chapter I will provide a critical examination of writings and research findings on allegations of sexual abuse in divorce, a categorization of the possible dynamics that may result in an allegation of sexual abuse in a divorce, guidelines for an assessment of the allegations that minimizes trauma to the child, and recommendations for disposition that take into account the child's needs both for safety and for relationships with her family.

Research on Sexual Abuse Allegations in Divorce

A number of assertions have been made about allegations of sexual abuse in divorce: first, that sexual abuse allegations in divorce are rampant; second, that they are mostly or entirely false; and third, that they are made by mothers against fathers either as acts of vindictiveness or to obtain sole physical and legal custody (Agar, 1987; Benedek, 1987; Blush & Ross, 1986; Gardner, 1987, 1991, 1992a, 1992b, 1995; Renshaw, 1987; Schuman, 1986).

These assertions will be examined using existing literature. A careful examination of these assertions requires attention to sample size, sample source, and criteria employed to determine the likelihood of sexual abuse of the various writings.

ARE ALLEGATIONS OF SEXUAL ABUSE IN DIVORCE RAMPANT?

With regard to the extent of sexual abuse allegations when couples divorce, cases from domestic relations courts involving custody disputes are the most appropriate sample source. There are three such studies with quite similar findings. In terms of both sample size and source, the most methodologically sound is a study conducted at the Association of Family and Conciliation Courts Research Unit (Thoennes, Pearson, & Tjaden, 1988; Thoennes & Tjaden, 1990). The researchers examined 9,000 cases where there was a divorce and a custody dispute. Cases came from 12 different states, but the researchers examined cases in depth from eight court jurisdictions with extensive court records. Out of the 9,000 disputed custody cases, only 1.9% (169 cases) involved allegations of sexual abuse.

Similar findings are noted by McIntosh and Prinz (1993), who studied cases from a single county domestic relations court. Out of 1,675 family court judgments in 1987, 603 involved custody and access disputes. Two percent of the custody disputes involved allegations of sexual abuse.

Finally, a recent study was conducted of family court cases in Canberra and Melbourne, Australia (Brown, Frederico, Hewitt, & Sheehan, 2000). The authors read court files, observed court proceedings, and interviewed court and other relevant staff. They found that cases of child abuse in the family court had doubled from 1993 to 1997. Nevertheless, from their record review of 200 cases, they found that only 5% involved child abuse of any sort. However, cases involving child abuse did not resolve as readily as cases on other child-related matters.

Writers who assert that the problem of these allegations is rampant present no data (Blush & Ross, 1986; Gardner, 1987, 1991, 1992a, 1992b, 1995; Renshaw, 1987; Underwager & Wakefield, 1988). Gardner states that he first noted this growing phenomenon in the late 1980s and has coined the phrase *parental alienation syndrome* to refer to these allegedly false cases. His publications are quite numerous but include no research data on this "epidemic." His books are self-published through his press, Creative Therapeutics, which does not publish anyone else's writings.

Similar assertions are found in the press, usually when a particular case is being covered (e.g., Agar, 1987). However, media generalizations are usually based upon interviews with individuals, such as Gardner, rather than a review of the research findings.

Thus, despite assertions to the contrary, actual data indicate that only a tiny minority of custody disputes involve allegations of sexual abuse. Others who have reviewed the empirical literature have come to comparable conclusions (Humphreys, 1997; McDonald, 1998; Penfold, 1995).

ARE SEXUAL ABUSE ALLEGATIONS IN DIVORCE USUALLY FALSE?

Percentages of unlikely or false cases reported in the literature vary depending upon research design and criteria used to assign a case to the "unlikely" or false category. The highest percentage is reported in a descriptive study of 18 cases by two psychiatrists, Benedek and Schetky (1985), only 14 of which were sexual abuse allegations in divorce cases. Ten of these cases (56% of 18 and 71% of 14) were determined to be false allegations, nine made by mothers. Benedek and Schetky gave these women psychiatric diagnoses, most frequently paranoid personality, but also asserted that their motivation was an attempt to get the ex-spouse out of their lives, vindictiveness, and "crying wolf." These findings probably need to be evaluated in light of Benedek's testimony (1987) in the *Morgan v. Foretich* (1988) case,[2] in which she was Foretich's expert. In that testimony, she stated that when asked to evaluate and provide testimony on a case (usually by the accused), she requests past investigative reports, evaluations, and previous court testimony. If, after reviewing the material, she believes the sexual abuse to have taken place, she informs the accused and refuses to work on the case. Conversely, if she believes, on the basis of the material supplied, that the abuse is questionable or unfounded, she agrees to serve as an evaluator and expert witness. Thus, the Benedek and Schetky study is probably a study, not of the full spectrum of allegations of sexual abuse in custody disputes, but of cases predetermined to be likely to be false.

There are other studies of small samples by psychiatrists. Kaplan and Kaplan (1981) reported on a single case they suggested was false, even though the children had testified in court to the allegations, and proposed *folie à deux* and programming as its etiology. Schuman (1986) cited seven cases that he judged to be false, six sexual abuse and one physical abuse, but did not provide information about the total size of the sample from which these cases were drawn. Green (1986) described 4 out of 11 cases (36%) from his private practice that he had determined to be false. On the basis of these four cases, he proceeded to describe characteristics of false allegations, such as ease in disclosure and looking to the mother before responding to questions. His article occasioned a challenge by Corwin et al. (1987), in part because one of the cases Green thought to be false was that of a boy whom two of the authors of the Corwin et al. article, on the basis of careful exploration and physical evidence, thought might well have been sexually abused. In addition, the authors pointed out the danger of generalizing from such a small sample. Green's article also led to a letter calling into question its conclusions that appeared in the *Journal of the American Academy of Child Psychiatry* (March 1988) and was signed by 19 mental health experts (Hanson, 1988).

In their large-sample study, Thoennes and Tjaden (Thoennes, 1988; Thoennes & Tjaden, 1990) used a Child Protective Services (CPS) disposition and the opinion of a court-appointed evaluator as their criteria of likelihood. In their review of case files, they found an opinion about likelihood in 129 of their 169 cases with an allegation of sexual abuse. The findings were 50% likely, 33% unlikely, and 17% uncertain. Faller and DeVoe (1995a), who examined 215 cases from a single tertiary care program, used opinion of a multidisciplinary team to determine likelihood. We categorized 72.6% of cases as likely, 20% as unlikely, and 7.4% as uncertain. Similar findings were reported by Jones and Seig (1988), with a comparable criterion of likelihood and a comparable sample source (Kempe National Center for the Prevention and Treatment of Child Abuse and Neglect), but with a sample of only 20 cases (70% likely; 20% unlikely; 10% uncertain). Finally, a study by Bala et al. (2001) examined written judicial opinions on 196 cases (262 children) in Canada. In 23% of cases, judges made a finding of abuse, and in 35% there was evidence of abuse but no finding. In 45% of cases, there was a judicial finding of no abuse.[3] Thus, results from the literature suggest that between one half and three fourths of allegations of sexual abuse in divorce are true.

A related issue of debate is whether the rate of false allegations is higher in divorce cases than in other types of sexual abuse cases. Using CPS substantiation rates as a comparison, Thoennes and Tjaden (1990) stated that the rate of false cases is no greater in divorce cases than in other reports of sexual abuse. The 50% substantiation rate in the Thoennes and Tjaden study is at least 10% higher than that typically reported by CPS (Peddle & Wang, 2001; U.S. Department of Health and Human Services, 2001; Wang & Daro, 1998). However, it is not clear whether their "unlikely category" (33%) is comparable to the category "unsubstantiated or unfounded" that CPS uses. Most sexual abuse cases where CPS fails to substantiate are ones in which there was insufficient information to make a determination.

In the Australian family court study cited above (Brown et al., 2000), 9% of child abuse cases were false, the same as the percentage of false cases reported to the child abuse registry (comparable to a report to CPS). These authors also cited another Australian study in a different family court that focused specifically on sexual abuse allegations, with a comparable percentage of false cases (Hume, 1997).

In contrast, when Jones and McGraw (1987) examined 576 CPS referrals in Denver County in 1983 (described in Chapter 2), they found that 6% of the allegations made by adults and 2% of those made by children were fictitious. Of the false allegations by adults, a large proportion were accusations made in the context of custody/visitation disputes. Troubled by the high percentage of false allegations involving custody disputes, Jones went to a source of cases having a larger proportion of divorce and custody/visitation disputes, the Kempe National Center for the Prevention and Treatment of Child Abuse and Neglect. This study (Jones & Seig, 1988), cited earlier, had a 20% false report rate, compared to 6% in the CPS sample studied by Jones and McGraw (1987).

Paradise, Rostain, and Nathanson (1988) reviewed sexual abuse cases from the Children's Hospital of Philadelphia over a 10-month period and six cases from the clinical practice of the first author. They selected 31 cases involving an allegation against a biological parent, 12 of which had a custody/visitation dispute and 19 of which did not. The substantiation rate for the former group was 67% and for the latter was 95%. The children in disputed custody cases were significantly younger (5.4 years) than those in the other biological parent cases (7.8 years). Young age of children when sexual abuse is alleged in divorce has been noted by other writers as well (Faller, 1991b; MacFarlane, 1986).

To date, the findings are mixed with regard to whether allegations in the context of divorce have higher propositions of unlikely cases than allegations of sexual abuse noted in other contexts.

ARE UNLIKELY ALLEGATIONS OF SEXUAL ABUSE MADE VINDICTIVELY AND KNOWINGLY?

Gardner (1992a, 1992b) has claimed not only that most allegations in divorce are false but that they are knowingly false and that 90% are made by mothers wishing to alienate children from fathers. However, as previously pointed out, he has provided assertions but presented no statistics. As already noted, Benedek and Schetky (1985) cited vindictiveness as one of the motivations behind false allegations, but they did not state how many cases in their study this dynamic applied to, nor did they state how this dynamic and others they noted integrated with the psychiatric diagnosis given to the women. Thoennes and Tjaden (1990) classified 8 cases (total N:9,000; 42 cases with allegations of sexual abuse determined unlikely) as calculated false cases on the basis of reports in court files, but they noted that only about half of their cases had sufficient information to determine the motivation of the allegation. In an additional 10 cases, Thoennes and Tjaden determined that the accuser was "disturbed." Faller and DeVoe (1995a) characterized most false cases (N:45) as misinterpretations and classified only 10 cases (of 215 cases studied) as calculated false cases. We based the determination of a calculated false allegation upon what the individual making the false statement said. However, our unit of analysis was the suspect-child dyad, and we noted that four false allegations were made and admitted by a single person.

Thus, data-reliant reports suggest that calculated false allegations are rare (Faller & DeVoe, 1995a; McDonald, 1998; Penfold, 1995; Thoennes & Tjaden, 1990). Moreover, they appear to be a minority of the false allegations in divorce cases.

WHAT HAPPENS WHEN "PROTECTIVE PARENTS" RAISE CONCERNS ABOUT SEXUAL ABUSE?

There are a number of individual reports in which parents raising concerns of sexual abuse have ultimately lost custody to the suspected abuser (Ducote, 2000; Goldsmith, 2000; Kaufman, 2000). However, these reports do not tell us how common that outcome is.

Faller and DeVoe (1995a) recorded sanctions experienced by nonaccused parents. These sanctions included being jailed; losing custody to the alleged offender, a relative, or foster care; limitation or loss of visitation; admonitions not to report alleged abuse again to the court, CPS, or the police; and prohibitions against taking the child to a physician or therapist because of concerns about sexual abuse in the future. There were 40 cases (18.6%) in our study in which parents experienced negative sanctions associated with raising the issue of sexual abuse. Although we were aware that some parents experienced several sanctions, we merely documented whether the parent experienced a sanction. None of the sanctioned parents were categorized as having made a calculated false allegation. However, nine violated court orders, and one entered the Underground. A troubling finding is that sanctioned cases scored significantly higher on a composite scale of likelihood of sexual abuse[4] and were significantly more likely to have medical evidence than cases without sanctions.

Neustein and Goetting (1999) reported on outcomes in 300 cases referred to the Help Us Regain Our Children Research Center. These cases represented a subset, with extensive documentation, of more than 1,000 cases referred to this program. The program was set up to assist protective parents and professionals having difficulty with the legal system. The authors classified cases according to outcomes as follows:

1. Negative case outcome—the child was placed in primary legal and physical custody of the alleged abuser, had serious physical sequelae of sexual abuse, and had serious psychiatric sequelae. Twenty percent of cases fell into this category.

2. Moderate outcome—the child was in joint physical and legal custody or in sole custody of the protective parent with unsupervised visits with the alleged abuser, and the child demonstrated moderate mental health symptoms. Seventy percent of cases were classified as moderate outcome.

3. Positive outcome—the child was in sole or primary custody of the protective parent, had supervised visits with the suspected abuser, and experienced intermittent mental health symptoms. Ten percent of cases were so classified.

In Bala et al.'s (2001) study, which was of family court judges' written opinions, results were somewhat different. Of the 89 cases where judges made a finding that the allegation was unfounded, 18 parents (20%) who raised the issue lost custody. However, the authors stated that often these parents had mental health problems. In addition, one parent was charged and convicted of mischief for falsely reporting. On the other hand, in the 51 cases where judges made a positive finding of sexual abuse, 21 resulted in an order of no access (visits) and 16 resulted in supervised access. Thus, it appears that in 17 cases no orders were entered to protect children. The authors also stated that the abuser was criminally charged in only 3 cases.

How should these diverse and divergent findings be evaluated? First, the cases studied derive from very different sources—a tertiary case program that handles complex child welfare cases (Faller & DeVoe, 1995a), a program set up to serve those dissatisfied with the domestic relations courts because these courts are not protective of children (Neustein & Goetting, 1999), and written opinions of Canadian family court judges (Bala et al., 2001). Nevertheless, the research to date suggests that parents raising concerns about sexual abuse risk an unprotective and punitive reaction from the domestic relations court.

About 10 years ago, I discussed such cases with Louise Armstrong, a pioneer in raising consciousness about the problem of child sexual abuse (e.g., *Kiss Daddy Goodnight*, 1976). Her response to me was surprising at the time. She said she had been approached recently, after giving a talk, by a nurse who said she had concerns that her ex-spouse was sexually abusing their daughter on visitation. Armstrong advised the nurse to say nothing to authorities about the sexual abuse concerns but rather to move from the East Coast to the West Coast, where she would be able to find a good job. I was taken aback that she did not trust the legal system to respond appropriately to the nurse's concerns about sexual abuse. In the meantime, I have come to understand her response.

Variations in Relationships Between Sexual Abuse Allegations and Divorce

There appear to be a variety of relationships between a sexual abuse allegation and divorce. For example, Thoennes and Tjaden (1990) noted that some allegations are raised during divorce and others after divorce, resulting in a request to change visitation. The following categorization is based upon clinical observation and case record review in cases described by Faller (1991b) and Faller and DeVoe (1995a). This work suggests at least four possible circumstances that may result in an allegation of sexual abuse as a marriage is dissolving or after it has dissolved: (a) the nonoffending parent finds out about sexual abuse and decides to divorce the offending parent, (b) there is long-standing sexual abuse that is revealed only in the context of divorce, (c) there is sexual abuse that has been precipitated by the marital dissolution, and (d) the allegation is false.

DISCOVERY OF SEXUAL ABUSE PRECEDES DIVORCE

In our research, 14.4% of cases were classified as ones in which sexual abuse discovery preceded divorce (Faller & DeVoe, 1995a). However, there appears to be variability in how women come to the decision to end the marriage.

In some cases, the woman learns of the sexual abuse from the children, from others in the family, or from observation. She then leaves the offender, taking the children, and files for divorce (Berliner, 1988; Corwin et al., 1987). The sexual abuse may come to professional attention only when issues of visitation with the offending parent are being decided in the domestic relations court.

In other cases, upon discovery of sexual abuse, the woman contacts professionals, such as the police, CPS, a minister, or a therapist. And in still others, the nonoffending parent learns of the sexual abuse only when an outside agent, such as the school, protective services, or the police, informs her. In the latter two instances, the sexual abuse is known to authorities before the woman initiates divorce action, and often these professionals are instrumental in the mother's decision to divorce.

It appears that when the woman independently chooses to protect her children by ending a marriage, the first circumstance cited, her motivations are more likely to be questioned. In these cases, she may be accused of falsely alleging sexual abuse in order to restrict the father's access to the children. In cases where professionals are involved before the divorce filing, the woman may have ignored sexual abuse or required persuasion by authorities to act in a protective way, indicators that she may be an inadequate parent.

The example below illustrates one mother's process of decision making when she learned of sexual abuse.

Case Example: Mrs. P, an African American mother residing in an impoverished inner-city environment, had three of her seven children living with her, Ursula, 10, Doreen, 4, and Laticia, 2. Three of her children were with her mother in Louisiana, and a fourth, who was mentally retarded, was in a residential facility.

Mr. P was her second husband and the father of Doreen and Laticia. Although he did not beat Mrs. P as her first husband had, Mr. P had a hard time holding a job and he spent money foolishly. He also expected her to wait on him. When he got an opportunity to go to Florida and work for his uncle, she encouraged him to do this. She thought that being on his own with some responsibility would help him grow up. The plan was for Mrs. P to stay behind and continue in her job as a nurse's aide for the time being, but she and the children were to join Mr. P at the end of the school year.

After Mr. P's departure, Ursula and Doreen told their mother about the pussy game Mr. P played with them. He would chase them until he caught them, throw them on the couch, and then rub their vaginas, asking, "Doesn't that feel good?" Sometimes he would take his penis out and masturbate. When Mrs. P first heard about the pussy game, she tried to contact her husband to get his explanation before deciding what to do. She was unable to reach him. (Later she found out that he was with another woman.) After some reflection, she concluded that her girls would not lie about such a thing and went to Legal Aid to get an attorney to file for divorce. She also informed her family and his about the allegations.

It was 2 years before the divorce case came to court, during which time Mr. P had not seen his daughters or sent any child support. Mr. P had a new partner, whom he introduced as his fiancée. He claimed that Mrs. P had made up the allegations because she did not want his daughters to come and visit him and his fiancée in Florida for the summer but that the girls wanted to come.

The judge interviewed the two older girls in chambers, and they described the pussy game to him. The judge made a finding that Mr. P had sexually abused his daughter and stepdaughter. Mr. P was ordered to pay back child support and was given 1-hour supervised visits monthly.

In this case, the mother's initial reaction was to give the father the benefit of the doubt, but, upon reflection, she concluded that the children were telling the truth and that she wanted to end the marriage. That decision might not have been so easy if he had been in the home at the time or had been a more dependable partner. Her choice of informing family members, who might also have children endangered by Mr. P, rather than going to the police, may reflect reservations African American families have about involving such agents in their lives.

DIVORCE PRECEDES DISCOVERY OF SEXUAL ABUSE

Early clinical literature describes classical incest as a pattern of father-daughter incest that persists for years. It is reported by the victim only when she reaches adolescence and is able to free herself of the incestuous relationship, or it is revealed when the couple divorces (Berliner, 1988; Faller, 1988a). Thus, it appears that clinicians observed as early as the 1960s that sexual abuse that has been long-standing might not surface until marital breakup.

The reasons for revelation after the marriage ends appear to be several. First, the child may feel safe enough at that time to report sexual abuse, which has been ongoing, because the perpetrator no longer is able to punish her for the disclosure (Berliner, 1988). Second, if the offender's ability to prevent revelation was based on manipulation of his relationship with the child, his absence after divorce may attenuate his capacity to manipulate. Third, the child may have kept the secret in order to keep the family together; after the marriage breaks up, the motivation to keep the secret vanishes. Fourth, the mother may have consciously or unconsciously avoided looking into certain behavior that was present during the marriage, but, as the marriage dissolves, she is able or willing to consider the implications of these observations. Fifth, the mother may have known about the sexual abuse during the marriage but may have been fearful of making it known or may have chosen to tolerate it because there were other benefits in the marriage. In our research, a quarter of cases fell into this category (Faller & DeVoe, 1995a). In two thirds of these cases the children raised the issue of sexual abuse, and in one third the custodial parent did.

In the example below, the reason for the mother acknowledging the possibility of long-standing sexual abuse of her four children was probably the fourth one mentioned.

> *Case Example*: Mrs. N had left her second husband, who was the father of her three younger children and the stepfather of the oldest, because she said he was really strange and had crazy spells. She indicated that she was concerned about sexual abuse because some things that had happened during the marriage now worried her. She stated when her youngest daughter, Jane, was 2½, she asked her mother to rub her vagina. When her mother refused, the child said that her daddy did that and that it felt good. Mrs. N also reported discovering her 4-year-old daughter, Sally, masturbating and putting her fingers in her vagina. When Mrs. N told her not to do that, the child replied that her father had said it was okay and had showed her how to do it. Mrs. N said that during the marriage she had worked nights as a nurse and would come home and find her husband in the bed with their children, Eric, 5, and the two girls. On one occasion, the girls had their nightclothes off. However, at the time, she thought nothing of it because the weather was hot. Frequently, her husband slept in the nude.
>
> At the time Mrs. N made these reports, she was also concerned because the children had been involved in a lot of sexual play, including oral sex. Interviews with the children confirmed sexual abuse of the three younger children. The stepson, who was 12, denied any involvement. However, the three children described him taking part in group sex with them and their father.

In this case, the mother made a number of observations that might be indicative of sexual abuse but realized their implications clearly only after she had made a decision to get out of the marriage and indeed after she had extricated herself from a relationship where she was constantly worrying about her husband's depression and unpredictable mood swings.

DIVORCE PRECEDES SEXUAL ABUSE

Divorce is usually a traumatic experience for all parties: husband, wife, and children. In this context, behavior not exhibited under other circumstances may develop that may include sexual abuse. The offending party may be either the mother or the father, although, as with other types of sexual abuse, the abuser is more likely to be a male. In our research, 27% of cases fell into this category (Faller & DeVoe, 1995a).

There may have been behavioral indications of sexual attraction to children during the marriage, but these urges appear to be held in check by the structure of the marriage. For example, the offending parent may have engaged in an unusual amount of touching and caressing of the child, may have engaged in tongue kissing, or may have slept with the child. In addition, there may be reports of the father experiencing erections when wrestling or involved in other body contact with the child or while bathing with the child.

One of the consequences of divorce is the loss of family structure. Often, there is no longer another adult around to monitor parental behavior. Both parents have unsupervised access to the child—one during visitation and the other as a custodial parent. Rules that regulate sleeping arrangements, bedtime, and bathing may no longer exist. This lack of structure and boundaries may increase risk for the expression of sexual feelings toward children.

Two other dynamics, observed clinically, may contribute to sexual abuse as a marriage dissolves. The parent who becomes the abuser may feel a tremendous emotional loss with separation from the spouse. In my experience, the offending parent is usually not the instigator of the divorce and often is bewildered and overwhelmed by the marital demise. In this vulnerable psychological state, the parent turns to the child to get his emotional needs met, and because this parent has some sexual attraction to children, the relationship becomes sexual. Second, the parent who becomes an abuser often is very angry at the spouse for destroying the marriage and for other perceived or actual transgressions. The parent may not have the opportunity to express that anger directly or may have such an opportunity but still be driven by the need to retaliate. The child then becomes the vehicle for the expression of anger toward the partner. Evidently, because of the intensity of these feelings, physical injury may result from the sexual maltreatment.

It is my clinical observation that the offender is in such a state of emotional turmoil that he may not be able to control his sexually abusive behavior even when he is aware that his ex-spouse, protective services, or the court is monitoring his contact with the child. Therefore, reincidences sometimes occur in this type of sexual abuse, even when the visits are partially supervised. These reincidences also may be variously interpreted as a mechanism for keeping the ex-spouse involved, as a cry for help, as defiance against those trying to exercise control, or as a way to make the abuse more exciting (for some abusers more risky sex is more exciting).

The following case example appears fairly typical of sexual abuse arising in the context of divorce:

Case Example: Mr. and Mrs. X had been married 10 years. They were both stockbrokers. Initially, they were both highly successful and had a typical dual-career marriage. They wanted children but thought this would not be possible after Mrs. X's second miscarriage. However, she conceived for the third time and, after a difficult pregnancy, delivered a healthy baby girl, Alice. Mrs. X had to return to work when Alice was 6 weeks old or else face a major career setback. This was very difficult for her, as her boss refused to take her parental duties into account, frequently scheduling noon meetings, when Mrs. X planned to go home and nurse Alice, and weekend work sessions. At this time, Mr. X left the stockbrokering business and opened a manufacturing company with other members of his family, using capital supplied by Mrs. X.

He was described as a devoted father, although the only care of Alice that interested him was bathing. He typically took baths with her, often spending an hour in the bath playing with her. He did not heed Mrs. X's assertions that this was inappropriate and continued to insist on his bathing time with Alice.

His business venture was unsuccessful, and he had to declare bankruptcy. Alice was 3 at the time. Initially, he searched for other jobs but felt that the ones he was offered were not good enough. He became preoccupied with a scheme to start another business. He spent long days at home working on these plans. He wanted to invest the family savings in this business, but Mrs. X refused to allow this.

A housekeeper cared for Alice until the X's could no longer afford her. Mr. X then had the responsibility of caring for Alice and the house. Mrs. X would return from work to a messy house, a dirty child, and no dinner. Often Mr. X remained in his pajamas the entire day. Mrs. X threatened to divorce her husband if he did not find a job. He blamed her for his situation, saying that if she would let him use the savings then he would have a job. She refused him sex. He became physically violent with her, throwing her up against the wall and pulling her hair. This behavior took place in front of Alice.

Mrs. X filed for a divorce, and Mr. X left the home, moving in with his parents. He returned to the house on several occasions. He begged for reunification, but he also threatened to assault Mrs. X and attempted to break in. She called the police.

Nevertheless, because Mr. X had always been good with Alice, Mrs. X allowed him liberal visits. Then Alice, now 4, began to return from visits with a red and sore vagina. Eventually Alice described to her mother her father rubbing her tushie and trying to put his dinky in her. Mrs. X took her to the county sexual abuse expert, who confirmed, on the basis of Alice's statements, that she had been sexually abused by her father. The expert filed a report with protective services.

Mrs. X took the expert's report to the circuit court, which had jurisdiction over the divorce and visitation, and demanded that the father's visits be stopped. They were suspended while another evaluation was conducted of Alice and her parents by an expert in disputed custody cases. That expert found both parents to be very self-absorbed people and found no evidence on the child's psychological tests that she had been sexually abused.

The father's visits were reinstated. Upon return from the first visit, Alice stated her father had rubbed her tushie, and there was medical evidence consistent with repeated fondling.

The family was then ordered to be evaluated by a second, more prominent expert in sexual abuse. The father failed to keep his appointments. However, the expert found evidence from the interview with the child that she had been sexually abused by her father and no evidence, on the basis of interviews with the mother, that she had fabricated the allegation. When the father was told the results of the evaluation by his attorney, he physically assaulted his attorney and fired him.

The expert in child custody asked to see the child again and was granted permission. She found evidence of inappropriate sexual interaction between the child and the father.

The court ordered that the father's visits be supervised by the Friend of the Court. However, he failed to visit his daughter and sought a new attorney to litigate the matter further.

Mr. X's bathing behavior with his daughter could be evidence of his physical and sexual attraction to her. Clearly, he was heavily invested in her and probably took solace in that relationship as he perceived his wife to be unsupportive, sexually rejecting, and destructive of his efforts to become gainfully employed again. Evidence of his anger at his wife is found in his violence, uncharacteristic of his behavior earlier in the marriage. The violence escalated after the separation but was accompanied by pleas for reunification, evidence of how bereft he felt by the loss of his wife. This is also a case where, despite the supervision of the court, Mr. X reabused his daughter on the first visit after reinstatement of visitation.

FALSE ALLEGATIONS IN THE CONTEXT OF A DIVORCE AND/OR CUSTODY OR VISITATION DISPUTES

As noted earlier, although research findings are mixed (e.g., Jones & McGraw, 1987; Thoennes & Tjaden, 1990), allegations of sexual abuse made in the context of divorce may be more likely to be false than allegations in other situations. Most false allegations come from adults rather than from children (Bala et al., 2001; Berliner, 1988; Faller, 1988a; Faller & DeVoe, 1995a; Jones & McGraw, 1987).

The risk for false allegations in divorce can be understood by contrasting it with that of other intrafamilial abuse situations. In the latter, a major issue is convincing nonabusive family member(s) that the perpetrator did abuse the child. A mother may find it very difficult to believe that someone to whom she is married could sexually victimize her children. Quite the opposite situation may occur when parents are divorcing. These adults may be convinced that their ex-spouses are capable of almost anything, including sexual abuse. Therefore, the adult may overreact to suspicious occurrences rather than underreacting to them.

There are several variations in this pattern. First, under the stress of divorce and its aftermath, parental perceptions may become distorted (Benedek & Schetky, 1985). Parents often perceive their ex-partners as very pathological persons. Occasional drinking episodes may become redefined as chronic alcoholism. A desire for certain sexual activities or for frequent sexual activity may be labeled perversion. An incident of the use of physical force in an argument may result in the ex-spouse's being labeled a batterer. Having developed a distorted view of the ex-partner, the parent may conclude that anyone who is an alcoholic, a pervert, or a batterer would also sexually abuse a child. Alternatively, the child may say something, such as "Daddy touched me," "Daddy hurt me," or "Daddy takes baths with me," that leads the parent with the distorted perception to conclude that the child is describing sexual abuse. In addition, these parents may have distorted perceptions of the child in relationship to the ex-spouse. For example, when the child returns from a visit and doesn't seem particularly disturbed, the parent may conclude that the child has been drugged or brainwashed by the alleged offender. Because the ex-partner has such a disturbing effect on the parent, it must be the same for the child, and if not, the ex-spouse must have manipulated the child in some devious way.

Second, the parent or others may observe behavior by the child that could indicate sexual abuse but could have other explanations as well. Typical examples are resistance to visits with the alleged abuser, having nightmares before or after the visits, wetting the bed, masturbating, or engaging in other unusual behaviors related to visits or the alleged abuser. These behaviors could be related to the stress of the divorce, the fear of losing the custodial parent if the child evidences loyalty to the alleged abuser, or an appreciation that the custodial parent would welcome negative reactions to or comments about the alleged abuser. Even masturbation may not be related to sexual abuse. Masturbation is normal among children (and adults). Only excessive masturbation is regarded as possibly symptomatic of sexual abuse, but what is normal may be viewed by a parent as excessive. Furthermore, self-stimulation feels good, and children may need to comfort themselves in a divorce situation. Especially if their parents are too preoccupied to comfort them, they may resort to self-comfort in the form of genital stimulation.

Third, parents may perceive correctly that their children have been sexually abused but may incorrectly attribute it to their ex-partners. The child may evidence precocious sexual knowledge, engage in sexual behavior, or present with physical evidence of having been sexually abused. In several cases I have evaluated, it was fairly clear, on the basis of medical or behavioral evidence, that the child had been sexually abused, and the mother was convinced that the estranged father was the perpetrator. However, after a careful evaluation, it appeared that a stepfather, boyfriend, or other relative was the offender, not the father, or that the child had acquired precocious sexual knowledge from other sources.

Finally, the parent may consciously lie in making the allegation. As noted in the research section of this chapter, these situations appear to be rare (Faller, 1991b; Faller & DeVoe, 1995a; Jones & McGraw, 1987; Nicholson & Bulkley, 1988; Thoennes & Tjaden, 1990). In my experience, conscious lies are more common about the new partner of the ex-spouse than about the ex-spouse him- or herself, although they are rare in both cases. They appear to be motivated by the desire to get the accused parent out of the lives of the child and the accusing parent. Consciously fabricated allegations may also be made as counterallegations by an accused parent (Faller & DeVoe, 1995a).

In the example below, there is evidence both of distortion and of attributing the sexual abuse to the wrong party.

Case Example: Mrs. L made accusations that her ex-husband, Mr. M, was sexually abusing their 4-year-old daughter, Kathy, on visits. She became concerned because her daughter had a sore vagina and said her daddy had hurt her down there. Mrs. L also described him as an alcoholic and said he had Vietnam veteran's syndrome.

Kathy was interviewed and said that her daddy had touched her and her stepbrother. She could give no detail beyond this statement. Mr. M's visits were suspended and a protective services investigation was undertaken. Mr. M's three stepchildren were interviewed but denied any sexual abuse by their stepfather.

Mr. L and Mrs. L, Mr. and Mrs. M, and Kathy were then sent to a multidisciplinary team for evaluation. Even before being asked, Kathy told the interviewer in a rote fashion that her daddy had touched her and that she had told her mother. She said her daddy was bad. No further details were forthcoming. Somewhat later in the interview, she was asked about her stepfather, Mr. L, and described in detail sexual abuse by him. She said that he sat her on the kitchen table and took off her panties. He put his finger in her hole and then he put his peter in her hole. This hurt and made blood come out. She said her mom was at the store and her little brother was outside. She had told her mother, but her mother said her real daddy had done this. She also said that her stepfather hit her little brother with a belt and that he had pushed her little brother down the stairs. Kathy added that she was a bad girl. She got lots of "whuppins" and had to spend a lot of time in her room.

Interviews with the four adults and assessments of the interaction between Kathy and the two sets of adults yielded the following information. Mr. M, Kathy's father, appeared to be quite intelligent and to have a good relationship with her. He could also describe his stepchildren in detail and seemed to understand them. His wife said their relationship with him was good. Mr. M had been in Vietnam but did not appear to be suffering from posttraumatic stress disorder. He said that when he had been married to Mrs. L, he used to have parties with his work mates, and they drank lots of beer. When Mrs. L was his wife, she had an affair with his best friend and left him. He had drunk more after that but drank little now. Mrs. M appeared warm and nurturing and interacted very appropriately with Kathy.

Mr. L was diagnosed with antisocial personality disorder, and he reported a history of being wrongly accused of raping a 4-year-old girl. He had recently been fired from his job after repeated absences and a fight with his boss. He did not interact with Kathy at all during the family interaction session and described her in very negative terms. Mrs. L did interact with Kathy, but this consisted of Mrs. L's complaining about coming to the evaluation and making negative comments about Mr. M. She appeared to be a very dependent woman who had a tendency to distort reality. She said that Mr. M had it in for her: He had reported her for neglect and had told the Friend of the Court that she was a prostitute. Mrs. L had been reported twice for neglect, but not by Mr. M. He had described to the court worker how their marriage had ended but had not said Mrs. L was a prostitute.

At the end of the interviews, the evaluators were not sure whether Kathy had been sexually abused or by whom, but they thought her relationship with her father and stepmother should be fostered. They recommended gradually increasing visits with the father and his family and careful monitoring of the situation.

Six months later, while Kathy was having an extended summer visit at her father's, she began to complain of sexual and physical abuse by her stepfather. There was another protective services investigation. Custody was switched to the father with visitation with the mother.

On two separate visits by Kathy to Mrs. L, Mrs. L made reports to the Friend of the Court that Kathy was being sexually abused by her father. Upon return from a visit with her mother, Kathy had physical evidence of forced penetration and said her stepfather had sexually abused her.

An evaluation by an expert in sexual abuse was initiated. Kathy's statements about her stepfather were graphic, and she denied any involvement with her father. She also again described injury to her brother, age 2. He was assessed and current injuries and old scars were found. The expert concluded that Kathy had been sexually abused and that victimization by the stepfather but not the father was most consistent with the evidence.

This is obviously a complicated case. However, it appears that Mrs. L's perceptions of her ex-husband are somewhat distorted, and there is a paranoid quality about them. Examples of the former are her description of him as an alcoholic and as suffering from Vietnam veteran's syndrome. Of course, his functioning may have been much worse when the marriage dissolved. Paranoia is suggested by her belief that he was the source of the protective services referrals. Mrs. L seems to have perceived rightly that her daughter had been sexually abused but to have had a need to believe that her ex-husband rather than her current husband was the abuser.

CAUTIONARY NOTE

I have described four variations in patterns of allegations of sexual abuse when there is also a divorce or parental discord. Other professionals have reported comparable patterns (e.g., Berliner, 1988; Corwin et al., 1987), but there are also other categorizations of sexual abuse and divorce (e.g., Thoennes & Tjaden, 1990). Moreover, there may be other patterns that have not been defined in the literature.

Evaluating Allegations of Sexual Abuse in Divorce

Somewhat different strategies should be employed to evaluate allegations of sexual abuse in divorce with custody and visitation issues than in other sexual abuse cases. The general approach I recommend is one described in Chapter 6 as the multimodal model.

APPROACHES TO ASSESSMENT FOR DIVORCE CASES

As in other cases, the child interview or interviews are central to determining the likelihood of sexual abuse (Berliner, 1988; Bresee, Stearns,

Bess, & Packer, 1986; Corwin, 1988), but interviewers will weigh the evidence supporting sexual abuse against competing hypotheses that the child may have been programmed, may be misinterpreting experiences, or may be attributing abuse to the wrong offender more heavily than in other sexual abuse cases.

Interviews with and testing of the accused and nonaccused parents, which may not be part of other sexual abuse assessments, are important in assessing allegations in divorce. However, because child interviews remain central, adult interviews may be more useful in determining why rather than whether sexual abuse occurred, if it did, what intervention is appropriate, and what the treatment prognosis is.

Understanding the history and the context of the allegations is important. This involves acquiring and reviewing prior reports to CPS and the police, information from the domestic relations court files about the marriage and divorce, and reports from previous evaluators of the family, the child, and allegations of maltreatment.

Obtaining a variety of perspectives can also assist the evaluator. Thus, telephone or face-to-face interviews with other relatives, baby-sitters, therapists, school personnel, and friends of the family and its members are useful.

Psychological testing can shed light on the overall functioning of family members and on specific aspects of functioning. Testing can be conducted on both adults and children, but it is usually more useful with adults. However, test findings alone cannot be used to rule in or rule out sexual abuse, except in very rare instances. Testing gives an additional dimension to understanding the individuals tested and can be integrated with interview and other findings.

SEXUAL ABUSE VERSUS CUSTODY AND VISITATION ASSESSMENTS

Before discussing the specifics of interview strategies in divorce cases, I will differentiate an assessment of an allegation of sexual abuse in divorce from an assessment to determine custody and access in divorce. If there is a concern about sexual abuse, this issue must be resolved before issues of custody and access are addressed. This principle also applies to situations in which other types of abuse are alleged, including domestic violence.

Custody and visitation assessments differ from those to assess allegations of sexual abuse in a number of respects. Evaluators of custody and visitation in divorce respond to child custody statutes, which generally set forth multiple criteria to be considered in making custody decisions. These may include the capacity to provide the child with education and religious guidance, the ability to provide materially for the child, the length of time the child has been with that parent, and the physical and mental health of the parent (Committee on the Family, Group for the Advancement of Psychiatry, 1980). Some custody statutes specifically address abuse, but the majority do not. In addition, child custody evaluations place a lot of emphasis on parent-child attachment and what is seen in parent-child interaction. As will be discussed below, using such interactions in sexual abuse cases is controversial (Corwin, 1988; Faller et al., 1991). Finally, when there is an accusation of sexual abuse, the emphasis is on protecting the child, whereas resolution of a custody dispute is often a compromise that gives something to each parent.

SPECIFIC TECHNIQUES FOR DIVORCE CASES

Special considerations and approaches for assessing allegations of sexual abuse in custody/visitation disputes will include additional techniques that may be useful and some differences in emphasis. The focus will be on four areas: the child interview, the interview with the nonaccused parent, the interview with the accused parent, and assessment of the parent-child relationship.

The Child Interview

As in other cases, the statements and/or behavior of the child will be the primary determining factors in assessing the allegation. The evaluator will be looking for data in the areas discussed in Chapter 7, including the child's ability to describe the context of the victimization, the child's account of the sexual abuse itself, and the child's emotional state when recounting the maltreatment. However, there are four ways in which this child interview may differ from child interviews in other cases.

First, in this type of a case, the evaluator will want to minimize possible pressure on the child to make a false positive statement. In most intrafamilial sexual abuse cases, the evaluator takes pains to see that the child is not influenced to conceal sexual abuse. This may be done by not having the alleged offender present when the child is seen and by having the child accompanied by a supportive adult. In divorce cases, there is concern that the victim not only might be coerced not to disclose but also might be influenced to assert that something occurred when it did not. It is as important to prevent undue influence on the child as it is to avoid discrediting the evaluation because of perceived influence.

To these ends, it may be appropriate to have a neutral party, such as the child's therapist or school counselor, the child protection worker, or a family friend, bring the child to the evaluation. However, logistically, using a neutral transporter may be difficult. If the evaluator must choose one parent to bring the child, it should be the nonaccused parent. The reason for this choice is that, so far, clinical and research findings indicate that an offender trying to influence a child not to tell is a much more common phenomenon than an accusing parent influencing a child to make a false allegation. Also, if the child is young or anxious, having that child brought by someone other than a parent may be inappropriate and counterproductive. Such a strategy may result in additional trauma to the child and may inhibit disclosure.

Second, although current practice with all sexual abuse allegations is to interview the child alone, such a practice is particularly important in divorce cases when parental influence is a concern. If the child is anxious, the parent may be allowed to stay for the initial part of the interview, when the evaluator asks about neutral topics or plays with the child, but the parent should leave before the issue of sexual abuse is addressed.

However, there will be times when this approach does not work and the evaluator must keep the parent in the room or have the parent return after having departed. For example, the child may be too anxious or may refuse to talk to the interviewer but nevertheless may indicate that something has happened. The interviewer may then ask the child if she thinks it would be easier to talk with the parent there. If it is necessary to have the parent in the room, it is best for the parent to sit behind the child and be silent. Periodically, the interviewer can ask the child if it is all right for the parent to leave.

Third, a useful approach to abuse-focused inquiry in divorce cases is to question the child about all important adult figures in her life, not merely the accused. Roughly the same questions should be asked about all these individuals (see Chapter 5 for "people-focused questions"). There are at least five reasons for gathering details about the child's relationships with all important adults. First, this strategy avoids bias and pursuit of a single hypothesis to the exclusion of others. Second, the positive and negative qualities of all these relationships are important to seeking children's best interests. Third, sometimes there are multiple offenders. In some situations, women may become involved with more than one partner who is sexually attracted to children (Faller, 1988a). Fourth, as already noted in this chapter, mothers may correctly perceive that their children have been sexually abused but may wrongly attribute it to the father. Finally, sometimes the children themselves will indicate that they have been sexually abused but will attribute it to someone who is less valued or less feared than the actual perpetrator. The less valued or feared person could be the father, the stepfather, or someone else.

Fourth, it may be appropriate for the interviewer to try, in a nonaccusatory way, to determine if anyone has suggested to the child what to say. For example, the evaluator may ask the child what mom said about coming here today and whether she said anything about what the child should say. However, the fact that the child says "yes" doesn't mean the allegation is false. The evaluator should ask for more information. Similarly, if the child says her mother said for her to tell the evaluator that "daddy put his fingers in her peepee," this reply should be a cue to ask additional questions, such as "Is that something that really happened to you or not?" There are other approaches for assessing for adult influence. The evaluator can ask the child if people talk about the abuse at the child's house, and if so, what they say. It may also be appropriate, after the child has made a specific allegation, to ask if that is something she really remembers or if it is something she has been told about. Finally, it may be useful to ask the child if the disclosed abuse is something that is real or just pretend.

Fifth, in disputed custody/visitation cases, the evaluator will focus even more than in other cases on the alleged victim's ability to provide detail. Therefore, a simple statement that "he touched me" will not be sufficient to confirm abuse. Descriptions of the sexual acts, an indication of sexual knowledge beyond that expected for the child's developmental stage, and an account told from a child's viewpoint should be sought. Further, the child's ability to describe the specifics of the context of the abuse will assist the evaluator in deciding whether the child is attributing the abuse to the correct perpetrator. The absence of detail about the abuse or the context could signal a coached allegation. The factors used to substantiate sexual abuse are discussed in Chapter 7.

Interview With the Nonaccused Parent

The interview with the nonaccused parent is the part of the assessment where most adjustments must be made when allegations of sexual abuse come in the context of a divorce and/or custody/visitation dispute. If the nonaccused parent is alleging the sexual abuse, the evaluator will want to pay careful attention to the basis of those concerns, the reaction of this parent to the possibility of sexual abuse, and the parent's functioning.

Therefore, the evaluator will want to hear exactly what made the parent think the child might be sexually abused (Bresee et al., 1986). Often a chronology of signs of possible victimization is useful and can be elicited by asking the parent to begin with the first observation that led to concern and to follow with subsequent events.

Persuasive evidence includes observations of the child's sexual behavior and the child's attribution of her knowledge of these acts to the alleged offender. In addition, the child's specific statements about sexual activities with the alleged offender and physical indicators of sexual abuse documented by a physician are quite compelling.

On the other hand, parental reports of children's statements that could refer to nonsexual experiences, reports of nonsexual symptomatic behavior, and reports of nonsexual, inappropriate activity by the accused parent are not persuasive. Examples of the first might be the child's saying "Daddy hurt me" or "I don't like daddy; he's bad." Nonsexual symptoms might include the child's not wishing to go for visits, having nightmares, wetting the bed, doing poorly in school, having problems with peers, displaying behavior problems, and experiencing mood changes. Nonsexual inappropriate parental behavior reported by the accusing parent may include that the child does not have a set bedtime on visits, is watching R-rated movies, is not eating nutritious meals, is sleeping with the alleged offender, or is bathing with that parent. The latter two examples are worrisome but not, by themselves, indicators of sexual abuse.

The case example that follows is one in which the parent gives quite persuasive information.

Case Example: Mrs. R, at the direction of protective services, brought her 4-year-old son, Mike, to be evaluated for possible sexual abuse by his father. When asked what first made her think he might have been sexually abused, she recounted the following incident. Mike had one of his friends from nursery school over to spend the night. They were taking a bath together, and Mrs. R caught Mike licking the anus of his friend. She asked him what he was doing, and he said playing a game. She then asked where he learned the game, and he said from his dad. He said his dad did this to him and had him do it to other people when he visited.

In this case, the mother gave graphic and specific details of the incident that triggered her concern. She seems to have very good reason to think her son has been sexually abused.

In addition to the source of concern about sexual abuse, the nonoffending parent's reaction to this information may be important in ruling out the likelihood that she manufactured the allegation. Typically, coming to believe that someone has sexually abused a child takes time: That is, the initial reaction to an accusation against someone close or close to the child is disbelief. If the nonaccused parent indicates disbelief that the alleged offender would do such a thing, reports thinking the child was mistaken, or asks the evaluator to confirm that the abuse didn't occur, then it is unlikely that this parent is making up the allegation. In contrast, if the adult reports that her initial reaction was that she knew it all along, or that it would be just like the alleged offender to sexually maltreat a child, this may signal reporter distortion. Of course, it is important to examine the facts of the case to see if the immediate conclusion that the alleged offender must have done it is or is not justified. If the alleged offender has previously sexually abused children, then such a conclusion may be very appropriate.

There are also a number of aspects of the nonoffending parent's functioning that may shed some light on the truth or falsehood of the allegation. However, it must be emphasized that findings in these areas are not conclusive of a false allegation. They are more helpful in understanding why the false allegation was made if the child interviews do not yield evidence supportive of sexual abuse. Moreover, to muddy the waters further, positive findings (i.e., problems) in the functioning of the accusing parent may be consistent with the dynamics of sexual abuse as well as those of a fabricated allegation.

If, on the basis of the child interview, the evaluator thinks perhaps the mother has coached the child to make a false allegation, the evaluator should assess her personality to see if findings are consistent with falsely accusing someone of sexual abuse. The evaluator will be looking for deficits in superego functioning or lack of conscience and empathy. If the accusing parent appears to have a serious personality disorder, the person may have made up the allegation. However, finding that the mother has a personality disorder does not rule out sexual abuse. An adult with such functioning deficits may be at increased risk for marrying a sexual abuser.

A childhood history of unresolved sexual victimization is another characteristic that may play a role in a false allegation. The childhood experience may result in distortions of events or hypervigilance (Bresee et al., 1986; Jones & McGraw, 1987), so that sexual maltreatment is imagined. However, sexual victimization can also signal increased vulnerability to having children who are sexually abused. A woman who has been sexually abused may feel uncomfortable with normal adult sexual relationships and may unwittingly choose a partner who does not make sexual demands because his primary sexual attraction is to children. In addition, a woman with a background of sexual victimization may not be as sensitive to risk situations as other women and, without meaning to, may place her children at risk.

Some authors have described mothers who make false allegations as hysterics (Benedek & Schetky, 1985; Blush & Ross, 1986). The argument they make is that these women overreact to signs that may be indicators of sexual abuse or that they distort what they observe and wrongly assume the child has been sexually abused. This appears to be true in a few cases. However, caution must be used in drawing this conclusion. Most mothers are upset when they think their children have been sexually abused. One would be concerned about them as parents if they were not. Moreover, the process of a divorce is likely to cause adults who ordinarily cope well to become quite distraught. Therefore, a parent who both is caught up in a divorce and has discovered her child has been sexually abused may look hysterical.

To conclude, in custody and visitation disputes, it is useful to alter the evaluation of the mother somewhat, assuming she is the accusing parent, but findings must be interpreted with care and in light of the results of the child interviews and other data.

Interview With the Accused Parent

There are also some alterations in the interview with the accused in divorce cases, but not as many as in the interview with the nonaccused parent. Whenever the accused in a sexual abuse case is interviewed as part of the evaluation process, he should be given an opportunity to provide an explanation for the allegations. This opportunity is perhaps more important in divorce cases than in others because of the possible risk of a false allegation based upon misinterpretation. As noted earlier, essentially benign behavior by the accused and children's reactions to their parents' divorce and disagreements may be misconstrued as signs of abuse. Child care behavior, such as assisting children with toileting, bathing, and dressing, may be misperceived as sexual behavior. The following case example probably illustrates misinterpretation of child care behavior.

Case Example: The noncustodial and accused parent in this case was the mother, Mrs. B. She left her husband to "find herself," leaving him with the care of three children. Mr. B was very upset with his wife. She had boyfriends, of whom he disapproved, but wanted regular visitation with the children. Although he was frequently concerned about her living situation, he allowed liberal visitation with the children.

Mr. B met a woman, and she and her 3-year-old son moved in with him. She was a help in caring for his three children but became concerned that all three of them had been sexually abused. She encouraged Mr. B to have them evaluated, and she and Mr. B questioned the children extensively. On the basis of concerns about sexual abuse, the court ordered a full family evaluation.

When Emma, age 5, came to be evaluated as part of the family evaluation, she said her "mommy 'bused me with her fingers and a bottle." Specifically, she reported that her mother had rubbed her vagina when she was in the bath, using her bare hand. Emma resisted this. In addition, Emma said her mother had made her lie on the bed and had tried to put her sister's deodorant bottle up her vagina. Emma hated this.

Mrs. B was subsequently interviewed and was asked first about rubbing her daughter's vagina when she was in the bath. She stated that she had to wash Emma because Emma did not wash herself well and continually got rashes. When asked if she used a washcloth or her hand, she stated, "I do just like I do with myself; I use my hand with soap on it." She said Emma does not like this and struggles when she washes her. Mrs. B was then told that Emma said she put a deodorant up her vagina. Mrs. B replied that she had to put A&D ointment on Emma after her bath. She had to "lay her on the bed and pull her legs apart" to do this. Emma fought and struggled when she put the ointment on her.

Although there is no way of knowing for sure what went on in Mrs. B's head when she engaged in these behaviors with Emma, her activities were probably motivated by a felt need to clean and medicate Emma. Most professionals would advise Mrs. B not to wash with her bare hand but to use a washcloth or, better still, to get Emma to wash herself. Despite a conclusion that these behaviors were probably in the service of child care, Emma experienced these behaviors as unpleasant and came to view them as sexual abuse after they were so defined by Mr. B and his girlfriend.

In addition to asking the accused about an explanation for the allegation, the interviewer should gather information that could be related to the other relationships between divorce and abuse allegations described above: (a) discovery of sexual abuse precedes divorce; (b) divorce precedes discovery of sexual abuse; and (c) divorce precedes sexual abuse. Information most likely to be provided by the accused relates to the third dynamic. His description of his feelings associated with the marital dissolution and the physical arrangements when he has contact with the child will probably be the most useful information.

ASSESSING THE PARENT-CHILD RELATIONSHIP

As noted in Chapter 6, there are those who argue that an accusation of sexual abuse can be decided on the basis of the interaction between the child and the parents (Gardner, 1992a, 1992b; Green, 1986; Guyer, 1983; Haynes-Seman & Baumgarten, 1994). In this section, I will reiterate and elaborate on the cautionary remarks in Chapter 6 in the discussion of the parent-child interaction model as an approach to assessing sexual abuse allegations.

Those who think the veracity of an abuse allegation can be ascertained by observing parent-child interactions assert that children who make false allegations may have symbiotic relationships with accusing parents and will turn to them for guidance during the interview (e.g., Green, 1986). Further, they state that sexual abuse is unlikely if the interaction between the alleged offender and the child appears to be appropriate (e.g., Haynes-Seman & Baumgarten, 1994). According to these professionals, children who have been sexually abused will interact in a sexual or provocative way with the abusive parent (Haynes-Seman & Baumgarten, 1994) or, alternatively, will be frightened and will avoid the offender (Gardner, 1992a, 1992b).

As noted in Chapter 6, there are even a few evaluators who believe that the child and the alleged abuser should be brought together and that the child should be asked to repeat the allegations to the offending parent (Benedek, 1987; Gardner, 1992a, 1992b; Green, 1986), although they do not necessarily agree about how to interpret the child's response.

The quality of the parent-child relationship is important for case disposition, regardless of whether sexual abuse is found, but there are serious practical and ethical obstacles to its use in a decision about the likelihood of sexual abuse. The limitations of what can be learned from observing the parent-child interaction will be addressed first. This will be followed by a discussion of the advisability of having a confrontation between the child and the accused parent, including asking the child to repeat the accusations.

Practical Obstacles to Accurately Interpreting Parent-Child Interactions

There are quite a few practical difficulties in assessing parent-child interactions. First, evaluators should be cautious about making too much of parent-child interaction during a circumscribed time frame in their presence. This is not to discount what is observed but to appreciate its limitations. What will be seen is one parent-child interaction but certainly not the entirety of the relationship and perhaps not what is typical. In addition, the evaluator's presence is likely to have an effect. A child may feel safe or alternatively inhibited in the presence of another adult. Moreover, because the accused parent will be very aware he is being scrutinized, he is likely to be on his best behavior.

Second, in some cases, the parent-child interaction observed will be the first contact for many months because visits have been curtailed following the sexual abuse allegation. Therefore, the evaluator may see an interaction distorted by the absence of contact. The interaction may also be affected by the custodial parent's opinion of the alleged offender. Thus, the child may express fear of or anger at the alleged offender; alternatively, the child may engage spontaneously, depending on the child's reaction to contact. These reactions may be independent of whether the parent sexually abused the child.

Third, it is worth bearing in mind that there are many aspects to a parent-child relationship other than the sexual abuse, if it has occurred. These are probably more apt to be displayed during the evaluation than the sexual aspect. Moreover, although sexual abuse or its possibility are of overriding salience to evaluators and other adults, the abuse issue may not be very salient to the child.

Fourth, the differences between an appropriate parent-child relationship and a sexualized one may be quite subtle; a potentially sexual interaction may be misunderstood to be an appropriate one. A parent can be quite invested in the child, a positive attribute, but as a vehicle for meeting the parent's needs, including sexual needs. Parents who are sexually abusive often are capable of being nurturing. The sexual interaction between adult and child may have evolved from appropriate hugging, caressing, and kissing. Moreover, as noted in Chapter 6, many sexual abusers are quite adept at playing appropriately with children. This may be because they are more comfortable with children than with adults and function on a regressed, childlike level.

For all of the above reasons, it is risky to rely on observations of parent-child interaction in determining whether a child has been sexually abused. Such observations will tell the evaluator something about the parent-child relationship but not all there is to know. Moreover, those observations may be open to a variety of interpretations, and, as noted in Chapter 6, the little research that exists indicates that evaluators, regardless of their level of experience, are not accurate at differentiating abusive from nonabusive interactions.

Ethical Considerations in Using Parent-Child Interactions

As mentioned, in addition to practical problems with relying on parent-child interactions, there are ethical considerations. The primary one that is the child may perceive such an encounter as a betrayal. If the child has trusted the evaluator enough to disclose sexual abuse, and then the evaluator requires the child to face the abuser, the child may experience this as a violation of her trust. The child was led to believe that it was safe to tell and then suddenly discovered that it was not. Children who have been sexually abused already have experienced betrayal by adults; the evaluator exacerbates the child's trust problems. Even when the child is not required to repeat her accusations to the accused, she will probably experience the parent-child interaction as a betrayal. However, most certainly if the child is required to confront the offender with the abuse, she will feel betrayed. It is curious that some writers think this confrontation appropriate, even though, in other sexual abuse cases, it is considered counterproductive because it usually leads to denial of actual sexual abuse. In therapy, such a confrontation may be a treatment goal, but use of this strategy usually requires a great deal of work and preparation.

Finally, there may be other ways of ascertaining the quality of the relationship between the child and the alleged offender. One is by asking the children what they like about the parent, what they dislike, whether they want to see that parent, and under what circumstances. A less desirable approach is asking the nonoffending parent; this is less desirable because the view may be biased. However, if the nonoffending parent says the relationship in the past was good, then there is good justification for maintaining and facilitating it. There may also be other people who can provide useful information—for example, other relatives, therapists, neighbors, and teachers.

Strategies for Protecting the Child

In this section, I will discuss how to manage cases where no sexual abuse is found, where sexual abuse is found, and where sexual abuse is uncertain. In discussing cases where sexual abuse is found, the rationale for fostering contact with the offender, the challenges of deciding when contact is appropriate, and strategies for facilitating contact will be described.

NO SEXUAL ABUSE IS FOUND

If, as a result of a careful assessment, there is no significant indication of sexual abuse, then the decision about custody should be based on criteria in the child custody statute, and visitation with the noncustodial parent (assuming this is the accused parent) should be liberal and unsupervised. However, if there has been a lot of turmoil surrounding the accusation, initially short and perhaps even supervised visits should precede unsupervised and liberal contact. Often the accused parent can be persuaded of the efficacy of this gradually increased access both out of empathy for the child and as a way of protecting himself against renewed allegations.

SEXUAL ABUSE IS FOUND

There is a lack of consensus in the field about what plan is preferable if sexual abuse is found. My opinion is that it is rarely in the child's best interest to totally sever contact with the abusive parent. Cases where that might be appropriate are those where the parent is dangerous or where contact is markedly traumatic for the child. A dangerous parent would be one who is a compulsive sexual abuser, who endeavors to molest the child even in the context of supervised visits, or who is likely to inflict physical harm on the child, the nonoffending parent, or a person supervising the visits. A determination that the visits are markedly traumatic to the child should be made by a neutral party, and a number of visits should be attempted before such a decision is made. Even when a decision to sever contact is made, there may come a time in the future when some contact with the offender is in the child's best interest.

Reasons for Allowing Contact Between the Child and Her Abuser

There are several reasons for a practice of trying to preserve the child's relationship with the offending parent. First, as noted earlier, there are many aspects to the relationship other than the sexual abuse, and these may well be worthy of preservation. One way of viewing the issue of sexual abuse is to appreciate that no parent is perfect, yet one does not sever the relationship because parents have problems. Sexual abuse can be viewed as one of many parental problems that children must be protected against, but the existence of problems does not rule out contact.

A second reason for maintaining the relationship is that it affords the child an opportunity to work through feelings about the sexual abuse as well as the divorce. Contact with the offender can serve as a stimulus for this processing.

A third and related reason is that access will encourage a realistic view of the offending parent. Without the contact, the child may come to view the parent as either all bad or all good. Either perception is problematic.

Possible Dispositions When the Parent Is an Abuser

When sexual abuse is substantiated, a possible disposition is no contact with the child until the offending parent has successfully completed treatment. In the abstract, this sounds like a sensible approach. However, problems may arise. Often the offender does not follow through on treatment and de facto relinquishes his relationship with the child. A different problem is that the offender may be pronounced cured when his problem has not been addressed. This may happen when his treatment is divorced from that of the victim and the nonoffending parent or when he seeks treatment from a clinician who lacks experience in treating sex offenders. The offender may deny that he has sexually abused the child and be believed by his therapist. The offender's therapist may unwittingly become the offender's advocate and recommend liberal contact. Therefore, as with other sex abuse treatment, contact between the offender's therapist and others in the family or their therapists is important.

Another possible disposition is supervised visits with the offender. Under ideal circumstances, the offender will also receive therapy. As a rule, these visits should be short and should not include overnights. The choice of a person to supervise will be very important and may prove an obstacle to visitation. Relatives provide the most flexibility. However, two problems may arise with relative supervision. If they are the nonoffending parent's relatives, the offender may find his relationship with them too difficult to allow for comfortable visits. On the other hand, if the relatives are the offender's, they may disbelieve or discount the importance of the sexual abuse and not provide the victim with adequate protection. As noted earlier, with this type of sexual abuse, there may be risk of subsequent maltreatment, despite court involvement and the vigilance of agencies and the nonoffending parent. One situation where reabuse may occur is when visits are supervised by the offender's relatives.

Additional potential supervisors of visits are persons from agencies who have responsibility for case management, such as CPS or the domestic relations court. An emerging service is one involving professional supervisors for visitation in CPS and divorce cases. Moreover, in some cases, a therapist involved with the family may furnish visit supervision. The advantages of these people as supervisors are that they are neutral and therefore likely to be acceptable to both parents and that they will be protective. The major disadvantages are the limited time they have available, the fact that their involvement may be time limited, and the cost of this type of supervision.

Another possibility is a jointly agreed-upon supervisor. This might be a friend of the family, a professional or paraprofessional who is moonlighting, or someone else. Problems that may occur in this arrangement are that the parents usually must pay for this service and that sometimes the person withdraws the service, particularly if there is a lot of hostility or if there are other difficulties around contact.

Finally, the issue of visit supervision may be resolved if the offender acquires a new partner. That person may become the supervisor of visits. Although the new partner shares with the offender's relatives the vulnerability of not being sufficiently protective, that partner's presence may decrease the potential for future sexual abuse because the offender's needs are being met by the new partner.

Unsupervised visits are rarely recommended in this type of sexual abuse because of the risk for reincidence. Liberal access should be resumed only when the offender has completed treatment successfully and the child wants the contact. Even then, contacts should be carefully monitored and extended and unsupervised access gradually introduced.

SEXUAL ABUSE IS UNCERTAIN

In addition to cases where sexual abuse is found and cases where it is not found are those where evaluators just cannot tell whether the child has been sexually abused. For a variety of reasons, these appear to occur at higher rates in custody/visitation disputes. The first is the young age of many victims (Faller, 1988a; Hewitt, 1991; MacFarlane, 1986; Paradise et al., 1988). MacFarlane first called attention to the very young age of some alleged victims in divorce situations and to the fact that, because of this, it may not be possible to determine whether the child has been sexually abused. In a study that compared characteristics of different kinds of intrafamilial sexual abuse cases, the mean age at evaluation for a sample of children sexually abused by a noncustodial father was 5.4 years. This was significantly younger than the age of victims of sexual abuse by biological fathers in intact families (8.7 years) and stepfathers (9.9 years) (Faller, 1988a). The second reason for inconclusive findings regarding sexual abuse is that children may be evaluated multiple times, and their accounts may be contaminated by this process. The third is the concern that they may have been pressured to say they were sexually abused when they were not.

A considerable dilemma is what to do regarding contact with the alleged offender when the results of evaluation are inconclusive. Hewitt (1991) has written a very sensible article that describes a strategy employed with seven cases of preschool children where the results of evaluations were inconclusive. She suggested the following. First, there is a meeting with the child to develop a list of acceptable and unacceptable touching from the child's viewpoint. Second is a meeting with the nonaccused parent to give her an opportunity to develop a similar list, to deal with her anxieties around resumed visits, and to teach her ways of asking nonleading questions and seeking help should further concerns arise about sexual abuse. Third is a meeting with the alleged offender to elicit a list of appropriate and inappropriate touching from him. Fourth is a meeting with the nonaccused parent and child to clarify appropriate and inappropriate touch and the child's strategy for telling should there be any inappropriate touching. Finally, there is a carefully orchestrated meeting between the child and the alleged offender in which they go over the list of appropriate and inappropriate touching and the alleged offender gives the child permission to tell should anyone, including himself, engage in bad touching. The evaluator then supervises several subsequent visits. Following that, unsupervised visits are introduced gradually, but there are meetings with the child alone to allow that child to disclose any inappropriate behavior on visits. Hewitt recommended involvement for at least a year and cited follow-up data on five cases, none of which had additional referrals for sexual abuse by the alleged offender. For further discussion of how to handle uncertain cases and cases involving young children, see Hewitt (1999).

Conclusion

The problem of sexual abuse allegations in custody/visitation disputes is complex. Such charges have the potential of being very damaging to children, regardless of their validity. Children must deal not only with the trauma of divorce but with the additional impact of an allegation and/or experience of sexual abuse.

Notes

1   For the sake of readability, the masculine pronoun will be used for the accused parent and the feminine for the nonaccused parent. However, I recognize that in a number of cases a woman is accused and a man does the accusing. The term *accusing parent* is not used because the person

making the allegation in many instances is someone other than a parent, often the alleged victim or a professional who has involvement with the victim.

2   *Morgan v. Foretich* (1988) was a very high-profile case in the 1980s. Eric Foretich, the father, was accused of sexually abusing his daughter, Hilary Morgan. Elizabeth Morgan, the mother and a plastic surgeon, went to jail three times, once for more than 2 years, and eventually sent the child to New Zealand to protect her daughter from unsupervised visits with the father.

3   The reader will note that the percentages add to more than 100%.

4   Items included in the scale were confirming characteristics in the child's statements, medical evidence, police evidence, conviction, confession, confirming evidence from another professional, and confirming information from a caretaker.

References

Abel, G., & Rouleau, J. (1990). Male sex offenders. In M. Thase (Ed.), *Handbook on outpatient treatment of adults: Nonpsychotic mental disorders* (pp. 271-290). New York: Plenum.

Abrams, S., & Abrams, J. (1993). *Polygraph testing of the pedophile.* Portland, OR: Ryan Gwinner.

Achenbach, T. (1993). *Child behavior checklist.* Burlington: University Medical Education Associates, University of Vermont College of Medicine.

Achenbach, T., & Edelbrock, C. (1983). *Manual for the Child Behavior Checklist and Revised Child Behavior Profile.* Burlington: University of Vermont College of Medicine.

Achenbach, T., Edelbrock, C., & Howell, C. (1987). Empirically-based assessment of behavioral/emotional problems of 2–3 year old children. *Journal of Abnormal Child Psychology, 15,* 629-650.

Adoption and Safe Families Act, 42 U.S.C.A. §§ 620, 670, et seq. (1997).

Agar, S. (1987, February 22). Daddy hurt me. *Free Press Magazine,* pp. 10-20.

American Academy of Child and Adolescent Psychiatry. (1997). *Guidelines for the evaluation of child and adolescent sexual abuse.* Washington, DC: Author.

American Association for the Protection of Children. (1985). *Highlights of official child neglect and abuse reporting, 1983.* Denver, CO: American Humane Association.

American Association for the Protection of Children. (1986). *Highlights of official child neglect and abuse reporting, 1984.* Denver, CO: American Humane Association.

American Association for the Protection of Children. (1987). *Highlights of official child neglect and abuse reporting, 1985.* Denver, CO: American Humane Association.

American Association for the Protection of Children. (1988). *Highlights of official child neglect and abuse reporting, 1986.* Denver, CO: American Humane Association.

American Association for the Protection of Children. (1989). *Highlights of official child neglect and abuse reporting, 1987.* Denver, CO: American Humane Association.

American Professional Society on the Abuse of Children. (1995). *Guidelines for the use of anatomical dolls.* Chicago: Author.

American Professional Society on the Abuse of Children. (1996). *Guidelines for the psychosocial evaluation of children suspected of being sexually abused.* Chicago: Author.

American Psychological Association. (1994). Guidelines for child custody evaluation in divorce proceedings. *American Psychologist, 49,* 667.

Applin, B., & Hunt, D. (2001, January). *Sexual exploitation of children and the Internet.* Presentation given at the Fifteenth Annual San Diego Conference on Responding to Child Maltreatment, San Diego.

Armstrong, L. (1976). *Kiss daddy goodnight: A speak-out on incest.* New York: Pocket Books.

August, R., & Foreman, B. (1989). A comparison of sexually abused and non-sexually abused children's behavioral responses to anatomically correct dolls. *Child Psychiatry and Human Development, 20*(1), 39-47.

Bala, N., Paetsch, R., Trocme, N., Schuman, D., Tanchak, M., & Hornick, J. (2001). *Allegations of child abuse in the context of parental separation: A discussion paper.* Research Report, 2001-FCY-4E Ottawa: Department of Justice, Canada.

Barden, R. C. (1995, January 5). Letter to Henry Hyde, Chairman of Judiciary Committee, signed by 30 professionals; accompanying draft statute. Available from R. Christopher Barden, 4025 Quaker Lane North, Plymouth, MN, 55441, tel. (612) 371-3296.

Barnitz, L. (2001). Effectively responding to the commercial sexual exploitation of children: A comprehensive approach to prevention, protection, and reintegration services. *Child Welfare, 80,* 597-610.

Barth, R., Courtney, M., Berrick, J. D., & Albert, V. (1997). *From child abuse to permanency planning: Child welfare service, pathways, and placements.* Hawthorne, NY: Aldine de Gruyter.

Barth, R., Yeaton, J., & Winterfelt, N. (1994). Psychoeducational groups for foster parents with sexually abused children. *Child and Adolescent Social Work Journal, 11,* 405-424.

Bays, J., & Chadwick, D. (1993). Medical diagnosis of the sexually abused child. *Child Abuse and Neglect 17,* 91-110.

Becker, J. (1985, November). *Evaluating and treating adolescent sexual offenders.* Paper presented at the Seventh National Conference on Child Abuse and Neglect, Chicago.

Bench, L. L., Kramer, S., & Erickson. S. (1997). Chapter 15: A discriminant analysis of predictive factors on sex offender recidivism. In B. Schwartz & H. Cellini (Eds.), *The sex offender: New insights, treatment innovations, and legal developments* (pp. 15-1 to 15-12). Kingston, NJ: Civic Research Institute.

Benedek, E. (1987). Court testimony, *E. Morgan v. E. Foretich, V. Foretich, D. Foretich,* Alexandria, Virginia, U.S. District Court, February 18, Civil Action No. 86 0944.

Benedek, E., & Schetky, D. (1985). Allegations of sexual abuse in child custody and visitation disputes. In E. Benedek & D. Schetky (Eds.), *Emerging issues in child psychiatry and the law* (pp. 1-25). New York: Brunner/Mazel.

Benedek, E., & Schetky, D. (1987). Clinical experience: Problems in validating allegations of sexual abuse. Part 1: Factors affecting the perception and recall of events. *Journal of the American Academy of Child and Adolescent Psychiatry, 26,* 912-915.

Benedict, M., Zuravin, S., Somerfield, M., & Brandt, D. (1996). The reported health and functioning of children maltreated while in family foster care. *Child Abuse and Neglect, 20,* 561-571.

Berliner, L. (1988). Deciding whether a child has been sexually abused. In E. B. Nicholson & J. Bulkley (Eds.), *Sexual abuse allegations in custody and visitation cases* (pp. 3-32). Washington, DC: American Bar Association.

Berliner, L. (1998). The use of expert testimony in child sexual abuse cases. In S. Ceci & H. Hembrooke (Eds.), *Expert witnesses in child abuse cases.* Washington, DC: American Psychological Association.

Berliner, L., & Conte, J. (1993). Sexual abuse evaluations: Conceptual and empirical obstacles. *Child Abuse and Neglect, 17,* 111-125.

Berliner, L., & Saunders, B. (1996). Treating fear and anxiety in sexually abused children: Results of a controlled 2 year follow-up study. *Child Maltreatment, 1*(4), 294-309.

Besharov, D. (1986). "Doing something" about child abuse: The need to narrow the grounds for state intervention. *Harvard Journal of Law and Public Policy, 8,* 459-566.

Bienenfeld, F. (1988). *Child custody mediation.* New York: Science and Behavior Books.

Bikel, O. (Director & Producer). (1993, July 20 & 21). Innocence lost. *Frontline.* New York: Public Broadcasting Service.

Bloom v. Braun, 317 Ill. App. 3d 720; 739 N.E.2d 925 (2000).

Blush, G., & Ross, K. (1986). *Sexual allegations in divorce: The SAID syndrome.* Unpublished manuscript, Mt. Clemens, MI.

Boat, B., & Everson, M. (1994). Exploration of anatomical dolls by non-referred pre-school-aged children: Comparisons by age, gender, race, and socioeconomic status. *Child Abuse and Neglect, 18,* 139-154.

Bolen, R., & Scannapieco, M. (1999). Prevalence of child sexual abuse: A corrective metanalysis. *Social Services Review, 73*, 281-313.

Bourg, W., Broderick, R., Flagor, R., Kelly, D., Ervin, D., & Butler, J. (1999). *A child interviewer's guidebook.* Thousand Oaks, CA: Sage.

Boychuk, T., & Stellar, M. (1992). *Videotaped forensic interview of the school aged child.* Unpublished manuscript. Available from Tasha Boychuk, Ph.D., Center for Child Protection, St. Joseph's Hospital, Phoenix, AZ.

Bradley, A., & Wood, J. (1996). How do children tell? The disclosure process in child sexual abuse. *Child Abuse and Neglect, 20*, 881-891.

Braga, W., & Schimmer, R. (1993). *Sexual abuse and residential treatment.* New York: Haworth.

Brainerd, C., & Ornstein, P. (1991). Children's memories for witnessed events. In J. Doris (Ed.), *The suggestibility of children's recollections* (pp. 10-20). New York: American Psychological Association.

Bremner, J. D., Krystal, J., Southwick, S., & Cahrney, D. (1995). Functional neuroanatomical correlations of the effects of stress on memory. *Journal of Traumatic Stress, 8*, 527-554.

Bresee, P., Stearns, G., Bess, B., & Packer, L. (1986). Allegations of child sexual abuse in child custody disputes: A therapeutic assessment model. *American Journal of Orthopsychiatry, 56*, 560-568.

Britton, H., & O'Keefe, M. A. (1991). Use of nonanatomical dolls in the sexual abuse interview. *Child Abuse and Neglect, 15*, 567-573.

Brown, T., Frederico, M., Hewitt, L., & Sheehan, R. (2000). Revealing the existence of child abuse in the context of marital breakdown and custody and access disputes. *Child Abuse and Neglect, 24*, 849-859.

Bruck, M., Ceci, S., Francoeur, E., & Renick, A. (1995). Anatomically detailed dolls do not facilitate preschoolers' reports of a pediatric examination involving genital touching. *Journal of Experimental Psychology: Applied, 1*(2), 95-109.

Bruck, M., Ceci, S., & Hembrooke, H. (1998). Reliability and credibility of young children's reports: From research to policy and practice. *American Psychologist, 53*, 136-151.

Bull, R. (1995). Innovative techniques for questioning children, especially those who are young and those who are learning disabled. In M. Zaragoza, J. Graham, G. Hall, R. Hirschman, & Y. Ben-Porath (Eds.), *Memory and testimony in the child witness* (pp. 179-194). Newbury Park, CA: Sage.

Burgess, A. (1984). *Child pornography and sex rings.* Lexington, MA: Lexington.

Burgess, A., Baker, T., & Hartman, C. (1996). Parents' perceptions of their children's recovery 5 to 10 years following day-care abuse. *Scholarly Inquiry for Nursing Practice, 101*, 75-92.

Bybee, D., & Mowbray, C. (1993). An analysis of allegations of sexual abuse in a multi-victim day-care center case. *Child Abuse and Neglect, 17*, 767-783.

Cage, J. (1988). Criminal investigation of child sexual abuse cases. In S. Sgroi (Ed.), *Vulnerable populations: Evaluation and treatment of sexually abused children and adult survivors* (Vol. 1, pp. 127-228). Lexington, MA: Lexington.

Campagna, D., & Poffenberger, D. (1988). *The sexual trafficking in children.* Dover, MA: Auburn House.

Cantlon, J., Payne, G., & Erbaugh, C. (1996). Outcome based practice: Disclosure rates of child sexual abuse comparing allegation blind and allegation informed structured interviews. *Child Abuse and Neglect, 20*, 1113-1120.

Carlson, N., & Riebel, J. (1978). *Family sexual abuse: A resource manual for health services professionals.* Minneapolis: University of Minnesota, Department of Family Practice and Community Health.

Carnes, C., Gardell, D., & Wilson, C. (2000). Addressing challenges and controversies in child sexual abuse interviewing. The Forensic Evaluation Protocol and Research Project. In K. C. Faller (Ed.), *Maltreatment in early childhood: Tools for research-based intervention* (pp. 83-104). New York: Haworth.

Carnes, C., & LeDuc, D. (1994). *Forensic evaluation of children.* Huntsville, AL: National Children's Advocacy Center.

Carnes, P. (1984.) *The sexual addiction.* Minneapolis, MN: CompCare.

Cavanagh-Johnson, T. (1988). Child perpetrators: Children who molest other children: Preliminary findings. *Child Abuse and Neglect, 12,* 219-229.

Cavanaugh-Johnson, T. (1997). *Sexual, physical, and emotional abuse in out-of-home care: Prevention skills for at-risk children.* New York: Haworth.

Ceci, S., & Bruck, M. (1993). The suggestibility of the child witness: A historical review and synthesis. *Psychological Bulletin, 113,* 403-439.

Ceci, S., & Bruck, M. (1995). *Jeopardy in the courtroom.* New York: American Psychological Association.

Ceci, S., Huffman, M., Smith, E., & Loftus, E. (1994). Repeatedly thinking about a non-event: Source misattributions among preschoolers. *Consciousness and Cognition, 3,* 388-407.

Ceci, S., Loftus, E., Leichtman, M., & Bruck, M. (1994). The role of source misattributions in the creation of false beliefs among preschoolers. *International Journal of Clinical and Experimental Hypnosis, 62,* 304-320.

Chaffin, M., & Stern, P. (2001, June). *Child abuse in the 1980s: What were we thinking?* Presentation given at the National Colloquium of the American Professional Society on Child Abuse, Baltimore.

Child Abuse Prevention and Treatment Act, 42 U.S.C. 5101-5107 (1974).

Child Abuse Prevention, Adoption, and Family Services Act, Pub. L. No. 100-294 (1988).

Children of the Underground Watch. (2001). Editorial: Underground mother arrested. www.members.aol.com/underwatch/. Accessed July 29, 2002.

Clarke-Stewart, A., Thompson, W., & Lapore, S. (1989, April). *Manipulating children's interpretations through interrogation.* Paper presented at the Society for Research on Child Development, Kansas City, KS.

Cohen, J., & Mannarino, A. (1996). Treatment outcome study for sexually abused pre-schoolers. *Journal of the American Academy of Child and Adolescent Psychiatry, 35,* 42-50.

Cohn, D. (1991). Anatomical doll play of preschoolers referred for sexual abuse and those not referred. *Child Abuse and Neglect, 15,* 455-466.

Colby, I., & Colby, D. (1987a). Videotaped interviews in child sexual abuse cases: The Texas example. *Child Welfare, 66,* 25-34.

Colby, I., & Colby, D. (1987b). Videotaping the child sexual-abuse victim. *Social Casework, 68,* 117-121.

Committee on the Family, Group for the Advancement of Psychiatry. (1980). *Divorce, child custody, and the family.* San Francisco: Jossey-Bass.

Conte, J., & Berliner, L. (1986). *The impact of sexual abuse on children.* Final Report No. MH37133. Bethesda, Md.: National Institute of Mental Health.

Conte, J., & Berliner, L. (1988). The impact of sexual abuse. In Lenore Walker (Ed.), *Handbook on sexual abuse of children* (pp. 72-93). New York: Guilford.

Conte, J., Sorenson, E., Fogarty, L., & Dalla Rosa, J. (1991). Evaluating children's reports of sexual abuse: Results from a survey of professionals. *American Journal of Orthopsychiatry, 61,* 428-437.

Corwin, D. (1988). Early diagnosis of child sexual abuse: Diminishing the lasting effects. In G. Wyatt & G. Powell (Eds.), *The lasting effects of child sexual abuse* (pp. 251-270). Newbury Park, CA: Sage.

Corwin, D., Berliner, L., Goodman, G., Goodwin, J., & White, S. (1987). Child sexual abuse and custody disputes: No easy answers. *Journal of Interpersonal Violence 2(1),* 91-105.

Crewdson, J. (1988). *By silence betrayed.* New York: Harper & Row.

Cross, T., De Vos, E., & Whitcomb, D. (1994). Prosecution of child sexual abuse: Which cases are accepted? *Child Abuse and Neglect, 18,* 661-677.

Cross, T., & Saxe, L. (1992). A critique of the validity of polygraph testing in child sexual abuse cases. *Journal of Child Sexual Abuse, 1(4),* 19-33.

Cross, T., & Saxe, L. (2001). Polygraph testing and sexual abuse: The lure of the magic lasso. *Child Maltreatment, 6*(3), 195-206.

Cross, T., Whitcomb, D., & De Vos, E. (1995). Criminal justice outcomes of prosecution of child sexual abuse. *Child Abuse and Neglect, 19,* 1231-1442.

Dallam, S. (2001). Crisis or creation? A systematic examination of the "False Memory Syndrome." *Journal of Child Sexual Abuse, 9*(3/4), 9-36.

Daro, D. (1988). *Confronting child abuse.* New York: Free Press.

Daro, D., & Cohen, A. (1984). *A decade of child maltreatment and evaluation efforts: What we have learned.* Paper given at the Second National Conference of Family Violence Researchers, Durham, NH.

Davies, D., Cole, J., Albertella, G., McCulloch, L., Allen, K., & Kekevian, H. (1996). A model for conducting forensic interviews of child victims of abuse. *Child Maltreatment, 1*(2), 189-200.

Davin, P., Hislop, J., & Dunbar, T. (1999). *Female sexual abusers.* Orwell, VT: Safer Society Press.

De Young, M. (1984). Counter-phobic behavior in multiply victimized children. *Child Welfare, 63,* 333-339.

De Young, M. (1986). A conceptual model for judging the truthfulness of a young child's allegation of sexual abuse. *American Journal of Orthopsychiatry, 56,* 550-559.

Deblinger, E., Lippman, J., & Steer, R. (1996). Sexually abused children suffering from post traumatic stress symptoms: Initial treatment outcome studies. *Child Maltreatment, 1*(4), 310-321.

Deitrich-MacLean, G., & Walden, T. (1988). Distinguishing teaching interactions of physically abusive from nonabusive parent-child dyads. *Child Abuse and Neglect, 12,* 469-480.

DeLoache, J. (1995). The use of dolls in interviewing young children. In M. Zaragoza, J. Graham, G. Hall, R. Hirschman, & Y. Ben-Porath, (Eds.), *Memory and testimony in the child witness* (pp. 160-178). Newbury Park, CA: Sage.

Detrich, A., & Carpenter, M. (1997, Dec. 14-17). Children of the Underground. *Pittsburgh Post-Gazette,* pp. 1-26.

DeVoe, E. R., & Faller, K. C. (1999). Characteristics of disclosure of children who may have been sexually abused. *Child Maltreatment 4*(3), 217-227.

DeVoe, E. R., & Faller, K. C. (2002). Disclosure patterns in children who may have been sexually abused. *Child Maltreatment, 81*(1), 5-32.

Doueck, H., English, D., DePanfilis, D., & Moote, G. (1993). Decision-making in Child Protective Services: A comparison of selected risk assessment models. *Child Welfare, 72,* 441-452.

Drake, B. (2000). How do I decide whether to substantiate a report? In H. Dubowitz & D. DePanfilis (Eds.), *Handbook for child protection* (pp. 113-117). Thousand Oaks, CA: Sage.

Dubowitz, H., & DePanfilis, D. (Eds.). (2000). *Handbook for child protection.* Thousand Oaks, CA: Sage.

Ducote, R. (2000). What I have learned at the courthouse. In E. St. Charles & L. Crook (Eds.), *Expose: The failure of family courts to protect children from abuse in custody disputes* (pp. 11-140). Los Gatos, CA: Our Children Our Future Charitable Foundation.

Dunkerley, G., & Dalenberg, C. (2000). Secret-keeping in black and white children as a function of interviewer race, racial identity, and risk for abuse. In K. C. Faller (Ed.), *Maltreatment in early childhood: Tools for research-based intervention* (pp. 13-36). New York: Haworth.

Duquette, D. (1981). Legal aspects of child abuse and neglect. In K. C. Faller (Ed.), *Social work with abused and neglected children.* New York: Free Press.

Duquette, D. (1990). *Advocating for the child in protection proceedings: A handbook for lawyers and court appointed special advocates.* San Francisco: Jossey-Bass.

Duquette, D. (2000). Legal representation of children in protection proceedings: Two distinct lawyer roles are required. *Family Law Quarterly, 34,* 441-466.

Duquette, D., Faller, K. C., & D'Aunno, L. (1988a). *Child Protective Services in Michigan: Recommendations for policy and practice.* Ann Arbor: University of Michigan, Interdisciplinary Project on Child Abuse and Neglect.

Duquette, D., Faller, K. C., & D'Aunno, L. (1988b). Putting protective services in its place. In D. Duquette, K. C. Faller, & D'Aunno, L. (Eds.), *Child Protective Services in Michigan: Recommendations for policy and practice*. Ann Arbor: University of Michigan, Interdisciplinary Project on Child Abuse and Neglect.

Duquette, D., & Ramsey, S. (1987). Representation of children in child abuse and neglect cases: An empirical look at what constitutes effective representation. *Journal of Law Reform, 20*, 341-407.

Eberle, P., & Eberle, S. (1986). *The politics of child abuse*. Secaucus, NJ: Lyle Stuart.

Ehrensaft, D. (1992). Preschool child sexual abuse: The aftermath of the Presidio case. *American Journal of Orthopsychiatry, 62*, 234-244.

Eisen, M., Goodman, G., Davis, S., & Qin, J. (1999). Individual differences in maltreated children's memory and suggestibility. In L. Williams & V. Banyard (Eds.), *Trauma and memory* (pp. 31-46). Thousand Oaks, CA: Sage.

Eisen, M. Goodman, G., Qin, J., & Davis, S. (1998). Memory and suggestibility in maltreated children: New research relevant to evaluating allegations of abuse. In S. Lynn & K. McConkey (Eds.), *Truth in memory* (pp. 153-180). New York: Guilford.

Elliott, D., & Briere, J. (1994). Forensic sexual abuse evaluations of older children: Disclosures and symptomatology. *Behavioral Science and the Law, 12*, 261-277.

Elliot, M. (1993). *Female sexual abuse of children: The ultimate taboo*. London: Longman.

Everson, M. (1996, January). *Models for forensic assessment of children who may have been sexually abused*. Paper presented at the San Diego Conference: Responding to Child Maltreatment, San Diego, CA.

Everson, M. (2000). *Forensic interviewing think tank*. Paper presented at the San Diego Conference: Responding to Child Maltreatment, San Diego, CA.

Everson. M., & Boat, B. (1994). Putting the anatomical doll controversy in perspective: An examination of the major doll uses and related criticisms. *Child Abuse and Neglect, 18*, 113-130.

Everson, M., & Boat, B. (1996). Concerning practices using anatomical dolls. *Child Maltreatment, 2*(1), 96-104.

Everson, M., Hunter, W., & Runyan, D. (1989). Maternal support following disclosure of incest. *American Journal of Orthopsychiatry, 59*, 197-207.

Fahlberg, V. (1997). *Creating kinship*. Portland, OR: Doughy Center.

Faller, K. C. (Ed.). (1981). *Social work with abused and neglected children: A manual of interdisciplinary practice*. New York: Free Press.

Faller, K. C. (1984). Is the child victim of sexual abuse telling the truth? *Child Abuse and Neglect, 8*, 473-481.

Faller, K. C. (1985). Unanticipated problems in the United States child protection system. *Child Abuse and Neglect, 9*, 63-69.

Faller, K. C. (1986). *Case management using home based devices with high risk families*. Ann Arbor: University of Michigan, Interdisciplinary Project on Child Abuse and Neglect.

Faller, K. C. (1988a). *Child sexual abuse: An interdisciplinary manual for diagnosis, case management, and treatment*. New York: Columbia University Press.

Faller, K. C. (1988b). Children who are sexually abused by more than one person. *Victimology, 12*, 21-29.

Faller, K. C. (1988c). Criteria for judging the credibility of children's statements about their sexual abuse. *Child Welfare, 67*, 389-401.

Faller, K. C. (1988d). The spectrum of sexual abuse in daycare: An exploratory study. *Journal of Family Violence, 3*, 283-298.

Faller, K. C. (1990). *Understanding child sexual maltreatment*. Newbury Park, CA: Sage.

Faller, K. C. (1991a). Polyincestuous families: An exploratory study. *Journal of Interpersonal Violence, 6*, 310-322.

Faller, K. C. (1991b). Possible explanations for child sexual abuse allegations in divorce. *American Journal of Orthopsychiatry, 61*, 86-91.

Faller, K. C. (1993a). *Child sexual abuse: Intervention and treatment issues.* Washington, DC: U.S. Department of Health and Human Services.

Faller, K. C. (1993b, Fall). Ritual abuse: A continuum of belief. *Believe the Children Newsletter,* pp. 2-3.

Faller, K. C. (1994a). Child sexual abuse allegations: How to decide when they are true. *Violence Update, 4*(6), 2-4, 8-11.

Faller, K. C. (1994b). Extrafamilial sexual abuse. In S. Kaplan & D. Pelcovitz (Eds.), *Child and adolescent clinics of North America* (pp. 713-727). New York: W. B. Saunders.

Faller, K. C. (1994c). Ritual abuse: A review of the research. *APSAC Advisor, 7*(2), 1, 19-27.

Faller, K. C. (1995). A clinical sample of women who have sexually abused children. *Journal of Child Sexual Abuse, 4*(3), 13-30.

Faller, K. C. (1996a). Interviewing children who may have been abused: A historical perspective and overview of controversies. *Child Maltreatment, 1*(2), 4-18.

Faller, K. C. (1996b). *Study guide: Evaluating children suspected of having been sexually abused.* Newbury Park, CA: Sage.

Faller, K. C. (1997). The polygraph, its use in decision-making about child sexual abuse: An exploratory study. *Child Abuse and Neglect, 21,* 993-1008.

Faller, K. C. (1998a). *The flexible interview: The University of Michigan model for interviewing children who may have been sexually abused.* Unpublished manuscript. Ann Arbor: University of Michigan School of Social Work.

Faller, K. C. (1998b). *Interviewing for sexual abuse: A forensic guide.* New York: Guilford.

Faller, K. C. (1999, April). *Assessing children who may have been sexually abused: What can the research tell us?* Paper presented at the Colloquium Series on Child Welfare, State University of New Jersey at Rutgers, School of Social Work.

Faller, K. C. (2000a). Child maltreatment and protection in the United States. *Journal of Aggression, Trauma, and Maltreatment, 2*(4), 1-12.

Faller, K. C. (Ed.). (2000b). *Maltreatment in early childhood: Tools for research-based intervention.* New York: Haworth.

Faller, K. C., & Corwin, D. (1995). Children's interview statements and behaviors, professional consensus and research findings for the identification of sexually abused children. *Child Abuse and Neglect, 19,* 71-82.

Faller, K. C., & DeVoe, E. (1995a). Allegations of sexual abuse in divorce. *Journal of Child Sexual Abuse, 4*(4),1-25.

Faller, K. C., & DeVoe, E. (1995b). *Final report: Computer assisted interviewing with children who may have been sexually abused.* Available from K. C. Faller, University of Michigan School of Social Work, 1080 S. University, Ann Arbor, MI, 48109-1066.

Faller, K. C., Froning, M., & Lipovsky, J. (1991). The parent-child interview: Use in evaluating child allegations of sexual abuse by a parent. *American Journal of Orthopsychiatry, 61,* 552-557.

Faller, K. C., & Henry, J. (2000). Child sexual abuse: A case study in community collaboration. *Child Abuse and Neglect, 24,* 1215-1225.

False Memory Syndrome Foundation. (1992). *The false memory syndrome phenomenon.* Philadelphia: Author.

False Memory Syndrome Foundation. (1998). Legal Corner. *False Memory Foundation Newsletter, 7*(4), 6-8.

Farley, R. (2001, January). *Advanced investigation in child sexual abuse and child exploitation cases.* Paper presented at the Fifteenth Annual San Diego Conference on Responding to Child Maltreatment, San Diego, CA.

Finkel, M. (1989). Anogenital trauma in sexually abused children. *Pediatrics, 84,* 317-322.

Finkelhor, D. (1979a). *Sexually victimized children.* New York: Free Press.

Finkelhor, D. (1979b). What's wrong with sex between adults and children? *American Journal of Orthopsychiatry, 49,* 692-697.

Finkelhor, D. (1984). *Child sexual abuse: New theory and research.* New York: Free Press.

Finkelhor, D., Hotaling, G., & Sedlak, A. (1992). The abduction of children by strangers and nonfamily members: Estimating the incidence using multiple methods. *Journal of Interpersonal Violence, 7,* 226-243.

Finkelhor, D., & Jones, L. (2001, January). *Sexual solicitation of children over the Internet.* Research symposium presented at the San Diego Conference on Responding to Child Maltreatment, Center for Child Protection, San Diego, CA.

Finkelhor, D., Mitchell, K., & Wolak, J. (2000). *Online victimization: A report on the nation's youth.* Washington, DC: National Center for Missing and Exploited Children.

Finkelhor, D., Moore, D., Hamby, S., & Straus, M. (1997). Sexually abused children in a national survey of parents: Methodological issues. *Child Abuse and Neglect, 21*(1), 1-10.

Finkelhor, D., Williams, L., & Burns, N. (1988). *Nursery crimes: Sexual abuse in day care.* Newbury Park, CA: Sage.

Fivush, R. (1993). Developmental perspectives on autobiographical recall. In G. Goodman & B. Bottoms (Eds.), *Child victims, child witnesses* (pp. 1-24). New York: Guilford.

Fivush, R., & Shukat, J. (1995). Content, consistency, and coherence of early autobiographical memory. In M. Zaragoza, J. Graham, G. Hall, R. Hirschman, & Y. Ben-Porath (Eds.), *Memory and suggestibility in the child witness* (pp. 5-23). Thousand Oaks, CA: Sage.

Fontes, L. (1995). *Sexual abuse in nine North American cultures.* Newbury Park, CA: Sage.

Freedom of Information Act, 5 U.S.C. § 552 (1974).

Freyd, J. (1993). Personal perspectives on the delayed memory debate. *Family Violence and Sexual Assault Bulletin, 9*(3), 28-33.

Friedrich, W. (1990). *Psychotherapy with sexually abused children and their families.* New York: Norton.

Friedrich, W. (1993). Sexual victimization and sexual behavior in children: A review of recent literature. *Child Abuse and Neglect, 17,* 59-66.

Friedrich, W. (1994, January). *Standardized measures for assessing child sexual abuse.* Workshop presented at the Eighth Annual San Diego Conference on Responding to Child Maltreatment, San Diego, CA.

Friedrich, W. (1997). *The Child Sexual Behavior Inventory.* Lutz, FL: Psychological Assessment Resources, Inc.

Friedrich, W. (1999). *The Child Sexual Behavior Inventory.* Lutz, FL.: Psychological Assessment Resources.

Friedrich, W., Berliner, L., Butler, J., Cohen, J., Damon, L. & Shafram, C. (1996a). Child sexual behavior: An update with the CSBI-3. *APSAC Advisor, 9*(4), 13-14.

Friedrich, W., Berliner, L., Butler, J., Cohen, J., Damon, L., & Shafram, C. (1996b, July). *Normative sexual behaviors: CSBI-3.* Paper presented at Trauma and Memory: An International Research Conference, Durham, NH.

Friedrich, W., Grambsch, P., Broughton, D., Kuiper, J., & Beilke, R. (1991). Normative sexual behavior in children. *Pediatrics, 88,* 256-264.

Fromuth, M., & Burkhart, B. (1987). Childhood sexual victimization among college men: Definitional and methodological issues. *Victims and Violence, 2,* 241-253.

The funding fount [Editorial]. (2001, July 10). *Wall Street Journal,* p. A14.

Gallagher, B. (1999). The abuse of children in public care. *Child Abuse Review, 8,* 357-365.

Galtney, L. (1988, June 13). Mothers on the run. *U.S. News and World Report,* pp. 22-32.

Gardner, R. (1987). *The parental alienation syndrome and the differentiation between fabricated and genuine child sexual abuse.* Cresskill, NJ: Creative Therapeutics.

Gardner, R. (1991). *Sex abuse hysteria: Salem witch trials revisited.* Cresskill, NJ: Creative Therapeutics.

Gardner, R. (1992a). *The parental alienation syndrome.* Cresskill, NJ: Creative Therapeutics.

Gardner, R. (1992b). *True and false allegations of child sex abuse.* Cresskill, NJ: Creative Therapeutics.

Gardner, R. (1995). *Protocols for the sex-abuse evaluation.* Cresskill, NJ: Creative Therapeutics.

Gil, E. (1982). Institutional abuse of children in out of home care. *Children and Youth Services, 4*(1, Suppl. 3), 7-12.

Goldsmith, S. (2000). Little girl's hell. In E. St. Charles & L. Crook (Eds.), *Expose: The failure of family courts to protect children from abuse in custody disputes* (pp. 113-122). Los Gatos, CA: Our Children Our Future Charitable Foundation.

Goldstein, S. (1987). *Sexual exploitation of children.* New York: Elsevier.

Goodman, G., Aman, C., & Hirschman, J. (1987). Child sexual and physical abuse: Children's testimony. In S. J. Ceci, M. P. Toglia, & D. Ross (Eds.), *Children's eyewitness testimony* (pp. 1-23). New York: Springer-Verlag.

Goodman, G., Bottoms, B., Qin, J., & Shaver, P. (1994). *Characteristics and sources of allegations of ritualistic child abuse. Grant No. 90CA1405.* Final report to the National Center on Child Abuse and Neglect. Washington, DC: National Clearinghouse on Child Abuse and Neglect.

Goodman, G., & Clarke-Stewart, A. (1991). The suggestibility of children's testimony: Implications for sexual abuse investigations. In J. Doris (Ed.), *The suggestibility of children's recollections* (pp. 92-105). New York: American Psychological Association.

Goodman, G., Hirschman, J., Hepps, D., & Rudy, L. (1991). Children's memory for a stressful event. *Merrill-Palmer Quarterly, 37,* 109-158.

Goodman, G., Pyle-Taub, E., Jones, D. P. H., England, P., Port, L. K., Rudy, L., & Prado, L. (1992). Testifying in criminal court. *Monographs of the Society for Research on Child Development, 57*(5, Serial No. 229). Chicago: University of Chicago Press.

Goodman, G. S., Quas, J. A., Batterman-Faunce, J. M., Riddlesberger, M. M., & Kuhn, J. (1997). Children's reactions to and memory for a stressful event: Influences of age, anatomical dolls, knowledge, and parental attachment. *Applied Developmental Science, 1*(2), 54-75.

Goodwin, J., Sahd, D., & Rada, R. (1980). Incest hoax. In W. Holder (Ed.), *Sexual abuse of children* (pp. 37-46). Englewood, CO: American Humane Association.

Gordon, B., Ornstein, P., Nida, R., Follmer, A., Crenshaw, C., & Albert, G. (1993). Does the use of dolls facilitate children's memories of visits to the doctor? *Applied Cognitive Psychology, 7,* 459-474.

Gorey, K., & Leslie, D. (1997). Prevalence of child sexual abuse: Integrative review and adjustment for potential response and measurement bias. *Child Abuse and Neglect, 21*(4), 391-398.

Graffam-Walker, A. (1994). *Handbook on questioning children.* Washington, DC: American Bar Association.

Gray, E. (1993). *Unequal justice: The prosecution of child sexual abuse.* New York: Free Press.

Green, A. (1986). True and false allegations of sexual abuse in child custody disputes. *Journal of the American Academy of Child Psychiatry, 25,* 449-456.

Groth, N. (1979). *Men who rape.* New York: Plenum.

Groth, N., & Stevenson, T. (1990). *Anatomical drawings.* Dunedin, FL: Forensic Mental Health Associates.

Guyer, M. (1983). False allegations of child abuse. Class presentation, University of Michigan Law School, Ann Arbor.

Hanson, G. (1988). The sex abuse controversy: Letter to the editor. *Journal of the American Academy of Child and Adolescent Psychiatry, 27,* 258.

Haralambie, A. (1993). *The child's attorney.* Chicago: American Bar Association.

Haralambie, A. (1999). *Child sexual abuse in civil cases.* Chicago: American Bar Association.

Hare, R. D. (1991). *The Hare Psychopathy Checklist: Revised manual.* Toronto: Multi-Health Systems.

Haynes-Seman, C., & Baumgarten, D. (1994). *Children speak for themselves.* New York: Brunner/Mazel.

Hechler, D. (1988). *The battle and the backlash.* Lexington, MA: Lexington.

Heiman, M. (1992). Annotation: Putting the puzzle together: Validating allegations of child sexual abuse. *Journal of Child Psychology and Psychiatry, 33*(2), 311-329.

Heriot, J. (1996). Maternal protectiveness following disclosure of sexual abuse. *Journal of Interpersonal Violence, 11*, 181-194.

Herman, J. (2000). *Incest.* Boston: Cambridge University Press.

Hewitt, S. (1991). Therapeutic case management of pre-school cases of alleged but not substantiated sexual abuse. *Child Welfare, 70*, 59-67.

Hewitt, S. (1999). *Assessing allegation of sexual abuse in preschool children: Understanding small voices.* Thousand Oaks, CA: Sage.

Hibbard, R. A., & Hartman, G. (1990). Emotional indicators in human figure drawings of sexually victimized and nonabused children. *Journal of Clinical Psychology, 46*, 211-219.

Hibbard, R. A., Roghmann, K., & Hoekelman, R. A. (1987). Genitalia in children's drawings: An association with sexual abuse. *Pediatrics, 79*, 129-37.

Hobbs, G., Hobbs, C., & Wynne, J. (1999). Abuse of children in foster and residential care. *Child Abuse and Neglect, 23*, 1239-1252.

Holden, C. (1989). Science in court. *Science, 243*, 1658-1659.

Holder, W. (2000). How do I assess risk and safety? In H. Dubowitz & D. DePanfilis (Eds.), *Handbook for child protection* (pp. 27-32). Thousand Oaks, CA: Sage.

Hollingsworth, J. (1986). *Unspeakable acts.* New York: Congdon & Weed.

Home Office. (1992). *Memorandum of good practice on video recorded interviews with child witnesses in criminal proceedings.* London: Her Majesty's Stationery Office.

Hoorwitz, A. N. (1992). *The clinical detective.* New York: Norton.

Horner, T., Guyer, M., & Kalter, N. (1993). The biases of child abuse experts. *Bulletin of the American Academy of Psychiatry and the Law, 21*, 261-292.

Hudson, J. A., & Fivush, R. (1987). *As time goes by: Sixth graders remember a kindergarten experience* (Emory Cognition Project No. 13). Atlanta: Emory University Department of Psychology.

Huffman, M., Crossman, A., & Ceci, S. (1997). Are false memories permanent? An investigation of long term effects of source misattributions. *Consciousness and Cognition, 6*, 482-490.

Hume, M. (1997). *Child sexual abuse allegations in the Family Court.* Unpublished master's thesis, University of South Australia Humanities and Social Sciences.

Humphreys, C. (1997). Child sexual abuse in the context of divorce: Issues for mothers. *British Journal of Social Work, 27*, 529-544.

Hunter, W., Coulter, M., Runyan, D., & Everson, M. (1990). Determinants of placement for sexually abused children. *Child Abuse and Neglect, 14*, 407-417.

Indian Child Welfare Act, 25 U.S.C.A. 1912 (e) & (f) (1978).

Jackson, H., & Nuttall, R. (1997). *Childhood abuse: Effects on clinicians' personal and professional lives.* Newbury Park, CA: Sage.

Jampole, L., & Webber, M. (1987). An assessment of the behavior of sexually abused and non-sexually abused children with anatomically correct dolls. *Child Abuse and Neglect, 11*, 187-192.

Jenny, C. (1996). Medical issues in sexual abuse. In J. Briere, L. Berliner, J. Bulkley, C. Jenny, & T. Reid (Eds.), *The APSAC handbook on child maltreatment* (pp. 195-205). Newbury Park, CA: Sage.

Jones, B. J. (1995). *The Indian child welfare handbook.* Chicago: American Bar Association.

Jones, D., & McGraw, E. M. (1987). Reliable and fictitious accounts of sexual abuse to children. *Journal of Interpersonal Violence, 2*, 27-46.

Jones, D., & McQuiston, M. (1985). *Interviewing the sexually abused child.* Denver, CO: Kempe National Center for the Prevention and Treatment of Child Abuse and Neglect.

Jones, D., & Seig, A. (1988). Child sexual abuse allegations in custody or visitation cases: A report of 20 cases. In E. B. Nicholson & J. Bulkley (Eds.), *Sexual abuse allegations in custody and visitation cases* (pp. 22-36). Washington, DC: American Bar Association.

Jones, L., & Finkelhor, D. (2001, January). *The decline in child sexual abuse cases.* Washington, DC: Department of Justice, Office of Juvenile Justice and Delinquency Prevention.

Jonker, F., & Jonker-Bakker, P. (1991). Experiences with ritualistic child sexual abuse: A case study from the Netherlands. *Child Abuse and Neglect, 15*, 191-196.

Jonker, F., & Jonker-Bakker, P. (1997). Effects of ritual abuse: The results of three surveys in the Netherlands. *Child Abuse and Neglect, 21,* 541-556.

Kadushin, A. (1980). *Child welfare services* (3rd ed.). New York: Macmillan.

Kadushin, A., & Martin, J. (1988). *Child welfare services* (4th ed.). New York: Macmillan.

Kalichman, S. (1993). *Mandated reporting of suspected child abuse.* Washington, DC: American Psychological Society.

Kaplan, S. L., & Kaplan, S. J. (1981). The child's accusation of sexual abuse during a divorce and custody struggle. *Hillside Journal of Clinical Psychiatry, 3,* 81-95.

Katz, S., Schoenfeld, D., Levanthal, J., & Cicchetti, D. (1995). The accuracy of children's reports with anatomically correct dolls. *Developmental and Behavioral Pediatrics, 16*(2), 71-76.

Kaufman, P. (2000). The role of mental health professionals in family courts. In E. St. Charles & L. Crook (Eds.), *Expose: The failure of family courts to protect children from abuse in custody disputes.* Los Gatos, CA: Our Children Our Future Charitable Foundation.

Keary, K., & Fitzpatrick, C. (1994). Children's disclosure of sexual abuse during formal investigation. *Child Abuse and Neglect, 18,* 543-548.

Kelley, S. J. (1988). Ritualistic abuse of children: Dynamics and impact. *Cultic Studies Journal, 5,* 228-236.

Kelley, S. J. (1989). Stress responses of children to sexual abuse and ritualistic abuse in day care centers. *Journal of Interpersonal Violence, 4,* 502-513.

Kelley, S. J. (1990). Parental stress response to sexual abuse and ritualistic abuse of children in day-care centers. *Nursing Research, 39,* 25-29.

Kelley, S. (1992a, January). *Ritualistic abuse: Recognition, impact, and current controversy.* Paper presented at the San Diego Conference on Responding to Child Maltreatment, San Diego, CA.

Kelley, S. (1992b). Stress responses of children and parents to sexual abuse and ritualistic abuse in day care centers. In A. W. Burgess (Ed.), *Child trauma I: Issues and research.* New York: Garland.

Kelley, S. (1993). Ritualistic abuse of children in day care centers. In M. Langone (Ed.), *Recovery from cults* (pp. 340-351). New York: Norton.

Kelley, S. J. (1994). Abuse of children in day care centers: Characteristics and consequences. *Child Abuse Review, 3,* 15-25.

Kelley, S. J. (1996). Parents' perceptions of their children's recovery 5 to 10 years following day-care abuse: Response. *Scholarly Inquiry for Nursing Practice, 10,* 93-96.

Kelley, S. J., Brandt, R., & Waterman, J. (1993). Sexual abuse of children in day care centers. *Child Abuse and Neglect, 17,* 71-89.

Kleinheksel, K. (1988, June.) *The role of law enforcement in investigating child sexual abuse.* Workshop delivered at the conference "A Community Approach to Child Sexual Abuse," Ann Arbor, MI.

Kline, D., & Overstreet, H. M. (1972). *Foster care of children: Nurture and treatment.* New York: Columbia University Press.

Kroth, J. (1979). *Child sexual abuse.* Springfield, IL: Charles C Thomas.

Kuenhle, K. (1996). *Assessing allegations of child sexual abuse.* Sarasota, FL: Professional Resources Press.

La Foutaine, J. (1994). *The extent and nature of organised and ritual abuse: Research findings.* London: Her Majesty's Stationery Office.

Lamb, M. (1994). The investigation of child sexual abuse: An interdisciplinary consensus statement. *Child Abuse and Neglect, 18,* 1021-1028.

Lamb, M., & Sternberg, K. (1999, March). *Eliciting accurate investigative statement from children.* Paper presented at the Fifteenth National Symposium on Child Sexual Abuse, Huntsville, AL.

Lanning, K. (1990). Ritual abuse: A law enforcement view. *Roundtable, 2*(2), 14-16.

Lanning, K. (1992). Investigator's guide to allegations of "ritual" child abuse. In *The False Memory Syndrome Phenomenon.* Philadelphia: False Memory Syndrome Foundation. 3508 Market St., Suite 128, 19104.

Lawson, L., & Chaffin, M. (1992). False negatives in sexual abuse disclosure interviews. *Journal of Interpersonal Violence, 7*, 532-542.

Leavitt, F. (1994). Clinical correlations of alleged satanic abuse and less controversial sexual molestation. *Child Abuse and Neglect, 18*, 387-392.

Leberg, E. (1997). *Understanding child molesters*. Thousand Oaks, CA: Sage.

Leichtman, M., & Ceci, S. (1995). The effects of stereotypes and suggestions on preschoolers' reports. *Developmental Psychology, 31*, 568-578.

Lilly, G. (1978). *An introduction to the law of evidence*. St. Paul, MN: West.

Loftus, E., & Ketchem, K. (1991). *Witness for the defense*. New York: St. Martin's.

Long, G. (1988). Legal issues in child sexual abuse: Criminal cases and neglect and dependency cases. In L. A. Walker (Ed.), *Handbook on sexual abuse of children*. New York: Springer.

Lykken, D. (1987). The detection of deception. In L. Wrightsman, C. Willis, & S. Kassin (Eds.), *On the witness stand* (Chapter 2, pp. 37-47). Newbury Park, CA: Sage.

Lyon, T. (2002). Scientific support for expert testimony on the child sexual abuse accommodation syndrome. In J. Conte (Ed.), *Critical issues in child sexual abuse* (pp. 107-138). Newbury Park, CA: Sage.

Lyon, T., & Saywitz, K. (1999). Reducing maltreated children's reluctance to answer hypothetical oath-taking questions. *Law and Human Behavior, 25*, 81-92.

MacFarlane, K. (1986). Child sexual abuse allegations in divorce proceedings. In K. MacFarlane & J. Waterman (Eds.), *Sexual abuse of young children* (pp. 121-150). New York: Guilford.

Mansell, L. (1990). *Naptime*. New York: William Morrow.

Margolin, L. (1991). Child sexual abuse by nonrelated caregivers. *Child Abuse and Neglect, 15*, 213-221.

Marshall, W., Laws, D., & Barbaree, H. (1990). *Handbook on sexual offending*. New York: Plenum.

Masson, G. (1984). *The assault on the truth*. New York: Farrar, Straus, Giroux.

Mathews, R., Matthews, J., & Speltz, K. (1989). *Female sexual offenders: An exploratory study*. Orwell, VT.: Safer Society Press.

Mayer, R. (1991). *Satan's children: Case studies in multiple personality*. New York: G. P. Putnam.

Mayhall, P., & Norgard, K. (1983). *Child abuse and neglect: Sharing responsibility*. New York: John Wiley.

McCann, J., Voris, J., & Simon, M. (1992). Genital injuries resulting from sexual abuse: A longitudinal study. *Pediatrics, 89*, 307-317.

McCarty, L. (1981.) Investigation of incest: An opportunity to motivate families to seek help. *Child Welfare, 60*, 679-689.

McCormack, A., & Selvaggio, M. (1989). Screening for pedophiles in youth oriented community agencies. *Social Casework, 70*, 37-42.

McDermott-Steinmetz, M. (1997). *Interviewing for child sexual abuse: Strategies for balancing forensic and therapeutic factors*. Notre Dame, IN: Jalice.

McDonald, M. (1998, Spring). The myth of epidemic false allegations of sexual abuse in divorce cases. *Court Review, 4*(2), 1-14.

McFadden, E. J. (1984a). *Fostering the child who has been sexually abused: Instructor's manual*. Ypsilanti: Eastern Michigan University, Institute for the Study of Children and Families.

McFadden, E. J. (1984b). *Preventing abuse in foster care*. Ypsilanti: Eastern Michigan University, Institute for the Study of Children and Families.

McFadden, E. J. (1989). The sexually abused child in specialized foster care. *Child and Youth Services, 12*, 91-105.

McFadden, E. J., & Ryan, P. (1986, August). *Abuse in family foster homes: Characteristics of the vulnerable child*. Paper presented at the Sixth International Congress on Child Abuse and Neglect, Sydney, Australia.

McFadden, E. J., & Ryan, P. (1991). Maltreatment in family foster homes: Dynamics and dimensions. *Child and Youth Services, 15*, 209-231.

McIntosh, J. A., & Prinz, R. J. (1993). The incidence of alleged sexual abuse in 603 family court cases. *Law and Human Behavior, 17,* 95-101.

Melton, G. (1987, July). *Overview of legal research.* Paper presented at the Family Violence Research Conference for Practitioners and Policymakers, Durham, NH.

Mendel, M. (1995). *The male survivor.* Thousand Oaks, CA: Sage.

Michigan Governor's Task Force on Children's Justice and the Family Independence Agency (1998). *Michigan forensic interviewing protocol.* Lansing, MI: Author.

Miranda v. Arizona, 384 U.S. 436 (1966).

Moore, D., Gallup, G., & Schussel, R. (1995). *Disciplining America's children: A Gallup poll report.* Princeton, NJ: Gallup Organization.

Moreau, D. (1987a). Concepts of physical evidence in sexual assault investigations. In R. Hazelwood & A. Burgess (Eds.), *Practical aspects of rape investigation* (pp. 61-94). New York: Elsevier.

Moreau, D. (1987b). Major physical evidence in sexual assault investigation. In R. Hazelwood & A. Burgess (Eds.), *Practical aspects of rape investigation* (pp. 95-136). New York: Elsevier.

Morgan v. Foretich, 846 F. 2d 941 (4th Cir. 1988).

Morgan, M. (1995). *How to interview sexual abuse victims.* Thousand Oaks, CA: Sage.

MSNBC. (2002). A call for help [Slide show]. www.msnbc.com/modules/slideshow/980424 underground/980424underground.asp. Accessed July 29, 2002.

Murphy, C. A., & Murphy, J. K. (1997). Polygraph admissibility. *Update: National Center for Prosecution of Child Abuse, 10*(1/2), 1-2.

Myers, J. E. B. (1994). *The backlash: Child protection under fire.* Newbury Park, CA: Sage.

Myers, J. E. B. (1997). *Mother's nightmare: Incest.* Thousand Oaks, CA: Sage.

Myers, J. E. B. (1998). *Legal issues in child abuse and neglect practice* (2nd ed.). Thousand Oaks, CA: Sage.

Myers, J. E. B., Bays, J., Becker, J., Berliner, L., Corwin, D., & Saywitz, K. (1989). Expert testimony in child abuse litigation. *Nebraska Law Review, 68,* 1-145.

Myers, J. E. B., Goodman, G., & Saywitz, K. (1996). Psychological research on children as witnesses: Practical implications for forensic interviews and courtroom testimony. *Pacific Law Journal, 27,* 1-822.

Nathan, D. (1987, September 29). Are these women child molesters? *Village Voice, 32*(39), 19-23, 27-31.

National Association of Counsel for Children. (2001a). *Advocacy for children and families: Moving from sympathy to empathy.* Denver: Author.

National Association of Counsel for Children. (2001b). NACC recommendations for representation of children in abuse and neglect cases. In *Advocacy for children and families: Moving from sympathy to empathy.* Denver: Author.

National Center for the Prosecution of Child Abuse. (1997). *Child Abuse and Neglect State Statute Series* (5 vols.). Washington, DC: NCCAN Clearinghouse.

National Child Abuse and Neglect Data System. (2001). *Child maltreatment, 1998.* Washington, DC: Government Printing Office.

Neustein, A., & Goetting, A. (1999). Judicial responses to the protective parent's complaint of child sexual abuse. *Journal of Child Sexual Abuse, 8*(4), 103-122.

New Jersey v. Michaels, 136 N.J. 299; 642 A.2d 1372 (1994).

Nicholson, E. B., & Bulkley, J. (Eds.). (1988). *Sexual abuse allegations in custody and visitation cases.* Washington, DC: American Bar Association.

North Carolina v. Kelly, 118 N.C. App. 589; 456 S.E.2d 861; disc. Rev. denied 341 N.C. 442; 461 S.E.2d 764 (1995).

Nunno, M., & Motz, J. (1988). The development of an effective response to the abuse of children in out-of-home care. *Child Abuse and Neglect, 12,* 521-528.

Nunno, M., & Rindfleisch, N. (1991). The abuse of children in out of home care. *Children and Society, 5,* 295-305.

Oates, K. Jones, D., Denson, D., Sirotnak, A., Gary, N., & Krugman, R. (2000). Erroneous concerns about child sexual abuse. *Child Abuse and Neglect, 24,* 149-157.

Okerblom, J. (n.d.). Satanism: Truth vs. myth. In *The False Memory Syndrome Phenomenon.* Philadelphia: False Memory Syndrome Foundation, 3508 Market St., Suite 128, 19104.

Paradise, J., Rostain, A., & Nathanson, M. (1988). Substantiation of sexual abuse charges when parents dispute custody or visitation. *Pediatrics, 81,* 835-839.

Peddle, N., & Wang, C.-T. (2001). *Current trends in child abuse reporting and fatalities: The results of the 1999 Fifty State Survey.* Chicago: Prevent Child Abuse America.

Pence, D., & Wilson, C. (1994). *The team investigation of child sexual abuse: An uneasy alliance.* Newbury Park, CA: Sage.

Penfold, P. S. (1995). Mendacious moms or devious dads? Some perplexing issues in child custody/sexual abuse allegation disputes. *Canadian Journal of Psychiatry, 40,* 337-341.

Peters, S., & Wyatt, G. (1986). Prevalence. In D. Finkelhor & Associates (Eds.), *Sourcebook on child sexual abuse.* Newbury Park, CA: Sage.

Petit, M., & Curtis, P. (1997). *1997 CWLA stat book: Child abuse and neglect: A look at the states.* Washington, DC: Child Welfare League of America.

Petronio, S., Reeder, H., Hecht, M., & Ros-Mendoza, T. M. (1998). Disclosure of sexual abuse by children and adolescents. *Journal of Applied Communications Research, 24,* 191-199.

Pfeiffer, S. (1999, August 27). SJC avoids judge's order for an Amirault hearing. *Boston Globe,* p. 3.

Plass, P., Finkelhor, D., & Hotaling, G. (1997). Risk factors for family abduction: Demographics and family interaction characteristics. *Journal of Family Violence, 12,* 333-348.

Poole, D., & Lamb, M. (1998). *Investigative interviews of children,* Washington, DC: American Psychological Association.

Poole, D., & Lindsay, S. (2001). Children's eyewitness reports after exposure to misinformation from parents. *Journal of Experimental Psychology Applied, 7*(1), 27-50.

Poole, D., & White, L. (1991). Effects of question repetition on the eyewitness testimony of children and adults. *Developmental Psychology, 27,* 975-986.

Poole, D., & White, L. (1993). Two years later: Effects of question repetition on the eyewitness testimony of children and adults. *Developmental Psychology, 29,* 844-853.

Poole, D., & White, L. (1995). Tell me again and again: Stabilities and change in the repeated testimonies of children and adults. In M. Zaragoza, J. Graham, G. Hall, R. Hirschman, & Y. Ben-Porath (Eds.), *Memory and testimony in the child witness* (pp. 24-40). Newbury Park, CA: Sage.

Portland State University. (1996). Cohort II Report. www.cwp.pdx.edu/cohort2/study2.html. Accessed January 1999.

Pruett, K., & Solnit, A. (1998). Psychological and ethical considerations in the preparation of the mental health professional as expert witness. In S. Ceci & H. Hembrooke (Eds.), *Expert witnesses in child abuse cases* (pp. 123-135). Washington, DC: American Psychological Association.

Quinsey, V. (1993). *APSAC Study guide: Assessment of sexual offenders against children.* Newbury Park, CA: Sage.

Rabinowitz, D. (1999, June 30). Finality for the Amiraults. *Wall Street Journal,* pp. 1-4.

Raskin, D., & Yuille, J. (1989). Problems in evaluating interviews of children in sexual abuse cases. In S. Ceci, D. Ross, & M. Toglia (Eds.), *Perspectives on children's testimony* (pp. 184-207). New York: Springer Verlag.

Reed, L. D. (1996). Findings from research on children's suggestibility and implications for conducting child interviews. *Child Maltreatment, 1*(2), 105-120.

Reid, J. E., & Inbau, F. E. (1977). *Truth and deception: The polygraph technique* (2nd ed.). Baltimore: Williams & Wilkins.

Renshaw, D. (1987). Child sexual abuse: When wrongly charged. *Encyclopedia Britannica Medical and Health Annual, 10,* 301-303.

Risin, L., & Koss, M. (1987). The sexual abuse of boys. *Journal of Interpersonal Violence, 2,* 309-323.

Rosencrans, B. (1997). *The last secret: Daughters sexually abused by mothers.* Brandon, VT: Safer Society Press.

Rosenthal, J., Motz, J., Edmondson, D., & Groze, V. (1991). A descriptive study of abuse and neglect in out of home care. *Child Abuse and Neglect, 15,* 249-260.

Russell, D. (1983). The incidence and prevalence of intrafamilial and extrafamilial sexual abuse of female children. *Child Abuse and Neglect, 7,* 133-146.

Russell, D. E. H. (1986). *The secret trauma: Incest in the lives of girls and women.* New York: Basic Books.

Russell, D., & Bolen, R. (2000). *The epidemic of rape and child sexual abuse in the United States.* Thousand Oaks, CA: Sage.

Ryan, G., & Lane, S. (1997). *Juvenile sexual offending.* San Francisco: Jossey-Bass.

Ryan, P. (1984). *Fostering discipline: Instructor's manual.* Ypsilanti: Eastern Michigan University, Institute for the Study of Children and Families.

Ryan, P., McFadden, E. J., & Wiencek, P. (1988, April). *Analysis of level of agency services as related to maltreatment in family foster homes.* Paper presented at the North Central Sociological Association, Pittsburgh, PA.

Ryder, D. (1992). *Breaking the circle of satanic ritual abuse.* Minneapolis: CompCare.

St. Charles, E., & Crook, L. (Eds.). (2000). *Expose: The failure of family courts to protect children from abuse in custody disputes.* Los Gatos, CA: Our Children Our Future Charitable Foundation.

Sas, L., & Cunningham, A. (1995). *Tipping the balance to tell the secret: The public discovery of child sexual abuse.* Unpublished work available from the London Court Clinic, 254 Pall Mall St., Suite 200, London, Ontario, Canada N6A 5P6, tel. (519) 679-7250.

Sassoon, D. (1988). The sexual trafficking of children: Silence and taboo trigger its growth and continuation. *Action for Children, 3*(1), 1, 10.

Satanic cults and children. (1987, November 19). *Geraldo,* Show No. 44. New York: Investigative News Groups, Inc.

Satanic worship. (1988, February 17). *Oprah,* Show No. W373. Chicago: WLS-TV.

Satanism. (1986, September 30). *Oprah,* Show No. 8607. Chicago: WLS-TV.

Saunders, B. (1997). Medical and mental health experts in legal cases. In P. Stern (Ed.), *Preparing and presenting expert testimony in child abuse cases.* Thousand Oaks, CA: Sage.

Saunders, B., Kilpatrick, D., Lipovsky, J., Resnick, H., Best, C., & Sturgis, E. (1991, March). *Prevalence, case characteristics, and long-term psychological effects of sexual assault: A national survey.* Paper presented at the annual meeting of the American Orthopsychiatric Association, Toronto.

Saunders, B., Villeponteaux, L., Lipovsky, J., Kilpatrick, D., & Veronen, L. (1992). Child sexual abuse as a risk factor for mental disorders among women: A community survey. *Journal of Interpersonal Violence, 7,* 189-204.

Saxe, L., Dougherty, D., & Cross, T. (1987). The validity of polygraph testing: Scientific analysis and public controversy. *American Psychologist, 40,* 355-366. Reprinted in L. Wrightsman, C. Willis, & S. Kassin (Eds.), *On the witness stand* (pp. 14-36). Newbury Park, CA: Sage.

Saywitz, K., Geiselman, R., & Bornstein, G. (1992). Effects of cognitive interviewing and practice on children's recall performance. *Journal of Applied Psychology, 77*(5), 74-84.

Saywitz, K., Goodman, G., Nicholas, E., & Moan, S. (1991). Children's memory for a genital examination: Implications for child sexual abuse cases. *Journal of Consulting and Clinical Psychology, 59,* 682-691.

Schumacher, R., & Carlson, R. (1999). Variables and risk factors associated with child abuse in daycare settings. *Child Abuse and Neglect, 23,* 891-898.

Schuman, D. (1986). False allegations of physical and sexual abuse. *Bulletin of the American Academy of Psychiatry and Law, 14,* 5-21.

Schwartz, B., & Cellini, H. (Eds.). (1995). *The sex offender: Corrections, treatment and legal practice.* Kingston, NJ: Civic Research Institute.

Sedlak, A., & Broadhurst, D. (1996). *Third national incidence study of child abuse and neglect.* Washington, DC: U.S. Department of Health and Human Services, Administration on Children, Youth, and Families, National Center on Child Abuse and Neglect.

Sgroi, S. (Ed.). (1982). *Handbook of clinical intervention in child sexual abuse.* Lexington, MA: Lexington.

Sgroi, S., Porter, F., & Blick, L. (1982). Validation of sexual abuse. In S. Sgroi (Ed.), *Handbook of clinical intervention in child sexual abuse.* Lexington, MA: Lexington.

Sink, F. (1988a). A hierarchical model for evaluation of child sexual abuse. *American Journal of Orthopsychiatry, 58,* 129-35.

Sink, F. (1988b). Studies of true and false allegations: A critical review. In B. Nicholson & J. Bulkley (Eds.), *Allegations of sexual abuse in divorce and custody disputes* (pp. 37-47). Washington, DC: American Bar Association.

Sivan, A., Schor, D., Koeppl, G., & Noble, L. (1988). Interaction of normal children with anatomical dolls. *Child Abuse and Neglect, 12,* 295-304.

Snow, B., & Sorenson, T. (1990). Ritualistic child abuse in a neighborhood setting. *Journal of Interpersonal Violence, 5,* 474-487.

Sorenson, T., & Snow, B. (1991). How children tell: The process of disclosure in child sexual abuse. *Child Welfare, 70,* 3-15.

Starr, R. (1987). Clinical judgment of abuse proneness based upon parent and child interactions. *Child Abuse and Neglect, 11,* 87-92.

Steele, N. (1995). Cost effectiveness of treatment. In B. Schwartz & H. Cellini (Eds.), *Chapter 4: Sex offender: Corrections, treatment and legal practice* (pp. 4-1 to 4-15). Kingston, NJ: Civic Research Institute.

Stein, T. (1991). *Child welfare and the law.* New York: Longman.

Steinberg, M., & Westhoff, M. (1988). Behavioral characteristics and physical findings: A medical perspective. In K. C. Faller (Ed.), *Child sexual abuse: An interdisciplinary manual for diagnosis, case management, and treatment* (pp. 244-264). New York: Columbia University Press.

Stern, P. (1997). *Preparing and presenting expert testimony in child abuse cases.* Thousand Oaks, CA: Sage.

Sternberg, K., Lamb, M., Davies, G., & Wescott, H. (2001). The memorandum of good practice: Theory versus application. *Child Abuse and Neglect, 25,* 669-681.

Sternberg, K., Lamb, M., Hershkovitz, I., Yudilevitch, L., Orbach, Y., Esplin, P., & Hovav, M. (1997). Effects of introductory style on children's abilities to describe experiences of sexual abuse. *Child Abuse and Neglect, 21,* 1133-1146.

Steward, M. S., Steward, D. S., Farquhar, L., Myers, J., Welker, J., Joye, N., Driskill, J., & Morgan, J. (1996). *Interviewing young children about body touch and handling.* Chicago: University of Chicago Press.

Stickel, G. (1993). *Archaeological investigations of the McMartin Preschool site: Manhattan Beach, California.* 186 pp. Available from E. Gary Stickel, Ph.D., Department of Archeology, University of California at Los Angeles.

Stone, L., & Stone, D. (1992). Ritual abuse: The experiences of five families. In D. Sakheim & S. Devine (Eds.), *Out of darkness: Exploring Satanism and ritual abuse* (pp. 175-184). New York: Lexington Books.

Summit, R. (1983). The child sexual abuse accommodation syndrome. *Child Abuse and Neglect 7,* 177-193.

Terry, W. (1991, January). *Perpetrator and victim accounts of sexual abuse.* Paper presented at the conference "Health Science Response to Child Maltreatment," Center for Child Protection, San Diego. Available from William Terry, M.D., 343 N. Allumbaugh St., Boise, ID 83704.

Thoennes, N. (1988, April). *Sexual abuse allegations in custody disputes.* Paper presented at the National Conference on the Victimization of Children, Anaheim, CA.

Thoennes, N., Pearson, J., & Tjaden, P. (1988). *Allegations of sexual abuse in custody and visitation cases.* Denver, CO: Association of Family and Conciliation Courts Research Unit.

Thoennes, N., & Tjaden, P. (1990). The extent, nature, and validity of sexual abuse allegations in custody/visitation disputes. *Child Abuse and Neglect, 14,* 151-163.

Thompson, W., Clarke-Stewart, A., & Lapore, S. (1997). What did the janitor do? Suggestive interviewing and the accuracy of children's accounts. *Law and Human Behavior, 21,* 405-426.

Toth, P., & Whalen, M. (1987). *Investigation and prosecution of child abuse.* Alexandria, VA: National Center for the Prosecution of Child Abuse.

Underwager, R., & Wakefield, H. (1988). *Accusations of child sexual abuse.* Springfield, IL: Charles C Thomas.

Undeutch, U. (1989). The development of statement reality analysis. In J. Yuille (Ed.), *Credibility assessment.* Dordrecht, the Netherlands: Kluwer.

United States v. Paterson, 71 F. Supp. 2d 695 (S. Dist. Tex. 1999).

U.S. Department of Health and Human Services. (1981). *Executive summary: National study of the incidence of child abuse and neglect.* Washington, DC: Government Printing Office.

U.S. Department of Health and Human Services. (1988). *Study findings: Study of the national incidence and prevalence of child abuse and neglect.* Washington, DC: Government Printing Office.

U.S. Department of Health and Human Services, Children's Bureau. (1998). *Child maltreatment 1996.* Washington, DC: Government Printing Office.

U.S. Department of Health and Human Services, Children's Bureau. (2001). *Child maltreatment 1999.* Washington, DC: Government Printing Office.

Valliere, P., Bybee, D., & Mowbray, C. (1988, April). *Using the Achenbach Child Behavior Checklist in child sexual abuse research: Longitudinal and comparative analysis.* Paper presented at the National Symposium on Child Victimization, Anaheim, CA.

Van der Kolk, B. (1994). The body keeps score: Memory and the psychobiology of posttraumatic stress. *Harvard Review of Psychiatry, 1,* 253-265.

Van der Kolk, B., & Fisler, R. (1995). Dissociation and the fragmentary nature of traumatic memories: Overview and exploratory study. *Journal of Traumatic Stress, 8,* 505-526.

Vandervort, F. (2000). Representing children in protection proceedings: Learning from Michigan's experience. *ABA Child Law Practice, 19*(10), 153.

Victims of Child Abuse Act, 18 U.S.C. 223 (1990).

Walsh, W. (2001, April). *Investigating child sexual exploitation.* Paper presented at the National Symposium on Child Sexual Abuse, Huntsville, AL..

Wang, C.-T., & Daro, D. (1998). *Current trends in child abuse reporting and fatalities: Results of the 1996 annual Fifty State Survey.* Chicago: National Committee to Prevent Child Abuse.

Wang, C.-T., & Harding, K. (1999). *Current trends in child abuse reporting and fatalities: Results of the 1997 annual Fifty State Survey.* Chicago: National Committee to Prevent Child Abuse.

Wang, C.-T., & Harding, K. (2000). *Current trends in child abuse reporting and fatalities: Results of the 1998 annual Fifty State Survey.* Chicago: Prevent Child Abuse America.

Ward, T., Hudson, S., & Marshall, W. (1995). Cognitive distortions and affective deficits in sex offenders: A cognitive deconstructionist interpretation. *Sexual Abuse: Journal of Research and Treatment, 7*(10), 67-83.

Warren, A., & Lane, P. (1995). Effects of timing and type of questioning on eyewitness accuracy and suggestibility. In M. Zaragoza, J. Graham, G. Hall, R. Hirschman, & Y. Ben-Porath (Eds.), *Memory and testimony in the child witness* (pp. 44-60). Newbury Park, CA: Sage.

Warren, A., Woodall, C., Hunt, J., & Perry, N. (1996). "It sounds good in theory, but . . . ": Do investigative interviewers follow guidelines based on memory research? *Child Maltreatment, 1*(3), 231-245.

Waterman, J., Kelly, R., McCord, J., & Oliveri, M. K. (1989a). *Manhattan Beach Molestation Study.* Grant No. 90CA1179. Summary for NCCAN Grantees' Meeting, March 1989. Unpublished report, University of California, Los Angeles, Department of Psychology.

Waterman, J., Kelly, R., McCord, J., & Oliveri, M. K. (1989b). *Supplementary material: Manhattan Beach Molestation Study*. NCCAN Grant No. 90CA1179. Unpublished document, University of California, Los Angeles, Department of Psychology.

Waterman, J., Kelly, R., Oliveri, M. K., & McCord, J. (1993). *Behind the playground walls: Sexual abuse in preschools*. New York: Guilford.

Wehrspann, W., Steinhauer, P., & Klajner-Diamond, H. (1987). Criteria and methodology for assessing credibility of sexual abuse allegation. *Canadian Journal of Psychiatry, 32*, 615-623.

Weinberg, S. K. (1955). *Incest behavior*. New York: Citadel.

Wells, S. (2000). How do I decide to accept a report for Child Protective Services investigation? In H. Dubowitz & D. DePanfilis (Eds.), *Handbook for Child Protection Practice* (pp. 3-6). Thousand Oaks, CA: Sage.

Wexler, R. (1990). *Wounded innocents*. New York: Prometheus.

White, S., Strom, G., Santilli, G., & Halpin, B. (1986). Interviewing young sexual abuse victims with anatomically correct dolls. *Child Abuse and Neglect, 10*, 519-529.

Williams, V. (1995). Response to Cross and Saxe's "A critique of the validity of polygraph testing in child sexual abuse cases." *Journal of Child Sexual Abuse, 4*(3), 55-72.

Wilson, C., & Steppe, S. (1986). *Investigating sexual abuse in daycare*. Washington, DC: Child Welfare League of America.

Wong, B., & McKeen, J. (1990). A case of multiple life-threatening illnesses related to early ritual abuse. *Journal of Child and Youth Care*, Special issue: *In the shadow of Satan: The ritual abuse of children*, 1-26.

Wood, B., Orsak, C., Murphy, M., & Cross, H. (1996). Semistructured child sexual abuse interviews: Interview and child characteristics related to credibility of disclosure. *Child Abuse and Neglect, 20*(1), 81-92.

Wood, J., & Garven, S. (2000). How sexual abuse interviews go astray: Implications for prosecutors, police, and child protection services. *Child Maltreatment, 5*(2), 109-118.

Wyatt, G. (1985). The sexual abuse of Afro-American and white American women in childhood. *Child Abuse and Neglect, 9*, 507-519.

Yapko, M. (1994). *Suggestions of abuse*. New York: Simon & Schuster.

Young, W., Sachs, R., Braun, B., & Watkins, R. (1991). Patients reporting ritual abuse in childhood: A clinical syndrome. Report of 37 cases. *Child Abuse and Neglect, 15*, 181-189.

Yuille, J. (n.d.). *The step-wise interview*. Available from John Yuille, PhD, Department of Psychology, University of British Columbia.

Yuille, J. (1988). The systematic assessment of children's testimony. *Canadian Psychology, 29*(3), 247-259.

Zaragoza, M. (1991). Preschool children's susceptibility to memory impairment. In. J. Doris (Ed.), *The suggestibility of children's recollections* (pp. 27-39). New York: American Psychological Association.

Zellman, G., & Faller, K. C. (1995). Reporting child abuse. In J. Briere, L. Berliner, C. Jenny, & T. Reid (Eds.), *APSAC handbook on child maltreatment* (pp. 359-382). Thousand Oaks, CA: Sage.

Zuravin, S., Benedict, M., & Somerfield, M. (1993). Child maltreatment in family foster care. *American Journal of Orthopsychiatry, 63*(4), 589-596.

Name Index

Abel, G., 57
Abrams, J., 69
Abrams, S., 69
Achenbach, T., 37, 182, 232
Adoption and Safe Families Act, 64
Agar, S., 241, 242
Albert, G., 154
Albert, V., 191, 206
Albertella, G., 105, 107–108, 142, 164
Allen, K., 105, 107–108, 142, 164
Aman, C., 107, 175
American Academy of Child and Adolescent
    Psychiatry, 76, 147, 187, 243
American Association for the Protection
    of Children, 11–12, 217
American Professional Society on the Abuse
    of Children, 76, 126, 129, 165, 187
American Psychological Association, 76
Applin, B., 22
August, R., 128

Baker, T., 223, 230, 232, 234–235
Bala, N., 173–175, 237, 244, 246–247, 254
Barbaree, H., 64, 100
Barden, R. C., 89
Barnitz, L., 27
Barth, R., 191, 205–206
Batterman-Faunce, J. M., 150
Baumgarten, D., 145–146, 265
Bays, J., 49, 52, 81, 86, 99–100, 141, 178, 184
Becker, J., 49, 57, 64, 81, 86, 99–100
Beilke, R., 44
Bench, L. L., 57
Benedek, E., 145, 164, 238, 241–243,
    245, 254, 263, 265
Benedict, M., 192, 196, 200
Berliner, L., 37, 49–51, 64, 81, 86, 99–100, 146,
    153, 164, 243, 248–249, 254, 257–258

Berrick, J. D., 191, 206
Besharov, D., 65
Bess, B., 257–258, 261, 263
Best, C., 15
Bienenfeld, E., 87
Bikel, O., 216, 223
Blick, L., 164
Bloom v. Braun, 32
Blush, G., 238, 241–242, 263
Boat, B., 128–129, 174
Bolen, R., 3, 16, 24
Bornstein, G., 105–106, 122
Bottoms, B., 29–31
Bourg, W., 105, 110, 142, 164
Boychuk, T., 106, 108–110, 111 (table), 120
Bradley, A., 151, 159
Braga, W., 205
Brainerd, C., 152–153
Brandt, D., 192, 196
Brandt, R., 216, 224
Braun, B., 30
Bremner, J. D., 153
Bresee, P., 257–258, 261, 263
Briere, J., 51
Britton, H., 128
Broadhurst, D., 11–13
Broderick, R., 105, 110, 142, 164
Broughton, D., 44
Brown, T., 242, 244
Bruck, M., viii, 62, 150, 154, 174, 215
Bulkley, J., 255
Bull, R., 106
Burgess, A., 26–29, 223, 230, 232, 234–235
Burkhart, B., 16, 25
Burns, N., 26, 29–30, 36, 215–222, 224,
    226–228, 230–231, 234–235
Butler, J., 37, 105, 110, 142, 164
Bybee, D., 29–31, 216, 223–224, 232

Cage, J., 68, 70
Cahrney, D., 153
Campagna, D., 26–27
Cantlon, J., 106, 159
Carlson, N., 46
Carlson, R., 216, 220, 222, 224, 226, 229
Carnes, C., 60, 142
Carnes, P., 57
Carpenter, M., 239
Cavanaugh-Johnson, T., 41, 192, 205
Ceci, S., viii, 62, 150, 152, 154, 164, 174, 215
Cellini, H., 57, 64, 100
Chadwick, D., 52, 141, 178, 184
Chaffin, M., 29, 52, 151, 154, 160, 172, 187
Child Abuse Prevention, Adoption, and
    Family Services Act, 56, 59
Child Abuse Prevention and
    Treatment Act, 11, 56, 84
Children of the Underground Watch, 239
Cicchetti, D., 149, 151
Clarke-Stewart, A., 150, 152–154
Cohen, A., 64
Cohen, J., 37, 64
Cohn, D., 128
Colby, D., 147
Colby, I., 147
Cole, J., 105, 107, 108, 142, 164
Committee on the Family, Group for the
    Advancement of Psychiatry, 258
Conte, J., 51, 128, 130, 153, 164, 187
Corwin, D., 49, 81, 86, 99–100, 146, 164, 174,
    243, 248, 257–259
Coulter, M., 160
Courtney, M., 191, 206
Crenshaw, C., 154
Crewdson, J., 16, 24, 27–28, 32, 216, 223
Crook, L., 239
Cross, H., 151
Cross, T., 68–69, 86, 144, 178, 184
Crossman, A., 152
Cunningham, A., 99, 155, 157, 160,
    177, 181, 183
Curtis, P., 3

Dalenberg, C., 161, 183
Dalla Rosa, J., 128, 130, 164, 187
Dallam, S., 88
Damon, L., 37
Daro, D., 4, 11–12, 14, 64, 244
D'Aunno, L., 65, 81, 87
Davies, D., 105, 107–108, 142, 164

Davies, G., 110, 123
Davin, P., vii
Davis, S., 149, 151, 154
De Vos, E., 86
De Young, M., 164, 194–195
Deblinger, E., 64
Deitrich-MacLean, G., 146
DeLoache, J., 127
Denson, D., 172, 174–175
DePanfilis, D., 63
Detrich, A., 239
DeVoe, E., 52, 123, 144, 151, 153,
    159, 173–174, 237–238, 243,
    245–247, 250–251, 254–255
Doueck, H., 63
Dougherty, D., 68, 69, 144, 178
Drake, B., 62
Driskill, J., 121, 122, 126, 130, 151–153
Dubowitz, H., 63
Ducote, R., 238, 245
Dunbar, T., vii
Dunkerley, C., 161, 183
Duquette, D., 65, 81, 84, 87

Eberle, P., viii
Eberle, S., viii
Edelbrock, C., 182, 232
Edmondson, D., 192, 197
Ehreinsaft, D., 223
Eisen, M., 149, 151, 154
Elliot, M., vii
Elliott, D., 51
England, P., 86
English, D., 63
Erbaugh, C., 106, 159
Erickson, S., 57
Ervin, D., 105, 110, 142, 164
Esplin, P., 106–107, 159
Everson, M., 128–129, 142, 146, 154,
    158, 160, 174

Fahlberg, V., 191
Faller, K. C., vii, 3, 11, 23, 26, 28–32, 49, 52,
    57, 62, 65, 69, 81, 86, 87, 99–100,
    106, 108, 118, 123, 129, 141,
    143–146, 150–151, 153, 159–160,
    162, 164, 172–178, 180–182, 184,
    187, 191, 194, 196, 209, 214, 215–217,
    219–220, 222, 224, 226–231, 237–238,
    243, 245–247, 249–251, 254–255,
    259–260, 270

False Memory Syndrome Foundation,
    viii, 31, 88
Farley, R., 22
Farquhar, L., 121–122, 126, 130, 151–153
Finkel, M., 141
Finkelhor, D., 3, 13, 15, 22, 24, 26–27,
    29–30, 36, 215–222, 224, 226–228,
    230–231, 234–235
Fisler, R., 153
Fitzpatrick, C., 159–160
Fivush, R., 152–153
Flagor, R., 105, 110, 142, 164
Fogarty, L., 128, 130, 164, 187
Follmer, A., 154
Fontes, L., 160
Foreman, B., 128
Francoeur, E., 150, 154
Frederico, M., 242, 244
Freedom of Information Act, 71
Freyd, J., 31
Friedrich, W., 37, 44, 131, 174, 182, 231
Fromuth, M., 16, 25
Froning, M., 145–146, 259

Gallagher, B., 192
Gallup, G., 13
Galtney, L., June, 239
Gardell, D., 60
Gardner, R., viii, 145–146, 164,
    174–175, 238, 241–242, 245, 265
Garven, S., viii
Gary, N., 172, 174–175
Geiselman, R., 105–106, 122
Gil, E., 191–192
Goettmg, A., 238, 246–247
Goldsmith, S., 245
Goldstein, S., 68
Goodman, C., 149, 151, 154
Goodman, G., 29–31, 49, 86, 107, 111 (table),
    121, 122, 146, 150–153, 172, 175,
    187, 243, 248, 257
Goodwin, J., 49, 146, 151, 243, 248, 257
Gordon, B., 154
Gorey, K., 16
Graffam-Walker, A., 110, 123
Grambsch, P., 44
Gray, E., 86
Green, A., 164, 243, 265
Groth, N., 57, 130, 209
Groze, V., 192, 197
Guyer, M., 164, 238, 265

Halpin, B., 128
Hamby, S., 13
Hanson, G., 243
Haralambie, A., 84, 87
Harding, K., 11, 12, 65
Hare, R. D., 68
Hartman, C., 223, 230, 232, 234–235
Hartman, G., 131
Haynes-Seman, C., 145–146, 265
Hechler, D., viii, 65, 216, 223
Hecht, M., 158, 160, 177, 183
Heiman, M., 164
Hembrooke, H., 215
Henry, J., 23, 86
Hepps, D., 152
Heriot, J., 160
Herman, J., 175
Hershkovitz, I., 106–107, 159
Hewitt, L., 242, 244
Hewitt, S., 270–271
Hibbard, R. A., 131
Hirschman, J., 107, 152, 175
Hislop, J., vii
Hobbs, C., 192, 196–197, 199, 213
Hobbs, G., 192, 196–197, 199, 213
Hoekelman, R. A., 131
Holden, C., 93
Holder, W., 63
Hollingsworth, J., 30, 216, 217, 223
Home Office, 106, 108, 114
Hoorwitz, A. N., 144, 164
Horner, T., 164
Hornick, J., 173–175, 237, 244,
    246–247, 254
Hotaling, G., 27
Hovav, M., 106–107, 159
Howell, C., 182
Hudson, J. A., 152
Hudson, S., 209
Huffman, M., 62, 150, 152
Hume, M., 244
Humphreys, C., 242
Hunt, D., 22
Hunt, J., 151
Hunter, W., 160

Inbau, F. E., 69
Indian Child Welfare Act, 102

Jackson, H., 8–9
Jampole, L., 128

Jenny, C., 141
Jones, B. J., 102
Jones, D., 63, 86, 151, 172, 174–175,
   180, 186, 187 (figure), 237, 243–244,
   253–255, 263
Jones, L., 13, 22
Jonker, F., 30
Jonker-Bakker, P., 30
Joye, N., 121–122, 126, 130, 151–153

Kadushin, A., 191
Kalichman, S., 65
Kalter, N., 164
Kaplan, S., 243
Katz, S., 149, 151
Kaufman, P., 238, 245
Keary, K., 159–160
Keiley, S. J., 31
Kekevian, H., 105, 107–108, 142, 164
Kelley, S., 30, 31, 219, 224,
   226–227, 229–230
Kelley, S. J., 30, 31, 216, 224, 230–231, 234
Kelly, D., 105, 110, 142, 164
Kelly, R., 29–31, 216–217, 219, 223–224,
   226–232, 234
Ketchem, K., viii
Kilpatrick, D., 3, 15
Klajner-Diamond, H., 164
Kleinheksel, K., 68
Kline, D., 191
Koeppl, G., 128
Koss, M., 15, 24–25
Kramer, S., 57
Kroth, J., 64
Krugman, R., 172, 174–175
Ktystal, J., 153
Kuenhle, K., 144, 164
Kuhn, J., 150
Kuiper, J., 44

La Foutaine, J., 31
Lamb, M., 105–107, 109–110, 113,
   122–123, 125, 159, 161, 182
Lane, P., 122
Lane, S., 41
Lanning, K., 29, 31
Lapore, S., 150, 154
Laws, D., 64, 100
Lawson, L., 52, 151, 154, 160, 172, 187
Leavitt, F., 30–31
Leberg, E., 57, 68, 100

LeDuc, D., 142
Leichtman, M., 62, 150, 154, 164
Leslie, D., 16
Levanthal, I., 149, 151
Lilly, G., 100
Lindsay, S., 150
Lipovsky, J., 3, 15, 145–146, 259
Lippman, J., 64
Loftus, E., viii, 62, 150, 154
Long, G., 81
Lykken, D., 68, 69
Lyon, T., 99, 149, 151

MacFarlane, K., 245
Mannarino, A., 64
Mansell, L., 216, 217, 222
Margolin, L., 220, 222, 235
Marshall, W., 64, 100, 209
Martin, J., 191
Mathews, R., vii
Matthews, J., vii
Mayer, R., 32
Mayhall, P., 65, 71, 141
McCann, J., 141, 184
McCarty, L., 62
McCord, J., 29–31, 216–217, 219,
   223–224, 226–232, 234
McCormack, A., 210
McCulloch, L., 105, 107–108, 142, 164
McDermott-Steinmetz, M., 105,
   142, 164–165
McDonald, M., 242, 245
McFadden, E. J., 192, 194, 196–197, 200,
   203, 205–206, 209, 270
McGraw, E. M., 63, 151, 172, 174–175,
   186–187 (figure), 244, 253–255, 263
McIntosh, J. A., 242
McKeen, J., 32
McQuiston, M., 180
Melton, G., 100
Mendel, M., vii
Michigan Governor's Task Force on
   Children's Justice and the Family
   Independence Agency, 106, 109, 164
Miranda v. Arizona, 71
Mitchell, K., 22
Moan, S., 121–122, 150–151, 153, 172, 187
Moore, D., 13
Moote, G., 63
Moreau, D., 70
Morgan, J., 121–122, 126, 130, 151–153

Morgan, M., 105, 142, 164
Morgan v. Foretich, 243, 272
Motz, J., 192, 197
Mowbray, C., 29–31, 216, 223–224, 232
MSNBC, 239
Murphy, C. A., 68
Murphy, J. K., 68
Murphy, M., 151
Myers, J., viii, 29, 49, 56, 81–82, 86,
     99–101, 111 (table),121–122, 126,
     130, 147–148, 151–153, 238

Nathan, D., 31
Nathanson, M., 244, 270
National Association of Counsel for
     Children, 84
National Center for the Prosecution
     of Child Abuse, 24, 55–56, 58, 65,
     81, 86, 143
National Child Abuse and Neglect Data
     System, vii
Neustein, A., 238, 246–247
New Jersey v. Michaels, 31, 215
Nicholas, E., 121, 122, 150–151,
     153, 172, 187
Nicholson, E. B., 255
Nida, R., 154
Noble, L., 128
Norgard, K., 65, 71, 141
North Carolina v. Kelly, 31, 215
Nunno, M., 192
Nuttall, R., 8–9

Oates, K., 172, 174–175
O'Keefe, M. A., 128
Okerblom, J., 31
Oliveri, M. K., 29–31, 216–217, 219,
     223–224, 226–232, 234
Orbach, Y., 106–107, 159
Ornstein, P., 152–154
Orsak, C., 151
Overstreet, H. M., 191

Packer, L, 257–258, 261, 263
Paetsch, R., 173–175, 237, 244,
     246–247, 254
Paradise, J., 244, 270
Payne, G., 106, 159
Pearson, J., 241
Peddle, N., 11, 12, 244
Pence, D., 55, 143–144

Penfold, P. S., 242, 245
Perry, N., 151
Peters, S., 3
Petit, M., 3
Petronio, S., 158, 160, 177, 183
Pfeiffer, S., 216
Plass, P., 27
Poffenberger, D., 26, 27
Poole, D., 105, 107, 109, 122,
     125, 150, 182
Port, L. K., 86
Porter, F., 164
Portland State University, 4
Prado, L., 86
Prinz, R. J., 242
Pruett, K., 90, 93
Pyle-Taub, E., 86

Qin, J., 29–31, 149, 151, 154
Quas, J. A., 150
Quinsey, V., 209

Rabinowitz, D., 216
Rada, R., 151
Ramsey, S., 84
Raskin, D., 215
Reed, L. D., 107, 123
Reeder, H., 158, 160, 177, 183
Reid, J. E., 69
Renick, A., 150, 154
Renshaw, D., 241, 242
Resnick. H., 15
Riddlesberger, M. M., 150
Riebel, J., 46
Rindfleisch, N., 192
Risin, L., 15, 24–25
Roghmann, K., 131
Ros-Mendoza, T. M., 158, 160, 177, 183
Rosencrans, B., vii
Rosenthal, J., 192, 197
Ross, K., 238, 241–242, 263
Rostain, A., 244, 270
Rouleau, J., 57
Rudy, L., 86, 152
Runyan, D., 160
Russell, D., 3, 15, 24
Russell, D. E. H., 194
Ryan, G., 41
Ryan, P., 192, 194, 196–197, 200, 203,
     205, 209, 270
Ryder, D., 32

Sachs, R., 30
Sahd, D., 151
Santilli, G., 128
Sas, L., 99, 155, 157, 160, 177, 181, 183
Sassoon, D., 27
Saunders, B., 3, 15, 50, 64, 74
Saxe, L., 68–69, 144, 178, 184
Saywitz, K., 49, 81, 86, 99–100, 105–106,
    111 (table), 121–122, 149–151,
    153, 172, 187
Scannapieco, M., 3, 16
Schetky, D., 145, 164, 238, 242, 245, 254, 263
Schimmer, R., 205
Schoenfeld, D., 149, 151
Schor, D., 128
Schumacher, R., 216, 220, 222, 224, 226, 229
Schuman, D., 173–175, 237, 241, 243–244,
    246–247, 254
Schussel, R., 13
Schwartz, B., 57, 64, 100
Sedlak, A., 11–13, 27
Seig, A., 237, 243–244
Selvaggio, M., 210
Sgroi, S., 62, 64, 164, 176
Shafram, C., 37
Shaver, P., 29–31
Sheehan, R., 242, 244
Shukat, J., 153
Simon, M., 141, 184
Sink, F., 151, 164
Sirotnak, A., 172, 174–175
Sivan, A., 128
Smith, E., 62, 150
Snow, B., 29–30, 49, 99, 151, 153,
    160, 172, 177, 183, 187
Solnit, A., 90, 93
Somerfield, M., 192, 196, 200
Sorenson, E., 128, 130, 164, 187
Sorenson, T., 29–30, 49, 99, 151, 153, 160,
    172, 177, 183, 187
Southwick, S., 153
Speltz, K., vii
St. Charles, E., 239
Starr, R., 146
Stearns, G., 257–258, 261, 263
Steele, N., 57, 64
Steer, R., 64
Stein, T., 87, 101
Steinberg, K., 106, 107, 110, 113, 123, 159
Steinberg, M., 70
Steinhauer, P., 164

Stellar, M., 106, 108–110, 111 (table), 120
Steppe, S., 236
Stern, P., 29, 100
Stevenson, T., 130
Steward, D. S., 121, 122, 126, 130,
    151, 152, 153
Steward, M. S., 121, 122, 126, 130,
    151, 152, 153
Stickel, C., 29, 30
Stone, D., 32
Stone, L., 32
Straus, M., 13
Strom, G., 128
Sturgis, E., 15
Summit, R., 49, 99, 183

Tanchak, M., 173–175, 237, 244,
    246–247, 254
Terry, W., 151
Thoennes, N., 173, 237, 241,
    243–245, 247, 253, 255, 257
Thompson, W., 150, 154
Tjaden, P., 173, 237, 241, 243–244, 245,
    247, 253, 255, 257
Toth, P., 85
Trocme, N., 173–175, 237, 244,
    246–247, 254

Underwager, R., 174, 242
Undeutch, U., 164
United States v. Paterson, 32
U.S. Department of Health and Human
    Services, 4, 11, 12, 244

Valliere, P., 29, 31, 216, 232
Van der Kolk, B., 153
Vandervort, F., 84
Veronen, L., 3, 15
Victims of Child Abuse Act, 85
Villeponteaux, L., 3, 15
Voris, J., 141, 184

Wakefield, H., 174, 242
Walden, T., 146
Walsh, W., 27
Wang, C. T., 4, 11–12, 14, 65, 244
Ward, T., 209
Warren, A., 122, 151
Waterman, J., 29–31, 216–217, 219,
    223–224, 226–232, 234
Watkins, R., 30

Webber, M., 128
Wehrspann, W., 164
Welker, J., 121, 122, 126, 130, 151–153
Wells, S., 56
Wescott, H., 110, 123
Westhoff, M., 70
Wexler, R., viii
Whalen, M., 85
Whitcomb, D., 86
White, L., 122, 125
White, S., 49, 128, 146, 243, 248, 257
Wiencek, P., 194, 196, 203, 209
Williams, L., 26, 29–30, 36,
    215–222, 224, 226–228, 230–231,
    234, 235
Williams, V., 178
Wilson, C., 55, 60, 143, 144, 236
Winterfelt, N., 191, 205

Wolak, J., 22
Wong, B., 32
Wood, B., 151
Wood, J., viii, 151, 159
Woodall, C., 151
Wyatt, G., 3, 15
Wynne, J., 192, 196–197, 199, 213

Yapko, M., viii
Yeaton, J., 191, 205
Young, W., 30
Yudilevitch, L., 106, 107, 159
Yuille, J., 106–107, 109–110, 113,
    129, 164, 215

Zaragoza, M., 150
Zellman, G., 65
Zuravin, S., 192, 196, 200

Subject Index

Abuse-specific drawing task, for child, 133 (table), 134
Achenbach's Child Behavior Checklist, 50
Adolescent offender, 220
Age:
  affect on interview, 159
  affect on suggestibility, 154
  maximum for victim, 23–24
  offender/victim differential, 23, 25
Allegations of sexual abuse, assessing:
  affect of child memory/suggestibility on, 149–154
  child interview model, 142–143
  joint investigation model, 143–144
  multimodal model, 144–145
  parent-child interaction model, 145–147
  videotaping interview for, 147–149
  See also Allegations of sexual abuse, possible explanations for
Allegations of sexual abuse, possible explanations for:
  actual experience, 172
  attention seeking, 175–176
  benign activity misinterpreted, 172–173
  coaching/programming child, 174, 263
  communication problems, 173–174
  exaggeration of abuse by child/adult, 176
  fantasizing by child, 175
  identification of wrong offender, 175
  lying by child, 174
  minimization of abuse by child/adult, 176–177
  sexual knowledge of child, 174–175
  statement/behavior of child misinterpreted, 173
  See also Allegations of sexual abuse, assessing

American Academy of Child and Adolescent Psychiatry, 147
American Professional Society on the Abuse of Children, 147
Analogue studies, 150–152
Anatomical doll, 127–130, 129 (table)
Asymptomatic child, of sexual abuse, 51–52
Attorney, role of:
  in child protection proceedings, 83–85, 92
  in civil damages proceedings, 87–90
  in criminal proceedings, 85–86
  in divorce/domestic relations proceedings, 86–87
  in personal injury case, 88–90

Backlash, against cases of sexual abuse, viii–ix, 14, 31–32
Behavior problem, as indicator of sexual abuse, 50–51
Bias, of professional, 8–9, 164
Bogus pipeline effect, 69

CAPTA. See Child Abuse Prevention and Treatment Act
CBCL, 232, 236
Child Abuse Prevention and Treatment Act (CAPTA), viii, 11, 84
Child advocacy center, 142
Child Behavior Survey. See Child Sexual Behavior Inventory
Child interview
CPS and, 60
  documenting, 60, 147–149
  exit interview, for foster child, 212
  flexibility in, 105–106
  for evaluating sexual abuse allegations in divorce, 257–258, 259–261
  law enforcement and, 5, 7

scope of information gathering in,
134–136
See also Allegations of sexual abuse,
assessing; Child interview, media
use in; Child interview, questions
for; Child interview,
structure/protocol of
Child interview, media use in:
advantages of, 125–126
anatomical doll, 127–130, 129 (table)
anatomical drawing, 130, 131 (table),
132 (figure)
child drawing, 130–134, 133 (table),
135 (figure)
disadvantages of, 126–127
See also Allegations of sexual abuse,
assessing; Child interview; Child
interview, questions for; Child
interview, structure/protocol of
Child interview, questions for:
checklist inquiry area/appropriate sample,
137 (table)–139 (table)
coercive, 112 (table), 124
direct, 112 (table), 121, 151, 153, 154
externally derived, 111 (table), 120
facilitative cues, 111 (table), 114–115
focused, 111 (table), 115–119
follow-up, 111 (table), 115
general/invitational, 111 (table),
113–114, 150, 151
leading, 112 (table), 123, 150
misleading, 107, 112 (table), 123–124, 150
multiple-choice, 111 (table), 119–120
questioning typology, 110–113, 111
(table)–112 (table)
repeated, 112 (table), 122–123
See also Allegations of sexual abuse,
assessing; Child interview; Child
interview, media use in; Child
interview, structure/protocol of
Child interview, structure/protocol of:
abuse-focused stage, 108, 109
closure stage, 108–109
initial phase, 107–108, 109
multiphase interview, 109
outline of, 106 (table)–107
principles, 110
See also Allegations of sexual abuse,
assessing; Child interview; Child
interview, media use in; Child
interview, questions for

Child interview model, for assessing sexual
abuse allegations, 142–143
Child protection agency, as abuse statistics
source, 11
Child protection proceedings, role of attorney
in, 83–85, 92
Child Protective Services (CPS):
attorney for, 83, 92
backlash against, viii
confidentiality issue for, 58–59
goals of, 62–64
joint investigation with law
enforcement, 5, 7, 143–144
limitations of, 65
reporting requirements for, 56–58
responsibilities of, 4
role in sexual abuse case (example), 5–7
role of, 59–61
statistical data on cases, 3, 11–13
Child Sexual Behavior Inventory (CSBI),
37–38, 44, 174, 182
Child sexual maltreatment, extent of:
incidence rates, 10–14
prevalence of, 14–17
Child welfare worker, responsibilities of, 3
Child-centered approach, to sexual abuse
case, 7–10, 32
Child-parent relationship, assessing, 265–266
ethical considerations in, 267
parent-child interaction model, 145–147
practical obstacles in, 266–267
Children's Advocacy Center, 60
Circumstantial sexual abuse. See
Opportunistic sexual abuse
Civil damages case, 81–82
role of attorney in, 87–90
Classical incest, 249
Coercive question, in child interview,
112 (table), 124
Competency, of child during
interview, 182–183
Confidentiality:
of law enforcement files, 71, 72n6
of reporter, 58–59, 74
waiving, 71note1, 100
Consent, defining, 24–25
Counterphobic behavior, 195
Country Walk (day care center), 30,
217–218, 223
Court data, as child abuse statistics
source, 11